End Time Pro

The Church Age

by Derek Walker

INDEX

*Introduction

This book is Part 2 of a series of 3 books (it was originally intended to be a 4-Part Series) providing a systematic presentation of Bible Prophecy, describing future events in their chronological order, and showing how God is working out His Purposes and fulfilling His Promises and Covenants.

Part 1 gave the 10 foundational principles (keys) for understanding the prophetic scriptures, and established the overall Framework of Bible Prophecy, giving a detailed explanation of Daniel's 70 Weeks and the Olivet Discourse of Christ.

Parts 2 and 3 build on this foundation. Part 2 covers what the Bible has to say about the Church Age and the Rapture of the Church, which is followed by the Judgment Seat of Christ. It also covers the Biblical teaching on Life after Death. All of these things have a direct bearing on how we live our Christian lives today.

Part 3 covers the events of the Tribulation, the Battle of Armageddon and the Second Coming of Jesus Christ to judge and rule the world. Then it brings the story to its glorious conclusion with Christ's Millennial Reign and the Eternal State.

The study of Bible Prophecy is all the more relevant and important in the light of the fact that we are living in the last of the last days, the final generation of the Church Age (this is something we established in Part 1). This means that the Coming of our Lord Jesus to receive us to Himself is very close, so that we need to make sure we are living holy lives before Him, and seizing every opportunity to serve Him and share the Gospel, for immediately after the Rapture we will all stand before Him to give an account of our lives, and receive our eternal rewards. Thus we can see that studying Bible Prophecy helps us to understand the times in which we are living, and wakes us up, giving us a sense of urgency, so that we do not waste our lives, because we have the wrong priorities and pursue the wrong causes.

Since we are living in the last of the last days, this means we are living in both exciting and dangerous times. The Church was given the Great Commission by her Lord almost 2000 years ago, to preach the Gospel and make disciples of all nations. Since then the torch has been handed down from one generation to the next, and now it is in our hands, and we have been given the honour of running the last lap before He returns. The Bible indicates that the final days of the Church Age will see a great soul-harvest across the whole world through the preaching of the Gospel (James 5:7-8, Matt 24:14, Mark 13:10). Therefore these are exciting days, full of opportunity. But the Bible also tells us these will be dangerous times, with evil on the increase, as the world heads toward the Judgments of the Tribulation: **"Know this, that in the last days** (of the Church Age) **perilous** (dangerous) **times will come. For men will be lovers of themselves, lovers of money, boasters, proud, blasphemers, disobedient to parents, unthankful, unholy, unloving, unforgiving, slanderers, without self-control, brutal, despisers of good, traitors, headstrong, haughty, lovers of pleasure rather than lovers of God, having a form of godliness but denying its power. From such turn away!"** (2Timothy 3:1-5).

The danger of living in such a dark world is not just the threat of persecution, but the peril to our own souls, that comes by compromising with the world-system, allowing our hearts to harmonise with its values and standards. If we are not strong in the Word of God, we will come under the spirit of this world. Therefore as this Age comes to its close there will be an increasing division between the light and the darkness, with the light becoming brighter and the darkness becoming darker. The only way to be free from the power of darkness, and to be shine in the darkness, is to embrace the light of Christ, which shines by His Spirit through the Word.

Christ calls His Church (1) to Himself in HOLINESS by the Great Commandment to love Him with all our heart (Matt 22:37), and (2) to embrace and join with Him in His mission of EVANGELISM to the world by the Great Commission (Mark 16:15-20, Matt 28:18-20), shining our light in the darkness - the main way we love the lost (Matt 22:38). God's Word and His prophetic Scriptures in particular, will enlighten you to understand His Purpose for the Church and the special times in which we live, so that you will know how to focus your energies to accurately fulfil God's Plan for your life. They will strengthen, stabilise, inspire and equip you to be fruitful in fulfilling His will in these last of the last days: **"We have the PROPHETIC WORD confirmed, which you do well to heed as a LIGHT that shines in a DARK place** (the world), **until the Day dawns** (at Christ's Return) **and the Morning Star rises in your hearts** (at the Rapture)"** (2Peter 1:19).

*Chapter 1 - The Value and Importance of Bible Prophecy

Did you know that we can know the future? God is the only One who knows it and He has revealed much of it through His Word. So we can only truly know the future by studying Bible Prophecy and that is exactly what we will do in this book. The study of the End Times is called Eschatology and it reveals how God will work His purposes out in bringing all things to their final destiny. Bible Prophecy is future history and so it reveals God's nature, power and glory, just as much as Bible history does through the record of God's previous interactions with mankind. Since Bible Prophecy is just as much God's Word as Bible History we can be sure that all that the Bible predicts will come to pass. The fact that much Bible Prophecy has already been fulfilled adds to our confidence that the rest of it will be fulfilled also. So, get ready for an exciting trip into the future!

2Timothy 3:16,17: **"ALL Scripture is given by inspiration of God, and is profitable for doctrine, for reproof, for correction, for instruction in righteousness, that the man of God may be complete, thoroughly equipped for every good work."** All Scripture is inspired by God and a great deal of Scripture is about Bible Prophecy. Eschatology (the study of the 'last things') is over a quarter of the Bible. So it must be very important to God and very relevant to our lives. It is not a side issue purely for specialists, as many think. So the fact that God inspired so much prophetic scripture, must mean that it has great importance and benefit for our lives and that He expects us to study it diligently. Since it is a big subject, it means we have got a lot of ground to cover in this book. We need to study the subject systematically to see how all the scriptures fit together and agree perfectly in presenting a vision of the future.

Prophecy exalts Jesus

One of the greatest things that Bible Prophecy will do for us is to reveal and exalt the Lord Jesus Christ and cause us to glorify God. Revelation 19:10: **"Worship God. For the testimony of Jesus is the spirit of Prophecy."** So, the spirit of prophecy is to testify to Jesus, so that we worship Him as God. Jesus is the central figure of Bible Prophecy, so studying it will reveal more of Jesus to us and inspire us in our lives. We know a lot about Jesus from what He did in the past, so likewise we will learn a lot about Jesus from what He will do in the future.

Prophecy reveals God's Sovereignty

Bible Prophecy gives us a bigger picture of God. It reveals His wisdom, power and sovereignty. Despite all the suffering and evil going on in the world around us, God is working out His purposes, fulfilling His Promises and Covenants and establishing His Kingdom over all. He is not making it up as He goes along. He knows the end from the beginning. So we are not to be overly disturbed by events, because we know where history is going.

Through Bible Prophecy the Lord God unveils the future. This makes it a very exciting subject, which glorifies God. Isaiah 46:9,10: **"Remember the former things of old, for I am God, and there is no other; I am God, and there is none like Me, declaring the end from the beginning, and from ancient times things that are not yet done, saying: 'My counsel shall stand, and I will do all My pleasure."** God declares ahead of time what He is going to do, so when it comes to pass this proves that He is sovereign over all. Only God can declare the end from the beginning, for He alone is the eternal I AM, the Alpha and Omega, existing outside time and seeing all things as present. Therefore the many prophecies that have already been fulfilled are a major proof that the Bible is the Word of God.

Everything that God does in the past, present and future is connected. What He began in Genesis He will bring to perfect fulfilment in Revelation. If we do not understand Bible Prophecy we will have a very limited knowledge of God's Purposes, for it reveals the ultimate destiny of all things. It gives us the big picture and overall perspective by which we can understand what God is doing and where history is heading. Thus everything in the past and present only makes sense in the light of Bible Prophecy.

Prophecy imparts Hope

Bible prophecy also imparts HOPE. Now hope is our vision and confident expectation for the future based on God's Word. 1Corinthians 13:13 names 3 essential attributes we must have: **"Now abide faith, hope and love, these three, the greatest of these is love."** Of course we need to be strong in love and faith, but it is also important for us to be strong in hope. Often hope is treated as being less important but we need Bible hope. Without it we are lacking in of the 3 essential spiritual attributes and it is the study of Bible Prophecy that builds our hope.

Hope is not wishful thinking, it is what we know will happen based on God's Promises, and this hope covers, protects and directs our minds and thoughts, holding us steady in the fight and keeping us on course through life.

This is why 1Thessalonians 5:8 commands us to put on: **"the hope of salvation as a helmet."** We put on this helmet by studying Bible Prophecy, which will cover our minds with hope from God's Word. Looking through the visor of the helmet of hope causes us to be focused on what God is doing in the world, so that we see things from His perspective, which also protects us from the negative thoughts that come from focusing on the darkness of this world.

There are 2 aspects of hope. First, there is the hope for our personal life, that God's promises will come to pass in our own lives. Then there is the bigger aspect of hope on the bigger scale of what is going to happen in this world, where is this world heading, and what is the ultimate destiny of all things, and it's Bible prophecy that gives us this hope. It protects our mind and anchors and stabilises our soul, especially when we are sailing through the stormy waters of troubled times. As Hebrews 6:19 says: **"This hope we have as an anchor of the soul, both sure and steadfast."** Here our soul is compared to a ship. If it is anchored by hope to the promises of God, then even in a storm of wind and waves, we will remain strong, stable and steady, and not be shipwrecked. While everything is being shaken around us Hebrews 12:28 describes the difference that hope makes: **"Since we are receiving a Kingdom which cannot be shaken, let us have grace, by which we may serve God acceptably with reverence and godly fear."**

The words of Bible Prophecy also give us comfort, peace and assurance for the future. After talking about our hope for the rapture it says in 1Thessalonians 4:18: **"Therefore comfort one another with these words."**

Some people think Bible Prophecy is just for specialists and fanatics who do not study anything else, and so they avoid the subject, thinking they are better off focusing on practical teachings rather than on Bible Prophecy. However, this is a false distinction, because a healthy dose of Bible Prophecy is very practical for your life. It will put something in you that nothing else will, and I trust that through this book, you will become greatly strengthened and deepened in your spiritual life,

God emphasised the importance of Bible Prophecy by making the last Book of the Bible, the Book of Revelation, a Book entirely devoted to End Time Prophecy. He further underlined the importance of this Book this by its starting and the finishing verses. Revelation 1:3: **"Blessed is he who reads and those who hear the words of this prophecy, and keep those things which are written in it; for the time is near."** This is the only Book where God promises a blessing for those who read, hear and keep it. So there must be a special blessing connected with the study of Bible Prophecy.

The very last words of the Book of Revelation are Revelation 22:18-19: **"For I testify to everyone who hears the words of the Prophecy of this Book: If anyone adds to these things, God will add to him the plagues that are written in this book; and if anyone takes away from the words of the book of this prophecy, God shall take away his part from the Book of Life, from the holy city, and from the things which are written in this book."** It is hard to imagine how God could have used stronger language to emphasise the importance of this book of Prophecy, yet how many people just avoid reading it? These verses also declare that this is the end of the Bible, that the Word of God is now complete, so nothing more can be added to it. So if any cult or religion comes along and claims that its writings are also the Word of God, whether it be the Koran, the writings of Ellen White, the book of Mormon and other writings by Joseph Smith, or the traditions of Popes and Church Councils, you can safely reject these claims, for they are false according to these final verses of Revelation, which make it clear that the Bible was completed with the Book of Revelation.

God gives strong warnings that those who add to Scripture will come under a curse. The common factor with all these groups who add extra writings to Scripture is that these other writings introduce a different way of salvation than that revealed in the Bible, which is through trusting in Christ alone. These other groups use the extra writings to twist the Bible and change the Gospel so that salvation is made to be dependant on works, which usually include membership of and conformity to the cult in question. The Bible says that those who trust in their own works are under a curse. Thus the main danger of adding to Scripture is that these other writings will turn you away from the true Way of Salvation to another way that is no way, from the true Gospel to another gospel, that is no gospel, from the simplicity of the Gospel of grace and faith in our Lord Jesus Christ, to the complexity of a man-made religious system, where you can never be sure of your salvation, thereby keeping you in bondage to it through fear.

If God finishes Revelation by saying if anyone adds to or takes away from its words, then He will add curse and take away blessing, then it is clear that God is not happy with us messing with this Book. In other words, it is of great importance and we need it to treat it as most holy and take it seriously, just as it is, in its plain literal meaning. If we take away its plain meaning and instead add spiritualised meanings to its words then we are ignoring the warning of its final verses.

Bible Prophecy gives us Mental Health

Bible Prophecy also adds to our mental health, for it gives us the big picture, the grand scheme, the panoramic view of God's Purposes. You see we can get so involved in our own little problems that we tend to get a very self-centred view of the world. We get so caught up in our small world, that we lose perspective and get overwhelmed with small things and so lose the bigger vision of how God is working all things out to fulfil His eternal Purpose. Bible prophecy is healthy for us for it expands our vision and understanding of the bigger picture, enabling us to see things through God's eyes. Bible Prophecy magnifies our view of God as Lord over all, which helps us to trust Him to work all the things in our life for our good. A literal translation of Romans 8:28 says: **"we know that God causes all things to work together for good, to those who are loving Him, who are called according to His Purpose."** In bad situations we should declare that God is working this problem for our good. God did not cause the bad things to happen, but He is well able to turn it around for our good. Bible Prophecy helps us to see our lives as a meaningful part of the bigger picture of what God is doing and bringing forth, enabling us to believe that He is working all things work together for our good.

Bible Prophecy gives us focus

Bible Prophecy gives focus to our lives today. Understanding God's overall Plan gives us wisdom to guide our lives today and the causes to which we give ourselves. It helps us not to be self-centred but to get involved in something bigger than ourselves. It gives us direction so that we flow with His Purposes for this time and keeps us from wasting time on things with no eternal value. If we do not understand what God is doing in the bigger picture, we will tend to give ourselves to the wrong things and waste a big part of our life. So Bible Prophecy is very practical in giving us wisdom to guide our lives.

Jesus is coming soon!

Studying Bible Prophecy heightens our awareness of the times and seasons, especially that Jesus is coming soon. The soon Return of the Lord is a major point that I want to emphasise in this book. I believe we have a lot of good evidence that we are living near the end of the Church Age and that Jesus will return in our lifetimes. Understanding Bible Prophecy will give us the realisation that at any time soon Jesus is going to return and that we are going to stand before Him and give an account and receive rewards for our faithfulness. This realisation will be a major motivation for us to live a life pleasing to God in holiness, and make it count with a fruitful ministry of fulfilling the Great Commission, for the present time is short. It will move us up a higher gear in our lives with the Lord. So this book will bring this hope alive in a way that will energise your life in the Lord. It will confirm that we are now living in the end times very near to the Close of this Age! It will motivate you to take every opportunity that comes our way to share the Gospel, for we need to make the best of the short time we have.

It is a privilege to live in these End Times. We are in a relay race and we have been chosen to run the last lap. The baton has been handed to us. We must be aware of our special calling to live in these days and run our race to the maximum without being distracted and pulled off course, and Bible Prophecy will equip us to do this. Jesus has not returned yet, because the harvest of the Church Age is not yet complete (James 5:7-8), He wants as many people as possible to be saved (2Peter 3:9, 1Timothy 2:4) and that is why we are still here - to bring the Gospel to them, for it is the Power of God unto salvation. Bible Prophecy helps us to understand that our purpose is not to take over the world and Christianise it as Dominion Theology teaches, but rather to reap a final soul harvest before the Lord returns.

Bible Prophecy also provides strong warnings for the lost in the light of the Lord's imminent Return. This world is not going to carry on as it is forever. It has a very limited time left, and God is giving the lost the opportunity now to hear the Gospel and turn to God, but soon it will be too late. This should stimulate us to witness to them, to warn them about sin and Hell, and to win them to Christ.

*Chapter 2: The Structure of Time

Before we focus on the Church Age and discover God's central Purpose for it, we will first see how the Church Age fits into God's overall Structure of Time.

God does not make everything up as He is going along; He has sovereignly ordained a Structure of Time by which He operates. In Part 1 we saw the Bible teaches that when Jesus returns He will establish His Messianic Kingdom on earth, in fulfilment of the vision of all the Old Testament prophets. The New Testament confirms the prophecies of this Kingdom, and fills in the one missing piece of information, that it will last 1000 years, the Millennium (Revelation 20:1-6).

This is of great significance, for the Jewish belief at that time, was that God structured time according to the principle of 1000 years being a DAY to the Lord. Psalm 90:4: **"1000 years in Your sight are like yesterday when it is past."** The Creation Week is a Type or Blueprint for the whole of history, so just as there were 7 days of Creation, so there are 7000 years of human history. Just as the Week consists of 6 days followed by 1 day of rest, so there are 6000 years followed the final 1000 years when the earth enters into rest under the rule of Messiah.

For 6 DAYS or 6000 years the earth has been labouring under the curse and rule of sinful man, but when Messiah comes there 1 DAY or 1000 years when the earth enters into blessing and rest. Therefore this Messianic Kingdom Age is also called the DAY of the Lord. Please note that the term 'the Day of the Lord' has 2 end-time applications. There is the shorter 'Day of the Lord' (the Tribulation), and the longer Day of the Lord, which is the Messianic Kingdom. The context will always make it clear which is intended.

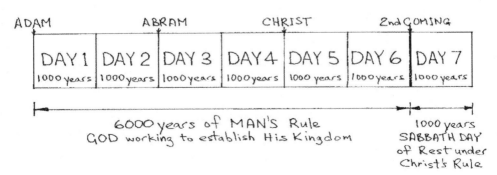

Now this Jewish belief in a 7000 year Plan of God based on Creation Week was well-known in the time of Christ, so when John said that the Messiah will return and reign for exactly 1000 years, he was clearly endorsing this belief, saying that Jesus will return and inaugurate the Sabbath Day of history. Any other length of time would have contradicted this belief, but by saying it was 1000 years God was confirming He is operating according to a Timetable based on Creation Week where 1 DAY = 1000 years.

The apostle Peter also gave his confirmation in <u>2 Peter 3:8</u>: **"Beloved, do not forget this one thing** (do not be ignorant of this one fact)**, that with the Lord one day is as 1000 years, and 1000 years as one day."** So 1000 years to man = 1 DAY to God.   <u>Then he said in v9</u>: **"The Lord is not slack concerning His promise** (to return)**, as some count slackness, but is longsuffering toward us, not willing that any should perish but that all should come to repentance."**

He is talking about the timing of the Lord's Return, saying that although He seems to be waiting a long time it is not because He is careless or reluctant to fulfil His promise, but that He wants as many as possible to be saved. However He is not going to wait forever, because He is operating to a Timetable, and the key to this Timetable is the fact that 1 DAY = 1000 years. No wonder the early Christians also had this belief along with the Jewish rabbis, which continued as a strong belief throughout church history. So God demonstrates His sovereignty over history by governing it according to His Timetable:

(1) There were 2000 years from Adam to Abraham - the first 2 DAYS.

(2) There were 2000 years from Abraham to Christ, in His 1st Coming - the next 2 DAYS. The first 4 DAYS are called the Former Days

(3) The next 2000 years or 2 DAYS must be from Christ's 1st Coming to His 2nd Coming, because according to this pattern Jesus must return at the end of the 6th DAY of history.

(4) The final 1000 years are the Sabbath DAY of history, the Millennial DAY of the Lord. The last 3 DAYS are called the Latter Days.

You may be thinking that we have already had 2000 years from Christ and nothing happened. This is a common confusion based on the fact we count years from Christ's Birth and so when the year 2000 passed many assumed the idea must not be valid. However, the key turning point when a new DAY was born, when the latter DAYS began, when the dispensation changed was not Christ's Birth, but His death and resurrection in AD 33. If we going to measure the 2000 years, we must count them from this date, not from His birth. So we have not reached the end of the 2000 years yet, but we are certainly getting close!

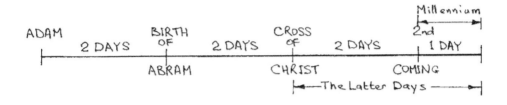

So history is modelled on the CREATION WEEK of 7 DAYS, which is a Type of a WEEK of history of 7000 years. God divides human history into 7 periods of 1000 years. If a DAY with the Lord is as 1000 years, then we can think of these as 7 DAYS of a WEEK, the great WEEK of history modelled on Creation Week. Since the Church Age has been going for almost 2000 years already, it means that we stand very near the end of the 6 DAYS or 6000 years, and therefore the final SABBATH DAY OF REST (the Millennium) is about to begin when Jesus, the Lord of the Sabbath will rule (Mark 2:28). This is one of many reasons (along with all the Signs of the Times described in Part 1) why we can know that we are truly living in the last of the Last Days, and that Jesus is coming soon!

Now it is important to say that no man KNOWS (including believers) the exact day or year when the Lord will return: **"But of that day and hour NO ONE knows, not even the angels of Heaven, but My Father only...Watch therefore, for YOU** (believer) **do NOT KNOW what hour YOUR LORD is coming. Therefore you also be ready, for the Son of Man is coming at an hour you do NOT EXPECT"** (Matthew 24:36,42,44). Thus not only do we not know when He is coming, we do not know when He is not coming, because He will come when we do not expect Him. This phrase is designed to destroy all human reasonings as to why the Lord cannot come soon. His Coming is imminent, which means He could come at any time. Therefore it is foolish and wrong to try and predict dates. This typology is not the basis for prediction, but it does confirm Jesus is coming soon.

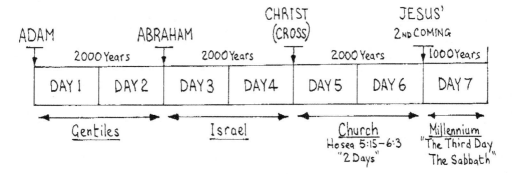

*(1) God began by dealing with mankind as a whole in the 2000 years or 2 DAYS from Adam to Abraham. This is **the Age of the Gentiles**.

*(2) Then the next 2000 years from Abraham to Christ is **the Age of Israel**. Starting with Abraham and continuing with Isaac and Jacob (Israel) and his 12 sons He formed the special, separated Nation of Israel and revealed Himself to them and through them. These 2 DAYS ended with the Death of Christ. The 4 DAYS or 4000 years from Adam to Christ are the Former DAYS.

*(3) After the Resurrection of Christ, we entered the LATTER Days. The next 2000 years or 2 DAYS is **the Age of the Church**, the body of Christ, a new body of people called out of both Israel and the nations. These will end with the Second Coming of Christ, at the end of 6 DAYS from Adam.

*(4) When Christ returns to the earth He will personally reign here as King of kings. This is **the Age of Christ**. According to Revelation 20, He will reign for 1000 years or 1 DAY. This is the Sabbath DAY of history when the earth enters her rest. This final DAY completes the Divine Week of 7 DAYS or 7000 years.

*(5) Finally, at the end of time, there will be a new heaven and earth and all the redeemed will be united into one People of God for all Eternity.

Thus in the outworking of God's Plan of Redemption and in His management of mankind, **God deals with 3 distinct groups: (1) the Gentiles (2) Israel and (3) the Church.** We have seen how the focus of God's Plan of Redemption has changed from group to group through the Ages. Within God's overall ultimate purpose He has a distinct plan, purpose and programme for each group and manages them accordingly in the various dispensations.

3 Confirmations of this Structure of Time

We will now see 3 fascinating confirmations of this Structure of Time and the fact that 1 DAY with the Lord = 1000 years to man. To learn more about the Structure of Time I recommend my book 'The Keys of Time'.

*1. The first 4 DAYS or 4000 years from Adam's sin to Christ's death are typified by the setting aside of the Passover Lamb 4 days before being sacrificed. In Exodus 12 the Passover lamb was set aside on the 10th day and sacrificed on the 14th. Likewise, Jesus was set apart as the Lamb of God from the foundation of the world 4 DAYS, or 4000 years before He was sacrificed on the Cross for us.

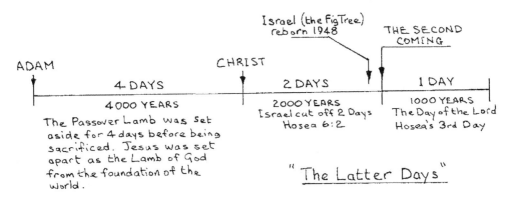

*2. There is a wonderful prophecy in Hosea that there are 2 DAYS or 2000 years between Christ's ascension to His Second Coming.

Hosea 5:14-6:3 is a prophecy of the Messiah: **"For I (the Messiah) will be like a lion to Ephraim, and like a young lion to the house of Judah."** Jesus came to Israel as a LION, as their KING, but they reject Him - therefore Israel comes under judgement: **"I, even I, will tear them** (cut them off) **and go away** (back to heaven); **I will take them away** (from the land), **and no one shall rescue."** This predicts that after the Messiah comes Israel will be scattered to the nations. This is exactly what happened, because she rejected Jesus. Then in continues in Hosea 5:15: **"I will return to my Place** (His ascension to the right hand of God the Father) **UNTIL they acknowledge their offence** (of rejecting His Messiahship)." The UNTIL means that He will return after a time, when Israel repents. Then it goes on to describe their repentance: **"Then they will seek My face; in their Affliction** (Tribulation) **they will earnestly seek Me."** This is a prophecy that in the Tribulation Israel will eventually realise who Messiah is.

Then Hosea 6:1 gives us the words that the leaders of Israel will use to call the nation to repent and return to the Messiah: **"Come, and let us return to the LORD; for He has torn** (judged), **but He will heal us; He has stricken, but He will bind us up."** They realise that He had judged them for their unbelief but that now He was about to raise them up again.

Next in Hosea 6:2, He gives a clue as to how long it will be between when the Messiah left them and judged Israel and when He will restore them: **"AFTER 2 DAYS** (2000 years) **He will revive us. On the 3rd DAY** (the 1000 year Millennium) **He will raise us** (Israel) **up that we may live in His sight."**

This prophecy predicts that the Messiah will come to Israel, and then return to heaven - this has been fulfilled. It then predicts He'll revive them spiritually at the end of 2 DAYS, that is 2000 years. Then it says He will raise them up again as a nation on the 3rd DAY so they will live in His sight. We will see in the next verse that He revives, restores and raises up Israel at His 2nd Coming. So what is the 3rd DAY of 1000 years? It's the 1000-year reign of Christ when Israel will be fully restored in faith as the chief nation and live in the Presence of God.

Hosea 6:3 says that the Messiah will personally restore Israel by His return in power and glory: **"Let us know, let us press on to know the Lord. His going forth** (out of Heaven) **is established as the morning sunrise."** This is speaking of His 2nd Coming, when He appears as the glorious Sun of Righteousness to start a new DAY of human history, as Malachi 4:2 says: **"The Sun of Righteousness shall arise with healing in His wings."** When it says: **"His going forth from Heaven is established as the Sunrise"** it means His glorious appearing is certain and will be at a fixed time. Just as you know when the sun will rise in the morning, that it is sure to come at an appointed time, so likewise the Coming of the Messiah to save Israel. What is this fixed time for the Lord's Return to restore repentant Israel? Hosea 6:2 hints it will be AFTER 2 DAYS or 2000 years from His ascension to Heaven in AD 33.

Finally, v3 describes the spiritual blessings in the 3rd DAY, the Millennium: **"He will come to us as the rain, like the latter and former rain on the earth."**

So, Hosea 5:15-6:3 speaks of Christ being rejected, then going to Heaven for 2 DAYS (2000 years) before returning to a repentant Israel to revive and restore her, and then pour out His blessings upon the earth for the 3rd Millennial DAY.

We are presently near the end of 2000 years from His First Coming! There were 4 DAYS (about 4000 years) from Adam to the Cross. Here Hosea predicts there will be 2 DAYS (about 2000 years) from the Cross to the Second Coming. This makes 6 DAYS, leaving 1 more DAY of 1000 years, the Sabbath DAY of rest, the Millennium, the 3rd DAY of Hosea's prophecy. Therefore we stand near the end of 2000 years from the Cross and we see Israel restored to the land in preparation to be restored to the Lord!

*3. The Parable of the Good Samaritan

Another gem is found in the Parable of the Good Samaritan in <u>Luke 10</u>, which Jesus gave to show what it means to love your neighbour, and to answer the question: **"What can I do to have eternal life?'** (v25).

First, Jesus showed the man that he was not good enough to save himself, as he did not love his neighbour as God required. At that time there was a mutual hatred between Jews and Samaritans, so by proving that the Samaritan was his neighbour, Jesus convicted him of his sin of racial prejudice. Thus Jesus helped him to take the first step to be saved by getting him to stop trusting in himself for salvation, but instead look to a Saviour. Then having shot down his false hope of saving himself, Jesus also revealed the true way of salvation, for this parable also contains a wonderful Picture of Salvation by Grace alone. It shows that we can only have eternal life by receiving it as a free-gift from Jesus.

The parable is an allegory where every detail has a meaning. JESUS is the GOOD SAMARITAN, Who alone fulfils the picture of the good neighbour, sacrificially loving and showing mercy - even to His enemies. There can only be

ONE Who can fulfil the Parable - JESUS. We are like the man left for dead. We cannot save ourselves. Our only hope is to be saved by the Good Samaritan.

v30a: **"Then Jesus answered and said: "A certain man went down from Jerusalem to Jericho."** This man represents all of us in Adam. This was a dangerous journey in a barren desert wilderness called 'the red and bloody way', a perfect hunting ground for thieves, with sudden turns and cliffs, making it easy to hide and suddenly attack a traveller. It was crooked and downhill all the way, descending from 2300 feet above sea level to Jericho, 1300 feet below sea level, the lowest place on earth. It was foolish of him to go alone. It was his fault he was robbed. He represents all of us in Adam: **"All we like sheep have gone astray, we have turned everyone to his own way"** (Isaiah 53:6).

This is a perfect picture of the road the man took when he went away from God in sin. He was created to dwell in Jerusalem, the city of peace, the city of the Great King where God rules and where His Presence dwells, where man had fellowship with God. But man sinned and foolishly walked away from God down the road of certain death, as it says in v30b:

v30b: **"and He fell among thieves and they stripped him of his clothes, wounded him, and they departed, leaving him half-dead."** He was beaten, stripped naked and left to die. What a picture of man in his sin! Jesus chose this story to show how sinful man is totally helpless and unable to save himself - he desperately needs a Saviour. Man had put himself outside God's protection, where satan and the curse could steal all of God's blessings from him. We were stripped of our robe of righteousness, our peace (wholeness) of mind and body, but worst of all we were left 'half-dead', for we died spiritually, and were about to die physically also and enter into eternal death. God said to Adam in Genesis 2:17: **"in the day you eat it, you shall surely die** (literally: 'dying you shall die')." There are 2 deaths - man's spirit died at once and his body started to die. He was half-dead. This is a picture of all men without Christ, helpless, hopeless, unable to save ourselves. Our only hope was to be saved by the Good Samaritan - Jesus!

After showing the failure of the Law and Religion to save in v31-32, CHRIST'S FIRST COMING to save the lost is described in v33: **"But a certain**

Samaritan as He journeyed came to where he was. When he saw him he had compassion on him." This Samaritan is a picture of Jesus. The twist of the story was Samaritans were hated enemies of the Jews (v37). Likewise, Jesus was "despised and rejected of men" (Isaiah 53:3). We were enemies of God but He still loved us. "As He journeyed He came to where he was." Jesus came to us on purpose, for He was on a mission from the heavenly Jerusalem. "The son of man came to seek and save the lost" (Luke 19:10). We couldn't come to God, or save ourselves. We were dying, powerless to move. But when were unable to come to Him, God, in the Person of Jesus, came to us. He humbled Himself to become a man to identify with us and humbled Himself further to enter into our death to lift us up and bring us to God. He found us, reached down to us and saved us from our sin and death.

"When he saw him he had compassion on him." Jesus saw us lying in sin and sickness, helpless, on the point of death and was moved with compassion for us. When we had no power to save ourselves, He became our neighbour, a fellow human being, and came to us to save us. His love for us caused Him to come near and humble himself to identify with us, to get down in the dirt and raise us up.

Then in v34a we see how this man was saved: "He went to him and bound up his wounds POURING in OIL and WINE." On the Cross, Jesus fully identified with us and became 'unclean' for us, bearing our sin, curse, sickness and death upon Himself, in order to save, heal and restore us. By His wounds we are healed. He also poured in the OIL and the WINE, a picture of the Holy Spirit. Jesus poured His SPIRIT into us when we ask and receive Him.

The OIL and WINE speaks of the 2-fold Ministry of the Holy Spirit

(1) OIL represents the Spirit in the New Birth.

(2) WINE represents the Baptism and Fullness of the Spirit. God wants our cup to run over with the abundant life, anointing, power and joy of the Spirit

Ephesians 5:18: "Be not DRUNK with WINE, wherein is excess; but be (being) FILLED with the SPIRIT." He compares being filled with the Spirit to drinking wine. As you get filled you will overflow with rivers of life flowing out of you (John 7:37-39). This dual ministry of the OIL and WINE is described in Matthew 9:17: "Neither do men put new wine into old wineskins else the wineskins break, and the wine runs out, and the wineskins perish: but they put new wine into renewed wineskins, and both are preserved." The wineskins represent our spirits, designed to contain and pour out the wine of God. But because of the Fall they became old and unable to hold the life and Spirit of God. They can only be renewed by rubbing them in OIL (a picture of the new birth) , and then they can hold the new WINE (the fullness of the Spirit). Our renewed wineskins are able to receive and pour out God's wine. The OIL is given once, but the WINE continually, so now we must continue to DRINK. The man received some wine when he was saved, but later in the story, he could drink as much as he wanted in the Inn, with the Innkeeper filling his cup as often as he requested.

v34b: "and He set him on his own animal." Jesus lifted us out of the Pit and made us sit with Him in heavenly places in His Kingdom!

The man had wanted to know how he could have eternal life. Jesus first showed him he could not save himself, as he did not truly love his neighbour as God required. Instead he was like the hopeless dying man in the story, who was not saved by his own efforts or merits, but simply by receiving the ministry of the Good Samaritan. In his pride he could have rejected that help saying: "Leave me alone and let me die." Likewise, all we have to do to be saved is to receive the saving ministry of Jesus. So in this parable Jesus did answer the question of how to have eternal life, by revealing that salvation by grace received through faith alone. We must see ourselves as that helpless dying man, who cannot save himself. Only Jesus, our Good Samaritan can save us. Risen again He is ready to pour out His oil and wine into us. All we have to do is receive His saving grace.

At this point we might expect Jesus to finish the parable, as He had made His main point, but He continues to add more details. Why? It must be because He is using this allegory to give us some key information about the Church Age.

v34: "He brought him to an inn and took care of him." There was an inn halfway between Jerusalem and Jericho, so people could break their journey. Having saved us Jesus took us to the Inn, a picture of the Church, a place of protection, peace and safety from robbers, and fellowship with fellow travellers, a place of good food and drink, where you can regain strength, be restored and help others who have been rescued by the Good Samaritan. Jesus instituted the Church as the place He takes care of us.

<u>v35</u>: **"On the next day, when he DEPARTED he took out 2 DENARII and gave them to the INNKEEPER and said: "take care of him and whatever you spend over that, I will repay when I COME AGAIN."**

The Good Samaritan departed to go back to Jerusalem. Likewise, having come to save us, Jesus returned to the Heavenly Jerusalem, but He didn't leave us alone, but entrusted us into the care of the Innkeeper - a picture of the Holy Spirit. They knew each other well. He said to the Innkeeper: "I will be coming back, but in the meantime take care of him and give him whatever he needs."

To cover the cost of this He gave the Innkeeper 2 denarii, which was 2 days wages (for labourers were paid a DENARIUS a DAY - see Matthew 20:2). The clear hint is that he was going to return after 2 days. He would go up to Jerusalem and then after 2 days return to the inn. This speaks of Jesus coming the first time to save us, then going back to the Heavenly Jerusalem for 2 DAYS or 2000 years. Then He will come again and take us back to the Heavenly Jerusalem with Him (John 14:1-3). So, Jesus is coming soon! Having died to save us and give us His oil and wine, and ascended to the Heavenly Jerusalem, our Good Samaritan has promised to return for us after 2 DAYS (2000 years).

Thus 2 denarii confirm that this present Age is about 2000 years!

This then is another confirmation that we are very close to the return of Jesus. He promised to return after 2 DAYS, and we are living very close to the end of the 2000 years from when He departed to heaven. So we need to realise we are living in exciting times with the world is heading rapidly towards its climax. Very soon Jesus our Good Samaritan is going to return for us from the heavenly Jerusalem.

Meanwhile Jesus has paid the price in full for His Spirit to give us every blessing, and we are invited to eat and drink at His table! Our Innkeeper is commissioned to give us all we need. He will keep filling our cup with new wine if we ask Him. It is up to us how much we want. We can continually receive an abundance of blessing for Jesus has paid the price. We just ask and freely receive what has been provided for us as a gift.

*Chapter 3: The Purpose of the Church Age

The primary Purpose of the Church-Age is a soul-harvest from the nations, and so to co-operate with His Purposes, we must make it our first priority to preach the Gospel. God's priority for this Age is the fulfilment of the Great Commission to preach the Gospel to every creature and disciple all nations. This is imperative because: **"the Gospel is the Power of God unto Salvation for everyone who believes"** (Romans 1:16). In this chapter, I want to fully establish this truth in your heart, because the enemy is constantly trying to divert our time and energy into other well-meaning activities, which will not bear eternal fruit. This issue very much relates to the prophetic scriptures, because your view on Prophecy will to a large extent determine your level of obedience to the Great Commission.

In this series of books, I am upholding the literal interpretation of Scripture, which leads to the Pre-Millennial and the Pre-Tribulation viewpoints. In Part 1 we established the truth of Pre-Millennialism (see also Appendix 5), which says that Jesus will come before the Millennium, and then He will establish His Kingdom on earth for 1000 years. The Purpose of the Church is to be a shining witness in a dark world, not to take over or Christianise the world. One tactic of the enemy is to divert the Church into 'Kingdom Now' or Dominion Theology, where the primary aim becomes establishing the Kingdom of God in the world, through taking over the mountains of the world-system, instead of preaching the Gospel. This is usually based on the false prophetic viewpoints of Post-Millennialism and/or Preterism.

In Appendix 5 and 6, I explain in more detail why this undermines and distracts us from fulfilling what Christ actually told us to – the Great Commission, replacing it with a vision that is more appealing to the flesh (transforming nations and taking over cities). The Bible says that the end-times will be like the days of Noah, with the Church courageously witnessing to a godless world, calling it to repent before Judgment falls in the Tribulation, and Christ comes personally to set up His Kingdom. These other viewpoints think that is too negative, and so replace it with a more positive vision of their own devising, namely, that the Church is called to fulfil the dominion mandate by establishing God's Kingdom on earth, and only then will Christ can come and reign. This results in a diminished emphasis on sharing the Gospel, substituting the Gospel with good works, social action, mercy ministries, reforming society and bringing institutions under God's Kingdom.

Now I need to clarify what I mean, in case you think I am saying that we should withdraw from the world into a holy huddle, and not get involved in mercy ministries, politics, social action, the media, education and so on. No, I am saying the opposite. We should be fully engaged according to our individual gifts and callings, but we should always hold before us that the ultimate aim is the salvation of souls through the Gospel. Our good works and our gifts will give us credibility and a platform from which we can share the Gospel. But because the Gospel is controversial, and not always well-received, the pressure always comes on us to just be good at what we do, show love by practical mercy and do our good works, but not share Christ. In other words we SUBSTITUTE our witnessing by our good works. We may run a food bank (which is good), but if we do not also use it as a way to share the Gospel, then we are not fulfilling the Great Commission, or bearing eternal fruit. We may think we are bringing the Kingdom of God into the world simply by living a Biblical lifestyle and following righteous principles in our business, but we are deceiving ourselves, for it is only through sharing the Gospel, that we can shine the light of Christ in this dark world and change men's hearts.

The issue is what is our ultimate aim? Is it to please men or to glorify God by winning souls, giving them the Gospel, so they will enjoy everlasting life in Heaven, rather than suffering everlasting punishment in Hell? If our ultimate aim is success in our field, rising to the top of our mountain, or to change society through political action, or to give practical help to as many people as possible, then we will always compromise the Gospel in order to achieve our goal, because sharing the Gospel will always seem to get in the way, because of the spiritual opposition of the world-system to the Gospel. This has been demonstrated again and again in history. Organisations that started out with a vision of salvation, offering practical help as a way to show love and gain a platform to be heard, end up focusing on social action and mercy, making the Gospel a secondary issue. By the way, we do not need to earn the right to share the Gospel, because Jesus has already authorised, commanded and sent us to do it. That should be enough for us.

It is not wrong to want God to raise us into higher positions in the world, because the higher you place a lamp, the greater the effect and the reach of its light. Jesus said: **"You are the LIGHT of the world. A city that is set on a hill** (the Church, where we join our lights together in unity) **cannot be hidden." Nor do they light a lamp and put it under a basket, but** (high up) **on a lampstand, and it gives LIGHT to all who are in the house"** (Matthew 5:14-15).

However, as you climb your mountain of success, the devil will always meet you on the way up (as he did with Jesus) and tell you that you can have what you want, as long as you do it his way, that is compromise, and not witness to Christ. Then even if you get to the top, you are no use to God anyway, because your light is not shining, for the only way we can shine our light is by sharing the Word of life (I prove this later in this chapter). Thus if our ultimate aim is our position and outward success, rather than being faithful in sharing the Gospel, we will embrace the rationalisations and excuses that allow us to compromise on God's Prime Directive, the Great Commission, and miss out from fulfilling our main call in life.

If you observe the example of Jesus, the apostles and the first Christians, their primary aim was not to transform society or gain high positions and influence, but to courageously preach the Gospel, even if it meant losing their position. Paradoxically, by taking this approach, through the salvation and discipleship of many souls, the result was often a great transformation of society, but that was not the primary focus. The reason for this success is that the true source of real transforming power is not our moral rectitude, good intentions or inspiring charisma, but Christ through His Word (Romans 1:16). So the moment we cease sharing the Gospel, treating it as a non-essential thing of secondary importance, (finding our fulfilment and satisfaction in doing good works, rather than obeying God's Commission) we lose all our real power to change lives and society, whereas those who hold fast to God's mandate and message, will not just save souls and bear fruit for eternity, but also transform their communities as a by-product.

Bible Prophecy plays an important role in helping us think straight and keep our priorities right. It reminds us that ultimately Christ will destroy this world-system (all the kingdoms of this world) and establish His Kingdom on earth. Then after the 1000 years, He will destroy this Universe and all that will be left from it will be the redeemed, who will enter the Eternal State. So our only lasting legacy will be the souls we have helped lead to Christ and disciple. Attempts to create utopia on earth independent from God are mere humanistic projects doomed to fail. Thus understanding Bible Prophecy correctly will give you God's revealed vision for the future (hope), which will keep you focused on God's agenda and priorities for your life in this present Church Age, and keep you on track in fulfilling His will for your life, protecting you from falling for satan's many devices to distract you from doing what God commands you to do – obeying the Great Commission.

We have noted how relevant the Pre-Millennial issue is for keeping us on track in fulfilling God's will for our lives. Understanding that God's Purpose for the Church Age is the fulfilment of the Great Commission in the salvation of souls, will cause us to align ourselves and our lives and use our gifts to fulfil His Purpose. If we truly understood how hopeless and sinful man is without God, then we will realise how absurd and useless it is to try to transform the world without the Gospel.

In this book (Part 2), we will particularly focus on a second truth of Bible Prophecy, that Jesus is coming to receive His Church in the Rapture, before the Tribulation starts. Many see this Pre-Tribulation belief as just an interesting theological issue, but without practical significance for our lives (which is how most people regard Bible Prophecy in general). But in fact believing it makes a big difference, because it means that Jesus' Coming is IMMINENT, that is, He could come at any time. This is a major doctrine of the New Testament, and is a major motivation in the New Testament for believers (1) to live HOLY LIVES (fulfilling the Great Commandment of loving God with all our hearts), and (2) to be zealous in SHARING the GOSPEL (fulfilling the great Commission), because Jesus could come at anytime and then we will have to stand before Him and give an account for our lives. This motivates us every day, to make sure that we are ready for His Coming, in fellowship with Him and serving Him, and witnessing to Him, and not wasting our lives because time is short. Again Bible Prophecy, correctly understood, gives us God's vision for the future and strengthens and clarifies our knowledge of God's purpose for our life, reminding us why we are here and emphasising what is truly important (what our priorities should be), so that we can align our life with God's revealed will, and stay on track in fulfilling our purpose.

The Ministry of Christ

To establish the Purpose of the Church and the Church Age, we first look at Jesus' own Mission and Ministry, for the Church's calling is to continue the Ministry that He started. Jesus had the Holy Spirit WITHIN Him from His conception and birth, but only received the Spirit UPON Him when He was baptised in the Spirit at His baptism, when He was sent and commissioned by God to fulfil his Ministry: **"Jesus was baptized; and while He prayed, Heaven was opened, and the Holy Spirit descended in bodily form like a dove UPON Him** (to empower Him for His ministry), **and a voice came from Heaven saying: "You are My beloved Son; in You I am well pleased** (this was His commission and authorization from His Father to represent Him in His Ministry)" (Luke 3:21-22).

From that time, Jesus started teaching the Word, preaching the Gospel and healing the sick in the Power of the Spirit: **"Jesus went about all Galilee, teaching in their synagogues, PREACHING the GOSPEL of the Kingdom, and healing all kinds of sickness and all kinds of disease among the people."** (Matthew 4:23, also 9:35, 11:5, Mark 1:14, Luke 7:22, 9:6, 20:1).

We are given a more detailed account of how He did this, when Luke describes His preaching in Nazareth: **"Jesus returned in the POWER of the SPIRIT to Galilee... He was handed the book of the prophet Isaiah. And when He had opened the book, He found the place where it was written** (in Isaiah 61:1-2a): **"The SPIRIT of the LORD is UPON Me, because He has (1) ANOINTED Me to PREACH the GOSPEL** (Good News) **to the poor; (2) He has SENT Me to HEAL the broken-hearted, to PROCLAIM LIBERTY to the captives and recovery of sight to the blind, to SET at LIBERTY those who are oppressed, to PROCLAIM the ACCEPTABLE YEAR of the Lord** (the Year of Jubilee). **"And He began to say to them: "Today this Scripture is fulfilled in your hearing"** (Luke 4:14,18-19,21). His Gospel Message was a proclamation that He was the Anointed One (Messiah) who fulfilled the Year of Jubilee. He declared the result of what happened at His baptism. He was (1) ANOINTED with the POWER of the Spirit UPON Him to preach the Gospel and heal the sick, and He was (2) SENT (commissioned, appointed and authorised) to preach the Gospel.

The Gospel is nothing more or less than the fulfilment of the Year of Jubilee (Leviticus 25), which was every 49 years (v8). During that time some men got into debt (a picture of sin), resulting in the loss of one's land (possession), and going into slavery. Until the Year of Jubilee when they could go free to reclaim their lost possession and rebuild their lives, having had all their debts (sins) forgiven. This took place on the Day of Atonement when the High Priest made the great sacrifice of the sin offering and took its blood into the holy of holies (v9). If the sacrifice was accepted, He would appear alive and proclaim the Good News that it was now the Acceptable Year of the Lord, the Year of God's Favour, because the price had now been paid, and men could be made acceptable to God through the Sacrifice.

The Year of Jubilee, which means 'trumpet blast' was then proclaimed throughout the land as the heralds and trumpeters went forth from town to town, proclaiming LIBERTY and FORGIVENESS (v9-10), on the basis of the Atoning Sacrifice. It was a year of grace, so that anyone who heard the trumpet and believed the Good News could receive their forgiveness from debt and be released from slavery and reclaim their lives, and return to reclaim their lost possessions, which were now released back to them (v10,13, 28,31,33, 54). So it was GOOD NEWS (Gospel) to the poor, who had lost their liberty, possessions and position. It is a proclamation of grace, that is, that salvation is offered as a free-gift to the poor (those who need it, and could not pay for it anyway), to be received by faith. It could be offered as a free-gift, for the price had been paid in full by the Sacrifice.

However wonderful this was, it was only a picture of the Great Jubilee that the Messiah would bring for all mankind, for we were all in sin-debt to God, and were slaves to sin, and had lost everything we had originally possessed (life, peace, righteousness, joy, health, the Presence of God, the Holy Spirit). Isaiah 61 predicts the Messiah would come to fulfil Jubilee, not just by being the Atoning Sacrifice (Isaiah 53), but also by being the first to proclaim the Year of Jubilee, that is, to preach the Gospel. In Luke 4, Jesus was claiming He was the Messiah who had come to fulfil Isaiah 61 and initiate the preaching of the Jubilee-Gospel. He declared the Good News that the authority and power of God was present upon Him to set them free from sin and restore their health, and it was a free-gift to them. Like the original Jubilee it was a NOW message, that is, when they heard the Jubilee Trumpet, they could immediately receive their forgiveness and walk free into a new life. Of course those who didn't believe the message stayed in bondage.

Once the High Priest and his Trumpeter made the original proclamation, the trumpet blasts multiplied throughout the land, as the trumpeters were sent to all the towns. Then when each new person received the Good News, they too sounded their shofar, declaring the Good News to others. Likewise, Jesus commissioned and sent His disciples to go into all the world and preach the Gospel (sound the Jubilee trumpet) to all people. This is the Great Commission. We are to declare that the Atoning Sacrifice is accepted and that forgiveness, liberty, healing, deliverance and restoration is now freely available through Christ, and that we are His authorised, empowered representatives, and His Spirit is upon us, so that we can heal the sick. We are called to continue the Jubilee Proclamation of the Gospel, which is the Power of God unto Salvation for all who believe (Romans 1:16), for until they hear the Trumpet of the Gospel they cannot believe in Christ and receive His blessing. The Gospel is described in terms of Jubilee in Acts 10:35-43, 1Corinthians 5:18-6:2. We preach: **"Behold, now is the acceptable time; behold, now is the day of salvation"** (6:2). Again we see that the Ministry of Jesus provides the Blueprint for our Ministry. We are to continue the Gospel Proclamation that He initiated.

As a practice run, Jesus first sent His apostles with the Gospel, empowering them to heal the sick (Matthew 10, Luke 9), and then the 70 (Luke 10), and then the whole Church (the Great Commission in Matthew, Mark, Luke, John and Acts). The Great Commission is our marching orders to continue His Ministry. It is a command not a suggestion. It is our divine authorization to preach the Gospel and make them disciples of Jesus. It defines His will for the Church in the present Age. It reveals His Purpose for the Church until He returns. It directs us in our use of His gifts. Notice He does not command us to take over the world but to preach the Gospel. We will rule and reign and have dominion with Christ in the future Age, but for now we are to humbly bear witness to the truth of Christ and His Gospel, just like Jesus and His apostles. Beware anyone downgrading the importance of preaching the Gospel, or substituting other activities for it, or saying: "we just need to witness by our life', for the only way people can be saved is through the Gospel.

*1. The Great Commission in John: **"Most assuredly, I say to you, he who believes in Me, the works that I do he will do also; and GREATER WORKS than these he will do, because I go to My Father."** We are not only called to do the same works as Jesus (preaching the Gospel, teaching and healing), but also GREATER WORKS, which is getting people BORN AGAIN and baptised in the Spirit, because Jesus could not do those works, because they only became available in the New Covenant through his death and resurrection.

John 20:21: **"Jesus said to them again, "Peace to you! As the Father has SENT Me, I also SEND you."** We have been given the same commission that God gave Jesus, to preach the Gospel and heal the sick with same commission. He has authorised us to go, and gives us the same power of the Spirit, within and upon us. On the evening of the resurrection He imparted the Spirit WITHIN them: **"When He had said this, He BREATHED on them, and said to them: "RECEIVE the Holy Spirit"** (John 20:22). This is Stage 1, when they were born again.

Next He started to prepare His disciples to receive stage 2 of the blessing of the Spirit, the Spirit UPON, which had to happen 50 days later, to fulfil Pentecost. That same evening at the start of the 40 days, He SENDS them on His Mission to preach the Gospel and promises them to give His POWER UPON them to fulfil it.

*2. The Great Commission in Luke 24:46-49: **"Then He said, "Thus it is written, and thus it was necessary for the Christ to suffer and to rise from the dead the third day, and that repentance and remission of sins should be PREACHED in His Name to all nations, beginning at Jerusalem. And you are My witnesses of these things. Behold, I send the Promise of My Father upon you; but wait in Jerusalem until you are clothed with POWER from on high."**

*3. The Great Commission in Mark. A week later they were gathered again in the Upper Room and this time Thomas was also there (John 20:26-29).

Mark 16:14-20: **"Later He appeared to the 11** (this means Thomas was there) **as they sat at the table;.. And He said to them: "Go into all the world and PREACH the GOSPEL to every creature. He who believes and is baptized will be saved; but he who does not believe will be condemned. And these Signs will follow those who believe. In My Name they will cast out demons; they will speak with new tongues... they will LAY HANDS on the SICK, and they will recover" ...And they went out and preached everywhere, the LORD WORKING with and confirming the Word through the accompanying Signs."**

*4. The Great Commission in Matthew. Sometime later when they went to Galilee Jesus appeared to them again and said: **"All authority has been given to Me in heaven and on earth. Go therefore** (with My AUTHORITY) **and make DISCIPLES of all the nations, BAPTISING them in the Name of the Father and of the Son and of the Holy Spirit, TEACHING them to observe all things** that I have COMMANDED you (including the Great Commission – which is a Command); and lo, I am WITH YOU always, even to the End of the Age (the Tribulation)." He draws His attention that He is WITH them in the Power and Anointing of His Spirit (as God was WITH Jesus, Acts 10:38), so that when we go, and preach and teach His Word, we will experience His Presence and Power. Thus the Spirit may be UPON us, but is only released when we obey (speak His Word).

*5. The Great Commission in Acts. "The former account (Luke's Gospel) I made, O Theophilus, of all that Jesus BEGAN both to DO and TEACH, until the day in which He was taken up, after He through the Holy Spirit had given commandments (the Great Commission) to the apostles whom He had chosen." This again proves that we are to continue the ministry that Jesus began to do. Then it describes His words at the end of the 40 days: "He commanded them not to depart from Jerusalem, but to wait for the Promise of the Father, "which" He said: "you have heard from Me; for John truly baptized with water, but you shall be baptized with the Holy Spirit not many days from now... But you shall receive POWER when the Holy Spirit has come UPON you; and you shall be My WITNESSES in Jerusalem, and in all Judea and Samaria, and to the end of the earth" (Acts 1:4, 5,8). They were authorised (sent) and empowered by the Spirit UPON to be His witnesses to the ends of the earth. They received this power a few days later on the day of Pentecost (Acts 2) and the rest of Acts records how the first Christians turned the world upside down by preaching the Gospel.

The Great Commission has not changed. We still have the same marching orders, and have the same authority and power of the Spirit as the early Church. We cannot keep this good news to ourselves. Empowered by the Spirit of God, we must make Jesus' last commandment our first priority.

That's why Jesus said in describing the Church Age in Mark 13:10: "The GOSPEL MUST first be PREACHED to all the nations." It is imperative that we preach the Gospel, for the salvation of souls from every nation is the central purpose of the Church Age. This Purpose is expressed even more clearly in Matthew 24:14: "And this GOSPEL of the Kingdom will be PREACHED in all the world as a WITNESS to all the nations, and then the End will come."

(Although from the context, the primary application of Matthew 24:14 is to the harvest of the Tribulation, whereas the primary application of Mark 13:10 is to the harvest of the Church Age, Jesus clearly presents these as 2 parallel truths which illuminate each other, showing there is a similarity in God's Redemptive Purposes for the Church Age and the Tribulation. It is 2 harvests, but the same God, and these 2 verses reveal that the heart and primary Purpose of God for both the Church Age and Tribulation is evangelism – to save as many as possible. Matthew 24:14 makes this explicit, by saying once this Purpose is fulfilled, God will bring the Age to its final end. Applying this thought to Mark 13:10, we can draw out its full meaning, by reading it as: **"The Gospel must first be preached to all the nations** (and then the 'End of the Age' or Tribulation will come)."

Even our prayers are to be governed by the need to fulfil God's primary Purpose - the fulfilment of the Great Commission, according to 1Timothy 2:1-4: **"I exhort as of first importance that supplications, prayers, intercessions, and giving of thanks be made for all men,** (especially) **for kings and all who are in authority, that we may lead a quiet and peaceable life in all godliness and reverence. For this is good and acceptable in the sight of God our Saviour, who desires (1) ALL MEN to be SAVED** (through the Gospel) **and (2) to come to the KNOWLEDGE of the TRUTH** (of God's Word through discipleship)."

Christ will only return for the Church, when He considers His Purpose fulfilled of gathering a great soul-harvest from all the nations, as James 5:7-8 confirms: **"be patient, brethren, until the Coming of the Lord. See how the Farmer waits for the PRECIOUS FRUIT of the earth, waiting patiently for it until it receives the early and latter rain. You also be patient. Establish your hearts, for the Coming of the Lord is at hand."** Notice that the Purpose of the Divine Farmer in this present Age is the bringing forth of the precious fruit of the earth (the souls of men), and so His Return to reap that harvest is connected with the fulfilment of the Great Commission. Everything else, like changing society, is secondary. If we are working with Christ, we will be primarily focused on winning precious souls and making disciples for Him – that's what will matter in eternity.

Revelation 5:9 confirms that God's Purpose for the Church-Age will ultimately be fulfilled. It describes the 24 elders, who represent the whole Church in Heaven, just after the Rapture, rejoicing and singing to the Lamb: **"You are worthy, for You were slain and have redeemed us to God by Your blood out of**

every tribe, tongue, people and nation." This proves there will be a soul-harvest from every nation before Jesus returns, in fulfilment of the Great Commission.

Next I want to show that the teaching of Jesus, especially when it is prophetic of the Church Age, confirms that His central Purpose is the Salvation of souls, and the resultant building of the Church, as each new soul is added.

The First Mention of the Church

In Matthew 16 Jesus prophesies the formation of His Church. Since this is the first mention it should describe her defining characteristics, nature and purpose.

Matthew 16:16: **"Simon Peter answered: "You are the Christ, the Son of the Living God."** This famous CONFESSION of faith in Jesus as the Divine Messiah, the Anointed One, is a pivotal moment in the Gospel, calling forth a response from Jesus in which He announced the formation of His Church.

Matthew 16:17: **"Jesus answered: "BLESSED are you, Simon Bar-Jonah for flesh and blood has not revealed this to you, but My Father who is in Heaven."** God had worked in Peter's heart and gave him a saving faith, as a result of which he was BLESSED with eternal life (salvation). This truth of the Deity of Christ, the One who is anointed to save us, is necessary for receiving eternal life, for salvation is through knowing, trusting in and confessing the Lord Jesus Christ. Peter gives us a wonderful picture of salvation. He is the BLUEPRINT for the rest of us who become part of the Church. For anyone to be saved, God must first reveal to them who Jesus is, that He is the unique God-man (John 1:1,14, 8:24, Romans 10:13). Then they must believe in Him, confessing Him as their Lord and God (John 20:28, Romans 10:8-9). Then they are blessed with eternal life!

Jesus then went on to say to Peter in Matthew 16:18: **"I also say to you, that you are Peter** ('petros' = 'small stone'**), and on this ROCK** ('petra' = massive rock = CHRIST Himself) **I will build MY CHURCH."** This is the first mention of the Church of Christ, something new and different from Israel, which had not yet come into existence. He used the future tense. The Church came into existence through His death and resurrection, and the RISEN CHRIST is her ROCK FOUNDATION (Psalm 118:21-23, Isaiah 28:16, Matthew 7:24-27, 21:37-42, Mark 12:10,11, Luke

20:17, Acts 4:10-12, Eph 2:20, 1Peter 2:6,7). This is confirmed by <u>1Corinthians 3:11</u>: **"No other FOUNDATION can any one lay than that which is laid, which is JESUS CHRIST."** So when Jesus said: **"Upon THIS ROCK I will build My Church"**, He was pointing to HIMSELF. The foundational ROCK is Jesus Himself and when we, like Peter, put our trust in Him as Savior and confess Him as Lord, we are built as a living stone upon the firm foundation of the true Rock, Christ, and become part of His Church, as Peter later said: **"Coming to HIM** (Jesus) **as to a LIVING STONE** (Foundation), **rejected indeed by men, but chosen by God and precious you also, as LIVING STONES, are being built up a spiritual HOUSE** (the Church)" (1Peter 2:4, see also 5-6). Using a play on words, Jesus gave Simon a new name: 'You are Peter', signifying the new nature that we receive when we believe in Him. He is a picture of one who is saved through faith in Christ and has become a new creation in Christ. 'Simon' meant 'reed', easily blown from one side to another, but now he is 'Peter' - a stone, stable, dependable. We receive the imparted nature of the Rock making us a living rock (stone) like Him. So He said to Peter: "I am the Rock, but you are Peter, a little stone, a living stone who is now built upon Me, the Rock, and you are a new creation with a new name, and you are part of My Church."

Thus when Peter believed and confessed his faith in Christ, Jesus could then use Peter as an example of how He will build His Church, with Himself as its Foundation, adding one living stone at a time, through them hearing the Gospel of Christ, and trusting Him as Savior and confessing Him as Lord and God. So when we receive Christ as Lord, like Peter, we become a living stone built upon the Rock, and together we become the Church, the Temple of the Living God. So the Church is God's Temple, where His Presence dwells, consisting of people built together as living stones on the Rock of Jesus, having received His life and nature.

So Jesus announced His central Purpose for this Age – the building of His Church through the Gospel and discipleship, and Peter is the blueprint for it:

(1) Peter received the REVELATION of Who Christ was (Matthew 16:17).

(2) Then he BELIEVED and CONFESSED that revelation that Jesus is Lord God. That is how we are built on the Rock and become part of His Church.

(3) As a result we are BLESSED, we receive the blessing of eternal life from God, through the New Birth, which involves a change of nature (signified by the change of Peter's name from Simon).

It is through the Gospel that God reveals to our heart by the Holy Spirit who Christ is, so that we believe that Jesus is the Christ (anointed Saviour), the Son of the Living God, and confess Him as our Lord. Someone is added to the Church as:

(1) They are CONFRONTED (through the Gospel) with the Person of Christ, Who asks them to respond to the question: "Who do you say I am?"

(2) They receive the REVELATION from Heaven (through the Holy Spirit) that Jesus is the Christ, the eternal Son of the Living God, our Savior and Lord.

(3) They believe this revelation and put their TRUST in Him (built on the Rock) CONFESSING Him as their Saviour and Lord, just as Peter did.

(4) Peter did not just privately confess Christ, but PUBLICLY before others and so this is also part of the process of building the Church. It is built by the public confession (testimony) and proclamation of this revelation of who Jesus is (through the Gospel), by believers like Peter. As we proclaim Christ, God's Spirit reveals the truth to men's hearts so they can believe, confess Jesus and be saved. Each one that comes to believe the truth about Jesus and puts their trust in Him will then, like Peter, confess and proclaim Him as the Son of God, resulting in others to believe and be saved, and so in this way the Church is built and grows.

Matthew 16:18,19: **"I will build My CHURCH and the Gates of Hades shall not prevail against it... I will give you the KEYS of the KINGDOM, and whatever you bind on earth will be bound having been bound in Heaven, and whatever you loose on earth will be loosed, having been in Heaven"** (this is the literal translation of v19). The Church carries His authority for the word translated 'church' is 'ecclesia' denoting a Governmental Assembly, and represents Christ and is an extension of God's Kingdom on earth. The Church has been given a mission and keys (authority) to fulfill that mission. The Keys of the Kingdom represent our authority to open the doors of Heaven to people, and to release the Power of God to them, through the preaching of the Gospel. We see how the apostles used those Keys in the book of Acts. He put the Church in the middle of a spiritual warfare and the battleground is men's souls. The world is under the power of the kingdom of darkness, but He gave us His authority to bind the power of the enemy and loose His Power to overcome the power holding men's souls in darkness. In the midst of all the false religions, philosophies and gods, we are to make the public proclamation of who Jesus is, and then the Spirit will also supernaturally reveal this to them (confirming the Word and convicting the world of the truth of sin, judgment and salvation in Christ – see John 15:26-27, 16:7-11).

When someone believes and becomes part of His Church, they are forgiven and born again and receive eternal life, setting them free from the power of Hades. So when they die they do not go down through the Gates of Hades, but up through the Gates of Heaven. Then as they confess their faith before men, God uses them to reach others, and so through their proclamation more are added to the Church and in this way the Church is built. By using the Keys of the Kingdom by proclaiming Christ we fulfill our mission of saving men from the kingdom of darkness, and make it possible for them to enter into God's Kingdom by faith. Matthew 16:18 also implies the Church will ultimately succeed in its Mission for the Gates of the enemy will not prevail against the Church. He has given us all we need to get the job done, the Power of His Spirit and the Authority of His Keys.

SHINING the LIGHT of CHRIST

One of the great Biblical pictures of witnessing and sharing the Gospel is shining the LIGHT of Christ. The whole world is under the power of darkness (1John 5:19) and its greatest need is for us to shine the LIGHT of the Gospel. This is what Jesus did: **"Jesus spoke to them again, saying: "I am the LIGHT of** (to) **the world. He who follows Me shall not walk in darkness, but have the light of life** (within him)" (John 8:12). **"I have come as a LIGHT into the world, that whoever believes in Me should not abide in darkness"** (John 12:46). Jesus then calls us to shine our light into the dark world: **"You are the LIGHT of the world"** (Matthew 5:14). This is a command to preach the Gospel. There is a common false teaching that we can shine the light of Christ without opening our mouths, because we can witness to Christ by just living moral lives and doing good works. This gives us an excuse to disobey Christ's Command to speak for Him in sharing the

Gospel and discipling believers. I want to prove you can only SHINE the LIGHT by your WORDS. This is something quite different from doing GOOD WORKS, which are also important. Our WITNESS is by definition VERBAL, but our WORKS are also important, because they back up our witness, giving it credibility. A witness in a trial necessarily gives verbal testimony, otherwise he is not being a witness at all. But when a witness testifies, his credibility is also tested to see if he is a trustworthy witness worth listening to, and that's where good works come in.

This common confusion between (1) our WITNESS, and (2) our WORKS arises from a common misinterpretation of <u>Matthew 5:16</u>: **"Let (1) your LIGHT** (witness) **so SHINE before men, so that (2) they may see your GOOD WORKS, and (3) GLORIFY your Father in Heaven** (through them accepting your witness and believing in Christ)**."**

The common mistake in reading Matthew 5:16 is to assume the SHINING of our LIGHT is the same thing as the GOOD WORKS. In other words, the false idea is that we SHINE our LIGHT by doing GOOD WORKS, which then makes our verbal witness unnecessary, or an optional extra, or at least something secondary to our good works. But this cannot be so, because obeying the Great Commission must be the primary thing, and our good works must be the secondary thing, for they back up our witness. You see, it is all about CHRIST and what He has done, not about us and what we do! Moreover, Christ tells us to SHINE our light BEFORE MEN, but a few verses later in Matthew 6:1-4, He tells that we are NOT to do our GOOD WORKS to be SEEN by MEN. In other words, letting our LIGHT SHINE before men must be a different thing to doing GOOD WORKS. So why does Jesus not make this distinction clearly? Simply because it was obvious to those listening, who knew the Old Testament Scriptures, that you shine the light through your words, and that your works are to complement this. Indeed I will give Scriptures from both the Old and New Testaments that establish this truth.

So what is Jesus saying here? He first said: **"You are the LIGHT of the world"** (v14). In other words, if you are saved, you have the LIGHT of Christ within you, so you have the ability to SHINE your LIGHT by testifying to Christ and speaking His Word. Then in v16, He commands us to SHINE our LIGHT before men, that is, to witness to Christ and His ability to transform their lives with our words. But He also points out that when you do this, they will automatically inspect your life and your works, to see if your witness has credibility. So He also emphasises the importance of our GOOD WORKS, because they need to see the life-changing reality of Christ in us. They do not expect to see perfection, but they expect to see some reality because Christ is in us, rather than empty hypocrisy. If you are not living a holy life, your sin will undermine your witness – it will be like a noise drowning it out. So if we shine the light of the Gospel, and then they see that backed up by a consistent life of love and good works, they will then be inspired to believe our witness, receive Christ and so glorify God for themselves.

When they believe and love God for themselves as a result of our witness that is them glorifying God, and this fulfils our ultimate purpose in this Age, to gather a harvest of souls for God, who are saved from Hell and have eternal life.

If someone asks: "Do I witness by my life or my lips?", I would say that it is like asking what is more important, the left wing or the right wing of an aeroplane? Both are vital. If we witness to Christ with our lips, but our life is unholy, they will reject our witness and even bring reproach upon Christ. If on the other hand we only do good works, but never glorify Christ with our lips, then we will get all the glory not Christ, for men will speak well of us, but God will not be glorified. So, we are to glorify God (1) through our life and (2) through our lips (light). So God commands us to witness with our lips, but also to live in such away that our lifestyle and our actions fit our words, so people will pay attention to our words. So good works are a supplement, but NOT a SUBSTITUTE for our verbal witness.

"Let your LIGHT SHINE" by opening your mouth. This also tells us what happens in the spiritual realm when we witness - we literally shine, we glorify God, for the Power of the Spirit radiates out of us whether we feel or realise it or not! The shining is the Power of the Spirit that goes forth as we share the Word. Remember that LIGHT always OVERCOMES the darkness because it is more powerful: **"the LIGHT SHINES in the darkness, and the darkness did not OVERCOME it"** (John 1:5). In the face of darkness, the answer is to shine the light of the Gospel, otherwise the darkness will prevail, which is why Paul said: **"I am not ashamed of the Gospel of Christ, for it is the Power of God to Salvation for everyone who believes"** (Romans 1:16). To be ashamed about something is to stay quiet about it, but we must proclaim the Gospel otherwise they will remain under the darkness, for it is only by sharing the Gospel that we release the light and power to them by which they can be saved. It is only by us shining the light of the Gospel that they can believe and receive salvation.

Daniel 12:3: **"Those who are wise** ("he who wins souls is wise" - Proverbs 11:30) **shall SHINE like the brightness of the firmament, and those who TURN MANY to RIGHTEOUSNESS shall SHINE like the STARS forever and ever."** This parallelism confirms that we shine by turning people to God. Notice how the eternal reward corresponds to how we function now – as if God is saying: "Because you have shone your light in this life to glorify Me to others, I will cause you to shine the light of My Glory for all eternity!"

Philippians 2:15-16: **"become children of God without fault in the midst of a crooked and perverse generation, among whom you SHINE as LIGHTS in the** (dark) **world, HOLDING FORTH the WORD of LIFE."** This verse proves that we SHINE by holding forth the WORD of God, but we must back up our words, by a holy life that is without fault. People receive God's life through the Word of God that we share, not through our works.

Isaiah 59 is a Prophecy of the New Covenant and how the blessing of God is passed on from generation to generation. Isaiah 59:21: **"As for Me" says the LORD, "this is My Covenant with them: My SPIRIT who is UPON you, and My WORDS which I have put in your MOUTH, shall not depart from your mouth, nor from the mouth of your descendants, nor from the mouth of your descendants' descendants," says the LORD, "from this time and forevermore."** This leads straight into Isaiah 60:1-3: **"Arise, SHINE; for your LIGHT has come! and the GLORY of the LORD is risen UPON you. For behold, the darkness shall cover the earth, and deep darkness the people; but the LORD** will arise **OVER** you, and His **GLORY** will be seen **UPON** you. The Gentiles shall come to your **LIGHT**, and kings to the brightness of your rising."

This shows that we SHINE in the darkness by speaking God's WORDS in the power of the SPIRIT. For our witnessing to be effective, for us to shine in the darkness of this world, we must do it in the Power of the Spirit. 2 things are necessary: the spoken WORD and the SPIRIT UPON us (which we receive when we are baptised in the Spirit). Notice that the SPIRIT UPON us is also described as His GLORY UPON us. We have His Spirit (Glory) upon us for others who are in the darkness, so that we can then SHINE His light by declaring His WORD to the world. When we do this, such is the power of the Word and Spirit, that many will be drawn to the light and receive Christ. Thus we are commanded to shine the light, by receiving the Spirit upon us and putting His Word on our lips.

2Corinthians 4:3-7: **"If our GOSPEL is veiled, it is veiled to those who are perishing, whose minds the god of this age has blinded, who do not believe, lest the LIGHT of the GOSPEL of the GLORY of Christ, who is the image of God, should SHINE on them. For we do not PREACH ourselves, but Christ Jesus the Lord, and ourselves your bondservants for Jesus' sake. For it is the God who COMMANDED** (spoke) **LIGHT to shine out of darkness, who has shone in our hearts to give the light of the knowledge of the glory of God in the face of Jesus Christ. But we have this treasure** (of the light of the Gospel, and the Power of the Spirit) **in earthen vessels, that the excellence of the Power may be of God and not of us."** This again proves that the Gospel contains the light and glory of Christ, and that we shine that light upon people when we share the Gospel, and when our words communicating that light penetrate into their heart, they are changed from darkness to light – this is the New Birth.

It is His SPIRIT that causes us to SHINE when we SPEAK His Word, for as we speak the power of the Spirit is released with our words. The connection between the SPIRIT and LIGHT was understood in ancient times, because the source of all LIGHT was OIL LAMPS. Thus it was understood that a lamp can only SHINE, because of the power of the OIL within and upon it. OIL is a type of the SPIRIT, and ANOINTING with OIL represents the SPIRIT UPON us. To shine, we must be anointed with the oil of the Spirit, and then ignite that oil by our words. The oil was invisible (hidden) within the lamp (the Spirit is within our spirit), but if a wick (representing our heart and soul) is soaked in the oil, the oil was also on the outside (the Spirit upon), for the wick came out of the MOUTH of the lamp. However even then there is no light unless the oil is ignited at the mouth. The Spirit (Oil) within us, not us in ourselves, contains the POWER of LIGHT ("we have this treasure in earthen vessels, that the excellency of the Power is of God and not of us"), but we have the power of IGNITION (Ro 1:16). We ignite our light by the Power of the Spirit, causing Him to shine, by speaking His WORDS.

This is what happened on the day of Pentecost. They already had the Oil of the Spirit WITHIN them, but now the Oil of the Spirit also came UPON them, and as they opened their mouths to glorify God and speak His words, the fire of God ignited upon them, and they began to shine. This fire was the manifestation of the Spirit within and UPON them. God was declaring that they were to be His lights (witnesses) to a dark world, and that He had given them His oil so that they might shine for Him, as they spoke His words. Although this fire is not normally seen by our natural eyes, this is what is actually happening in the spiritual realm: **"Then there appeared to them divided tongues, as of FIRE, and one sat UPON each of them. And they were all filled with the HOLY SPIRIT and began to SPEAK with other tongues, as the Spirit gave them utterance"** (Acts 2:3-4). These 2 verses describe the same experience from 2 viewpoints: (1) how it appears outwardly, with the Spirit igniting upon them (v3), and (2) how it was experienced inwardly, as the Spirit who is within them also now fills them (v4) and comes upon them, as they yield their tongues to Him to speak His Word. This means we must embrace His mission (to shine His light), and then (1) surrender our soul for His Spirit to fill and empower us, and (2) yield our tongue to Him to speak His words.

Now we can understand why the Churches are described as the Lord's Lampstands with Christ in their midst in Revelation 1:12,13,20: **"The Mystery of the 7 stars which you saw in My right hand, and the 7 golden Lampstands: The 7 stars are the angels** (pastors) **of the 7 Churches, and the 7 Lampstands which you saw are the 7 Churches"** (1:20). This introduces Christ's letters to the 7 Churches in Revelation 2-3, which represent the whole Church of Christ throughout Church History (see Appendix 2). In these letters Christ evaluates their faithfulness in fulfilling their ministry of being His anointed witness (light) to the world, through their words backed up by their works. This again proves that the purpose of the Church in this Age is to be God's light-bearer (witness) to the world. The 7 letters are Christ's assessment of how true the Churches have been to the Word, in keeping and spreading it, and in resisting false doctrine.

ROMANS 11

In <u>Romans 11,</u> Paul confirms that the major Purpose of this Age is a soul-harvest from the Gentiles, before God fulfils His purposes for Israel. He says in <u>v11</u> that by Israel's **"fall** (transgression of rejecting the Messiah) **salvation has come to the Gentiles."** Israel's unbelief has resulted in salvation going to the Gentiles in this Age. <u>v12</u>: **"their fall** (transgression) **is riches for the world and their failure riches for the Gentiles."** <u>v15</u>: **"their being cast away** (rejection) **is the reconciling of the world."** However God has not finished with Israel, for these same verses also speak of her future restoration. <u>v12</u> describes it as 'their FULLNESS' after 'their FALL' is over, and <u>v15</u> as 'their ACCEPTANCE' after 'their (time of) REJECTION' is over, which will be like 'LIFE from the DEAD.' Though Israel would seem to be dead spiritually and naturally she will rise again on both counts. Also in v23 Paul said the natural branches (Israel), that had been cut off from the place of Divine favour and anointing, will be grafted in again.

Then v25-26a: **"blindness in part has happened to Israel** (in this present Age) **UNTIL the FULLNESS of the GENTILES has come in; and so all Israel will be saved."** Thus the central purpose of this Age is the salvation of people from every nation, for this Age will continue until this purpose is fulfilled, for when the full number of the Gentile harvest has come into the Kingdom, Jesus will return to gather in this whole harvest to Heaven by the Rapture. Then, after "the fullness of the Gentiles" has been ingathered at the Rapture, the Tribulation will begin, in which God's central purpose will be the full Salvation of Israel, so that by its end: **"ALL Israel will be SAVED"** (her national salvation). In v26b-27 Paul shows how this future Salvation of Israel agrees with God's Purposes as revealed in Prophecy: **"as it is written: "The Deliverer will come out of Zion, and He will turn away ungodliness from Jacob; for this is My Covenant with them, when I take away their sins."** Jesus fulfilled this in His 1st Coming. He came out of Israel in fulfilment of the promises made to Israel, and established the New Covenant, the primary purpose of which is the Salvation of Israel from her sins (Isaiah 59:20-21, Jeremiah 31:31-34), and so it is fitting and necessary for Him to fulfil that purpose once the full Gentile harvest of this Age has come in.

The SOWER SOWS the WORD

Another Biblical description of the Church's primary Purpose and Mission in this Age as the preaching of the Gospel, is the sowing of seed and the reaping of the harvest. In Part 1, we saw that in Matthew 13, Jesus introduced the revelation of the Mystery Kingdom (the Church Age) that would come after His death and resurrection instead of the prophesied Messianic Kingdom, because Israel was rejecting Him. Through the Parables He revealed that this form of the Kingdom of God would be very different from the Messianic Kingdom, in which Christ would rule visibly over the nations, controlling their laws and politics. It was to be a spiritual kingdom established in the hearts of believers, which would be spread by the continued SOWING of the WORD of God in men's hearts, which Jesus had started. The Parable of the Sower was described as the foundational Parable describing how this Kingdom will operate and spread through the sowing of the Word, producing different responses in different people according to their heart condition. Thus we enter the Kingdom when we receive the Word planted in our heart and we are born again (1Peter 1:23-25, John 3:3-7). This Parable and the Parable of the Wheat and the Tares predict that the enemy will still be actively opposing God's Word, unlike in the Messianic Kingdom. Also they teach that this present Church Age will be an extended period of time, from the seed-time of sowing to the harvest-time of reaping, and that 'the Harvest' was at 'the End of the Age' (the Tribulation). So the harvest-time covers the whole Tribulation, starting with the ingathering of the fullness of the Gentiles in the Rapture, and ending with the ingathering of the Old Testament and Tribulation saints at the 2nd Coming. The reaping (harvesting) of the righteous is accomplished by their rapture or resurrection when they are offered up to God. Jesus was the first fruits of this ingathered harvest when He was resurrected and offered to God and accepted by God on our behalf, the guarantee of what will happen to the whole harvest. Also throughout the Tribulation all the unbelieving Tares will be removed from the earth by death and be thrown into the fires of Hades, but the saints who survive the Tribulation will be gathered into the Messianic Kingdom.

James 5:7: **"Be patient, brethren, until the Coming of the Lord. See how the farmer waits for the PRECIOUS FRUIT of the earth, waiting patiently for it** (the precious fruit)**, until it** (precious fruit) **gets the former and latter rains."**

This tells us what is important to God and what He is looking for from this Church Age – it is the precious fruit of the earth, that is, the precious souls of those who are born again in it. Christ's priority for this Age is the harvest. The reason He has not returned yet is that full number of the precious fruit is not yet in. This again proves that the Purpose of this Age is not taking over the world or changing society but the creation of precious fruit of the earth through the Gospel. When Jesus comes, He does it with the purpose of joyfully reaping and gathering this harvest into Heaven in the Rapture.

James also points out that as well as the SOWING of the SEED (the Word of God), it is necessary to have the RAIN of the SPIRIT to activate the SEED. So 2 things are necessary to be effective, the SEED (Word of God) and the HOLY SPIRIT, who causes the WORD to go forth with power and be fruitful. The SEED that must be sown into the EARTH is the WORD of the Gospel that must be planted in men's HEARTS. But the seed needs rain to bring forth fruit, otherwise it remains dormant. Thus 2 things are necessary for the full harvest. First, the SEED must be sown, and 2nd it must be watered by the RAIN. Rain was seen as the blessing of God, falling on the earth and activating the seed to grow and produce. Likewise, we need the blessing of the outpoured Spirit to fall on men's hearts and activate the Word in their hearts. Thus it is the Spirit working with the Word that brings forth the harvest. So as well as sowing the seed in evangelism, we need to water it with prayer, so the Spirit falls on them with convicting power, and they receive the Word and bring forth fruit. The Purpose of this Age is the precious fruit of the earth (the saved souls), so when this precious fruit is fully ready to be harvested, Jesus will return, but first, in order for it to be ready, it is necessary for this precious fruit to receive both the former and latter rains. Thus, it is essential for the Rain of the Spirit to work with the Seed of the Word to bring forth the fruit of the earth. So as we sow the gospel-seed in men's hearts, we should also PRAY for the anointing of the Spirit to soften their hearts and empower our words to them.

An Appeal for a balanced Eschatology of the Church Age

The main conflict in Eschatology (the study of the last things) is between 2 opposing approaches, one being all optimistic about the Church's ultimate victory over the world in the end times before Jesus returns, and the other being all pessimistic about the world's victory over the church (apostasy). Proponents from both sides believe that it must be either one or the other, and so the optimists mock the other side for their defeatism, and reject or reinterpret scriptures that seem to be pessimistic and the pessimists reject any talk of hope or great things such as revival for the church. So there is a polarisation of opinion. I would contend that this is due to inflexible thinking that's unable to hold 2 parallel truths together. The situation in the church and world according to Scripture is more complex than one or other of these positions, and that both sides have part of the truth concerning the Church-Age, and we should submit to Scripture and uphold the balance that it presents.

In studying the prophetic scriptures and using them to guide us in the time we live we are Watchmen, who are to look at the whole truth and not just the part that we want to see, but also the dangers, so that we can protect ourselves and those who hear our voice. If in our over optimism we shut our eyes to the enemy operating in darkness, and just focus on what is of the light, we are open to deception and will end up deceiving others. God asks you: **"Watchman, what of the night? Watchman, what of the night?"** The watchman said: **"The morning** (light) **comes, and also the night"** (Isaiah 21:11-12). This faithful Watchman saw both the light and the darkness and reported both. The prophetic scriptures reveal the increasing light of God's Kingdom advancing, as well as the increasing darkness in the world, as we head towards the Return of Christ. A balanced study of the Scriptures show that we should expect the world to get darker and darker as we approach the Tribulation, but also by contrast the true Church will get brighter and brighter. It is this balance that both the optimists and pessimists have trouble combining and yet it is scriptural.

In Genesis 15:5 God told Abraham that his seed would be like the stars of heaven, which shine against the darkness of night, so that the darker the night the brighter they shine (in Christ we are the seed of Abraham). This same picture is repeated in Daniel 12:3: **"Those who are wise shall shine like the brightness of the firmament, and those who turn many to righteousness like the stars forever and ever"** and Philippians 2:15-16: **"become blameless and harmless, children of God without fault in the midst of a crooked and perverse generation, among whom you shine as lights in the world, holding fast the word of life."** Notice that even with the stars shining their witness the world is still in darkness. We have grounds for optimism that the true Church is being restored in its doctrine and life, and will go from glory to glory, powerfully preaching the Gospel till Jesus returns, for He has commissioned us and is with us as we fulfil His Commission (Matthew 28:18 -20) and the Gospel will be preached to all nations (Mark 13:10, Matthew 24:14), so that Jesus will have a great soul- harvest from the nations before He comes in the Rapture (James 5:7-8, Romans 11:25, Rev 5:8-10).

However, as well as the light of the Gospel increasing, the Bible also talks about the darkness of sin and deception increasing in the world. We see this balance clearly in the prophetic Parable of the Tares (Matthew 13:24-30, 37 -43), where the seed of the Gospel is sown in the field, which is the world (v38), showing that the mission of the church is to sow the Gospel in the whole world, and that this will be achieved. But the enemy will also be able to sow his seed throughout the world, and both the Wheat and the Tares continue to grow together until the End. The Tares are not overrun by the Wheat, and the Wheat is not overrun by the Tares. Moreover the Master's Plan for this Church Age is revealed to be NOT one of judgment and dominion (removing the Tares by force) for He will do that Himself with His angels at the End. Rather His servants are to keep sowing the good seed. So it is neither a purely optimistic nor pessimistic vision for the Church Age but a combination of both.

We see how great darkness and light can coexist in Isaiah 61:1-2: **"Arise, shine; for your light has come! And the Glory of the Lord is risen upon you** (God's people), **for behold, the darkness shall cover the earth, and deep darkness the people; but the Lord will arise over you, and His glory will be seen upon you. The Gentiles shall come to your light, and kings to the brightness of your rising."** This applies to Israel, but both are in the New Covenant, Israel is a type of the Church, so it can also be applied spiritually to us.

Isaiah 59:20: **"So shall they fear the Name of the Lord from the west, and His glory from the rising of the sun; when the enemy comes in like a flood, the SPIRIT of the Lord will lift up a Standard against him."** v21,22: describes how this Standard will be raised against the enemy by the Spirit of God: **"The Redeemer will come to Zion, and to those who turn from transgression in Jacob" says the Lord"** (this is Christ's 1st Coming to establish the New Covenant of forgiveness from sin and the Holy Spirit within). Then v21 shows how this covenant will operate: **"As for Me," says the Lord, "this is My covenant with them: My SPIRIT who is upon you, and My WORDS which I have put in your mouth, shall not depart from your mouth, nor from the mouth of your descendants, nor from the mouth of your descendants' descendants" says the Lord: "from this time and forevermore."** As we declare the Gospel and God's Word with His Spirit upon us, we raise up the Standard of the Lord and release the light of the Gospel and power of God against the enemy. Again the picture is of us shining in the darkness, personally victorious over the darkness of sin and satan, but nevertheless the darkness still covers the world.

Against those who only see darkness for the Church Age, it is possible to be optimistic that through the preaching of the Gospel many souls will be saved, and that we will have times of refreshing and revival (Acts 3:19), as is happening. This does not contradict the imminence of the Rapture for only God knows when the fullness (full number) of the harvest of the nations is saved. In regard to other world events that still have to happen, imminence is preserved by the fact that the Rapture and Start of the Tribulation may be weeks, months or even years before the covenant with antichrist that signals the start of the last 7 years (Daniel's 70th Week). So believing in the Pre-Tribulation Rapture does not get in the way of our true mission of reaching the world with the Gospel and believing for revival and a great harvest of souls, for believing our Bridegroom could come at any time for us motivates us to live holy and to be urgent and zealous about fulfilling the Great Commission (the idea that the Rapture is an emergency exit for a defeated Church is a total misrepresentation). What is negative and defeatist about our wonderful Jesus coming for us once He considers the Church's Mission to be accomplished? It is true that the imminent Rapture does get in the way of the overoptimistic dominionist plans to take over the world, and that is why they dislike it so much, because it takes our eyes off their long-term aim of taking over the systems (institutions) of the world. But that's why the teaching of the imminent Rapture is so important - it focuses our minds on what we need to focus on (the harvest of precious souls), helping to keep us from getting off course into projects God never told us to do. We are not called to transform, take over or rule the world in this Age, rather we're to faithfully hold forth the Gospel and bring in a harvest of souls.

The Rapture also takes our eyes off earthly, fleshly ambitions (the love of this world) and focuses them instead on our heavenly home and citizenship, from where Jesus will come at any time soon and take us to be with Him. This helps us to not be too entangled in this world, but rather work for the treasure that is in heaven that will keep for all eternity, much of which is connected with us winning the eternal souls of men for God by being faithful to the Great Commission. The imminent Rapture also focuses us on the imminent Judgment Seat of Christ, when we will give an account and receive eternal rewards for obeying Him (preaching the Gospel) rather than doing something He did not command. It also focuses on the need to be faithful to God and walking in love rather doing whatever it takes to gain popularity power and influence in this world (which leads to certain compromise), for our real home is Heaven and our real future is in the next Age, where our dominion then will depend on our faithfulness now to the Great Commission. 1Corinthians 13 reminds us of how it is essential to follow after love above all, for it says without love 'we are nothing' and all our great works and supernatural powers 'will profit us nothing' (there will be no eternal reward).

The correct Eschatology is important because it gives us an understanding of God's purpose for this Age and how to live and prioritise in the light of that. It keeps us alert and on our toes, eager to be active fulfilling the mission God has given us, for Jesus could return at any time and we want Him to be pleased with us. It keeps us from building our own kingdoms and legacies and living as if we have all the time in the world, but instead focuses us on winning souls for His future Kingdom. It also warns us about the darkness of this world, which will only increase, so that we are on our guard and do not let it contaminate us.

In particular the warnings of apostasy, even coming into the Church through its desperation to fit in and be approved by the world, causes us to guard the Gospel and not compromise it. Under no circumstances can we tolerate another Jesus (than the God- man) or another Gospel of salvation by Christ alone, by grace alone, through faith alone. Neither dare we ever make agreements not to preach the Gospel so as not to offend a group of people for it is the power of God unto salvation (Romans 1:16). Without it we have nothing to offer the world that can change lives now and deliver them from an eternity of hell, releasing them into an eternity of joy in heaven. Getting people born again is truly the greater work to which Jesus calls us, and then we are to get them built up in the Word so they can win others. In this way we are to be fruitful, multiplying ourselves, through loving and ministering to people not trying to take over society. If we get enough people saved society will be changed as a by- product, but we must keep our main focus on shining forth the light of the Gospel, remembering Jesus is coming soon.

*Chapter 4: The Sequence of Pre-Tribulation Events

We have seen that we are living at a special time near the End of the Church-Age, and that we expect Jesus to come soon. We have the honour of being chosen to run the last lap of a relay race that started almost 2000 years ago. The baton has been handed to us, and we must run a good race looking to Jesus, who will meet us at the finishing line at His Return. In order to understand what God is doing in our times and co-operate with it, we now study the events that the Bible indicates will happen as the Church-Age comes to its close.

The Completion of the Church Harvest

The main Purpose of the Church-Age is a harvest from the nations, and so the special purpose for the final period of this Age must be the completion of this harvest through evangelism and prayer. Although this is true for the whole Church Age, it must be especially urgent for those living near the close of the Age. Jesus is waiting for the harvest to come to its fullness, so we should expect a final harvest of souls to come in before He returns. Thus God's priority for this Age is the harvest, as James 5:7 says: **"Be patient, brethren, until the Coming of the Lord. See how the farmer waits for the precious fruit of the earth until it** (the precious fruit) **gets the former and latter rains."**

The Latter Rain

In Israel the agricultural year started with the sowing of seed at the end of October, which is when the early or former rain began to fall, which softened the earth to help it receive the seed. It was also essential for seed's germination and early growth (Isaiah 30:23). Likewise, the rain of the Spirit softens the hearts of men, so they're able to receive God's Word. There were also rains over the wintertime, and then in March-April, just before the harvest-time, the latter rain would fall. These spring rains were essential in bringing the crops to their fullness, for an abundant harvest. For example in 2014, Israel had heavy winter rains, but hardly any latter rain. As a result the harvest was still disappointing despite all the winter rain. As the natural so the spiritual. The former RAIN is a picture of the outpouring of the SPIRIT at the start of the Church-Age, causing the harvest to get off to a great start. As the Church-Age comes towards its close when its harvest is ingathered at the Rapture, we should expect a great latter rain outpouring of the

Spirit, which is essential to bring forth the abundant final harvest that God desires. I believe the latter rain of the Spirit began in 1900 with the Pentecostal Outpouring, which then transformed the church-world through the charismatic movement. Today this is the fastest growing part of the Church. So the modern Pentecostal Outpouring is another sign of the end times.

Living as we do near the Close of the Church Age, we should expect and pray for more of this latter rain before the Lord returns, for it's essential for the final harvest from all nations. The SEED that must be sown into the EARTH is the WORD of the Gospel that must be planted in men's HEARTS. But the seed needs rain to bring forth fruit, otherwise it remains dormant. 2 things are necessary for the full harvest. First, the SEED must be sown, and 2nd it must be watered by the RAIN. Rain was seen as the blessing of God, falling on the earth and activating the seed to grow and produce. Likewise, we need the blessing of the outpoured Spirit to fall on men's hearts and activate the Word in their hearts. Thus it is the Spirit working with the Word that brings forth the harvest. So as well as sowing the seed in evangelism, we need to water it with prayer, so the Spirit falls on them with convicting power, and they receive the Word and bring forth fruit.

James 5:7 confirms these thoughts: **"Be   patient, brethren, until the Coming of the Lord. See the Farmer waits for the precious fruit of the earth, waiting patiently for it, until it** (the precious fruit) **gets the former and latter rains."** The purpose of this Age is the precious fruit of the earth (the saved souls), so when this precious fruit is fully ready to be harvested, Jesus will return, but first, in order for it to be ready, it is necessary for this precious fruit to receive both the former and latter rains. Therefore, it is essential for the Rain of the Spirit to work with the Seed of the Word in order to bring forth the fruit of the earth. So as we sow the gospel-seed in men's hearts, we should also PRAY for the anointing of the Spirit to soften their hearts and empower our words to them. A few verses later, James encourages us to do this, by pointing to Elijah's example of praying for rain as he says in James 5:16-18: **"The effective prayer of a righteous man can makes much power available, effective in its working."** We release the power of the Spirit through prayer. **"Elijah was a man with a nature like ours and he**

PRAYED earnestly… and the heaven poured RAIN and the earth produced its FRUIT." Note the sequence: (1) He PRAYED, which (2) released RAIN from heaven, so that (3) the earth produced its fruit. By saying Elijah was a man like us, James was saying we can do what Elijah did. In Christ we are just as righteous, so we too can release the rain of God's Spirit upon the souls of men by prayer, so that the word sown in their hearts produces fruit. The fact James was thinking of the salvation of souls is clear from the next verses (v19,20): **"he who turns a sinner from the error of his way will save a soul from death."**

So we are now in the time of the latter rain, so God's priority for us, all the more as the Rapture draws near, is the seed sowing of evangelism, supported by prayer that releases the anointing. Zechariah 10:1 agrees: **"ASK RAIN from the Lord at the time of the spring** (latter) **rain** (we're living in that time). **The Lord who makes the storm clouds; and He will give them showers of rain, crops in the field to each man."** Notice the end-result of the rain is a harvest of crops!

So one key to opening the windows of heaven to release the blessing of the latter-rain is PRAYER. Another key is PRAISE according to Psalm 67:5-7: **"Let the peoples praise You, O God; let all the peoples praise You. Then the earth shall yield its produce; God, our God, blesses us** (with rain). **God blesses us, that all the ends of the earth may fear Him."** Here the seed is in the earth, but it needs God's blessing of rain to fall upon the earth in order to activate the seed to produce its fruit. The key that releases the blessing, the rain, of God is the praises of the people. The result of this rain is a great soul-harvest, for when the blessing of rain is released: **"all the ends of the earth fear Him."** This is the earth yielding its produce. This works for us personally as well as in praying for others. The word may be sown in a heart but be dormant, not producing fruit. But when we praise God for His faithfulness to fulfil His Word, and thank Him for bringing it to pass, we activate and release the blessing and Spirit of God to activate the Word, and cause it to bring forth its fruit.

So the primary thing on God's heart to accomplish at this time at the end of the Church-Age is a great final harvest of souls, through the preaching of the Gospel and the latter rain of the Spirit, and we all have a part to play. The latter day outpouring of the Spirit resulting in multitudes coming to the Lord has been happening for over 100 years already, and yet great things are ahead. Later in this chapter we look at the Divine Intervention in the latter days when a regathered Israel is invaded from the north by Russia, Iran and Turkey, and point out that the result will be that God is glorified among all the nations. This implies that this event will trigger a final worldwide revival before Christ returns.

Israel re-established as a Nation

Next we move to a major world event that must happen in the time leading up to the Tribulation - Israel's Regathering to her Land and Rebirth as a Nation there, after being scattered to all the nations. This was fulfilled in 1948 and is one of the greatest miracles ever, made more remarkable by the fact that it was the fulfilment of many prophecies made over 2500 years ago! We've previously seen that this is the major Sign that shows we are within a man's lifetime of Christ's Return. Strangely many in the Church see no significance in the Rebirth of Israel (being blinded by replacement theology), and so call it just an accident of history. But many of these also claim a strong belief in the absolute Sovereignty of God, which they seem to ignore, when it comes to the modern State of Israel!

The condition of Israel over the last 2000 years up to the present day is perfectly explained and described by the Bible. The mystery of Israel to many is both her suffering and existence. Why she has suffered so much, and how she has continued to survive as a nation? As God's elect covenant people, whatever happens she can never be destroyed. But because of her rejection of Messiah, instead of receiving the Kingdom she came under Divine discipline and as a result was scattered to the nations and has suffered greatly (Luke 21:21-24). Despite her unbelief, God has not finished with her, and her discipline is only for a certain time, after which she will be restored. In fulfilment of the many prophecies that she must be regathered to her Land before the End of the Age (Tribulation), Israel was miraculously reborn in 1948. God did this in preparation for the Tribulation, which requires Israel to be back in the Land. In this future time, she will face her greatest ever suffering, but God's purpose is to have His final dealings with her to restore her to fellowship and faith, so that by the end of the Tribulation, she will repent and receive Jesus (Yeshua) as her Messiah, calling on Him for Salvation. He will then save Israel from destruction at His 2nd Coming, and establish His Kingdom, with Israel fully restored as chief nation. Thus, Israel's sufferings (past, present and future) and the origin and purpose of the Tribulation are explained by Israel's original rejection of the King and Kingdom.

As well as predicting the captivity of Israel to Assyria (722 BC) and Babylon (607-537 BC) because of idolatry (Deuteronomy 28:49), the prophets also predicted another dispersion of Israel - this time to all nations. This worldwide scattering of Israel would happen after they had returned from the previous dispersions: **"Then the LORD will scatter you among all peoples, from one end of the earth to the other"** (Deuteronomy 28:64, also 4:26,27). v65-68 describes the trouble they would face in the nations where they were scattered.

This was confirmed by Jesus in <u>Luke 21:24</u>: **"They will fall by the edge of the sword, and be led away captive into all nations. And Jerusalem will be trampled by Gentiles..."** This prediction was fulfilled in AD 70 and 135. The first time Israel went to Babylon for 70 years, but this time she was scattered to all nations for 1900 years. The first captivity was due to idolatry from which they later repented, so what sin could be so bad that it brought about a far greater discipline upon Israel? The only possible explanation is the national rejection of her Messiah - Yeshua! But God will regather her again and give her a second chance.

After warning Israel in <u>Deuteronomy 29:22-29,</u> that if they sinned God would remove them from the Land and disperse them to the nations, in <u>30:3-5,</u> He promised that He will ultimately regather them from all the nations: **"The Lord your God will bring you back from captivity, and have compassion on you, and gather you again from all the nations where the Lord your God has scattered you. If any of you are driven out to the farthest parts under heaven, from there the Lord your God will gather you, and from there He will bring you. Then the Lord your God will bring you to the Land which your fathers possessed, and you shall possess it"** (Deut 30:1-10 will only be completely fulfilled at Christ's Return after Israel's repentance, but we are seeing the beginnings of its fulfilment in our time). Such a worldwide Regathering could only take place after AD 70 following the worldwide dispersion that began that year.

<u>Leviticus 26</u> describes the 5 Cycles of Discipline God would apply to Israel if she sinned. The 4th Cycle was enemy domination and occupation, but if they continued to sin, God would move them into the 5th Cycle of expulsion from the Land (v27-39). This happened first in 607-537 BC with the Captivity in Babylon.

However, the prophecy also indicated that there would be another dispersion, this time not to just one nation, but to all the nations (v33,38). This was fulfilled in AD 70. However, again Israel is told that God will ultimately regather Israel from every nation. This regathering will be completed when she repents (v40-46).

Many of the prophets (especially Isaiah, Jeremiah and Ezekiel) predicted the return of Israel to their own Land from a worldwide captivity. This would require one of the greatest miracles of all time! Moreover, this dispersion and regathering was predicted by Jesus: they will fall by the edge of the sword, and be led away captive into all nations. **"And Jerusalem will be trampled by Gentiles <u>UNTIL</u> the times of the Gentiles are fulfilled"** (Luke 21:24). The 'UNTIL' indicates that the dispersion will only last for a definite period of time (called 'the Times of the Gentiles'), after which Israel will come back to the Land and regain control of Jerusalem. This was fulfilled in 1948 and 1967, so we have seen Jesus' prophecy come to pass in recent history! The Times of the Gentiles are therefore now over (with the exception of the 7 years of the Tribulation yet to run (see my book: 'The 7 Times of the Gentiles' for more explanation of this). In fact, **it was necessary for ISRAEL to be back in her Land before the Start of the Tribulation,** because the prophecies of this time assume that Israel is a Nation in the Land and in control of Jerusalem (e.g. Matthew 24, Daniel 9:26, Zechariah 12-14, Ezekiel 38,39, Revelation 7-19). **The stage must be set before the final scene begins**, so this requires the re-establishment of Israel as a Nation before the Tribulation begins. Bible Prophecy of the nations is all centred on Israel and the Land, so we should expect this miraculous event to be a major end-time Sign. The Return of Israel to her Land from all nations, and her Rebirth as a Nation is a major theme of Old Testament prophecy, which is why hundreds of years ago believers started to predict it, even when it looked impossible!

We have seen that Jesus gave the Rebirth of Israel as the main SIGN by which we'd know we were in the final generation before the Tribulation in the Parable of the Fig-Tree (Luke 21:29-32). In Jeremiah 24:5 the people of Israel in captivity are described as a collection of individual figs, rather than part of a Fig-Tree (nation) planted in the Land, but Jesus said when you see the Fig Tree rising up again know the end is near. Thus the Rebirth of Israel (1948) is a clear sign we're in the last days. The world has crossed over the threshold into the end times, the time of the fulfilment of the prophetic Word. The present Regathering of Israel from all nations is a prophesied work of God, signalling the end of the Time of the Gentiles, and the approach of the Kingdom being restored to Israel.

To fully understand the prophecies concerning the Regathering of Israel, it's important to know the prophets spoke of 2 divinely ordained international Returns:

(1) The initial Regathering from the nations would only be a partial regathering, and it will be in unbelief, in preparation for the Tribulation, through which God will bring Israel to repentance and faith in Christ by its end. This Regathering started last century and is still taking place now, as a major fulfilment of prophecy. This is the Fig Tree putting forth its leaves, but not yet bearing fruit, just as Jesus predicted. He brings her back to the Land, causing her to be a nation again, so He can restore her as a nation to the Lord, receiving a national salvation.

(2) The 2nd Regathering will happen after Israel has repented and received Christ. It will be a final and complete Regathering, with Israel in faith. It will be accomplished by Christ Himself at His 2nd Coming, and it will be in preparation for the Millennium, so that all Israel will be in the Land. This is pictured by the Fig Tree bearing fruit. Thus the Fig Tree (Israel) planted in the Land and putting forth leaves in spring is a Sign that soon she will be bearing her summer fruit.

Thus (1) Israel will return to the Land, and then (2) to the Lord. Then on the basis of her spiritual restoration Christ will complete her regathering and physical restoration in the Land. He will return and save her from her enemies and complete her restoration in the Messianic Kingdom. But prophecies of the 1st Regathering in Ezekiel and Zephaniah indicate that Israel will first have to endure much suffering and affliction in the Land before she receives Jesus as her Messiah.

We see these 2 International Regatherings in Isaiah 11. The chapter starts with the 1st Coming of Christ (v1-3), and then it jumps to the 2nd Coming and the Messianic Kingdom (v4-16). v11-12 describes the final Regathering of Israel from the nations at this time: **"It shall come to pass in that day that the Lord shall set His hand again the SECOND TIME to recover the remnant of His people who are left, from Assyria and Egypt, from Pathros and Cush, from Elam and Shinar, from Hamath and the islands of the sea. He will set up a banner for the nations, and will assemble the outcasts of Israel, and gather together the dispersed of Judah from the 4 corners of the earth."** Now since this Regathering of the remnant (in faith) is called the 2nd International Regathering, there must be a 1st International Regathering that happens beforehand.

The First Regathering must happen before the Tribulation, for Daniel 9:27 says that early in the Tribulation, the antichrist will make a covenant with Israel, which requires a regathered Jewish Nation in unbelief before the Tribulation. Isaiah calls it a covenant with death, bringing great suffering on Israel (28:14-22). Also the Olivet Discourse of Jesus (Matthew 24), which expounds and builds on Daniel's prophecy, shows Israel as a Nation in the Land during the Tribulation. Zechariah 12-14 gives a detailed prophecy of the Tribulation leading up to the 2nd Coming, from the viewpoint of Israel being in the Land at that time, and in the centre of the action. After tremendous suffering where 2/3 are killed (13:8), they realise that Jesus is their Messiah (12:10), receive cleansing from sin (13:1), then He returns to Jerusalem to save them from their enemies, concluding with His triumphant ascent on the Mount of Olives (14:1-5). The book of Revelation (especially chapter 11) also requires Israel to be a Nation in the Land.

Ezekiel 22:17-22 describes **the initial Regathering in unbelief before the Tribulation**, so that Israel is a Nation in the Land when the Judgments (Wrath) of the Tribulation begin. Another key passage describing Israel's return in unbelief in preparation for the judgments of the Tribulation followed by a national restoration to the Lord is Ezekiel 20:33-38: **"As I live" says the Lord God: "surely with a mighty hand, with an outstretched arm, and with fury** (wrath) **poured out, I will rule over you. I will bring you out from the peoples and gather you out of the countries where you are scattered, with a mighty hand, with an outstretched arm, and with fury poured out. And I will bring you into the wilderness of the peoples, and there I will plead My case with you face to face. Just as I pleaded My case with your fathers in the wilderness of the Land of Egypt, so I will plead My case with you" says the Lord God. "I will make you pass under the rod, and I will bring you into the bond of the** (New) **Covenant; I will purge the rebels from among you, and those who transgress against Me; I will bring them out of the country where they dwell, but they shall not enter the Land of Israel. Then you will know that I am the Lord."** This Regathering out of the nations is in unbelief, because it is done 'with wrath' and indeed the horrors of the Holocaust, when 6 million Jews died, created the world-conditions for Israel to become a State. He compares the present situation to when Israel came out of Egypt and became a Nation at Mt.Sinai. Because of their rebellion and unbelief they did not qualify to possess the Promised Land, but instead they came under a Judgment at Kadesh Barnea and had to dwell in the wilderness for 40 years, until they were in faith and Joshua could lead them into possession of the Land. Likewise, although many Jews have come out of the nations and have become a Nation in 1948, because of unbelief they don't yet qualify to possess the promised Messianic Kingdom, when they will possess the whole Land under the full blessing and protection of God. They are still 'in the wilderness' spiritually speaking. Instead they will come into a time of Judgment (the Tribulation) because the majority will choose to trust in antichrist's word rather than God's Word (Daniel 9:27), just as the majority trusted in the evil report rather than God's Word at Kadesh Barnea. Thus in this analogy the 40-years in the Wilderness is a type of the 7-year Tribulation. It was a period of judgment in which God purged out all those who did not believe, so that only those who believed (like Joshua and Caleb) could enter in. It was also a time when God directly pleaded His case to Israel, so that by the end of the 40 years Israel was in faith and so could possess her Land.

Likewise, the Tribulation will be a time of Judgment when God will purge out all the rebels from Israel, for they will not be permitted to enter the Kingdom. It will also be a time when God will plead His case to Israel bringing her to repentance, so that by the end of the Tribulation, Israel as a Nation will come to faith in her Messiah, and the Greater than Joshua will lead them into the Messianic Kingdom, when they will enjoy full possession of their Land and the fulfilment all the promises to Abraham. The Judgment aspect is described as 'passing under the rod', which describes what a shepherd does to inspect the sheep and separate his sheep from the rest. To enter the sheepfold the sheep must go through the shepherd and pass under his rod, symbolising submission to his authority. Those who are not his sheep are sent away. Likewise in the Tribulation, Yeshua, the Shepherd of Israel, will confront the Jews, separating the believers from the unbelievers. Only those who submit to His authority will enter the Kingdom, and the rest (the rebels) will be purged out, so that by the end ALL Israel will believe in Christ and be saved, and He will bring the whole Nation **"into the bond of the** (New) **Covenant"**, which in turn will spiritually qualify them to possess all the blessings of the Messianic Kingdom.

So because of Israel's unbelief this Regathering from the nations is described as being 'with wrath.' Her unbelief also means she can't yet possess her promises, but instead must enter a 'halfway' house (a wilderness state) until she is ready to enter into the fulfilment. Her continuing unbelief means she must enter a time of Judgment (the Tribulation) where she will face the direct dealings of God, designed to prepare her to enter into the fulfilment of her promises. This corresponds to Israel's 40 wilderness-years between leaving Egypt and entering the Land. Thus her unbelief means this Regathering is not just 'with wrath', but also 'for wrath', for she's been regathered as a nation in preparation for the Tribulation.

Zechariah 13:8-9 describes this purging of Israel in the Tribulation (resulting from the rejection of Christ, v7): **"It shall come to pass in all the Land"** says the Lord: **"That 2/3 in it shall be cut off and die, but 1/3 says shall be left in it. I will bring the 1/3 through the fire, and refine them as silver is refined, and test them as gold is tested. They will call on My Name, and I will answer them. I will say: 'This is My people'; and each one will say: 'The Lord is my God."** Jesus said about this time: **"he who endures to the end** (of the Tribulation) **shall be saved"** (Matthew 24:13). The context of this is Israel.

Zephaniah 2:1-3 also shows that the Regathering in unbelief happens before the Tribulation ('the Day of the Lord' in 1:14-18): **"Gather yourselves together, yes, gather together, O undesirable** (unbelieving) **Nation** (Israel), **before the decree is issued, or the day passes like chaff** (blowing the wicked away), **before the Lord's fierce anger comes upon you, before the Day of the Lord's anger comes upon you** (the Tribulation)**! Seek the Lord, all you meek of the earth, who have upheld His justice. Seek righteousness, seek humility. It may be that you will be hidden in the Day of the Lord's anger** (a hint of the Pre-Tribulational Rapture!)**."** Thus the 1st Regathering in unbelief in preparation for the Tribulation is described in Ezekiel 20:33-38, 22:17-22 and Zephaniah 2:1-3.

Ezekiel 36:16-21 describe Israel's sin and consequent scattering to the nations. Then v22-32 describes her cleansing and regeneration, but making it clear that there is a Regathering to the Land BEFORE this happens. Her physical restoration is a prelude to her spiritual restoration. v22-24 describe an initial Regathering with Israel in unbelief: **"Say to the house of Israel, thus says the Lord God: I do not do this for your sake, O house of Israel, but for My holy Name's sake, which you have profaned among the nations wherever you went. And I will sanctify My great Name, which has been profaned among the** nations, which you have profaned in their midst; and the nations shall know that I am the Lord, says the Lord God, when I am hallowed in you before their eyes. For <u>I will take you from among the nations, gather you</u> out of all countries, and bring you into your own Land." This Regathering is not for their sake (in response to their repentance and faith), for they are still in sin, but God does it 'for His own Name's sake' (for the honour of His Name), to demonstrate His faithfulness to fulfil His unconditional covenant promises to Israel (see also v32). The scattering of Israel to the nations has resulted in His Name being profaned, because it makes it look like the Biblical God of Israel is not powerful enough to fulfil His promises to His people. So in order to vindicate His Name and show His Faithfulness to His Everlasting Covenant with Israel, He will regather her, even while she is in unbelief, as a 1st step toward her restoration. <u>v25-27</u> confirm that this initial Regathering is in unbelief, because it is only after it happens that God will revive them spiritually: **"Then I will sprinkle clean water on you, and you shall be clean; I will cleanse you from all your filthiness and from all your idols. I will give you a new heart and put a new spirit within you; I will take the heart of stone out of your flesh and give you a heart of flesh. I will put My Spirit within you and cause you to walk in My statutes, and you will keep My judgments and do them** (this is when Israel enters the New Covenant at the end of the Tribulation)." At this point with Israel in faith, the Messiah will complete the Regathering of Israel from all from all the nations, so that all Jews will dwell in Israel in the Messianic Kingdom under the blessing of the New Covenant: **"Then you shall dwell in the Land that I gave to your fathers; you shall be My people, and I will be your God"** (v28). Israel will then enjoy all her covenant promises, including all of Israel dwelling in her whole Land in a state of righteousness, peace and prosperity (v28-31).

This is confirmed by the famous vision of the valley of scattered dry bones in the next chapter, for <u>Ezekiel 37:1-14</u> describes the restoration of Israel in the same <u>2 Stages</u>: (1) A physical Regathering of the scattered dead bones of Israel (in unbelief), so that they form a single body (nation), followed by (2) a spiritual Regeneration, enabling her to fully and permanently dwell in the Land.

<u>Ezekiel was told to prophesy twice, reflecting these 2 Stages of Restoration</u>.

(1) By the 1st Word of God, the scattered bones of Israel came together, sinews and flesh came upon them, and skin covered them, forming into a united entity; but **"there was no breath** (spirit) **in them"** (v1-8). This is the present Regathering of Israel in unbelief. But it's clearly a work of God, the result of His Command. **Then (2) by the 2nd Word of God**, the Breath or Spirit of God entered into them and they lived and stood upon their feet, an exceedingly great army (v9,10). This is the spiritual regeneration of Israel, resulting in her becoming a great and powerful nation in the Millennium. v14: **"I will put My Spirit in you, and you shall live, and I will place you in your own Land."**

For the interpretation, Ezekiel is told: **"These bones are the whole house of Israel"** scattered to the nations (v11), confirming that the prophecy is about the restoration of Israel. God will first bring them into the Land of Israel (v12), THEN be made to come alive spiritually (v13,14).

Thus Ezekiel 37 gives the same sequence, which also agrees with the way God man Adam, first forming his body, and then breathing the spirit into him.
(1) A physical Regathering of the scattered dead bones of Israel (in unbelief).
(2) A spiritual Regeneration once the nation is physically restored. First, Israel must be physically resurrected, by being regathered to her Land and joined together as a Nation. This is the first step leading to her spiritual restoration at Christ's Return, and full and permanent possession of the Land in the Millennium.

The first Stage is described in v7-8 as: 'A noise', then a 'rattling sound', then 'bones came together, bone to bone', then 'tendons and flesh appeared', then 'skin covered them', but 'there was no breath in them.' This forecasts a *gradual* coming together of the bones. The body of the Jews was scattered all over the graveyard that contains the bones of many other civilisations, now all dead. But "the dead bones" of Israel would be different; they would gradually leave the graveyard and once again become a living Nation. The regathering of Israel in recent history was not an instantaneous miracle, but one that occurred gradually until the nation was established in 1948. At the present time we are still in the first stage for Israel has not yet received the BREATH (SPIRIT) that can only happen through receiving her Messiah. So Israel's initial Regathering as a Nation is just a preparation for her national spiritual restoration, after which she will fully regathered to her Land, and permanently settled there in the Millennium.

Ezekiel 37:15-28 then describes life in the Millennium. Israel will be completely regathered from the nations (v21), and become one unified undivided kingdom under one king (v22), the resurrected David (v24,25). They will be holy unto God (v23) and dwell in the Land forever, never to removed again (v25), because they have received the everlasting New Covenant (v26), the spiritual basis for their blessings of being established and prospering in the Land, and for their being fruitful and multiplying. Moreover they will have a new Temple in the midst (v26-28), described in great detail in Ezekiel 40-48, and the Lord God (Jesus Christ in His Glory) will dwell among them and be their God (v27). The Glory of God will shine out of the Temple in their midst, by which all the nations will know that God has set Israel apart as His holy and chief nation (v28).

Ezekiel 38:1 - 39:16, the next chapters, describe a massive invasion from the north upon a regathered Israel before her national conversion and salvation. Then the next prophecy describes the Battle of Armageddon, when Christ returns (39:17-20), followed by the final physical regathering and spiritual restoration of Israel (39:21-29), in preparation for life in the Millennium (Ezekiel 40-48). Thus, Ezekiel 38 shows Israel initially regathered to her Land in the last days (v8), awaiting her final restoration, which will take place at Christ's Return.

Jeremiah 30:3-11 also describes an initial Regathering before the Tribulation: **"I will bring back from captivity My people Israel and Judah,' says the Lord. 'And I will cause them to return to the land that I gave to their fathers, and they shall possess it"** (v3). Then it describes the Tribulation (the time of Jacob's Trouble), but promises that Israel will be saved out of it: **"For thus says the Lord: 'We have heard a voice of trembling, of fear, and not of peace. Ask now and see, whether a man is ever in labour with child? So why do I see every man with his hands on his loins like a woman in labour and all faces turned pale? Alas! For that Day is great, so that none is like it; and it is the time of Jacob's Trouble, but he** (Israel) **shall be saved out of it"** (v5-7). 'Jacob' is the name for Israel in unbelief, so it is 'Jacob's Trouble' but by its end, 'Jacob' will turn into 'Israel' (his name when in faith) and so "all Israel will be saved" by the Lord's Return to destroy all their enemies (v8). He then completes Israel's Regathering and establishes the Davidic Kingdom (v9-11).

Jesus described this final Regathering at His 2nd Coming in Matthew 24:31: **"He will send His angels with a sound of a great trumpet, and gather together His elect** (Israel) **from the 4 winds."** By now "all Israel will be saved" and this final Regathering is to establish her in her Land for the Millennium, where she will be the chief nation. So the 1st Regathering is in preparation for the discipline of the Tribulation, and the 2nd will be in preparation for the blessings of the Millennium. Many prophecies will only be completely fulfilled by the 2nd Regathering, but the 1st Regathering is included within their scope including Isaiah 43:5-7 and Jeremiah 16:14-17, 23:7-8, 32:36-42.

Thus the present situation of Israel is in perfect agreement with the Prophetic Word, which predicts God will sovereignly and miraculously regather Israel, before she comes to faith. He does it for His own Name's sake. It also predicts that this reborn Israel and especially Jerusalem will be the centre of controversy among the nations, and that it will be an end-time sign to the nations of His Coming Kingdom when He will full restore Israel. Israel will increasingly be an issue that divides the people who know God's Word and Spirit, from those under the spirit of this world. Whether you working for or against God in these end-times will be greatly determined by your attitude toward Israel. Satan who controls the spirit of this world seeks to destroy Israel, for by so doing He would cause God's Word and Plan to fail. This is the spiritual cause of anti-semitism and the irrational hatred of the Jews and the repeated attempts in history to commit genocide against them. In the end-times, the world will increasingly be aligned against Israel climaxing in Armageddon, causing the issue of our attitude toward Israel to be increasingly decisive for our own spiritual lives. The true people of God will be revealed by their love for Israel and blessing of Israel. Romans 5:5 says God has poured His love into the hearts of those who are truly born again. Since God loves His people Israel with an everlasting love (Jeremiah 31:3) then we'll have that same supernatural love in our hearts if we're born again.

In the Judgment of the Sheep and Goats in Matthew 25:31-46, the sheep and goats are the surviving Gentiles at the 2nd Coming (v31-32). What distinguished the Sheep Gentiles from the Goat Gentiles is their attitude to a 3rd group whom Jesus called: **"My brethren"** (v40). v37-40: **"Then the righteous** (gentiles) **will answer Him, saying: 'Lord, when did we see You hungry and feed You, or thirsty and give You drink? When did we see You a stranger and take You in, or naked and clothe You? Or when did we see You sick, or in prison, and come to You?' And the King will answer and say to them: 'Assuredly, I say to you, inasmuch as you did it to one of the least of THESE MY BRETHREN, you did it to Me."** 'My brethren' must refer to Jesus' fellow Jews who have survived the Tribulation. Remember He is the Lion of the tribe of Judah! If 'My brethren' just meant believers then they would be identical to 'the sheep', so the sheep are being praised for caring for each other, but Jesus is praising them for caring for another group of people (Jews) who've faced extreme persecution during the Tribulation. Notice this passage emphasises that blessing Israel includes compassionate ministry to her giving practical help to meet her needs. As a result of blessing her in this way they are blessed by God (v34). By way of contrast the goats are cursed because they did nothing to bless the Jews in this way, when they were under attack and in great need. This lack of compassion was a manifestation of their unregenerate hearts. This is another demonstration that Genesis 12:3 is still in force: **"I will make you a great nation…I will bless those who bless you, and curse him who curses you."** Thus your attitude to the Jews and Israel will determine whether your life comes under blessing or curse.

Sadly, the anti-Semitic spirit of this world has invaded the church through replacement theology, which says God has cancelled His election of Israel and transferred it to the Church. This gives a basis for those who oppose Israel, for they can say they're doing God's will, for if God rejected Israel, then we should also. But Romans 11 is clear that although Israel is in unbelief she is still the elect nation of God, and that God will judge the gentiles who boast against her. We've also established the present Nation of Israel is no accident, but a miraculous fulfilment of prophecy, the result of a sovereign act of God, who's still fulfilling His purposes for Israel. Indeed all agree that Israel's scattering was a result of God's judgment, and whatever He does in blessing or cursing, no man can reverse. Therefore, the Rebirth of Israel must be God's work. Therefore, **we need to align ourselves with God's purposes for Israel and support and bless what God is doing** rather than opposing it, lest we find ourselves resisting God!

Therefore we should pray for Israel and seek her good. God commands this in Psalm 122:6-9, telling us that it will result in blessing for us and our families: **"Pray for the peace of Jerusalem: "May they prosper who love you. Peace be within your walls, prosperity within your palaces." For the sake of my brethren and companions, I will now say: "Peace be within you." Because of the house of the Lord our God I will seek your good."** We should align with God's revealed prophetic purposes by prayer as we see Daniel do in Daniel 9:2-4.

Isaiah 62:1,6,7: **"For Zion's sake I will not hold My peace, and for Jerusalem's sake I will not rest, until her righteousness goes forth as brightness, and her salvation as a lamp that burns.... I have set watchmen on your walls, O Jerusalem; they shall never hold their peace day or night. You who make mention of the Lord, do not keep silent, and give Him no rest till He establishes and till He makes Jerusalem a praise in the earth."**

As well as pray we should comfort Israel with practical compassionate help as we saw from Matthew 25:37-40.   Also Romans 11:31: **"Even so these also have now been disobedient, that through your mercy** (compassion) **they also may obtain mercy** (from God)."** Our compassionate ministry to the Jews will be a witness to them, helping to open their hearts to receive God's mercy through Christ. Romans 15:27 affirms that we should bless Israel in natural ways, which includes the giving of our finances, because we owe her a great debt of gratitude: **"It pleased them indeed, and they** (as Gentiles) **are their debtors. For if the Gentiles have been partakers of their spiritual things, their duty is also to minister to them in material things."** Paul practised this principle by making it a priority of his ministry to make a collection from all the Churches for the poor in the Church in Jerusalem, and brought it there himself at great personal risk.

What a great debt we owe to Israel, for they gave us our Bible and our Saviour, as Jesus said: **"Salvation is from the Jews"** (John 4:22), and Church history has only compounded this debt through prejudice and persecution. Therefore it is important to keep free from the spirit of world and Christian anti-semitism, whether racial, political or theological (replacement theology). This ministry of compassion that we owe to the Jewish people is also seen in Isaiah 40:1-2: **"Comfort, yes, comfort My people!" says your God. Speak comfort to Jerusalem."** Along with our actions our speech should comfort and support Israel as she face many enemies, and especially the Messianic Community in the Land. Our comforting words should include sharing the Gospel (v3-11), the Good News that her Messiah has come in the Person of Jesus, remembering that: **"the Gospel of Christ is the Power of God unto Salvation for everyone who believes, for the Jew first and also for the Greek."** Therefore it is right to support Jewish evangelism (for there is no other Way of Salvation than Christ).

Jeremiah 31 is a classic chapter on the restoration of Israel and gives a wonderful summary of what God commands us to do. Israel has a future based on God's unconditional election and everlasting love for her, therefore He will draw her again to Himself (v3) and restore her (v4-6). In v8-9 He says He will regather them **"from the ends of the earth"**, and in v7 He tells us what we should do: **"Thus says the Lord: "SING with gladness for Jacob, and SHOUT among the chief of the nations; PROCLAIM, give PRAISE, and PRAY: 'O Lord, SAVE Your people, the remnant of Israel!'"**

1. We are to rejoice and PRAISE God when we see Him fulfilling His promises to Israel. 2. We are to PRAY for Israel, particularly for their Salvation through Christ. 3. In the face of all the anti-Israel voices, we are to be loyal to Israel, for we are in covenant with the God of Israel. We are to speak for Israel and PROCLAIM God's Word concerning Israel. What we are to proclaim is given to us in v10: **"Hear the Word of the Lord, O nations, and declare it in the isles afar off, and say: "He (God) who scattered Israel will gather him, and protect him as a Shepherd does His flock."** Thus we should bless Israel: (1) by supporting evangelistic and mercy missions to her, and (2) spiritually through PRAYER, PRAISE and PROCLAMATION.

v31-34 describes the establishment of the New Covenant with the House (Nation) of Israel at the time of the 2nd Coming, which provides the spiritual basis for all the blessings of the Messianic Kingdom. (This spiritual restoration takes place after her initial physical Regathering, v27-28). He draws a parallel to when He established the Old Covenant with her at Sinai, constituting her as a Nation under God. Israel's acceptance of this Covenant as a Nation was a necessary preparation for her to possess her Land. Likewise, when Israel accepts the New Covenant, when as a nation she officially accepts Jesus as her Messiah at the end of the Tribulation, all Israel will be saved and be constituted as a Nation under Christ, and thereby she will be spiritually qualified to receive and possess the Messianic Kingdom. This is the national repentance of Israel, resulting in her national regeneration (salvation) and full restoration. Israel will not break the New Covenant as she did with the Old Covenant, for He will put His Law and Spirit in their hearts. In the Millennium every Jew will be saved and know the Lord (v34). Finally in v35-37 God gives the strongest possible guarantee that Israel has a future, saying that while the sun, moon and stars exist, Israel will remain a Nation before Him. He concludes that despite all their sins, He will never cast them away, because of His everlasting Covenant with them.

The RECAPTURE of JERUSALEM

The next major event prophesied for in the end-times before the Tribulation is Jerusalem coming back under Israel's control. This is necessary since prophecies of the Tribulation assume a Jewish Jerusalem. This was fulfilled in 1967. Jerusalem under Jewish control is another sign we are getting close to the Tribulation. Jerusalem's Recapture is highly significant, because it is the City of the Great King (Matthew 5:35, Psalm 48:2), the place of God's Throne on earth. Jesus will rule the world from Jerusalem, which is why it is the centre of spiritual warfare, and of the controversy of nations (Zechariah 12:2-3), leading up to Armageddon itself (14:2-3), and so this is why Jesus will return to Jerusalem (14:4). The restoration of Jewish sovereignty over Jerusalem was prophesied in Luke 21:24: **"Jerusalem will be trampled under foot by the Gentiles UNTIL the Times of the Gentiles are fulfilled."** This tells us that Jerusalem's Recapture in 1967 officially marks the end of the Times of Gentile Dominion over Israel, for Jerusalem is the God-ordained capital and seat of authority of Israel. The Times of the Gentiles began with Nebuchadnezzar in 600 BC and lasted over 2500 years. It was a period when God disciplined Israel by putting her under Gentile control. But now it is finished, the nations no longer have the right to exercise dominion over Israel and God will judge them if they try (see my book: "The 7 Times of the Gentiles.")

The Temple Rebuilt

Another thing that must take place before the Tribulation is preparations to rebuild the 3rd Temple, that will be operational in the Tribulation, and perhaps even the rebuilding itself, although that might take place early in the Tribulation.

*4 Passages of Scripture prove that there will be a Tribulation Temple

*(1) Daniel 9:27: **"He** (antichrist) **shall confirm a covenant with many** (the majority in Israel) **for one Week** (7 years); **but in the middle of the Week, he shall bring an end to sacrifice and offering** (in the Temple). **And on a wing of the Temple he will set up an Abomination that causes Desolation, until the end decreed is poured out on him."** This is Daniel's 70th Week. Antichrist makes a treaty with Israel near the start of this 7-year Tribulation, allowing Israel to worship in her Temple. Halfway through the 7 years he breaks this covenant, takes over the

Temple, stops the Jewish worship there, and puts up an idolatrous image of himself in the Temple, dedicating it to himself. In response to this desecration of His Temple, God pours out desolating judgments on his kingdom.

*(2) Matthew 24:15: **"When you see standing in the Holy Place** (of the Temple) **the Abomination that causes Desolation, spoken of by the prophet Daniel then let those in Judea flee."** This is part of the Olivet Discourse which started with Jesus prophesying the destruction of Jerusalem and the Temple, and the scattering of Israel to the nations as a result of her rejection of the Messiah (Matthew 23:37-24:2 Luke 21:6,20-24). But later when He describes the End of the Age (Tribulation), He says Israel will be back in the Land with a rebuilt Temple, thus setting the stage for the final act (this is why the Rebirth of Israel, the Fig Tree, is a major Sign of the approaching Tribulation). Although Daniel 11:31 refers to an abomination (idol) of desolation in the Temple this had already been fulfilled before the time of Christ by Antiochus Epiphanes (168 BC). But Jesus prophesied an Abomination of Desolation in the Temple, that was still in the future. Therefore He was speaking of an end-time Abomination, of which the previous one was just a type. He was referring to the Abomination of Daniel 9:27, saying that its fulfilment was still future (thus proving that this verse was not fulfilled by Christ, but awaits a future fulfilment by antichrist). He confirmed that the Abomination would be part of the sequence of Tribulation-events leading up to the 2nd Coming. Therefore Jesus Himself confirms that there will be a functioning Jewish Temple in the Tribulation, which antichrist will desecrate.

*(3) 2Thessalonians 2:4: **"He** (antichrist) **will oppose and will exalt himself over everything that is called god or is worshipped, so that he sets himself up in the Temple of God, proclaiming himself to be god."** This speaks of the same event when the antichrist takes over the Temple at Mid-Tribulation. Some see this 3rd Temple as not being in God's will, but here it is called: 'the Temple of God.' Jesus called it: 'the Holy Place.' God's purpose for this Temple is to reach Israel in the Tribulation with the Gospel, as seen in the next scripture.

*(4) Revelation 11:1-3: **"Then I was given a reed like a measuring rod. And the angel stood, saying: "Rise and measure the Temple of God, the altar, and those who worship there. But leave out the court, which is outside the Temple, and do not measure it, for it has been given to the Gentiles** (this is

where the Al-Aska Mosque is). **And I will give power to my 2 witnesses, and they will prophesy 1260 days, clothed in sackcloth.**" Again we see there will be a Jewish Temple in the Tribulation. The Temple Mount will be shared with the Gentiles, as agreed in her covenant with antichrist. It will be the ministry base for the 2 witnesses who preach Christ to Israel in the 1st half of the Tribulation, as they come to the Temple. So God will use the Temple (even the sacrifices) to remind the Jews that there is no forgiveness of sins without the shedding of blood, and to proclaim to them the Lamb of God has already been sacrificed for them. Since losing the Temple, Judaism has developed into a religious system of works-salvation, that's independent of sacrifice. It has forgotten man's sinfulness and our need for redemption by Messiah's blood. Thus this Temple will be a key part of God's Plan for Israel's Salvation. The 2 witnesses (under Divine protection) will operate at the Altar, which will be visited by all of Israel, witnessing to Christ and His Sacrifice. Thus they will evangelise Israel and bring many to faith.

The preparations for the Temple are well under way. The Temple Institute has been making all the necessary items for the Temple, including a Gold Menorah. Also a Levitical Priesthood has been prepared to carry out the Temple Ministry. This 3rd Temple must be built where the Dome of the Rock is now, because the Rock, called 'the Foundation Stone', is the location of the Holy of Holies. It even has a rectangular depression, that's the right size for the Ark of the Covenant. (see my book: 'Mount Moriah, Golgotha and the Garden Tomb'). This Temple must already be functioning early in the Tribulation. With modern technology a basic structure and altar can be set up very quickly. The Dome of the Rock, which presently stands on the Holy Place, is a monument to a false god, proclaiming in Arabic writing: 'God has no Son' (showing it is a manifestation of the spirit of antichrist). It is therefore a type of the final idol-abomination, which the antichrist will put at that same place (for further proof see my: '7 Times of the Gentiles'). The rebuilding of the Temple has only been possible since 1967, when Israel captured the Temple Mount. Although it is under Israeli sovereignty, to help maintain peaceful relations, she decided to allow its daily running to be left in the hands of the Muslim religious authorities. In the present religious and political situation, it seems impossible for the Temple to be rebuilt, especially as the Dome of the Rock would have to be destroyed, and that would start a war. Something dramatic must happen to change the international landscape, to make the Temple a possibility, and something must also cause the Dome to be destroyed, like a great earthquake, so that the Temple can be rebuilt. I will give a possible scenario for how this might all happen when we look at the next major Pre-Tribulation event.

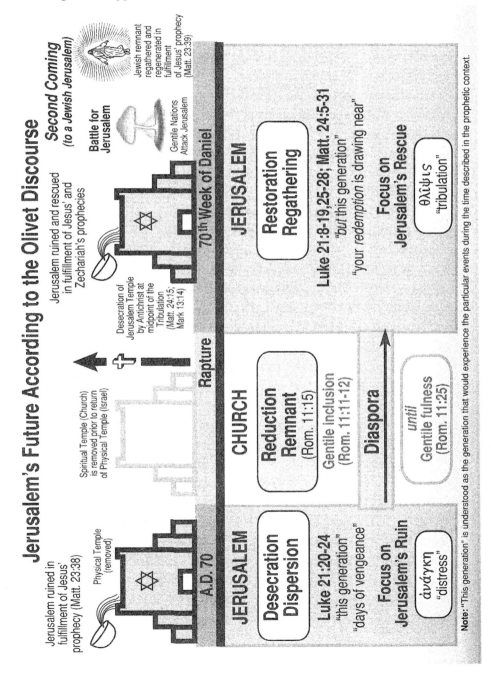

Jerusalem's Future According to the Olivet Discourse

Second Coming *(to a Jewish Jerusalem)*

Jewish remnant regathered and regenerated in fulfillment of Jesus' prophecy (Matt. 23:39)

Jerusalem ruined and rescued in fulfillment of Jesus' and Zechariah's prophecies

Battle for Jerusalem

Gentile Nations Attack Jerusalem

Desecration of Jerusalem Temple by Antichrist at midpoint of the Tribulation (Matt. 24:15; Mark 13:14)

Spiritual Temple (Church) is removed prior to return of Physical Temple (Israel)

Jerusalem ruined in fulfillment of Jesus' prophecy (Matt. 23:38)

Physical Temple (removed)

Rapture

70th Week of Daniel

JERUSALEM
- Restoration
- Regathering

Luke 21:8-19,25-28; Matt. 24:5-31
"but this generation"
"your redemption is drawing near"

Focus on Jerusalem's Rescue

θλίψις "tribulation"

CHURCH
- Reduction
- Remnant (Rom. 11:15)

Gentile inclusion (Rom. 11:11-12)

Diaspora

until Gentile fulness (Rom. 11:25)

A.D. 70

JERUSALEM
- Desecration
- Dispersion

Luke 21:20-24
"this generation"
"days of vengeance"

Focus on Jerusalem's Ruin

ἀνάγκη "distress"

Note: "This generation" is understood as the generation that would experience the particular events during the time described in the prophetic context.

The Temple Through Time

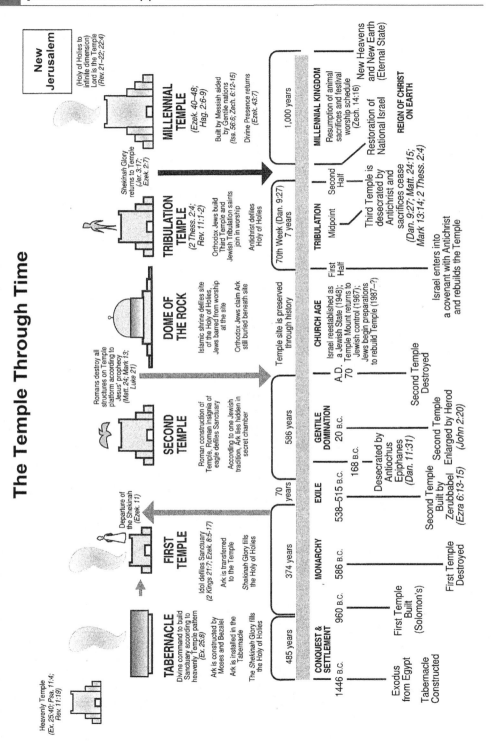

New Jerusalem

(Holy of Holies to infinite dimension)
Lord is the Temple
(Rev. 21–22; 22:4)

Heavenly Temple
(Ex. 25:40; Psa. 11:4; Rev. 11:19)

MILLENNIAL TEMPLE
(Ezek. 40–48; Hag. 2:6-9)

Built by Messiah aided by Gentile nations
(Isa. 56:6; Zech. 6:12-15)

Divine Presence returns
(Ezek. 43:7)

Shekinah Glory returns to Temple
(Jer. 3:17; Ezek. 2:7)

TRIBULATION TEMPLE
(2 Thess. 2:4; Rev. 11:1-2)

Orthodox Jews build Third Temple and Jewish Tribulation saints join in worship

Antichrist defiles Holy of Holies

DOME OF THE ROCK

Islamic shrine defiles site of the Holy of Holies, Jews barred from worship at the site

Orthodox Jews claim Ark still buried beneath site

Romans destroy all structures on Temple platform according to Jesus' prophecy
(Matt. 24; Mark 13; Luke 21)

SECOND TEMPLE

Roman construction of Temple, Roman insignia of eagle defiles Sanctuary

According to one Jewish tradition, Ark lies hidden in secret chamber

FIRST TEMPLE

Idol defiles Sanctuary
(2 Kings 21:7; Ezek. 8:5-17)

Ark is transferred to the Temple

Shekinah Glory fills the Holy of Holies

Departure of the Shekinah
(Ezek. 11)

TABERNACLE

Divine command to build Sanctuary according to heavenly Temple pattern
(Ex. 25:8)

Ark is constructed by Moses and Bezalel

Ark is installed in the Tabernacle

The Shekinah Glory fills the Holy of Holies

Temple site is preserved through history

| 485 years | 374 years | 70 years | 586 years | | | | 70th Week (Dan. 9:27) 7 years | 1,000 years |

CONQUEST & SETTLEMENT

1446 B.C.

Exodus from Egypt

Tabernacle Constructed

960 B.C.

First Temple Built (Solomon's)

MONARCHY

586 B.C.

First Temple Destroyed

EXILE

538–515 B.C.

Second Temple Built by Zerubbabel
(Ezra 6:13-15)

168 B.C.

Desecrated by Antiochus Epiphanes
(Dan. 11:31)

GENTILE DOMINATION

20 B.C.

Second Temple Enlarged by Herod
(John 2:20)

A.D. 70

Second Temple Destroyed

CHURCH AGE

Israel reestablished as a Jewish State (1948); Temple Mount returns to Jewish control (1967); Jews begin preparations to rebuild Temple (1987–?)

Israel enters into a covenant with Antichrist and rebuilds the Temple

TRIBULATION

First Half — Midpoint — Second Half

Third Temple is desecrated by Antichrist and sacrifices cease
(Dan. 9:27; Matt. 24:15; Mark 13:14; 2 Thess. 2:4)

MILLENNIAL KINGDOM

Resumption of animal sacrifices and festival worship schedule
(Zech. 14:16)

Restoration of National Israel

REIGN OF CHRIST ON EARTH

New Heavens and New Earth (Eternal State)

The Invasion of Israel from the North (Ezekiel 38)

Another major event that will probably happen before the Tribulation is a massive invasion of Israel from the North led by **Russia**, supported by **Iran**, **Turkey** and **many other Islamic nations**. It is described in detail in Ezekiel 38:1-39:16. My book: 'The Imminent Invasion of Israel' gives a full explanation.

The setting is Israel regathered to her Land in the Last Days, but before her national conversion. The invading armies will cover the Land like a cloud and it will seem hopeless. Israel will be totally overwhelmed, but God says: "You've come against '**My people**' and '**My Land**'", so in His wrath He (not Israel) will destroy this invading army with a combination of judgments, including **a massive earthquake**. This will be one of the greatest, most dramatic Divine Interventions ever, proving that Israel is still His covenant people and He is a covenant-keeping God. He will demonstrate His glory and magnify Himself in the sight of many nations, and they will know He's the Lord, the Holy One in Israel (38:23, 39:7), and that the God of the Bible, the God of Israel is still alive and well. It will be a catalyst for a worldwide revival. The world will be in awe, especially since this will be such a clear fulfilment of Bible Prophecy. This will give us a unique window of opportunity to share the Gospel, so we need to be ready.

This has never been fulfilled, and the setting and political alignments described perfectly fit the present time. Moreover Ezekiel 39:9 says that Israel will be burning the invader's weapons for 7 years. So it must take place at least 7 years before the 2nd Coming. So it could be very early in the Tribulation, but much more likely it will be before the Tribulation. I think it will happen soon.

2 Possible Scenarios that trigger this Invasion

*1. Israel must stop Iran developing nuclear weapons, otherwise they will be used against her. If Israel attacks Iran's nuclear facilities, or acts against Iran in a strong way, it would give Russia an excuse to gather a coalition of nations against Israel (this would give the operation diplomatic cover and respectability, rather than doing it alone). So this could be the catalyst for Ezekiel's war, giving this Russia-Muslim Coalition all the excuse they need to attack an unpopular Israel.

*2. Israel will annex a major part of the West Bank, which is the disputed territories of Judea-Samaria (including East Jerusalem). This also described as 'the mountains of Israel', which is the very place described in Ezekiel 38 as being the location of the invading armies which God destroys (they do not invade Israel proper). To minimize international opposition, they will do this in the name of international law, undoing Israel's claim, and establishing a Palestinian State, but the prophecy reveals that her real motives are economic and strategic. By doing this Russia will gain control of Israel's strategic position 'in the centre of the earth' (v12 - the middle of the middle east), and limit Israel's competition with Russia in selling oil and gas, for Russia' economy depends on that (Israel has great oil and gas reserves that have been recently discovered in perfect fulfilment of Deuteronomy 33:24). By doing this Russia can increase her grip on the Middle-East and thus the world energy market, upon which her fragile economy depends. The prophecy shows Russia ruled by a dominant leader (Gog), which is certainly the case at the moment. The other Islamic nations who will support Russia all want Israel destroyed, as they see her as their number one enemy, and a contradiction to their faith. When all these nations invade Israel, God will move quickly to decisively judge the invading nations, including sending a great earthquake, which is felt around the world (v19), which destroys the Dome of the Rock, making way for the rebuilt Temple. The invading armies are completely destroyed (19:4) and destruction will fall on their homelands, especially Russia (19:6).

Although Israel does not yet receive her Messiah, this Divine Intervention will cause her to reverence God and have a renewed confidence that He is the God of Israel. It will demonstrate to the world that God has not finished with Israel, and will judge all nations who curse Israel and come against Israel. The Jewish sages believed this War of Gog and Magog would usher in the Messianic era, and warned that those who witnessed Russia's preparations to invade Israel should prepare its heart for Messiah. This understanding will fuel their desire to build the 3rd Temple. Thus Israel's salvation from destruction will set the stage and strengthen moves to rebuild her Temple, creating a window of opportunity for her to do this, especially with the Islamic opposition (supported by Russia's military might) greatly weakened. Alternatively, the Temple will only be able to be rebuilt as part of the peace-treaty Israel makes with the antichrist. Either way this war will so change the political situation that what now seems impossible will suddenly happen. Thus God's defeat of these armies will create the political, military and religious conditions that will lead to Israel rebuilding her Temple.

This Divine Intervention will also trigger a REVIVAL of faith in the nations. Thus one of God's purposes for destroying the invading armies is described in 19:7: **"So I will make My holy name known in the midst of My people Israel, and I will not let them profane My holy Name anymore. Then the nations shall know that I am the Lord, the Holy One in Israel."** This will give the Church a great opportunity to reap a great soul-harvest, for on that day He will be glorified in the eyes of the whole world. In one moment, He will judge Russia and Islam, save Israel, proving to the most sceptical minds that a supernatural God exists. Millions of souls who've been deceived by secular humanism and Islam will suddenly realise the God of the Bible is alive. We must be ready to take advantage of this opportunity this will provide us to preach the Gospel. Islam will suffer a great blow, with many of its nations sharing in this Judgment. This politically orientated religion thrives on military and political success, but is also very sensitive to failure. It will be very difficult for Islam to explain its total defeat at the hands of God, and many Muslims will realise it must be false, causing them to turn to the Bible and accept Christ.

The breaking of the power of Russia and these Islamic nations will also create a power-vacuum enabling a new world power to arise, from which antichrist will emerge as its leader. Being clever, persuasive, deceptive and dynamic he will present himself as a friend-protector of Israel, enabling him to sign a covenant with her early in the Tribulation (Daniel 9:27), which is really part of his move to control the Middle East and then the world (Revelation 6:1-2).

World Politics leading up to the Tribulation

Bible Prophecy tells us what to expect in the time just before the Tribulation.

*1. The rise of Russia as a major power, as we've seen in Ezekiel 38-39.

*2. Israel back in her Land, and the centre of world controversy. At the end, God will judge the nations over **"the controversy of Zion"** (Isaiah 34:8, also Zechariah 14:2, Joel 3:2, Psalm 83). Zechariah 12:2-3 warns these nations that they will pay a heavy price for messing with Israel: **"Behold, I will make Jerusalem a cup of drunkenness to all the surrounding peoples, when they lay siege against Judah and Jerusalem. And it shall happen in that day that I will make Jerusalem a very heavy stone for all peoples; all who would heave it away will surely be cut in pieces, though all nations of the earth are gathered against it."**

Therefore in the time leading up to the end Israel must be the focus of much unwanted attention around the world and that is certainly true.

Psalm 83 describes an alliance of Islamic nations that will conspire and come against Israel in the last days. 3000 years ago it was prophesied that these nations would form a confederacy against Israel with the aim of destroying her as a nation. The Psalm calls for God's Judgment to fall on them: **"Do not keep silent, O God! Do not hold Your peace, and do not be still, O God! For behold, Your enemies make a tumult; and those who hate You have lifted up their head. They have taken crafty counsel against Your People** (Israel) **and consulted together against Your sheltered ones. They have said: "Come, and let us cut them off from being a Nation, that the Name of Israel may be remembered no more." For they have consulted together with one consent; they form a confederacy against You."** The ancient list of nations in v4-8 enumerates almost all the modern Islamic nations that oppose Israel's existence today. They form an inner ring of nations surrounding Israel in contrast to the invaders of Ezekiel 38 which form an outer ring, although these would have to go through the inner ring to reach Israel (**"the many** (other) **nations"** of v9?). Psalm 83 perfectly describes what's been going on constantly since 1948, which has been manifested through various wars. Some believe that it also prophesies a specific end-time invasion of Israel yet to come, different from the Ezekiel invasion, in which God will give Israel a great military victory in answer to the supplications at the end of the Psalm (v9-18). God's ultimate purpose in destroying these invaders is that these nations would come to know Him as the true God (v16,18).

*3. Isaiah 17 predicts the destruction of Damascus which is taking place now, as a reaping of the cursing of Israel that has come from Syria: **"Behold, Damascus will cease from being a city, and it will be a ruinous heap"** (v1).

*4. The possible rebuilding of literal Babylon in Iraq as antichrist's capital city (Revelation 18). Or Babylon could be symbolic of the kingdoms of this world, ruled over by antichrist, king of Babylon (since Babylon is the first world-power, the head of gold, in Daniel's vision of the gentile world-powers who would rule over Israel, Babylon is the name of all these empires taken together (as they form a unity in the statue of Daniel 2 and as a single 7-headed Beast in Revelation 13:1)

*5. Both Daniel and Revelation reveal that in the Tribulation a confederacy of 10 nations becomes the dominant world power under the antichrist, which establishes a One World Government for a brief time. So in the time leading up to the Tribulation, we'd expect to see the rise of a powerful empire that antichrist will take control of, the 2 main possibilities being (1) a Revived Roman Empire that comes out of Europe, or (2) an Islamic Caliphate (a Revived Ottoman Empire) coming out of the Middle East. Thus the present vision of a Federal Europe, which drives the growing economic and political union of the EU could be the forerunner of the final end-time beast, or else it could be that the modern resurgence and growth of Islam will ultimately produce a united confederacy of nations that will ultimately become antichrist's power-base in the Tribulation.

The present situation can be likened to a story about a woman in an old rented house. The whole area had been bought up for redevelopment, and the owner visited her and told her she could stay in her house until it was time for it to be knocked down. At that time he promised he would personally come to collect her and move her into a far better modern house. As the days went by the trucks and bulldozers started arriving and surrounding the house preparing to demolish it. When asked if she was worried, she said 'No, because before they start to demolish the house, the owner will come and take me to my new home.' Likewise, we can see all the Signs (bulldozers) coming into place as God is getting ready to demolish the kingdoms of this world, but we are not to fear but rather to lift up our heads in anticipation that the Owner of all things, Jesus is coming at any time to save us from the coming destruction (Luke 21:28), and personally escort us to a far better place, our mansion above (John 14:1-3)!

*Chapter 5: The Teaching of Jesus on the Rapture

It was Jesus who initiated the New Testament teaching on the Mystery Church Age (Matthew 13), and He also gave the foundational teaching for the Rapture of the Church, that is part of this Mystery (1Cor 15:51). The Rapture of the Church is the final event of the Church Age, the ingathering of the harvest of the Church, when Christ comes for His Bride (all believers in Christ, saved in the Church Age) and takes them to Heaven. The dead in Christ will be resurrected and we who are still alive will be raptured. The RAPTURE is the Coming of Christ for the Church in which He instantly 'catches up' all living believers to meet Him in the air and translates them into immortal bodies without experiencing death.

<u>Jesus said in John 14:1-3</u>: **"Let not your heart be troubled; you believe in God, believe also in Me. In My Father's House** (HEAVEN) **are many mansions; if it were not so, I would have told you. I go to prepare a place for you. And if I go and prepare a place for you, I will come again and receive you to Myself; that where I am, there you may be also."**

These are the words of a Bridegroom to His betrothed Bride, saying He will go away to Heaven, to prepare a home there for His Bride, where they will dwell together forever. He promises her that He will come again and receive her to Himself, to take her back to Heaven where their Marriage will take place. This foundational verse establishes a number of key truths about the Rapture, which distinguishes it from His Second Coming, when He returns in power and glory to take over the whole earth.

This is a Coming of Christ for believers only, unlike the 2nd Coming, which involves everyone. Its purpose is to be reunited with His Bride and take her to Heaven, whereas the purpose of the 2nd Coming is to judge His enemies and establish His Kingdom on earth. In John 14, Christ does not come and land on the earth and dwell (reign) here, as He does in the 2nd Coming (Zechariah 14:4), but He comes close to receive His Bride to Himself (in fact we will meet the Lord in the air - 1Thessalonians 4:15). He then returns with her to the place He has prepared in Heaven, where they abide during the period of Judgment on the earth, called the Day of the Lord, after which we will return with Him in His 2nd Coming (Revelation 19). Those who teach a Post-Tribulation Rapture, say that when Christ returns at the 2nd Coming, we will rise to meet Him in the Rapture, and then immediately do a U-turn and go back with Him to the earth. But this contradicts John 14, which says that when Jesus returns in the Rapture He takes us to Heaven.

Jesus also taught on the Rapture in His Olivet Discourse of Jesus, which we studied in Part 1 of this series. We saw that His teaching was structured to answer the 3 Questions in Matthew 24:3:

*Question 1 asked for **the Signs of the Temple's Destruction** (in AD 70), which Jesus answered in Luke 21.

*Question 2 asked: **"What will be the Sign of Your Coming?"**, which He answered in Matthew 24:4-31, by describing the events in the Tribulation.

*Question 3 asked: **"What is the Sign of the End of the Age?"**
This is a different question than Question 2, but their answers are connected. The End of the Age is the Tribulation, so Question 3 is: "what are the Signs by which we can know when we are living in the time just before the Tribulation?" In other words, how do we know we are in the last days of the Church Age? Jesus answers this in Matthew 24:32-44 and Luke 21:28-36.

Notice that answering Question 3 after Question 2 requires Him to go back in time, from v31, which describes the final Regathering of Israel at the 2nd Coming, to v32ff which describes the time leading up to the start of the Tribulation. This is what interests us the most, being very relevant to us, for we are live in that time, the last days of the Church Age. In Part 1, we proved that Jesus' answer to Question 3 perfectly fits our unique times, confirming that we live in the last of the last days. Jesus answered Question 2 first because He needed to refer to His answer to Question 2 in order to answer Question 3. He expressed the connection between the answer to Question 2 (the conditions and events in the Tribulation), and Question 3 (the conditions and events in the time just before the Tribulation) in terms of TREES, because developing trees express the continuity of history. He uses TREES to describe all the different SIGNPOSTS in the world. For in the TRIBULATION, all the trees will come to their fullness, and are bear their fruit, as trees do in the SUMMER - either good trees bearing good fruit, like Israel (the FIG TREE), or evil trees bearing evil fruit. Other 'Tribulation Trees', like the Tree of advanced Technology, are neutral in nature. Once we know what the Tribulation Trees look like in the Summer, we can then know when we are in the SPRING time just before the Summer, because in the SPRING all these trees are budding, putting forth LEAVES in preparation for them bringing forth their fruit in the SUMMER.

Luke 21:28-32: **"Now when THESE THINGS** (that come to their fullness in the Tribulation) **BEGIN to happen** (in the time just beforehand), **look UP and lift UP your heads, because your Redemption** (in the Rapture) **draws near." Then He spoke to them a Parable: "Look at FIG TREE** (Israel – see Luke 13) **and ALL THE TREES. When they are already budding** (putting forth leaves in the SPRING) **you SEE and know for yourselves that SUMMER is now near. So you also, when you SEE THESE THINGS** (that will be in full manifestation in the Tribulation) **happening** (budding, beginning to happen), **know that the KINGDOM of God** (the Tribulation-Summer when the Kingdom starts to invade earth) **is near. Assuredly, I say to you, this generation** (who see these trees budding) **will by no means pass away till all things take place."**

So these SIGNS are like the initial appearing of TREES in the Springtime when they put forth their leaves, which is the sign that Summer is near, when they will be bearing all their fruit. Likewise, when we see them all these things begin to happen together, we know we are in the Spring time, just before the Summer heat of the Tribulation, when they will come to their fullness. That is why He used TREES to represent the SIGNS of the Tribulation, because trees, like world-conditions develop in a continuous way, and so they also tells us when we are close to the Tribulation. In Part 1, we explained how this works for all the signs of the times, we are presently experiencing, proving that Jesus is coming soon.

So Jesus compares the SIGNS to TREES, which are fully developed and bearing fruit in the Summer. When you see them all blossoming and putting forth leaves together in the Spring, you know that Summer is near. Likewise, since we know the various world conditions in the Tribulation (the Trees in their fully developed form), we can know when we are in the time just before the Tribulation, for they cannot become this way overnight. So when you see all these world conditions begin to develop together you know the world is getting close to the Tribulation. Now we can understand why God inspired Questions 2 and 3 to be asked together as a 2-fold Question: *"What will be the Sign of Your Coming, and of the End of the Age?"* It is because the answer to the 3rd Questions comes directly from the answer to the 2nd Question. Jesus said that when you see the Fig Tree

(Israel back in the Land) and ALL the Tribulation Trees spring up together then you know the Tribulation is near. In fact He went further and said that everything will be fulfilled within a man's lifetime from when these Trees start appearing.

The Rapture of the Church

We've seen that after Jesus had answered Question 2 by giving the events of the Tribulation leading up to His 2nd Coming, He went back in time in order to answer Question 3 which asked for the Signs of the End of the Age (Tribulation). We now study the last part of His answer, which gives the **Disappearance of believers in the Rapture of the Church** as the final SIGN that the world will see before the Judgment of the Tribulation falls upon the whole world, which is.

In Luke 21:28 we saw He connected these Signs with the Rapture: **"When these THINGS (SIGNS) begin to happen, look UP and lift UP your heads, because your Redemption** (in the Rapture) **draws near."**

Many scriptures command the Church to wait, watch and look for the imminent Coming of Christ for us to take us to be with Him forever. Spiritually we are to be looking UP to heaven where Christ is and from where He will suddenly return for us. He has not told us exactly when He will return, so we always have to stay ready. For us who see the signs of the approaching Tribulation we have all the more reason to look UP, for surely Jesus must be coming soon. Clearly the response Jesus wants from us who see these Signs is to adjust our spiritual focus, looking up to Jesus in heaven in expectation of the imminent redemption of our body in the Rapture, so our focus is on Jesus and our whole life is guided and motivated by the consciousness that any day we will rise to meet Him and stand before His Judgment Seat. This will motivate us to greater holiness, good works and evangelism.

The Church is restraining the final manifestation of evil. So the removal of the Church will result in a final sudden release of evil causing the Tribulation to begin. In the Tribulation, God allows evil to come to its fullness and judges it. Thus the Rapture is the final Sign to the world that the Tribulation is about to start. The Rapture is imminent, which means no one can know when it will happen - it's God's secret. Although the Signs we have seen so far give the general time, they do not reveal the exact timing of the Start of the Tribulation.

That is what Jesus says next in <u>Matthew 24:36</u>: **"BUT of that day and hour** (of the start of the Tribulation) **no one knows, not even the angels of heaven, but My Father only."** Remember He is still answering <u>Question 3</u>, which asked about the timing of 'the End of the Age' or Tribulation. So God keeps the timing of the Rapture and Start of the Tribulation secret. He knows it, but does not reveal it to us, because we would probably misuse that knowledge. He wants to keep us on our toes, so that we always stay ready. He will come suddenly without warning, as a thief in the night. This is the Doctrine of Imminence - which is God's limitation on our knowledge of the time of the Rapture. He wants us to live as if Jesus could come anytime. So although we can't know the exact day of the Rapture, the general signs He gave us tell us that we are living very close to the end of the Church Age.

Then Jesus said in <u>Matthew 32:37</u>: **"For the Coming of the Son of Man will be just like the days of Noah."** Remember He is still answering Question 3 about the timing of the Start of the Tribulation, and having said no one can know its exact date, He now identifies it with the Coming of the Son of Man. This is saying that He will come to receive us in the Rapture before the Tribulation starts. In fact, the Rapture is the triggering event for the Start of the Tribulation. As we continue in His Prophecy, we will see that this truth is confirmed again and again.

Some assume 'the Coming of the Son of Man' here refers to the 2nd Coming, but that does not agree with the fact He is answering Question 3. Also the phrase: **"no one knows the day or hour"** always applies to the Rapture and NOT His 2nd Coming, because anyone in the Tribulation will be able to calculate the exact day of the Lord's Return. When Jesus said: **"the Coming of the Son of Man will be just like the days of Noah"**, He was saying the events in the time of Noah in connection with the Flood are a TYPE or picture of what will happen in the time around His Coming in the Rapture and the Start of the Tribulation. The most obvious parallel is that **the Flood is the Type of the Tribulation,** for the Flood was the only previous worldwide judgment, and likewise the Tribulation is a worldwide judgment. Those who assume He is comparing His 2nd Coming with Noah's Flood forget the fact that the whole Tribulation is a time of world-wide Judgment, which has its climax at the 2nd Coming.

In Matthew 24:37-39 Jesus compared His Coming to the days of Noah, making a 3-fold comparison, based on the 3 key phrases: 'BEFORE', 'the DAY', and 'the FLOOD'. Thus He is comparing (1) what happens before the main event, (2) what happens on the day of His Coming, and (3) the Judgment that falls immediately afterwards: **"The Coming of the Son of Man will be just like the days of Noah. For as in those days BEFORE the Flood they were eating and drinking, marrying and giving in marriage, until the DAY that Noah entered the Ark, and they did not understand until the FLOOD came and took them all away; so will the Coming of the Son of Man be."**

The Parallels between the time of the Flood and the Tribulation.

*1. He compared the general time BEFORE the Flood to the general time before His Coming.

*2. He compared what will happen ON THE SAME DAY as the Flood, immediately before it fell, to what will happen immediately before the Flood of Tribulation Judgement falls on the earth.

*3. He compared the FLOOD itself to the future judgment of the Tribulation, pointing out that it will be world-wide and therefore no one on earth will be able to escape its effects. He says that the result of both judgments is to take all the unbelievers away from the earth.

*1. The time just before the Flood tells us what it will be like in the time just before the Tribulation. Jesus compared the Last Days of the Church Age to the time of Noah. The days before the Flood of Tribulation Judgments fall on the whole world will be like the days of Noah before the Flood of God's judgment fell on the whole world. Thus the special characteristics of Noah's time will be repeated before the Tribulation. Jesus' characterised Noah's generation as just eating, drinking, marrying, giving in marriage. Now there's nothing wrong with these things in themselves, but there is no sign of any spirituality here. They were engrossed in their materialistic life and had no time for God. It indicates a society caught up in materialism and godlessness, forgetting God and pursuing purely natural things, and that certainly is a sign of modern life on earth. Also according to Genesis 6, great wickedness, corruption, lawlessness and violence covered the earth - a major public decline of all moral standards. v1 also speaks of a population explosion in Noah's time. So we'd also expect a population explosion in the time leading up to the Tribulation, and this has certainly happened in an unprecedented way in the last 100 years. Man was advanced in knowledge before the Flood, evidenced by Noah's ability to build such a huge ship. The last 100 years have been marked by rapid scientific progress. So Jesus compared what will happen in the final days of the Church Age before His Coming and the start of the Tribulation to the time of Noah before the Flood.

Noah preached the Gospel to the world using His Ark as a visual aid. Likewise, in the closing period of the Church Age the Gospel will be preached to all nations, as Jesus said in Mark 13:10. The great explosion in world missions started in about 1800. There was a final period of 120 years of Grace during which Noah preached the Gospel, declaring that judgment was coming, but that God had provided a Way of Salvation, which was the Ark, a Type of Christ, so that all who trusted in God's Provision for would be saved from destruction. Those who were in the Ark were saved, being under its covering, for the Ark took the beating of the Flood instead of them. God told Noah to cover the wooden Ark with pitch, which was a red resin, in order to make it waterproof. So none of the waters reached those inside. Also the Hebrew word for pitch is also the word for covering or atonement. So the Ark covered with red pitch is a picture of Christ covered with His atoning blood, and all who take refuge in Him, come under the covering of His blood and are saved, because He took all the judgment we deserved. But those who reject Him will be swept away when judgment falls. But the people in Noah's day were so immersed in their godless, materialistic lives that they ignored all the warnings, and so were totally taken by surprise, when the Flood suddenly fell.

Before the Flood, Jesus specifically described life in the world before the Flood as going on as normal, right up to the day of the Flood, eating and drinking, marrying and giving in marriage (v38). The people had no idea that judgement was about to fall even though Noah warned them. Likewise, as in the Days of Noah, just before the Tribulation life will be carrying on normally, and they will even be saying: 'Peace and Safety.' **Therefore it follows that life on earth, even up to the Day the Lord comes in the Rapture, will also be going on as normal.** This is a clear contrast to events just before His 2nd Coming, for at that time it is at the end of the Tribulation, with God pouring out His Bowls of Wrath and the Battle of Armageddon raging and the sun turning to darkness. Life will be anything but normal! Thus the Flood is a type of the whole Tribulation and not just the 2nd Coming, for in the days just before the 2nd Coming, described in detail in the Book of Revelation, anything but normal life is going on. This is the Great Tribulation, the worst time ever, and Jesus said if He did not cut it short all flesh would be destroyed. This also proves the Coming of Christ in these verses is not the 2nd Coming, but the Rapture, which is a separate event before the Tribulation.

So Jesus emphasised that life just before the Flood was going on as normal, so they were all taken by surprise when the Flood suddenly fell. There were no special signs that it was about to fall. Likewise, the world will be taken by surprise when the Rapture happens and the Tribulation-Flood suddenly falls on them. There will be no special signs that the Rapture is about to happen. So the Rapture itself is a SIGNLESS EVENT, which can happen at any time, and it will happen suddenly, without warning, when you least expect it. Although Jesus gave Signs to give us a general idea when we are in the season just before the Tribulation, He emphasised that there would be no specific Sign, by which we could know the exact date of the rapture. Don't think that something dramatic must happen before the Rapture as a final warning, like a global crisis. In fact the world will be saying 'peace and safety.' There will be no announcement from heaven saying: '10 days to the Rapture!' Life will be going on as normal and then we will suddenly disappear. So there is a major difference in the Signs for the Rapture and the 2nd Coming. The Rapture is imminent, coming suddenly at an unknown time without any specific Signs. The 2nd Coming comes after a whole series of specific signs that will enable people to know the exact day.

In Matthew 24:37-39 Jesus pointed to 3 similarities between the days of His Coming and the days of Noah. First, the time before His Coming will be similar to the time before the Flood. Second, the Day of His Coming to initiate a period of judgment is compared to the actual Day that Noah entered the Ark. Third, world-wide judgement will suddenly fall on the world on the Day of the Lord's Coming, just as the world-wide judgment of the Flood suddenly fell on the very day Noah entered the Ark. Again this cannot be talking about the 2nd Coming, as this comes as the climax of 7 years of escalating world-wide judgements.

*2. Let us now consider the 2nd point of similarity - the Day of His Coming, which initiates the judgment. This is compared with the day that Noah entered the Ark, which initiated judgment. Initially this does not seem like an obvious similarity, until you realise that the final Sign to the world that the Flood was about to fall, the final event before the Flood, was the disappearance of all the believers into the Ark, when God removed them from the scene of judgement and lifted them above it, as <u>Matthew 24:38-39 says</u>, they were living their normal life: **"until the day that Noah entered the Ark, and did not know until the Flood came and took them all away, so also will the coming of the Son of Man be."**

Likewise, the final event before the Tribulation-Flood falls, the final Sign to the world that the Tribulation is about to start, will be the disappearance of the believers into Christ, when He comes for them in the Rapture. Just as God called Noah into the Ark, so Christ will return and gather His own to Himself in the Rapture. God will remove the true Church from the earth by lifting us above the scene of Judgment, before pouring out His Tribulation Judgments. Remember that He is still answering Question 3: 'What is the Sign of the End of the Age?' Having said there are no specific Signs for His Coming in the Rapture, He points out that there will be a final specific Sign to the world for the Start of the Tribulation - the disappearance of the believers in the Rapture. However, this is not a warning Sign, for the Tribulation will start immediately after the Rapture, so anyone who misses the Rapture will have to go into he Tribulation. Just as God shut the Door as soon as Noah entered the Ark, so He will shut the Door straight after the Rapture.

Then to confirm He is talking about the Rapture, Jesus gave a classic description of this Rapture of believers that happens in conjunction with His Return in <u>Matthew 24:40-42</u>: **"Then there will be 2 men in the field; one will be taken and one will be left. 2 women will be grinding at the mill; one will be taken and one will be left. Watch therefore, for you do not know what hour YOUR LORD is COMING."** He is talking about the parallel event to Noah entering the Ark and disappearing from view. Jesus will come and take the believers to Himself in the Rapture. The rest must enter the Tribulation. Notice He tells believers to be constantly on the alert for His Coming as they do not know when it will be. That's imminence. This repeats the early statement that no man knows the day, showing He is still talking about the same event. Notice when He says to believers to be Ready for: **"YOUR LORD is coming"**, the implication that He is coming for them, to take them to Himself. This verse does not describe His 2nd Coming when He comes to take unbelievers from the earth in judgment, but His Coming in the

Rapture when He comes to TAKE His believers to be with Him. This is confirmed in the next verses.

Some relate these verses to the 2nd Coming based on the fact that the word 'taken' also appears in the previous verse to describe unbelievers in Noah's time being 'taken' from the earth in judgment. However, this is a trick of translation. The 2 words translated as 'took' and 'taken' in these verses are actually 2 different words in the original Greek, so this argument backfires, for if Jesus wanted to make connect these 2 things He would have used the same word. When it says 'one was taken another left' the word for 'taken' is the same word that is used for when Joseph 'took' Mary to be with him as his wife (Matthew 1:24). So this is speaking of Jesus coming to take us to be with Him. This is the first hint that the Rapture is the Bridegroom coming to take His Bride.

Another argument people use is it can't be talking about the Rapture, as Jesus didn't talk about the Rapture, as it was part of the Mystery. That was left for the Apostle Paul to do. But this is a false assumption for we have seen that Jesus started to reveal the Mystery in Matthew 13, and it was given to Paul to complete it. Also we will see Jesus taught on the Rapture in John 14:1-3. Related to this is the assumption that the whole Olivet Discourse is about Israel and has nothing to say about the Church. This is a clumsy unjustified assumption, as the apostles represented both Israel and the Church, so the context should determine who is in view in any scripture. In fact, Jesus talks about Israel, the nations and the Church.

The final proof that Matthew 24:40-42 CANNOT refer to the 2nd Coming is that it contradicts the other scriptures of the 2nd Coming, especially the Judgment of the Sheep and Goat in Matthew 25. These tells us that at His 2nd Coming Jesus will gather all living Gentiles to Jerusalem to be judged, where they all stand before Jesus and are separated into those who are taken from the earth, and those who continue alive into the Kingdom. Thus the 'one taken another left' separation at the 2nd Coming takes place in one place, Jerusalem, whereas the 24:40-42 separation takes place throughout the world, wherever people are working or sleeping.

Then in Matthew 24:43-44, Jesus compared His Coming in the Rapture to a thief coming suddenly in the night to take the valuable things from the earth: **"But know this, that if the master of the house had known what hour the THIEF would COME, he would have watched and not allowed his house to be broken into. Therefore you also be ready, for the Son of Man is coming at an hour you**

do not expect." This is the first time that Jesus compares His COMING to a THIEF, who comes secretly and suddenly, unannounced, without warning signs, TAKING the things that are precious to Him, and then going away unseen. This is in total contrast to His 2nd Coming when He comes openly and visibly in manifest glory. The Rapture is a totally different kind of event to the 2nd Coming. Comparing His Coming with the coming of a thief seems shocking, but although He is taking the precious things from the earth (us), He is not actually a thief because He only takes those who belong to Him, who have given their hearts to Him. But to the world it will seem as if a thief has come when we all suddenly disappear. So it will appear to the world after the Rapture has happened, that a thief has come and taken multitudes of people. Now it is true that Jesus comes to take the precious things from the earth (His people), but of course He is not really a thief, for He will only take what belongs to Him. **To the world, He will seem to come as a thief, but for Us He will come as the Bridegroom for His Bride**, to rescue her from danger before waging war on the world-system under the power of the evil one.

The 'master of the house' who would try and stop Jesus coming to take His Church must be satan, the god of this world (2Cor 4:4), the ruler of this world (John 16:11), for the whole world lies in his power (1John 5:19, Eph 2:2). This reveals one of the differences between His Coming in the Rapture and His 2nd Coming, that absolutely requires them to be distinct events at different times. The 2nd Coming is signposted in such a precise way that anyone in the Tribulation (including satan) will be able to know exactly when Jesus will return (from Daniel and Revelation). In other words, this event is not imminent for us as it is at least 7 years away, and it won't be imminent for those in the Tribulation, for they will know when it is. This is one reason why satan gathers the world's armies to Israel just before Jesus is due to return there - in order to resist His arrival: **"the beast, the kings of the earth, and their armies, gathered together to make war against Him who sat on the horse and against His army"** (Revelation 19:19). So in the case of the 2nd Coming the master of the house does try and stop Jesus breaking into 'his house', for he knows when He will come. Needless to say, all his attempts to resist Christ are in vain! On the other hand, Christ's Coming as a Thief in v40-43 is imminent, for a thief doesn't announce when he will come. He keeps it a secret, so He might come at any time. Therefore the master of this world is not able to prepare any special resistance to Christ's Coming in the Rapture. Thus the very point Jesus is emphasising is the imminence of this phase of His Coming.

Therefore He concludes in Matthew 24:44: **"Therefore YOU** (believers) **also be ready, for the Son of Man is coming at an hour you do not expect."** So He is coming when you do not think He will. This is a strong statement of the imminence of His Coming in the Rapture. Whatever theory you may have as to why Jesus cannot come yet is contradicted by this verse. It is designed to humble us, by pointing out our lack of knowledge, because He has not revealed it to us. The Doctrine Imminence says God has limited our knowledge in such a way that as far as we're concerned the Rapture could happen at any moment - therefore we always have to '**be ready**.' Thus not only do we not know when He is coming (v36), we do not know when He is not coming (v44)! Matthew 24:44 says that, not only does the world and satan not know, but believers also do not know, as Matthew 24:42 says: **"YOU** (believers) **do not know what hour YOUR Lord is coming."**

As a thief does not reveal when He is coming, so Jesus does not reveal the time of His Coming in the Rapture. His 2nd Coming on the other hand will have a clear 7-year Countdown, which Jesus outlined earlier in the Olivet Discourse. Therefore the Coming of the Lord in these verses is a distinct event from His public 2nd Coming. Actually I prefer to say that the 2nd Coming is in 2 Phases. **In the first Phase He comes FOR His Church in the Rapture, then 7 years later in the 2nd Phase, He will come WITH His Church in power and glory.** In the 1st Phase the Lord comes to initiate the Day of the Lord, the worldwide judgment of the Tribulation. In the 2nd phase the Lord comes on the Great and Awesome Day of the Lord, the climactic day of the Day of the Lord, to conclude and complete this worldwide judgment, and establish His Kingdom on earth.

Notice Jesus made repeated statements of Imminence since Matthew 24:36, confirming that He has been talking about the same event throughout - His Coming as a Thief to take the believers to Himself. **"But of that day and hour no one knows"** (v36), **"Watch therefore, for you do not know what hour your Lord is coming"** (v42), **"Therefore you also be ready, for the Son of Man is coming at an hour YOU do not expect"** (v44). Also this demonstrates this is the main feature of this phase of His Coming that He felt it was important to emphasise. Now previously in the same talk in Matthew 24:7-30, He described in great detail all the SIGNS leading up to the 2nd Coming, giving the 7-year Countdown according to Daniel's 70th Week. But now in <u>Matthew 24:36-44</u> He emphasises that His Coming is an imminent and therefore SIGNLESS event. There's only 1 solution to this paradox: His Coming is in 2 phases. He comes 1st as a thief, and 2nd in manifest glory.

We have seen that in v37-39, Jesus pointed to 3 similarities between the days of His Coming and the days of Noah: (1) just as in the days of Noah normal life went on until the day the waters of the Flood started to fall, so normal life will be going on right up to the day the Tribulation Judgments start to fall. It will happen suddenly with no special warning signs. (2) Just as the key event that marked the transition to sudden Judgment in the days of Noah was the disappearance of the believers into the Ark, so the key event that marks the transition into the Tribulation is the disappearance of the believers into Christ when He comes in the Rapture. So the final thing that will happen before the Tribulation Judgments fall will be the removal of the believers into Christ - the Ark of our Salvation.

*3. What happens immediately after. Just as Noah's Flood started to fall on the same day he entered the Ark, so the Tribulation Flood will start to fall on the same day as His Coming in the Rapture. In both cases it is a worldwide Judgment, so no one on earth will be able to escape it. Thus worldwide Judgment will suddenly fall on the world on the day of His Coming, just as the worldwide Judgment of the Flood suddenly fell on the very day Noah entered the Ark.

<u>1Thessalonians 5:2</u> agrees with this when it says: **"the Day of the Lord** (Tribulation) **will come just like a THIEF in the night** (the Rapture). **While they are saying, "Peace and safety!" then destruction will come upon them suddenly like labour pains on a woman with child, and they will not escape."** The fact that the Tribulation starts on the same day as the Rapture means that His Coming to remove the believers in the Rapture is what initiates the time of Tribulation Judgement. We can understand why there is this connection in 2 ways.

(1) 2Thessalonians 2 says the Church, indwelt by the Holy Spirit, is presently restraining the spirit of antichrist, but when the Restrainer is removed in the Rapture the forces of evil are released to come into full manifestation especially through the antichrist, and this is one of the special characteristics of the Tribulation.

(2) Another characteristic of the Tribulation is that it is a time of Divine Judgment and Wrath upon the whole world, like Noah's Flood. But God has promised the Church that He has delivered us from the Wrath of God, so it would not be righteous of God to subject the Church to the Tribulation Wrath of God. Therefore God must remove His believers to a place of safety before releasing His Judgment. Since this Judgment is upon the whole earth, He must first come and remove us from the earth, and then there is no more reason to delay His Judgment, so immediately after the Rapture He begins the time of Judgment. Therefore, it will be just as in the days of Noah. First, God separated and removed the believers, so that they were lifted above the waters of the Flood, above the scene of Judgment. Then, as soon as He had made the believers safe, He immediately released His Judgments on the earth. Likewise Jesus will return and lift us above the earth, removing us from the scene of Judgment, and then He will immediately start releasing the judgments of the Tribulation.

Jesus confirmed this in a similar passage in Luke 17 where He compared this time to the days of Lot. v28 says: **"It will be the same as happened in the days of Lot: they were eating, they were drinking, they were buying, they were selling, they were planting, they were building."** The days leading up to the Tribulation Judgement are likened to the days leading up to the judgment of Sodom and Gomorrah. From one point of view it is life as normal with no obvious sign that the judgment is about to fall. In fact these towns were very prosperous. But from another point of view we know there was great immorality that was not only accepted, but also publicly approved and promoted by the society.

Then Jesus said in Luke 17:29-30: **"but on the day that Lot went out from Sodom it rained fire and brimstone from heaven and destroyed them all. It will be just the same on the day that the Son of Man is revealed."** Again we see that God removed the believers from the scene of the Judgment, before releasing His Judgment on the cities. Clearly as in the days of Noah, God withheld His Judgment until He had removed the believers, for He would not be just in pouring out His wrath on the righteous. Now we can understand why the very same day the believers were removed, God's judgment fell from heaven. Jesus said that the same thing would happen when He comes to save us and reveal Himself to us in the rapture. First, He will remove us from the scene of Judgment, which is the earth, and then on the very same day He will initiate the Judgments of the Tribulation. It is significant from the story in Genesis 18 that Christ Himself came to earth with His angels to rescue Lot and to initiate the Judgment of the cities. He will do the same at the Tribulation. Since the time of Divine Judgment starts at the beginning of the Tribulation, not at its end, all these passages speak of a Coming of the Lord before the Tribulation, to save His own and initiate Judgment, as well as His Coming at the end of the Tribulation.

Matthew concludes this section of the Olivet Discourse with a Parable, which emphasises the importance of taking the doctrine of imminence seriously.

Matthew 24:45-51: **"Who then is a faithful and wise servant, whom his master made ruler over his household, to give them food in due season? Blessed is that servant whom his master, when he comes, will find so doing. Assuredly, I say to you that he will make him ruler over all his goods. But if that evil servant says in his heart: 'My master is delaying his coming' and begins to beat his fellow servants, and to eat and drink with the drunkards, the master of that servant will come on a day when he is not looking for him and at an hour that he is not aware of, and will cut him in 2 and appoint him his portion with the hypocrites. There shall be weeping and gnashing of teeth."**

This demonstrates the positive influence of believing in imminence on our behaviour. The good servant knew his master could come at any time, so was determined that his master will find him doing good when he comes, and so he maintained a constant faithfulness and so received a good reward at His Coming. The evil servant rejected imminence and assumed his master would DELAY his coming, so was not looking for his master. Without the consciousness of the master's imminent arrival, he felt free to behave badly and mistreat those under him, until the master took him by surprise. In this case his evil behaviour demonstrated an unregenerate spirit, although he called himself a Christian and had a position in the church. He was a hypocrite in that he professed outwardly to follow Christ, but that was not what was in his heart. So when the master returned he consigned him to a place of punishment with the rest of the unbelievers. Likewise, when Jesus returns He will consign all unbelievers (including 'Christian' ones to the wrath of the Tribulation on earth, and if they still do not repent, they will end up under everlasting wrath in hell.

We complete our study of the Olivet Discourse, with the concluding words of Jesus in the parallel passage in Luke 21, which emphasise that the Tribulation will be a worldwide judgment from which there will be no escape for those who are on the earth, just like the Flood in the days of Noah.

After describing the events of the Tribulation, Jesus said in Luke 21:34-36: **"Take heed to yourselves, lest that Day** (the Day of the Lord or Tribulation) **come upon you unawares. For it** (the Tribulation) **will come as a snare** (a trap that will suddenly snap tight) **shall it come on ALL those who dwell on the face of the whole earth** (it will be a world-wide Judgment). **Watch therefore and pray always, that you may be COUNTED WORTHY to ESCAPE** (through the Rapture) **ALL these THINGS** that **shall come to pass** (in the Tribulation)**, and STAND** (in a transformed body) **before the Son of Man."**

Jesus promises to provide an escape from the Tribulation-Trap, for those 'counted worthy.' They will escape from 'all these things' of the Tribulation that will come on all those who are on the earth. He doesn't talk about enduring through these things. This escape is the Rapture. Instead of going through the Tribulation, we will stand in our new bodies before the Son of Man, and give an account before the Judgment Seat of Christ. Since the events of the Tribulation come upon all those on the earth, the only way to escape all these things is to be removed from the earth, and this is exactly what Jesus will do in the Rapture to those counted worthy (righteous) through their faith in Christ. They will be lifted up from the earth and find themselves standing before the Son of Man in their glorified bodies. The only way to escape ALL these things is by a Pre-Tribulation Rapture, for a Mid-Tribulation or Postulation Rapture would only be an escape from SOME of these things. Now since the Tribulation is world-wide and affects ALL who dwell on the earth, and since these 'worthy' ones are promised an escape from 'ALL these things' that will take place on the earth, it is obvious that this escape must involve a removal from the scene of judgement, which is the whole earth, BEFORE 'all these things' of the Tribulation take place.

Thus the teaching of Jesus is that before the worldwide Judgment of the Day of the Lord falls, He will return as a thief to take the believers to Himself. So as far as the world is concerned, the initial act of Judgment of the Day of Lord is when Jesus gets up from sitting at the right hand of the Father and returns to receive His own to Himself. By removing the Church He is removing His restraint upon evil, allowing it to come to fullness in order for it to be judged. This action also allows Him to move in greater Judgment. Thus the Day of the Lord begins with the Coming of the Lord to rapture His Church and then continues to the end of the Tribulation as He continues to pour out His Judgments.

This agrees with the 2 examples Jesus used for this event:

(1) God removed Noah into the Ark before the Flood fell, raising him above the earth and the waters of judgment, rather than protecting him underwater.

(2) God removed Lot from Sodom, the scene of Judgement, before sending the Judgement down, rather than preserving him through the bombardment. There is no language here of preservation through Judgement.

Jesus confirms this in Revelation 3:10 where He does not just promise believers protection from Judgment, but deliverance from the very time-period of the Tribulation Judgment: **"I will keep you from the hour of trial which shall come upon the whole world, to test** (all) **those who dwell on the earth."** Therefore to fulfil this promise God must provide an escape FROM THE EARTH ITSELF for those counted worthy before the Tribulation begins. This exactly describes the Pre-Tribulation Rapture! Then He adds that once they have been removed from the earth their new location will be standing in the very Presence of Christ in their resurrection bodies.

Therefore Jesus will come to take His chosen ones to Himself, gathering them together to Himself just before 'all these things', that is all the events of the Tribulation come to pass on the earth. Thus Luke 21:34-36 is a plain statement of the Pre-Tribulation Rapture! Notice that these verses describing the removal or taking of true believers into the Presence of Christ before the Tribulation, confirms that when He talked earlier about one being taken and the other left behind, it was referring to the taking of believers in the Rapture, and not the taking of unbelievers in judgment at the 2nd Coming.

So, how one can be 'counted worthy' to be in the Rapture? This language agrees perfectly with the Gospel. No sinful man could actually be worthy of receiving salvation or anything from God. But it does not say they are worthy, but they are 'counted worthy' and there is only one way anyone can be 'counted worthy' of salvation or 'reckoned as righteous' before God, and that is through receiving the imputed righteousness of Christ as a free-gift. On the Cross Jesus accomplished the Great Exchange in Himself of our sin for His righteousness, so that when we receive Christ our sin was imputed to Him and His righteousness was imputed to us as a totally free-gift of His grace. Only in this way are we counted worthy of Salvation. The Rapture is part of our Salvation by Grace. It's not a reward for good works, because the judgment of our works for rewards happens after the Rapture at the Judgment Seat of Christ. Our spirit was saved when we were born again, our soul is now being saved by God's Word, and our body will be saved at the Rapture, thus completing our Salvation by Grace. So this isn't talking about a partial rapture where only the best Christians will make it but the rest must go through the Tribulation. This is unbiblical. We are not made worthy through our own efforts. We can only be counted worthy by accepting Christ and being clothed in His righteousness. All truly born again believers will be raptured and stand before Christ on that day. If you have prayed and accepted Christ then you will be counted worthy, because you have turned from trusting in yourself and your works, and put all your trust in Christ and His work for you.

*So how can you be RAPTURE READY?
(1) Receive Jesus as your Lord and Saviour.
(2) Prove the genuineness of your faith by a changed life.

If Jesus is truly your Lord and Saviour, you are in Christ, and you will go up in the Rapture. What will happen immediately after that is that you will stand before His Judgment Seat and receive your eternal reward based on your faithfulness to Him in this life, and this could happen at any time! Let the imminence of the Lord's Coming inspire you to a consistent holy life, so that you are ready to meet Him when He returns.

1John 3:1-3: **"Behold what manner of love the Father has bestowed on us, that we should be called children of God!... Beloved, now we are children of God; and it has not yet been revealed what we shall be, but we know that when He is revealed, we shall be like Him, for we shall see Him as He is. And everyone who has this hope in Him purifies himself, just as He is pure."**

*Chapter 6: The Romance of Redemption

It was Jesus who initially taught on the Rapture in the Olivet Discourse. We have seen that to the world His Coming in the Rapture will be like a THIEF in the NIGHT. Jesus also taught in John 14 that for the Church it will be like the BRIDEGROOM coming for His BRIDE to take us home and be with Him forever.

John 14 records His tender words as the Bridegroom promising His Bride, that although He must go away and prepare their marital home, He will come again to fetch her to be with Him. John 14:1-3: **"Let not your heart be troubled; you believe in God, believe also in Me. In My Father's house are many mansions; if it were not so, I would have told you. I go to prepare a place for you. And if I go and prepare a place for you, I will come again and receive you to Myself; that where I am, there you may be also."** This will be fulfilled in the RAPTURE. This is our blessed hope the glorious appearing of Jesus Christ for His Bride. He is coming soon to take us home. Redemption is a Divine Romance, which comes to a climax in the Rapture.

In those days, the Bride did not know exactly when the Bridegroom would return for her, so she had to prepare herself and always stay ready. Right now the Church needs to be preparing for that romantic moment when her Bridegroom comes and rescues her from the time of Tribulation, lifting her up into His Presence. The Tribulation is a time when Christ wages war on the world-system. What Bridegroom would leave His beloved bride in a place that He was about to bombard, if He had the power to extract her? Surely He will rescue her from this terrible time of God's outpoured Wrath!

Knowing the marriage customs of Bible times gives much insight into Bible Prophecy and the Romance of Redemption (God's ultimate purpose in saving us).

*1. The marriage is planned and arranged by the father of the Bridegroom, who chooses a bride for his son. Likewise the Father planned a marriage for His Son and chose the Church as his Bride.

*2. The Father negotiates with her family and a Bride Price is paid, representing her value. The price paid for the Bride was the Blood of Jesus. He came the first time to win His Bride by demonstrating His love, laying His life down for her and thus paying the Bride Price.

*3. Once the agreement was made, they would eat and drink wine together, signifying they were now in covenant. At this point the couple are BETROTHED. Likewise when we receive Christ, accepting His offer to belong to Him, we are BETROTHED to Him. Paul said in 2Corinthians 11:2: **"I betrothed you to one husband, so that to Christ I might present you (to Him) as a pure virgin."** We now belong to Christ, united to Him by covenant through His Blood, destined to become His wife.

*4. Gifts would be given to the Bride from the Bridegroom.
Likewise, gifts and blessings are poured upon us by Christ through the Holy Spirit.

*5. They may never have seen each other face to face.
We have not seen Jesus face to face, but we love Him and eagerly await His return.

*6. After the Betrothal the Bridegroom goes away to his Father's house promising to return. There he prepares the marital home. Only when the father says everything is ready can the son return. Likewise, Jesus has gone to Heaven to prepare a place for us and has promised to come back for us.

*7. Meanwhile the Bride makes herself ready to presented to Her Bridegroom in the beauty of holiness, her beauty not merely external, but that which comes from a devoted heart. She prepares her wedding dress to be dressed like a Queen. She wants him to be pleased when he looks upon her. She keeps herself pure, for all her hopes are now looking toward the day of her marriage when she will see her Bridegroom face to face and be with him forever. Likewise, we prepare ourselves for when we will see Him face to face as 1John 3:2-3 says: **"we know that when He is revealed, we shall be like Him, for we shall see Him as He is. And everyone who has this hope in Him purifies himself, just as He is pure."** We are sanctified by the Blood and the washing of the Word, so that when He returns we will be ready. Our wedding garment will be His glory corresponding to our good works, which He'll release in us at His Return when He rewards us according to our works.

*8. No one knows the exact time of the Wedding, which happens when the Bridegroom returns for His Bride. Even she does not know exactly when he'll come for her. She must stay ready even if he seems delayed. Likewise no one knows the time of Christ's Return for His Bride in the Rapture. He tells us: "I'm coming quickly." There's great excitement in heaven & earth as the time gets near.

*9. At the father's signal, when he judges all things to be ready, the bridegroom returns for His bride. Likewise when the Bride is ready and complete, when the full number are saved, then the Father will turn to the Son and says: "Go, get her, Son!"

*10. The Bridegroom dressed as a King goes in joyful procession with his friends to the Bride's house. There is great excitement. He enters the house and carries the Bride out, and brings her back to the place he has prepared for her.

Likewise, when Jesus returns for His Church it will be to TAKE His Bride home to be with Him forever. In the Rapture of the Church He comes in a joyful procession with shouts and trumpets and we will be lifted up to meet the Lord in the air. This is a romantic moment as He carries off His Bride, delivering her from the Tribulation, in order to be with Him forever.

*11. Back at his house, she makes her final preparations to be ready for brief family Wedding Ceremony, including putting on her wedding dress.

Likewise, back in Heaven, the Bride is prepared to be presented spotless and glorious to Christ. To be ready, she must go through the Judgment Seat of Christ first, where she is cleansed from all unworthy, dead works that she is wearing. She is also rewarded for her good works with a corresponding glory that will be released through her and that will radiate out of her, which is now her clothing.

*12. In the Wedding Ceremony the bride is unveiled and presented to the bridegroom in all her beauty and they see each other face to face, for until now she has been veiled. They are now MARRIED and she is His WIFE.

Ephesians 5:25-27: **"Christ loved the Church and gave Himself for her that He might sanctify and cleanse her with the washing of water by the word, that He might present her to Himself a glorious Church, not having spot** (no physical blemish) **or wrinkle** (no sign of age) **or any such thing** (no imperfection), **but that she should be holy and without blemish** (inwardly pure and perfect)."
Likewise, at this point Christ and His Church will be MARRIED, and the BRIDE will now become the WIFE of the Lamb and they will reign together forever as King and Queen. We will have our eternal marital home in the New Jerusalem.

In a vision of the Church in Heaven just before the 2nd Coming this Wedding Ceremony has already taken place. Revelation 19:7-8: **"Let us be glad and rejoice and give Him glory, for the Marriage of the Lamb has come** (happened)**, and His WIFE has made herself ready. And to her it was granted to be arrayed in fine linen, clean and bright, for the fine linen is the righteous acts of the saints."** Now having passed through the Judgment Seat of Christ where her dead works were consumed by fire, she is now dressed only in white glorious linen, shining with the Glory of God according to the reward she received for her good works that received approval at the Judgment Seat.

*13. The couple next go into a special bridal-chamber where the marriage is consummated. Likewise, the Church has 7 years in heaven before the Marriage Feast, of close 'face to face' fellowship with Christ where our union with Him will be brought to completion on every level, His glory filling our whole beings.

*14. They then appear together and lead a procession to the Marriage Feast. The herald cries: **"the Bridegroom comes!"** so that the invited guests know to come to the Feast. Christ will return to the earth with His Church, as HUSBAND and WIFE, in His 2nd Coming, for the Marriage Feast, which takes place on earth. In Revelation 19:7-8, we saw the WIFE in heaven dressed in white linen.

Then v9-14: **"Blessed are those who are called to the Marriage Supper of the Lamb!' ... Now I saw Heaven opened, and behold, a white horse. And He who sat on him was called Faithful and True** (the HUSBAND)**, and in righteousness He judges and makes war. His eyes were like a flame of fire, and on His head were many crowns...and His Name is called The Word of God. And the armies in heaven, <u>clothed in fine linen, white and clean</u> followed Him on white horses** (this is the WIFE according to the previous verses)**."**

This confirms that the Rapture must take place before the 2nd Coming.

*15. The invited guests join in the celebrations, which will last a week at the start of the Millennium. General invitations had already been sent out to friends to invite them to the Wedding so they could be ready to come. When it was time, they are bidden to come to the Feast. Among the Wedding-Guests for this Feast will be the believers on earth at the end of the Tribulation. During the Tribulation, the Gospel of the Kingdom will be preached inviting all people to be come and be part of this Feast and the Kingdom. But only those who are ready, who have received

Christ and have OIL in the LAMPS (that is, the Holy Spirit in their spirits), only these will be able to enter into the Feast and the Millennium. The unbelievers with no oil will be excluded. This is the scenario of the Parable of the 10 Virgins in Matthew 25, when Jesus returns with His Wife to earth at the end of the Tribulation for the Marriage-Feast. These virgins are not the Bride but the companions of the Bride in the Feast. They are the people alive on the earth when the Bridegroom returns with His Bride. When He comes He separates these ones into 2 groups depending on whether they are ready or not.

So the Rapture (7 years before) is part of a joyful wedding procession with shouts and trumpets as the Bridegroom comes to TAKE His Bride to Himself to be with Him forever face to face, fulfilling His love for her. He delivers His Bride from this evil world and lifts her up to a higher life with Him. In the time in between the betrothal and the wedding, the Bride must prepare to meet Him and be ready for when her bridegroom comes for her.

Pictures of this 'Romance of Redemption' are seen in Old-Testament Marriages, which are Types of Christ and the Church. Ruth is redeemed by **Boaz** and becomes his wife, and **Esther** who after a long period of preparation and beautification is presented before the King who then marries her. Other Marriages also contain pictures of the Rapture. For example:

*1. ADAM and EVE (Genesis 2:18-25). God had a Plan for us before sin came in, which was revealed before the Fall in the Marriage of Adam and Eve - a picture of Christ and the Church. His Plan is more than saving us from sin. It's for us to be eternally united with Christ as His Bride. Adam is a type of Christ. God's purpose revealed in Adam is fulfilled in Christ. It is not God's best for Christ to rule alone. So Genesis 2:21-22 says: **"The Lord God caused a deep sleep to fall on Adam, and he slept; and He took one of his ribs, and closed up the flesh in its place. Then the rib which the Lord God had taken from man He made into a woman, and He brought** (presented) **her to the man."** He received her as His wife saying she was: **"bone of my bone and flesh of my flesh"** (v23). Likewise, the Father provided a Bride for Jesus through His sleep of death. This 'sleep' represents an aspect of Christ's death that has nothing to do with sin. Rather, it is the laying down and giving up of His life to release it to us and to make His Bride. In death, His side was opened and out came blood and water. The Church was taken out of Christ being brought forth from His side. The Church was created from Christ's own life and spiritual DNA and so corresponds to Him and qualifies to be His Bride. Eve was formed out of a wound in Adam's side. She derived her life and nature from Adam. She was built and prepared by God to be presented to and meet her future Husband. She was perfect like him and became one with him, sharing his dominion. In all these ways, Eve is a picture of the glorious Church. At the Rapture the Church will be presented before Christ in perfection and with the same words of acceptance, Christ will own her as His Wife forever.

*2. ISAAC and REBEKAH (in Genesis 24) is another story of a marriage made in heaven - a picture of the Divine Romance. Isaac, the only beloved son of Abraham, who had previously been offered as a sacrifice in Genesis 22 is a type of Christ. They both experienced a death and resurrection after which they both received their bride. The Chief Servant (Eliazer, which means Helper) is a Type of the Holy Spirit and sent by the Father, to find a Bride for His son. Rebekah, the chosen Bride, is a type of the Church. Likewise, the Father sent the Spirit to the earth to find and call out a Bride. As the Gospel is preached He calls her to come to Jesus and receive Him as her Head. Meanwhile Isaac remained in his inheritance. Likewise, Jesus remains in Heaven while the Bride is being called and prepared. Finally, the Bride will be brought to the Bridegroom.

Rebekah responded positively to the Servant, who glorified Isaac, telling her all about him, his sacrifice, his character, his rich inheritance, and the promises and covenant from God that assured his future. She would be able to partake of all of these things in Isaac. This is a picture of the Spirit preaching the Gospel to every person, calling them to Christ. Then he proposed to her and called for a decision. If it was a 'no', he would go elsewhere. Rebekah believed him and said 'yes.' When we say 'yes' to Jesus, we are then betrothed to him, even though we've never seen him. Abraham had told the Servant to TAKE a wife for Isaac, which was only accomplished when she stood before Isaac. First, He called her. Then, He led her on a journey to Isaac leaving her old-life behind. Finally, she was presented to Isaac to be his wife. Likewise, the Spirit first calls us to Christ. Then, He takes us out of our old-life in the world and takes us on a new journey with Him that has a heavenly destination where we will stand before Jesus. Finally, at the Rapture we are taken into Christ's Presence to be His Wife.

The decision was Rebekah's. In v57 she was asked: **"Will you go with this man?"** And she said: **"I will go."** She decided to leave the old-life and start at once on the new journey with the Servant This journey is a picture of the present Christian life in this world. She was now following the leading of the Servant, who knew the way. Now Isaac was the most important One for her. Likewise, we are called to leave the old-life and walk in the Spirit, Who leads us closer to Jesus. On the journey she didn't see Isaac, but believed in him and was committed to him, rejoicing in the hope of seeing him. It was a long difficult journey of faith to reach her final destination and permanent inheritance. But she had a Personal Guide and Helper. On the journey the Servant told her all she wanted to know about Isaac and his inheritance. In the hardship she was inspired by the thought that the journey was temporary and soon she would be with her Isaac forever. Her thoughts were focused on when she would see him. The last time Isaac was seen was when he was sacrificed. The next time He is seen is when He comes to meet his Bride. He has been waiting for her and preparing a place for her. As Rebekah reached the end of her journey, Isaac came for her out of his dwelling place.

Likewise at the end of the 2000-year journey of the Church, Jesus will come out from heaven for His Bride. At the Rapture, Jesus will come down from heaven and signal the Spirit to take us up to meet Him in the air, just as Rebekah was taken up to meet Isaac. Then Rebekah saw Isaac for the first time, and he took Rebekah and she became his wife and he loved her. This speaks of the consummation of our salvation at the Rapture, when we will enjoy eternal face-to-face fellowship united with Him and sharing His glory, authority and inheritance as His beloved Wife. As Rebekah was brought into Isaac's presence, to dwell with him as his wife, so in the Rapture, we will be lifted up, transformed and presented before Christ as His glorious Bride. This is when the Marriage takes place, and we will be eternally united with Him as His wife.

The Song of Solomon

*3. A 3rd picture of the Divine Romance and my personal favourite is the SONG of SOLOMON, which gives a wonderful picture of the love relationship between Christ and the Church. It is the story of Solomon, who is a type of Christ. His beloved, Shulamith, is a type of the Church. Shulamith is the feminine form of Solomon, and both names mean peace. One day King Solomon, dressed as a Shepherd and not as a King, goes to the countryside and inspects his flocks. In his travelling, he comes across a young country girl who is looking after her family's vineyards and they fell in love. He initially presented Himself to her as a Shepherd lover because He wanted their relationship to be based on love, rather than on force, with her being overwhelmed by His kingly power. This is a picture of Christ's 1st Coming, clothed in a human nature, dressed as an ordinary man, with His majesty veiled. He didn't come as the King in all its glory, for then we would be forced to submit to Him because of His power. Rather He wanted a relationship with us based on love. He came dressed as the Good Shepherd wanting to win our heart with His love, not His power. He wants us to love Him for Who He is in Himself. The couple enjoy a wonderful courtship where He revealed Himself as a loving Shepherd. He declared his love for her and awoke her love under the apple tree. Likewise Christ demonstrated and declared His love for us under the Tree of Calvary.

Once they had got to know each other, at some point He would have had to give her an amazing revelation about Himself, saying: "There's something I have to tell you. I am not just a shepherd, I am also the King." She would have laughed, but as she looked at him again, she'd have realised he was serious. She had to trust him and accept it by faith without seeing His Majesty, and she did believe Him. Likewise, when Jesus tells us: "I am not just the Good Shepherd, I'm also the King of kings", we know He is true and we believe Him even though we have not seen His glory. Then Solomon proposed, she accepted and they became betrothed, declaring vows of undying love to each other. Then he said he had to go away up to Jerusalem to prepare a place for her in the royal palace and get everything ready for the wedding. But he also promised that when all was done He will return and take her to be with him as his wife. This is the promise Jesus gave us in John 14. Until she sees him again she has to trust his word and prepare herself for the great day when he returns for her, and not be discouraged by the ridicule of unbelievers. Likewise we must believe the Lord's promise to come back for us, and prepare ourselves for the day of the Rapture. You can imagine what happened when she told her family the young man she had been seeing was actually King Solomon, and that one day he will return and take her to Jerusalem! They really she was in a fantasy world, and so they put out to work hard in the vineyards. Likewise the world thinks we are crazy, when we say my Jesus is coming again as King of kings.

But one day Solomon returns in power and glory as described in chapter 3. This time, he is not dressed as a Shepherd, but as the King in all His glory with all his mighty men with him. Likewise Christ will return for us at the Rapture with His angelic guard of honour. The whole town asks: **"Who is this coming with such a great procession."** As it gets closer, they say: **"It is King Solomon on the day of his wedding with all his mighty men."** Then the procession turns in their little town, and as Shulamith looks, she recognises the King as her Shepherd-Lover. He has come for her! He gets out and walks to her house and lifts her up and takes her away back to Jerusalem where they are married and have a Wedding Feast. This is a wonderful picture of the Rapture of the Church, after which the unbelievers realise that she was telling the truth all the time.

The Song opens at the wedding feast with her now as the Queen, sitting at table with Solomon and the ladies of the court. She tells them her story, explaining why her skin is so tanned as her brothers had put her out to work hard in the vineyards. She tells them all about Solomon, and the story of their courtship up to that point and also their developing relationship including their first night together. It is the most beautiful picture in the Bible of the Divine Romance, which is why it is called the Song of Songs, just like the Holy of Holies.

*Chapter 7: Paul's Teaching on the Rapture

Having seen that Jesus taught the Pre-Tribulation Rapture, that is, the Rapture will happen just before the Tribulation starts. We will now go on to Paul's teaching on the Rapture. First of all, Paul taught that the Rapture is part of the Mystery in <u>1Corinthians 15:51-53</u>: **"Behold, I tell you a MYSTERY, we will not all sleep, but we will all be changed, in a moment, in the twinkling of an eye, at the last trumpet; for the trumpet will sound, and the dead will be raised imperishable, and we will be changed. For this perishable** (body) **must put on the imperishable, and this mortal** (body) **must put on immortality."**

This is logical because the whole Church-Age was a MYSTERY hidden in God in the Old Testament times and only revealed by Christ and the apostles. This Age ends with the RAPTURE of the Church from the earth. So the Rapture is part of the Mystery. This means the Rapture of the Church was not revealed in the Old Testament, and therefore Jesus was the first one to reveal it. Now the resurrection of the righteous dead when the Messiah comes to establish His Kingdom at the end of the Tribulation is not a Mystery, for this was clearly prophesied in the Old Testament, but what is new is the Rapture of the Living, their mortal bodies being changed to immortality. Since the Rapture is a Mystery it must be a distinct event from the resurrection of the dead at Christ's 2nd Coming. To explain this let us first of all define the Rapture:

*<u>DEFINITION</u>: **The RAPTURE is the Coming of Christ for the Church in which He instantly 'catches up' all living believers to meet Him in the air and translates them into immortal bodies without experiencing death.**

Not only was this transformation of living believers not prophesied in the Old Testament, but it seems to contradict the Old Testament prophecies of the Messianic Kingdom, for if all believers are raptured at the Lord's Return, there would be no one left to populate the Messianic Kingdom, for all unbelievers are killed at Christ's Return. The only solution to this paradox is that the 2nd Coming of Christ is in 2 phases. First He comes for His Church, to take us to be with Him in the Rapture, then after a period of time (actually 7 years) He will return in power to repossess the earth. During this time many will be saved and those who endure to the end of this time will inherit the Messianic Kingdom.

1Corinthians 15

1Corinthians 15:51-52 describes what will happen to us in the Rapture: **"Behold, I tell you a Mystery; we shall not all sleep, but we shall all be changed, in a moment, in the twinkling of an eye, at the last trumpet; for the trumpet will sound, and the dead will be raised incorruptible, and we will be changed."** 'Sleep' refers to the state of a Christian's body when it has died, because God will wake it up again on the resurrection morning. The event that Paul describes here applies to those believers who are alive at Christ's Coming in the Rapture. Paul himself had a strong hope of being in the Rapture for he says: **"WE will be changed."** He was not wrong in this, but had this hope because he correctly believed in imminence, that the Rapture could happen at anytime. This doctrine of immanency is also seen here when it says we will be changed 'in a moment'. This is the word 'atomos', which means an atomic second, the shortest possible moment of time. He also said it will happen in the twinkling of an eye, in the time it takes for a photon of light to reflect off your eye. In other words it will happen suddenly, with no warning. We will suddenly find ourselves standing before the Lord. Many times Jesus says: 'I am coming soon', but this is a poor translation. It really means: "I am coming suddenly or quickly"-again a statement of imminence. For us living in the end times we can also say 'Jesus is coming soon', because of all of the Signs of the Times that are fulfilled.

Then Paul describes the amazing change that will take place in our bodies in v53-57: **"For this corruptible** (body) **must put on incorruption, and this mortal** (body) **must put on immortality. So when this corruptible has put on incorruption, and this mortal has put on immortality, then shall be brought to pass the saying that is written: "Death is swallowed up in victory." O Death, where is your sting? O Hades, where is your victory?" … thanks be to God, who gives us the victory** (over death) **through our Lord Jesus Christ."**

Finally in v58 he applies this truth to our life: **"Therefore** (in view of the Rapture), **my beloved brethren, be steadfast, immovable, always abounding in the work of the Lord, knowing that your toil is not in vain in the Lord."**

The teaching on the Rapture is very practical. It will motivate you to be steadfast when things get hard, helping you fix your eyes on the prize at the end of your race. When it says your toil or labour in the Lord is not in vain, this is referring to the fact that when you are raptured you will stand before the Judgment Seat of Christ for rewards. The Rapture is the completion of our salvation when our bodies are saved from the presence and power of sin, and transformed into immortal bodies, just like that of Jesus Christ.

ICorinthians 15:20: **"Now Christ has been raised from the dead, the first fruits of those who are asleep."** The first fruits of a harvest represented the whole harvest. The offering up of the first fruits to God was the guarantee of the rest of the harvest. In other words, Jesus' Resurrection body is the prototype for our resurrection bodies.

1Corinthians 15:50: **"flesh and blood cannot inherit the Kingdom of God."** Therefore our new bodies will not have blood. Instead our body will be filled with the Glory of God. The glory of God in our spirits will be fully released in and through our bodies.

Philippians 3:20-21: **"Our citizenship is in heaven, from which we also eagerly wait for the Saviour, the Lord Jesus Christ who will transform our lowly body that it may be conformed to His glorious body, according to the working by which He is able even to subdue all things to Himself."**
Our bodies will be changed to be just like Jesus' resurrected glorified body! As the HEAD, so the BODY, for we are completely united to the HEAD forever.

Ephesians 5:27 says that after the Rapture we will be presented: **"a glorious church, not having spot or wrinkle or any such thing** (all marks of the Fall removed), **holy and without blemish."** Jude 24 says God is able to: **"present you faultless before the presence of His glory with exceeding joy."**

*Paul's letters to the Thessalonians are full of teaching on the Rapture.

1Thessalonians 1:10: **"We are to wait for His Son from Heaven** (not the antichrist from hell), **whom He raised from the dead, even Jesus, who delivers us from the wrath to come."** We are to wait for Jesus who will come for us. When He comes He 'delivers us from the wrath to come.' His delivering us from Wrath is directly connected to His Coming. Now Jesus has already delivered us from the Wrath of Hell by His Blood. So this Wrath to come must be a different Wrath. It must be the wrath of the Tribulation. So Jesus must come before the

Tribulation in order to deliver us from the Wrath of the Tribulation. So Jesus will come to deliver us from the Tribulation! We are not told to look for or expect the Tribulation and the antichrist, but to wait with expectancy for Christ to come and save us from it, by means of the Rapture, for we have been delivered from all judgement, wrath and condemnation. God has promised the Church deliverance from all of God's wrath, for Jesus has taken it all upon Himself. This includes the deliverance from the Tribulation, since it is a Time of Divine Wrath.

1Thessalonians 4

Later in 1Thessalonians 4 Paul describes how the Lord will do this. The classic passage on the Rapture is 1Thessalonians 4:13-18: **"But we do not want you to be uninformed, brethren, about those who are asleep, so that you will not grieve as do the rest who have no hope."** It seems that they understood about the Rapture of the living, and expected it to happen anytime. But they did not know what would happen to believers who die before the rapture. They were concerned that some of their departed brethren would miss out on this wonderful event.

v14: **"For if we believe that Jesus died and rose again, even so God will bring with Him those who have fallen asleep in Jesus."** Paul encourages them that the dead in Christ will be resurrected at the same time. Although their bodies are in the grave, their spirits are in heaven, and when Jesus returns He will bring their spirits with Him, and they will be reunited with their bodies and receive resurrection bodies.

v15: **"For this we say to you by** (according to) **the Word** (teaching) **of the Lord** (in other words Paul's teaching on the Rapture agrees with and expands the teaching of the Lord), **that we who are alive and remain until the Coming of the Lord, will not precede those who have fallen asleep."** He talks about 2 groups of believers, (1) those who are alive and (2) those who are sleeping at the Lord's Coming. He calls the 1st group: **"we who are alive"**, again showing that Paul believed in imminence and himself lived in the expectancy that he would be alive for the Rapture. Considering the Signs of the Times we have all the more reason to believe that we will be part of the rapture generation who will never die.

v16: **"For the Lord HIMSELF will descend from Heaven with a shout, with the voice of the archangel and with the Trumpet of God, and the dead in Christ will rise first."** 'HIMSELF' emphasises the personal nature of the Rapture. This is not something He can delegate for this is the Bridegroom coming to fetch His Bride. Notice the magnitude of this event - it is the Trumpet of God, not of an angel or man. Those who put the Rapture at Mid-Tribulation tend to identify the Rapture Trumpet with the 7th Trumpet of Revelation. But the 7th Trumpet is an angelic trumpet releasing judgment, whereas the Rapture Trumpet is the Trumpet of God calling a great assembly of believers to meet Christ in the air. He tells them there is no need to be concerned for those who have died in Christ, for they are not going to miss out. In fact they are going up first! Notice there is no partial rapture here. Those who go up are: 'the dead in Christ.' The only requirement is that they are in Christ. Being in the Rapture is part of our salvation by grace independent of our work. Therefore the only requirement for the living to go up is that they are in Christ. It will not be a dismembered Bride that will be presented to Christ.

v17: **"Then we who are alive and remain will be CAUGHT UP together with them in the clouds to meet the Lord in the air, and so we shall always be with the Lord."** We get the word 'rapture' from this verse. The word 'rapture' is from the Latin verb 'rapto' which was used to translate of the Greek word 'harpazo' translated as 'caught up'. It means 'to seize or snatch away' suddenly. We will all suddenly be caught up and find ourselves rising and meeting the Lord in the air. It will be a huge meeting in the air of the whole church whether dead or alive. No earthly stadium is big enough so God has use the atmosphere!

The Coming of the Lord and the 'catching up' to meet Him will be like a MAGNET coming down over a box of different materials. Only those with the same iron-nature as the magnet will go up. Things that look like they are made of iron, but are really plastic, will not go up. Thus plastic, pretend Christians will not go up. But anyone who is born-again, with Christ within them, will be drawn up to meet Christ in the clouds by a powerful attraction! When it says: **"so we shall always be with the Lord"** this reveals the purpose of the Rapture - the Divine Romance, the Bridegroom coming for His Bride to be with each other forever.

v18: **"Therefore comfort one another with these words."** The teaching of the Pre-Tribulation Rapture is a comfort. But if it is after the Tribulation, then they would not be concerned for those who fell asleep. In fact, they would be happy for them, as they will not have to go through the Tribulation.

1Thessalonians 5

In 1Thessalonians 4:15-18 the apostle Paul described the Rapture claiming that his teaching on this was according to the Lord's own teaching (v15). Then he continues on the same theme in 1Thessalonians 5 by addressing the issue of the timing of the Rapture and the Tribulation, using the same language and coming to the same conclusion as the Lord in His teaching.

v1,2: **"But concerning the times and the seasons** (the timing of the Rapture and the Tribulation) **brethren, you have no need that I should write to you** (for he had already taught them on this). **For you** (believers) **yourselves know perfectly that the Day of the Lord** (that is, the Tribulation)**, so comes** (starts) **as a THIEF in the night."** In agreement with the teaching of Jesus, Paul is saying here that the Day of the Lord will start suddenly, without warning, with the Lord's Coming as a Thief to take His own in the Rapture, according to the very language used by Jesus. 'The Day of the Lord' here is the Tribulation, for the whole Tribulation is a time when the Lord intervenes directly in Judgement.

This is confirmed by v3: which gives more detail about the start of the Day of the Lord, confirming that it refers to the Tribulation, not to the 2nd Coming of Christ: **"For when they** (the unbelieving world) **say: "Peace and safety!" then sudden destruction** (the Judgment of the Tribulation) **comes upon THEM** (on the world, not the church)**, as LABOUR PAINS upon a pregnant woman, and they shall not escape."** He describes the time just before the Day of the Lord as being apparently normal, where people are even saying: 'Peace and safety.' Then He describes the start of the Day of the Lord judgments as the sudden onset of labour pains, which then continue intensify until the Birth (the 2nd Coming). Thus the Day of the Lord is the time of labour pains, a classic definition of the Tribulation.

This is very the language Jesus used to describe the start of the Tribulation, comparing it with the sudden onset of Labour Pains (Matthew 24:8), from which there will be no escape, signifying that this is a worldwide Judgment that takes place over a period of time. So when v2 says 'the Day of the Lord' starts as a thief in the night, Paul is talking about the start of the Tribulation, and saying that it is initiated by the coming of a thief, which is the very language used by Jesus to describe His Coming in the Rapture. The Bible is consistent in its use of language. Paul knew the teaching of Jesus and was expounding it. So when Paul referred to the coming of a thief, he was speaking of the Rapture. So v2 says the Day of the Lord or Tribulation starts with the Coming of the Lord in the Rapture as a thief in the night. So this is a plain statement that the Tribulation begins suddenly with the Rapture, and it will be a total surprise to the world. This confirms the teaching of Jesus that the Tribulation will start immediately after the Rapture. This means that when the Thief comes He must remove something that had been preventing the Judgement, so that when it is removed the result is a sudden onset of destruction. This is speaking of the Church, which Jesus will remove from the earth when He comes. This also explains why there is a clear distinction between 'you' (believers) and 'them' (unbelievers) in this passage, for these 2 groups will experience the Rapture and Tribulation in 2 very different ways.

Notice that it is the unbelieving world, not the Church that experiences the Rapture as a thief in the night and the Tribulation as birth pains.

v2-4: **"The Day of the Lord** (the Tribulation) **so comes as a THIEF in the Night. For when THEY say: 'Peace and safety', then sudden destruction comes upon THEM** (not on us)**, as Labour Pains upon a pregnant woman. And THEY** (the unbelieving world) **shall not escape** (the Day of the Lord, unlike the Church, which will escape in the Rapture)**." But YOU, brethren** (believers have a different destiny)**, are not in darkness, so that this DAY** (the Day of the Lord or Tribulation) **should overtake YOU as a THIEF."** He clearly distinguishes the experience of believers (referred to as YOU) and unbelievers (referred to as THEY) in relation to the Day of the Lord. He specifically says that the sudden destruction of the Tribulation will come on THEM, but not on YOU (the Church). Notice how he contrasts the experience of believers and unbelievers. Having said unbelievers will experience His Coming as a thief, as they discover multitudes of people have suddenly been taken away from the earth, Paul affirms here that the believers will NOT experience His Coming as a Thief.

So the Day of the Lord will overtake unbelievers like a Thief, again confirming that the Tribulation is initiated by the Coming of the Lord as a Thief to take His own in the Rapture. The world will experience the Rapture as if a Thief has come, after a billion or more people are suddenly taken from the earth. On the other hand, the Church-Age believers will NOT experience the Rapture as the coming of a Thief, but as an escape from the darkness of the Tribulation, being rescued by our Bridegroom. So we will not have to face this time of Judgment. On the other hand the world will not escape the Day of the Lord Judgment, for it will suddenly come upon and overcome them. This will not be the experience of the Church because it will be raptured. So it is the Lord who initiates the time of worldwide Judgement called the Day of the Lord, by coming as a Thief to remove the Spirit-filled Church from the earth, and in so doing He will remove the restraining force on the antichrist and evil generally. This results in the birth pains of the Tribulation starting suddenly with great destruction all around the world, and intensifying until the Return of Christ.

Having said that the unbelievers will not escape the Labour Pains of the Tribulation, Paul affirms that the Tribulation will not overtake the believers (as a thief). He gives the reason for this difference. Unbelievers are in DARKNESS, that is, they are in the kingdom of darkness, which God starts to judge in the Tribulation. But believers are in the LIGHT, not the darkness, and so they do not come under the judgment of the Tribulation. So our experience of the Lord's Coming will be different from the world. For the world He is an unknown Thief who surprises them and removes the valuables from the earth, but for us, He is our Bridegroom coming for His Bride to take us home to Heaven.

He goes on to reaffirm that as sons of the light, we are not part of the kingdom of darkness, but the kingdom of light, so we do not belong to the darkness of the Tribulation, when the kingdom of darkness is being judged by the kingdom of light. Instead we belong in the Light of God's Glory. v5: **"You are all sons of**

light and sons of the day. We are not of the night nor of (the kingdom of) **darkness."** So we must make sure we are alert and ready for the Lord's Coming.

<u>v6-8</u>: **"Therefore, let us not sleep, as others do, but let us watch and be sober. For those who sleep, sleep at night, and those who get drunk are drunk at night. But let us who are of the day be sober, putting on the breastplate of faith and love, and as a helmet the HOPE of SALVATION."**

Hope relates to the future. So the hope of salvation is talking about our expectation of a future salvation, the salvation of our body, which takes place at the Rapture. So the salvation he is talking about here is not the salvation of our spirit, but of our body in the Rapture. We are to put on this hope as a helmet. A helmet covers our mind and directs our vision. These prophetic truths are a necessary part of our spiritual armour, protecting our mind. Whatever battles we face, we must have our helmet firmly fixed on our head, especially the vision of the imminent Coming of the Lord to save us in the Rapture.

Paul again talks about this future salvation when he concludes in <u>verse 9</u>: **"For God did not appoint us to Wrath** (to the Tribulation)**, but** (instead) **to obtain Salvation** (in the Rapture) **through our Lord Jesus Christ."** We are not appointed to wrath, but instead to obtain Salvation from this Wrath. So, we are not appointed to go through the Tribulation, but to receive Salvation from the Tribulation-Wrath, when Jesus returns for us in the Rapture. At that time we will also receive the Salvation of our bodies.

<u>v10</u> confirms that this salvation through Jesus is not something that has already happened, but something that will happen when Jesus comes for us in the Rapture: **"who died for us, that whether we wake or sleep** (whether we are alive or dead at the Rapture), **we should live together with Him."** This reflects the language of 1Thessalonians 4 that all believers, dead or alive, will receive a release of resurrection life in their bodies at the Rapture, and taken to be with Him forever. So instead of experiencing the wrath of the Tribulation, Jesus will return and save us in the Rapture, transforming our bodies and delivering us from this wrath by removing us from the earth.

Another confirmation that Paul has continued to talk about the Rapture in chapter 5 is in <u>verse 11</u>: **"Therefore comfort each other and edify one another**

just as you also are doing." This is very similar to what he said at the end of his classic description of the Rapture in chapter 4. Again we see that the Teaching of the imminent Pre-Tribulation Rapture is a great comfort and encouragement for believers inspiring us to be found ready when He comes.

The Thief in the Night

We conclude with a final look at the expression that Paul used to describe the Coming of the Lord in the Rapture: 'the thief in the night.' This term originates with Jesus who compared His Coming with sudden, unexpected coming of a thief. He said in <u>Luke 12:39,40</u>: **"If the master of the house had known what hour the THIEF would come, he would have watched... Therefore you also be ready, for the Son of Man is coming at an hour you do not expect."**

To the WORLD, THE RAPTURE will be the coming of a THIEF in the night, taking the precious things from the earth. But to the CHURCH the Rapture is the coming of the BRIDEGROOM for His BRIDE.

<u>Other verses also talk about the thief in the night</u>.

<u>2Peter 3:10</u>: **"the Day of the Lord will come like a THIEF."**

<u>In Revelation 3:3 Jesus says:</u> **"I will come like a THIEF, and you will not know at what hour I will come to you."**

<u>Revelation 16:15:</u> **"Behold, I am coming like a THIEF. Blessed is the one who stays awake."**

 What the comparison of the Rapture with the coming of a Thief tells us:
*1. The RAPTURE is IMMINENT, which means it can happen at any time. A thief does not tell the house what time he is coming, neither does he give them any kind of warning sign. Likewise the Rapture will be unannounced. There will be no special warning signs for it. Life will be going on as normal on the earth. Some say the Church must be glorious first, so it cannot happen for a long time, but the glorification of the Church can only be fulfilled after the Rapture. Whatever theory you may have why Jesus can't come yet, remember that He warned us that He would come at a time when we do not expect Him.

<u>Luke 12:40</u>: **"be ready, for the Son of Man is coming at an hour you do not expect."** So not only do we not know the time of the rapture, for Jesus said 'no man knows the day', but we also don't know any time when it can't take place, for

He said He will come at a time when we do n0t expect Him. He is saying that we cannot know, because He has not revealed it to us, so we can only speculate. So He deliberately keeps us in suspense, for He could come at any time.

Likewise Matthew 24:40 says: **"Be on the alert, for you do not know which day your Lord is coming."** He is talking to believers here, so it's not just the world that does not know the day. Then in v42 He said: **"be ready; for the Son of Man is coming at an hour when you do not think He will."**

*2. Like a thief in the night, Jesus will come when the world is in darkness and asleep. The Rapture will be unexpected. The world will be taken off guard and unprepared. The Rapture will happen suddenly and take the world by surprise, but those who are awake will are ready for Him

*3. Jesus comes like a thief to take the precious jewels (the believers) from the house (the earth). To the world, it will look like a thief has come, taking people from the earth. But He's not really a thief because He only takes what belongs to Him. We belong to Him, because He has purchased us with His blood. He is coming to claim His own - to snatch us away from the earth and take us back to His home in Heaven. The word used for the Church being 'caught up' is the same as that used for Philip's sudden translation in Acts 8 and Paul's 'catching up' to heaven in 2Corinthians 12

*4. The thief comes suddenly, takes what he wants and then leaves quickly. When Jesus says 3 times at the end of the Bible in Revelation 22: **"I am coming soon,"** this really means: **"I am coming quickly."** Remember we saw that the whole event will be over in a moment, in the twinkling of an eye. He will come, do His work and go unseen and the world and the world asleep in the darkness won't see Him or be aware of Him. All they will be aware of is that something valuable has been taken from them. Although 1Thessalonians 4 describes the Rapture as a noisy event, it will probably only be noisy in the Spirit, so only believers will hear the trumpet in their spirit calling them to rise to meet Jesus. As far as the world is concerned it will happen secretly, as if a thief had come. (It is possible that all will hear a short loud noise but not understand it).

On the other hand, His 2nd Coming will be totally different kind of event. When He comes at the end of the Tribulation it won't be as a thief. He will come publicly manifesting His power and glory, so that every eye will see Him. The 2 descriptions of His Coming, as a Thief and as the King of kings, are so opposite to each other, they could not be more different. Therefore they must be descriptions of 2 different phases of His Coming.

2Thessalonians 2

In our study of Paul's teaching on the Rapture, we now go to 2Thessalonians 2, which confirms that in the Tribulation, after the Church is removed, evil is allowed to come to its fullness through the antichrist, and God responds by increasingly pouring out His wrath on the world system.

2:1: **"Now brethren, concerning the Coming of our Lord Jesus Christ and our Gathering together to Him."** Clearly the Rapture is the subject under discussion. This is important to bear in mind in interpreting the next verses.

v2: **"that you not be quickly shaken from your composure or be disturbed either by a spirit** (a false prophecy) **or a message** (a false teaching), **or a letter as if from us, to the effect that the Day of the Lord** (the Tribulation) **has come."** Some were teaching that the Day of the Lord, the Tribulation, the time of antichrist's dominion, had already come. Again it's clear that the Day of the Lord here can't refer to the 2nd Coming, for they surely knew Christ hadn't yet returned in power and glory. Rather, they were troubled by the teaching that they were in the Tribulation, no doubt thinking one of the emperors like Nero was the antichrist. This would have been all the more troubling if they had been taught by Paul that they would be raptured before the Tribulation.

Remember that in 1Thessalonians 5, Paul had clearly defined 'the Day of the Lord' as the Tribulation, and it makes no sense that he changed the meaning of this expression in his 2nd letter. Many assume that 'the Day of the Lord' here refers to Christ's 2nd Coming in glory, but that makes no sense, because the idea that the 2nd Coming had already happened would have been silly. Jesus taught that when He returns the whole earth will see Him in His glory. Paul's disciples were well taught and would not have been disturbed by such reports. Some translations try and make sense of this by translating it as: "that the Day of the Lord is at hand", that is, it is about to happen, but this violates the normal meaning of the Greek used here. Also 'the Day of the Lord' here cannot mean 'the Rapture', for they were not troubled that the Rapture had come, because it had obviously not come. Neither were they troubled that the Rapture was about to come, for they would be happy about that, not troubled. The only meaning that makes sense and is consistent with other scriptures is that the Day of the Lord is the Tribulation. They were being troubled by people saying that the Tribulation had started. Some even used Paul's name in vain saying he'd written a letter to that effect. Naturally, they were troubled by this, for Paul had taught them that the Rapture will be before the Tribulation. But now this hope was disturbed by this report that they were now in the Tribulation, without being delivered from it by the Rapture as they had expected.

In the next verses, Paul puts them right by affirming the Pre-Tribulation Rapture. First of all he told them not to believe this false message in <u>v3</u>: **"Let no one in any way deceive you, for that Day** (the Day of the Lord, the Tribulation) **will not come until the APOSTASY** (or DEPARTURE) **comes first, and** (then) **the man of lawlessness** (the antichrist) **is revealed, the son of destruction."**

Much confusion has arisen around the word translated 'apostasy', which affects the whole meaning of this verse. Other translations have it as 'falling away.' It is the Greek word 'apostasia.' Its basic meaning is simply: 'Departure.' (Since the translation of 'apostasia' is so central to the correct interpretation of this passage, I have devoted Appendix 4 to this important issue). In fact, the oldest English translations translated it as 'Departure'. Now, in 1Timothy 4, Paul does talk a 'departure' or 'falling away' from the faith in the last days, referring to apostasy. Perhaps the translators assumed he was talking about the same thing here, and so translated it 'apostasy'. But this is an unjustified assumption. It does not say that the Departure in v3 is a Departure from the Faith. It does not explain what the departure is, but simply calls it THE Departure. Paul is talking about a specific Departure, but does not directly tell us what this Departure is and what it is from. Therefore, he thinks it should be obvious to the readers, as if we should know which Departure he is talking about. He cannot have assumed that they knew it was 'the Departure from the Faith' that he had described to Timothy, as 1Timothy had not even been written yet. Since he does not explain it in the verse, it must be clear from the context. Since he does not specify what this Departure is, rules of Bible interpretation dictate that we should look in the context of previous verses to see what Departure that Paul is talking about, and it is right there in v1, where he introduces the subject under discussion: **"concerning the Coming of our Lord Jesus Christ and our GATHERING together to Him."**

So let us translate the verse in a way that helps us to keep an open mind on this issue: **"for that Day will not come unless THE DEPARTURE comes first."** If we look in the context, it becomes obvious what this Departure is. Not only is there a Departure there, but Paul had even underlined the fact that it was the main subject under discussion! That's in v1 where he says: **"Now brethren, with regard to the Coming of our Lord Jesus Christ and our GATHERING together to Him."** What Departure is he talking about? Clearly it is the DEPARTURE of the Church from the earth in the RAPTURE. So we can translate v3 as follows: **"Let no one in any way deceive you; for the Tribulation will not come unless the RAPTURE comes first, unless the Departure of the Church happens first."** It is a plain statement of the Pre-Tribulation Rapture. The whole passage now makes sense. He is confronting the false teaching that they were in the Tribulation, by saying that was impossible, because the Tribulation cannot start until the Departure of the Church. Clearly the presence of the Church on earth prevents the Tribulation from happening, and Paul explains why this is the case in the next few verses.

So he is talking about the Rapture, the Departure of the Church from the earth. In v3 Paul is saying that the Tribulation will not start until the Rapture comes first, and then immediately after that the antichrist will be revealed, who is destined for destruction. We know from other scriptures that the start of the Tribulation is marked by the rise of antichrist on the world-stage. In Daniel 9:27 he is revealed at the start of the 7 years when He makes a covenant with Israel. When the 1st Seal is opened in Revelation 6, he is the Rider on the white horse going forth to conquer. So the Tribulation starts with the antichrist being revealed.

So the antichrist will only be revealed after the Rapture, and it also says this in v3: **"Let no one in any way deceive you, for that Day** (the Tribulation) **will not come until the DEPARTURE comes first, and** (then) **the man of lawlessness is revealed, the son of destruction."** They were worried that the Tribulation had started, which means they would have to face the antichrist. Paul's answer was that the Tribulation will only start and the antichrist will only be revealed after the departure of the Church, so they won't be there for the Tribulation or antichrist. Thus the Rapture happens first followed by the Tribulation when antichrist will be revealed. So the Tribulation can't begin and antichrist can't be revealed until the Church departs from the earth in the Rapture. So they have no grounds for concern.

In verse 4 Paul describes what antichrist will do when he becomes world-ruler at Mid-Tribulation: **"who opposes and exalts himself above every so-called**

god or object of worship, so that he takes his seat in the Temple of God, displaying himself as being God."

Then he explains why the antichrist cannot be revealed until the Church is removed. It is because the Holy Spirit through the Church is a powerful restraining force against the spirit of antichrist in <u>v6-8</u>: **"and now you know WHAT restrains him** (antichrist) **now that in his time he will be revealed. For the mystery of lawlessness is already at work; only HE who now restrains will do so until He is taken out of the way. Then that lawless one will be revealed…"**

There is a RESTRAINER holding back the revelation of antichrist until he is TAKEN OUT of the WAY. We know what is restraining the antichrist. It is the Church, empowered by the Holy Spirit. This Restrainer is 2-fold in nature, which is why it is called a WHAT in v6 (the Church) and a HE in v7 (the Holy Spirit). So the removal of the Restrainer is the Rapture, the Departure of the Church in v3, our gathering together unto Him (v1). When the Church is taken out of the way, then evil can come to its fullness, especially in the person of the antichrist. God allows it in order to judge it. So the Church is restraining the antichrist until it is taken out of the way and then the antichrist will be revealed. That is why he said in v3 that the departure of the Church must happen first, before the Tribulation begins and the antichrist is revealed.

Paul does not directly identify the Restrainer by name, which means it must be obvious from the context, as good communication requires. Other theories such as the Restrainer being human government have little basis in the context. Remember from v1 that the main subject of the whole passage is the Rapture, the 'taking away' of the Church from the earth. Therefore, when v6-7 talk about the Restrainer being taken out of the way, it must refer to the Church. This makes perfect sense for the Church is God's agent in the earth set in opposition to the spirit of antichrist and holding it back. By definition the spirit of antichrist tries to oppose, deny and replace the truth of Christ. It is the Church that is called to proclaim and exalt Christ, in direct opposition to the spirit of antichrist. Moreover if the Restrainer is not the Church, and its removal is not the Rapture, we have an oddity, in that Paul introduces the Rapture in v1 as the main subject under discussion, and then fails to mention it again, or even allude to it. This is clearly impossible, so the Rapture must be a central feature of the whole passage. When the 'Departure' is seen to be the Rapture, the whole passage fits together perfectly.

So what restrains the antichrist now is the Church, or more precisely the Holy Spirit through the Church. That's why the Restrainer is described as both a WHAT in v6 and a HE in v7. When the Church is removed then the restraining ministry of the Spirit through the Church will also cease. However, the Spirit is omnipresent God and so will continue to be present on the earth, enabling many to get saved in the Tribulation. These verses fit perfectly with v3, which said that the Departure of the Church must happen first and then the antichrist will be revealed. v7-8 says that the Restrainer must be taken out of the way first and then the antichrist will be revealed. Both verses talk about the removal of something and in both cases the result of this removal is the revelation of the antichrist. So they must be talking about the same event. In other words the Departure of the Church from the earth is the same as the Taking away of the Restrainer.

Paul's logic is now clear. First he said that the antichrist cannot be revealed until the Church is removed in the Rapture (v3), then he explained why this was the case. The Church functions as the Restrainer, holding back the revelation of antichrist, so he can only be revealed once the Church is taken out of the way (v6-8). Once the removal of the Restrainer is identified as the Rapture of the Church, then everything fits together perfectly, and it becomes clear this passage teaches a Pre-Tribulation Rapture. Any interpretation of this passage should be tested against v1, which says **the Rapture is the main subject**. Alternative explanations don't even mention the Rapture after v1, showing that something is wrong.

The passage finishes by describing antichrist's destruction at the Second Coming of Christ, v8: **"Then that lawless one will be revealed whom the Lord will slay with the breath of His mouth and bring to an end by the Appearance of His Coming."**

*Chapter 8: The Rapture in the Book of Revelation

The Morning Star

We now go on to the teaching of Peter and see that he also taught a Pre-Tribulation Rapture. He speaks of the Morning Star -which is a wonderful picture of the Rapture. 2Peter 1:19: **"We have (1) the PROPHETIC WORD confirmed, which you do well to heed as a light that shines in a dark place, UNTIL (2) the DAY DAWNS, and (3) the MORNING STAR arises in your hearts."**

This describes 3 Lights or Manifestations of Christ.

(1) In this present time we have His Light shining in our hearts through the Prophetic Word. If we are living by the Light of God's Word, we will not walk in darkness. Peter says we must live by this Word: **"UNTIL (2) the DAY dawns, and (3) the MORNING STAR rises in your heart."** This speaks of 2 different future manifestations of Christ's Glory, which compared to 2 natural lights, which are associated with the dawn of a new day. The DAY dawns at SUNRISE when the SUN appears and lights up the whole world. This is a picture of the manifestation of Christ in His 2nd Coming, when He will rise upon the whole world, and all shall see Him in His Glory. Malachi 4:2 describes the Return of Christ as the rising of the SUN of Righteousness covering the whole earth with His Glory (see also Hosea 6:3). His glory will shine outwardly and visibly, bringing a new DAY (the Millennium).

But shortly before the Dawn, while it's still dark, another light rises into view called the MORNING STAR. It is actually the planet Venus (or Sirius), which appears as one of the brightest stars, and is a Sign heralding the coming Dawn. Its appearance means the sun will soon rise and the new Day begin. It only appears to those who are awake and watching. Thus it is a manifestation to true believers only. All will see the Sun, but only some will see the Morning Star. Christ will arise and shine from within their hearts. Those who are not ready to see the Morning Star will miss it. After the appearance of the Morning Star the world remains in darkness for a short time before the Sun rises and all is revealed. The Morning Star is the Sign that the Sun (Jesus) is about to come and bring a new Day when all shall see Him in His glory

In Revelation 22:16, Jesus said: **"I AM the Bright Morning Star."** So the Morning Star is a Manifestation of the Glory of Jesus. Also in Revelation 2:28

Jesus promised believers: **"I will give him the Morning Star."** So this is a special future manifestation of the glory of Jesus that's only given to believers. These are 'romantic' words of love, for He is saying, as the Bridegroom to the Bride: "I will give you MYSELF, I will fill you with My glory."

Also notice that Peter says: **"the Morning Star will arise in your hearts"**, that is, in the hearts of believers. This is different from the Glory of Christ covering the earth at the 2nd Coming. This is a manifestation of Christ's Glory that originates in the hearts of believers. So while the world is asleep in the darkness before Sunrise, when all will see Christ's Glory, there will be a special manifestation of His Glory given to believers only. He will appear to them as 'the Morning Star' and His Glory will arise in their hearts.

So the Morning Star is the promise of the Glory of Christ manifested to and in believers in the Rapture, before the 2nd Coming.

This tells us that at the moment of the Rapture, the Glory of Christ will shine in our hearts. It will be manifested within us, and shine out of us. So at the Rapture, Jesus will release His Glory and resurrection power from within (**"Christ in us, the hope of Glory"**) which will transform our bodies and we rise to meet Him! His glory will be revealed in and through us, so that it arises in our hearts, transforming us. The same power that raised Jesus from the dead, the Holy Spirit, is already in our spirit, and on that day Jesus will give the command releasing the Morning Star Glory to surge out of our spirits, through our hearts, then transforming our mortal bodies into immortal bodies. This is the manifestation of the Morning Star. It will happen for us in the Rapture, and 7 years later the new Day will dawn on the earth when the Glory of Christ will cover the whole earth.

The Book of Revelation

John in the Book of Revelation also teaches the Pre-Tribulation Rapture.
In Revelation 1:19 Jesus gave John an outline of the whole Book:

(1) **"Write the things which you have seen"** = the vision of Christ in chapter 1.

(2) **"and the things which are** (now)**"** = the Church-Age in chapters 2-3, described by His 7 letters to the 7 churches (see also Appendix 2).

(3) **"and the things which will take place AFTER this** (after the Church Age)**."** These must be the things that will take place after the Church-Age, described in

chapters 4-22, which include the Church in Heaven (chapter 4-5), the Tribulation (6-18), the 2nd Coming (19), the Millennium and final Judgment (20), and the Eternal State (21-22). Now to confirm that the Church Age ends at the end of chapter 3 and the things that take place after the Church Age (including the Tribulation) start in chapter 4, let's go to Revelation 4:1, where John is called up by a Trumpet into Heaven, symbolic of the Rapture of the Church.

Revelation 4:1: **"After these things** (after the 7 letters describing the Church Age) **I looked, and behold, a door standing open in Heaven, and the first voice which I heard was like** (the sound of) **a trumpet speaking with me, saying: "Come up here, and I will show you things which must take place AFTER this."** These words are clearly introducing a new section of the book using the very same phrase as in 1:19, where John is told that He will be shown things that will take place after the Church-Age. Therefore Revelation 4:1 onwards must reveals events that will take place after the Church Age. As we read on we see that Revelation 4-19 describe the events of the Tribulation in great detail from their initiation in chapters 4-5 to their conclusion in chapter 19. Thus the Church-Age ends before the Tribulation begins. This is why Jesus promised in Matthew 28:19-20 that He would be with the Church, as we fulfil His Great Commission, UNTIL the Tribulation (the End of the Age).

Just as the Church Age will end with the Rapture of the Church into Heaven when we will hear the sound of a trumpet and the voice of Jesus calling us up to Himself, in exactly the same way John was raptured (caught up) to Heaven as a type of the Rapture of the Church (4:1). He is taken forward in time to see what happens after the Church-Age ends and observes firsthand the events of the Tribulation from above, just as the raptured Church will. Thus John's Pre-Tribulation Rapture is a type of the Pre-Tribulation Rapture of the Church. Having been on earth as a representative of the Church to receive revelation about the Church in its ministry on earth as Christ's Lampstand and Light (Revelation 2-3), John is then raptured to heaven (4:1) to view the Tribulation from above. Thus the timing of John's 'rapture' in the typology also supports a Pre-Tribulation Rapture. After the completion of the Church Age at the end of Chapter 3, John (as a type of the Church) is raptured to Heaven, and then observes the actions in Heaven (chapters 4-5), which initiate the Tribulation on the earth.

The 7 letters of Revelation 2 and 3 chart the whole course of the Church-Age, and give Christ's guidance, warnings and promises for the believers in the Church-Age. In particular, Revelation 3:10-11 clearly promises the true Church deliverance from the Tribulation by a Pre-Tribulational Rapture: **"Because you have kept My command to persevere, I also will keep you from the hour of trial** (the Tribulation) **which shall come upon the whole world, to test** (all) **those who dwell on the earth. Behold, I am coming quickly!** (the Rapture). **Hold fast what you have, that no one may take your crown** (at the Judgment Seat of Christ for rewards, straight after the Rapture)**."** Some say we will go through the Tribulation and here God promises that to protect us while we are in the Tribulation. But many believers will be killed by the antichrist, so I am not sure what kind of protection they are talking about! Notice, He does not just keep us from the Test or Trial in the sense of just protecting us in it. He says He will keep us from the Hour of Trial, from the very time-period itself. This Trial will come upon ALL who dwell upon the earth, so the only way to be delivered from it is to be removed from the earth. He must do this by means of a Pre-Tribulation Rapture. In fact in v11, Jesus confirms He will do this by means of the Rapture. Once the true Church is removed in the Rapture, whatever remains of the professing Church will be unbelievers, that will be part of the harlot. In Revelation 3:16 Jesus says He will totally reject and disown this apostate Church after the Rapture: **"So then, because you are lukewarm, and neither cold nor hot, I will vomit you out of My mouth."** The Lord would not cast out any who belonged to Him, so all true believers must be removed first (in the Rapture).

John sees the Throne of God in Heaven and 24 elders sitting on thrones. v4: **"Around the Throne were 24 thrones, and upon the thrones I saw 24 elders sitting, clothed in white garments, and golden crowns on their heads."** v10: **"the 24 elders will fall down before Him who sits on the throne and will worship Him who lives forever and ever, and will cast their crowns before the Throne."** The presence of these elders proves that Church is already in Heaven before the Tribulation begins, since it is the opening of the Book with 7 Seals in Revelation 5, which initiates the events of the Tribulation on earth.

An elder is a term that always describes a man of maturity and authority. Angels are never called elders. Neither do angels sit on thrones, whereas men do.

Angels are servants, whereas we will reign with Christ and judge angels. So these elders must be men. Eldership is a representative office of the Church for the elders of a local Church represent that whole Church. Likewise these are the chief elders of the universal Church, who must represent the whole Church.

So the fact they are called elders denotes that they represent a larger group of people, by virtue of their spiritual maturity. Their song in <u>Revelation 5:8-10</u> reveals who this larger group is: **"The 24 elders fell down before the Lamb, having golden vials full of odours, which are the prayers of saints. And they sung a new song saying: "You are worthy to take the Book, and to open its Seals: for you were slain, and have REDEEMED US to God by your blood out of every kindred, tongue, people and nation; and have made US kings and priests to our God, and WE shall reign on the earth."**

Firstly, notice the elders sing about how they have been redeemed by the blood of Christ. Therefore they are redeemed men. Secondly, they represent a larger group of people, who've also been redeemed, and who are from every nation, and who are kings and priests destined to reign on the earth. This is clearly a description of the Church, so these elders must represent the whole Church. So it is fitting that this term is used, for eldership is an established office of leadership in the church. By singing: **"You have redeemed US to God from every tribe"** these elders clearly identify with this larger group and represent them in their worship before God's Throne.

Another confirmation they are men is that they call themselves royal priests, which are men representing other men to God. We even see them acting as priests presenting the prayers of the saints before the throne. Only a human being can truly identify with and represent other men. The fact there are 24 elders points to David's organisation of priests into 24 divisions, with a chief priest over each division (1Chronicles 24). This indicates these elders are the chief priests over a larger royal priesthood. There is no biblical basis for identifying these elders as angels. They are men who represent the Church. Thus the Church (represented by the 24 elders) is present in Heaven, before the Tribulation begins.

Also these elders are REDEEMED, RESURRECTED and REWARDED men. They sing of their completed redemption (spirit, soul and body). They have already been rewarded, being clothed in white, shining ROBES of GLORY, and wearing golden CROWNS (of honour), and sitting on THRONES (positions) of authority (4:4). Overcomers are promised white robes in the resurrection (3:4-5,

19:8,14). Likewise throne-authority is only promised to men, not angels. Again it is promised to overcomers in the resurrection: **"To him who overcomes I will grant to sit with Me on My throne"** (3:21). Also the word 'stephanos' used for their 'crowns' denotes a victor's crown, given as a reward (as in 2:10). Eternal rewards are often described as crowns. Therefore this confirms they are not disembodied spirits, but men who've already been resurrected and passed through the Judgment Seat of Christ, where we'll all receive our rewards. What is true of the 24 elders must be true of the whole Church they represent. So the Church must already be raptured to Heaven at this point, before the Tribulation begins with the breaking of the 7 Seals. Thus the elders represent the whole Church in Heaven, having been raptured and passed through the Judgment Seat of Christ, and received their rewards. Thus, the Church is raptured and rewarded in Revelation 4, even before the Tribulation begins in Revelation 6!

Revelation 6-18 gives a detailed description of the events of the Tribulation on earth, but the Church on earth isn't mentioned once (not surprising since we have just seen her in heaven). Neither is the Church mentioned in any Old Testament prophecies of the Tribulation. Instead the focus is upon Israel. 'Saints' are mentioned, but this is a general term representing believers of all ages, so it is not specific to the Church (it is used many times in the Old Testament). Israel and the Jews are often mentioned, but not the Church. Why? Because she is no longer present! For example, compare: **"He who has an ear, let him hear what the Spirit says to the Churches"** (2:7,11,17, 29, 3:6,13,22) and: **"If anyone has an ear let him hear"** (13:9). Why are the Churches no longer mentioned? You know why! She must be absent from the earth. The absence of the Church in the Tribulation is most clearly seen in Revelation 7, where 144,000 Jewish evangelists, from the 12 tribes are sealed and anointed as God's witnesses (v1-8), to spearhead the Gospel during the Tribulation, resulting in much fruit (v9-14). They are identified as being of ISRAEL by their tribe rather than as a member of the CHURCH. The Church must be absent, to create this vacancy to be filled by Israel. It means that God will no longer be dealing with the Church as His witness and representative on the earth, but that He will turn again to the Nation of Israel. If the Church were present they would be in the Body of Christ, where nationality is not relevant (Galatians 3:28). Their membership of the Church would override and supersede any natural relationships. Why does God have to suddenly anoint a new group of witnesses? Because the Church has now left!

Thus we see Israel taking centre stage again, once the Church has left. This is consistent with other scriptures on the Tribulation in which Israel is the centre of the action. In the Tribulation God will complete His dealings with Israel, bringing her to faith in Christ, so that she can receive the Kingdom at His Return. The Tribulation is essentially Daniel's 70th Week, during which the final 7 years on Israel's clock will run, culminating in her complete restoration in the Kingdom. Daniel 9:24 specifically says that this counting of time relates to Daniel's people, Israel, which is why the Church-Age is not included in the count. Therefore the 70th Week relates to Israel and not the Church. This shifting from Israel to the mainly Gentile Church (in AD 33) and then back again to Israel in the Tribulation is exactly what Romans 11 teaches. Israel's temporary fall led to salvation going to the Gentiles (v11,12,15), and when the fullness of this (mainly) Gentile harvest has come in, then all Israel will be saved (v25-26). Thus after the harvest from the Church-Age has been ingathered at the Rapture, God will turn again to Israel in the Tribulation in order to bring her to repentance and salvation through Christ.

This focus on Israel (rather than the Church) in the Tribulation is not just seen in Revelation 7, but also in Revelation 11, where the 2 witnesses conduct their world-impacting ministry from the Temple Mount in Jerusalem. It is also seen in Revelation 12, which reveals the spiritual warfare in the Tribulation, for the central character under attack from the dragon is the WOMAN who brought forth the Messiah, who is ISRAEL. This attack culminates in the Campaign of Armageddon (Revelation 16-19) where all the nations gather to destroy ISRAEL. Then of course, Christ returns to Jerusalem to save Israel (Zechariah 14:4). In all of this action centred on Israel, there is no mention of the Church on earth.

We only see the Church again in Revelation 19:7-9 just BEFORE the 2nd Coming. And where is the Church then? Not on earth, but in heaven, with Christ, clothed in white shining linen. Now she is called His Wife. Thus the Rapture, Judgment Seat of Christ and Wedding must have already taken place before the 2nd Coming. It cannot be the same event. Then in Revelation 19:11-16, we see His Wife, the Church, return to earth from heaven with Christ at His 2nd Coming, as part of the armies in heaven, following Him and riding on white horses. She is identified by her clothing of shining white linen received at the Judgment Seat (v8).

Thus when Jesus returns to earth, He is already married and He returns with His Wife (the Church) to the Wedding Feast on earth (v9). Thus a period of time must elapse between the Rapture and the 2nd Coming to allow time for the Wedding, including the final Preparation of the Bride at the Judgment Seat, and her Presentation to Christ in glory; as well as for face-to-face time together before they go forth together to the Wedding Feast on earth (the Second Coming).

Then, <u>in Revelation 20:4</u>, after the 2nd Coming of Christ, it says: **"Then I saw thrones, and they sat on them, and judgment was committed to them."** This is the resurrected Church. Then it describes a separate group of believers who had not yet been raised: **"Then I saw the souls of those who had been beheaded for their witness to Jesus and for the Word of God, who had not worshipped the beast or his image, and had not received his mark on their foreheads or on their hands. And they lived and reigned with Christ for 1000 years."**

This describes the resurrection of the Tribulation martyrs, killed by the antichrist in the Tribulation. Now if the Tribulation was just part of the Church-Age and these believers were part of the Church, they would have been resurrected at the same time as the rest of the Church, rather than as a separate group. These Tribulation Martyrs were not part of the Rapture, therefore they must have been saved after the Rapture and then were killed by the antichrist in the Tribulation, which is why they have a separate resurrection from the Church after the Second Coming. This again confirms the Pre-Tribulation Rapture.

Finally, <u>Revelation 20</u> confirms there will be a literal Kingdom of God on earth for 1000 years, but if all believers are raptured at the 2nd Coming, only unbelievers will be left alive to populate the Millennium. But other scriptures tell us that Jesus will return as the Judge and will remove all unbelievers from the earth to a place of punishment, leaving no one left alive for the Kingdom!

This contradiction is most plain when you consider the Judgment of the Sheep and Goats in <u>Matthew 25:31-46</u>: **"<u>When the Son of Man comes in His Glory</u> (to the earth), and all the holy angels with Him, then He will sit on the Throne of His Glory. All the nations (gentiles) will be gathered before Him, and He will separate them one from another, as a shepherd divides his sheep (believers) from the goats (unbelievers). Then the King will say to those on His right hand: 'Come, you blessed of My Father, inherit the Kingdom... Then He** will also say to those on the left hand: 'Depart from Me, you cursed, into the everlasting fire."

v31 is crystal clear that this Judgment takes place at the 2nd Coming, before the Messianic Kingdom. The location of this Judgment must be the earth for Jesus returns to the earth to judge the world. Therefore the Throne that He will sit on is His earthly Throne, the Throne of David in Jerusalem for in the Kingdom He will reign over the earth from Zion. The population on earth at this time clearly consists of both believers (sheep) and unbelievers (goats), but this is impossible if all believers were raptured at the 2nd Coming! Neither can one argue that these sheep became believers after the 2nd Coming, for Jesus pointed to their lifestyle over a period of time as the evidence of their genuine faith. Moreover Scripture warns clearly that men must make their decision before Jesus returns, for after He returns it will be too late.

So a Post-Tribulation Rapture leads to 2 contradictions. First, there will be no sheep left in their natural bodies for this Judgment. Second, not only are there no sheep left to inherit the Kingdom, but in this Judgment Christ will also remove all the goats (unbelievers) from the earth, leaving no one to populate the Millennium! Therefore there must be a significant time between the Rapture of the Church and the 2nd Coming to allow for another significant soul-harvest to produce these surviving sheep at the 2nd Coming. This criterion is only satisfied by a Pre-Tribulation Rapture.

A final observation from Revelation showing that the Tribulation is a distinct period of time from the Church-Age is from the prayers of the martyrs. The first and prototype Martyr of the Church-Age was Stephen, who followed Christ's example of praying for God's mercy and forgiveness upon his murderers, saying: **"Lord, do not charge them with this sin"** (Acts 7:60). This is appropriate since the Church-Age is generally a time of grace, not judgment. However, the prayer of the Tribulation Martyrs is quite different, calling for judgment to fall on their murderers: **"How long, O Lord, holy and true, until You judge and avenge our blood on those who dwell on the earth?"** (6:10). This again is appropriate since the Tribulation is a time of Divine Judgement.

In conclusion, the Book of Revelation consistently teaches a Pre-Tribulation Rapture.

*Chapter 9: The Rapture-Tribulation Issue

There are 4 main views on when the Rapture will happen in relation to the 2nd Coming of Christ. Interestingly, the first 3 views all acknowledge the power of the Wrath Argument, that the Church been promised deliverance from Divine Wrath, and so they agree the Church will be raptured before His Wrath is poured out on the earth. But they differ from each other on when God starts to move in Judgement during the Tribulation.

<u>Therefore the first 3 views all see Christ's Coming as being in 2 Phases</u>: First, He will come FOR His Church in the Rapture, and then months or years later, He will come WITH His Church to the earth in power and glory.

This concept of 2 phases is supported by the great differences in the descriptions of the Rapture and 2nd Coming, indicating they are 2 distinct events rather than different aspects of the same event. This is similar to the Old Testament Prophets seeing both the 1st and 2nd Coming of Christ. Often prophecies of the Second Coming come right after prophecies of the first Coming, as if it might all be part of one big event. Nowhere does it explicitly say it is 2 Comings separated by a long time. But now it is obvious to us that the 2 visions are so different they must be 2 separate events.

<u>*Moreover, there are certain aspects that cannot be harmonised unless there are 2 phases to the 2nd Coming, with a significant time-interval in-between</u>.

*1. The description of life before the Rapture as going on normally, compared to the description of life before the 2nd Coming, which is anything but normal. Everyone will be saying: 'ARMA-GEDDON out of here!'

*2. Another difference is that one set of scriptures, which relate to the Rapture, teach imminence, that the Lord could come at any time. However, another set of scriptures which relate to the 2nd Coming, speak of a series of signs that must happen before the Lord can come, contradicting imminence. (We previously saw a clear example of this in Matthew 24). Some prophecies of His Coming say no man will know when it will happen. But anyone living in the last 7 years will be able to predict from the signs the exact day the Lord will return. The only way to reconcile this is by having 2 separate events, the first (the Rapture) being imminent, and the 2nd (the 2nd Coming) not being imminent, but coming after a set of signs (namely, the events of the Tribulation).

*3. When Jesus returns to judge the earth He will remove all the unbelievers from the earth as the Parable of the Tares, the Judgment of the Sheep and Goats, and the Wise and Foolish Virgins makes clear. Now if the Rapture happens at the same time as the 2nd Coming then all the believers will be in their new bodies, leaving no one to populate the Millennium!

*4. A number of important events related to the Church must take place in Heaven after the Rapture but before the 2nd Coming: (1) the Judgment Seat of Christ, followed by (2) our Presentation to Christ as His glorious Bride, followed by (3) the Wedding Ceremony. All points to a significant time interval rather than a simple U-turn in the atmosphere.

The Pre-Tribulation Rapture View

*The Pre-Tribulation View says the Rapture will be before the 7-year Tribulation. It is the consequence of following the Keys of Bible Prophecy, such as taking the prophetic scriptures literally, seeing the Church-Age as a Mystery that is distinct from Israel, and seeing the whole Tribulation as a special time of Divine Judgment. One major strength of the Pre-Tribulation view is that it is the only view that upholds Imminence, which is a major doctrine of the New Testament.

Imminence says the Lord could suddenly come for us at any time, so we are to look for Him, wait for Him and watch for His Coming, living every day in the expectancy that He could come any time and we will find ourselves standing before Him giving an account for our lives. Therefore this inspires us to holiness and evangelism, because we want to be found in fellowship with Him and faithfully serving Him when He comes, and indeed many New Testament scriptures motivate us using the doctrine of Imminence. None of the other views preserve imminence, because if the Rapture is at the End of the Tribulation then I know that Jesus cannot come for at least 7 years. Likewise if the Rapture is in the Middle of the Tribulation, then He cannot come for at least another 3.5 years.

The Mid-Tribulation Rapture View

*The Mid-Tribulation View says the Rapture will happen in the middle of the Tribulation. They say that the 1st half of the Tribulation is just the wrath of man and satan, but the wrath of God only happens in the 2nd half of the

Tribulation. There is little positive evidence of a rapture event at Mid-Tribulation. They just point to the catching up of the 2 witnesses at Mid-Tribulation as a symbol of the Rapture of the Church. They also point out that the 7th and last Trumpet in the Book of Revelation is blown at Mid-Tribulation, and that the Rapture happens at the Last Trump, so they deduce that the 7th Trumpet is the Rapture Trump. However, the 7 Trumpets of Revelation are blown by angels and release judgments, whereas the Rapture Trumpet is called the Trump of God, blown by the Lord Himself to call the Church to rise and meet Him in the air.

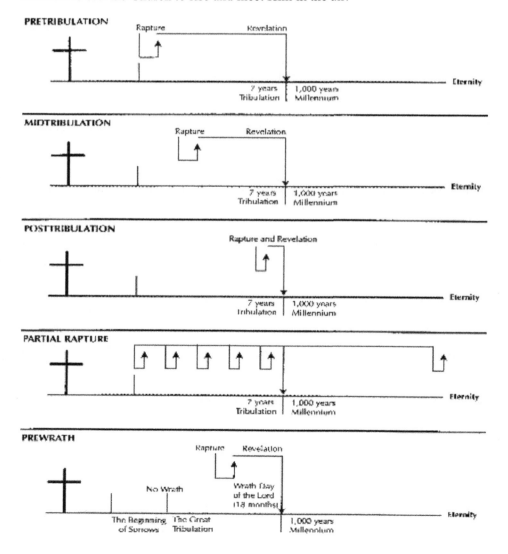

The Pre-Wrath Rapture View

*The Pre-Wrath View says the Rapture happens near the end of the Tribulation, but before the 7 Bowls of Wrath, and God only starts moving in judgement when He pours out these Bowls. This is a relatively new view and is quite complex when it comes to understanding all its details. Its key error is in not understanding that the whole of the Tribulation is called 'the Day of the Lord' and that God directly intervenes in judgement right from the start of the Tribulation, so that the whole Tribulation is a time of judgment and not just the final Bowls of Wrath. Revelation is clear that the events on earth in the Tribulation are initiated from heaven by the 7 Seals and 7 Trumpets, as well as the 7 Bowls. In fact, it is Christ who initiates the Tribulation and all its woes by breaking the Seals in Revelation 6. Later when we see the meaning of the Scroll with 7 Seals it will be obvious that Christ is moving forcefully in judgment against the world-system right from the start of the Tribulation.

The Post-Tribulation Rapture View

*The Post-Tribulation View says the Rapture and 2nd Coming happen at the same time. As Jesus returns we will rise to meet Him in the air, and then do a U-turn and come back with Him to earth. To support this idea that it is all part of a single event, they give an excellent analogy. In those days when a king came to a city, its leading citizens came out to meet him, and then they would return and enter the city with the king. So this is a picture of going up to meet Jesus in the Rapture and then immediately returning to the earth with Him. But what if the city is in rebellion to the king? Those loyal to the king will go out to greet him, but He will not be able to immediately enter the city. He will have to start a siege to overcome His enemies and forcefully recapture the city, and that is exactly what happens in the Tribulation. We will rise to meet King Jesus in the Rapture, but the world-system rejects Him as King, and so over the next 7 years there is a state of war. When Christ opens the Book, which is the Title Deed of the earth), He is asserting His right as owner to possess the earth and evict the evil tenants. He wages war by withdrawing His mercy (pulling the plug) from the various areas of the world-system, and by releasing direct judgments from heaven (e.g. the Trumpets). This is how to understand the Tribulation and this is why He will withdraw His beloved Bride first.

Now Jesus has the power to destroy His enemies in one day, so why take 7 years before He finally finishes the job at His 2nd Coming? It is because He wants to give them a final chance to be saved. By having 7 years of bombardments, constantly increasing in intensity, He creates the conditions whereby as many as possible can repent and be saved in the Tribulation.

Further Arguments for the Pre-Tribulation Rapture

We conclude by summarising some of the arguments for the Pre-Tribulation Rapture and explain why this is an important issue with vital practical application for our lives.

*1. The Wrath Argument is based on understanding the nature of the Tribulation as a time of worldwide Divine Judgement or Wrath - which is why it is called 'the Day of the Lord.' This is why Jesus compared the Tribulation to Noah's Flood. Although one characteristic of the whole Tribulation is the wrath of satan and man, with evil coming to fullness, its main characteristic is the Wrath of God, as revealed in the Seal, Trumpet and Bowl Judgments. All the events of the Tribulation are initiated by Christ in Heaven, even from its beginning, when He starts to break the Seals. This can be also seen in the whole structure of Revelation, which constantly switches back and forth between heaven and earth, showing us that the events (judgments) on earth are initiated from heaven.

Romans 5:9: **"Much more then, having now been justified by His blood we shall be saved from wrath through Him."** This is not just talking about being saved from Hell, but also from the Wrath of the Tribulation.

When Jesus came the first time He saved us from God's wrath by His death, but 1Thessalonians 1:10 says that when Jesus returns to the earth He does so with the purpose of delivering us (believers) from the Wrath of God coming on the earth: **"We are to wait for His Son to come from Heaven whom He raised from the dead even Jesus, who DELIVERS us from the Wrath to come."** Notice it doesn't say that *He delivered us* from wrath (which He did at the Cross), but that when He returns *He will deliver us* from the coming wrath. This can only mean that He delivers us from the Tribulation (He has already delivered us from Hell), so He will return to deliver the Church from the Tribulation. Later in chapters 4-5 Paul describes how He will do this by the Rapture. He concludes in 1Thessalonians 5:9:

"God did not appoint us to Wrath but to obtain Salvation (by the Rapture) **through our Lord Jesus Christ."** Thus our expectation is not the Wrath of the Tribulation, but the Coming of Christ. We are to look for the Rapture not the Tribulation. God has promised the Church in Christ total deliverance from God's wrath (John 5:24, Romans 5:9, 8:1, 1Thessalonians 1:10). Therefore since the Tribulation is a worldwide judgment, He must first remove us from the scene of judgment, namely the earth, just as He removed Noah into the Ark before sending the Flood, just as He removed Lot from Sodom before raining down the fire and brimstone. Thus the principle of God removing believers before judgment is seen in 2 pictures of end-time wrath, which Jesus specifically used to describe to His Coming, comparing it to the days of NOAH and LOT (Luke 17:26-30). In both cases the believers were removed from the scene of judgment to safety before Judgment fell. God always makes a way of escape for believers and since the Tribulation will come upon the whole earth, the only possible escape from it is by the Rapture. Therefore, believers will be removed from the earth before the judgments of the Tribulation fall. We will be removed to safety before judgment falls on them. Would a loving bridegroom subject his bride to His wrath before the wedding? Would Christ subject His own Body (and therefore Himself) to His own wrath? The belief that we need to go through Tribulation-wrath and persecution to be purified is a Protestant Purgatory, which is equally heretical as the Catholic version, in denying the sufficiency of the work of Christ. It would mean that His Blood is not enough! We are purified by His Word, Spirit and Blood not by the antichrist and the Tribulation! And what about those who have died and missed this vital Tribulation-purification?

*2. The AMBASSADORS Argument. In the Tribulation, God's Kingdom starts waging war on the kingdoms of this world, for He is taking back the earth by force, and by its end He will destroy all earthly kingdoms and establish His Kingdom over all. This is pictured in Daniel 2, which interprets Nebuchadnezzar's dream of a giant statue, representing the main Gentile Powers that dominate Israel. The statue stood until a STONE cut out without hands (representing the Messiah) struck the image on its feet of iron and clay, and broke them in pieces (v34). Then v35 says: **"Then the iron, clay, bronze, silver and gold were crushed together and became like chaff; the wind carried them away so that no trace of them**

was found. And the stone that struck the image became a great Mountain and filled the whole earth." This Mountain represents the Messianic Kingdom, according to the interpretation in v44: **"in the days of these kings the God of heaven will set up a Kingdom which will never be destroyed; it will break in pieces and consume all these kingdoms, and it will stand forever."**

God does not use maximum force and finish the job in 1 day, but spreads the war over 7 years of increasing bombardment to save as many as possible. The Tribulation begins when Christ starts to move against the kingdoms of this world by breaking the Seals. Now when a nation is about to declare war on another nation, it first removes its ambassadors, before hostilities begin. So likewise God will remove His ambassadors before the Tribulation.

*3. The Psalm 110:1 Argument.

This is confirmed by Psalm 110:1: **"The LORD said to my Lord: "SIT at My right hand, UNTIL I make Your enemies Your footstool."** So Jesus will sit at the Father's right hand UNTIL the time comes for His enemies to be judged and put under His feet. Thus He sits for the duration of the Church Age, but will rise from His Throne to take new action during the Tribulation. The fact He will no longer be permanently seated indicates that He Himself will carry out this judgment, when the Father releases Him. So the action that will signal and initiate a new phase of history when God starts to forcefully put His enemies under foot will be when Jesus rises from His Throne. He will do this when He returns to the earth to fetch His Bride in the Rapture and this will initiate the Tribulation.

It is significant that when Jesus initiates the Judgments of the Tribulation by breaking the Seals, He is STANDING, not SITTING. Revelation 5:5-7: **"Behold the Lion from the tribe of Judah, has overcome so as to open the Book and its 7 Seals …and I saw in the midst of the throne…a Lamb STANDING…And He came and took the book out of the right hand of Him who sat on the Throne."** The fact that Jesus stands to break the seals at the start of the Tribulation indicates that it is now a new phase of history, where He is no longer sitting. According to Psalm 110 this change of posture means He is now starting to put His enemies under His feet. He is personally starting to take action to intervene in world-events, moving in judgment, for it is the Day of the Lord.

*4. The 70 Weeks Argument. Another reason for the Pre-Tribulation Rapture of the Church comes from Daniel's 70 Weeks, which says that God allocated 490 years on Israel's Clock to fulfil His purposes for Israel. We saw that because Israel rejected the Messiah, God stopped Israel's Clock in AD 33, and brought in the Church as His representatives for the new Church Age, so now God measures time by the Church Clock. But God has not finished with Israel, and there are still 7 years left to run on Israel's Clock by the end of which Israel will be saved and the Messianic Kingdom established (this is the 70th Week). So at some point in the future God will restart Israel's Clock for her last 7 years to run as the Tribulation. During this time of Daniel's 70th Week Israel will again be God's representative and God will fulfil His purposes for Israel. The fact that God will measure time by Israel's Clock in the Tribulation, rather than by the Church's Clock, can only mean that the Church will stop being God's representative on earth. So the Church-Age must end before the Tribulation begins. Thus the Rapture must happen before the Tribulation, so that the baton can be handed back to Israel, for these last 7 years are primarily to do with Israel, as Daniel's 70 Weeks tells us. We see this transfer of anointing back to Israel in the anointing and sealing of the 144,000 Jewish evangelists at the start of the Tribulation. So when the Church Age has finished at the Rapture then God will turn back to Israel and restart her Clock. By the end of these 7 years Israel will fully repent and the Kingdom will be restored to her through the Coming of her Messiah (Daniel 9:24).

From Israel's point of view God inserted the Church Age as a parenthesis within the time of Israel, which delays, but does not cancel God's plans for Israel. It's like a paragraph inserted in a sentence before its end. It doesn't replace or change the main sentence, but delays its end and adds something extra. For example: **"Jim painted the room all morning** (except for a 20 minute tea break) **and finished it at noon."** Likewise: **"ISRAEL** (CHURCH) **ISRAEL."** So Israel has 7 years left to run on her Clock, which can only start again after the Church-Age is finished at the Rapture. Since the Tribulation is part of the time of Israel, the Church-Age must end before it begins (the paragraph must end before the rest of the sentence can resume). When the true Church is raptured (the ingathering of the fullness of the Gentiles), He will graft Israel back in again into the Olive Tree (the place of anointing as His representative) and will complete His plan for her: "all Israel will be saved" (Romans 11:23-27). Thus Israel's clock will restart and the 70th Week will run its course, by the end of which Israel will be fully restored and the Millennial Kingdom established (Daniel 9:24). Those who believe the Church goes through the Tribulation misunderstand the nature of the Tribulation and blur the distinction between Israel and the Church by spiritualising prophecy. The purpose of the Tribulation is to prepare Israel for the Kingdom, and to be a time of worldwide judgment. Neither purposes have any relation to the Church.

*5. A significant interval is needed between the Rapture and 2nd Coming because the Church in Heaven must go through certain events: *1. The Judgment Seat. *2. The Presentation of the Church to Christ. *3. The Marriage.

*6. Millennial Population Argument. Many scriptures make it clear that Jesus will remove all unbelievers from the earth at His 2nd Coming, so that only believers will enter His Kingdom on earth. But if all the believers are raptured at or near the end of the Tribulation, then there will be nobody left in their natural bodies to populate the Millennial Kingdom on earth! This is a major problem, especially for the Post-Tribulation view, for it will be too late for the unsaved once Jesus returns. Their chance to repent is before He comes again.

(1) Jesus said the Tribulation, which climaxes in the 2nd Coming, will be like the Days of Noah, when all unbelievers were killed, and only the believers were allowed to populate the new earth.

(2) In the Parable of the Tares in Matthew 13:37-43, Jesus made this very point. He compared the world to a field with 2 kinds of seed, the good seed, who are the sons of God; and the tares (the sons of the evil one). In the End of the Age (the Tribulation), which is the harvest time, all tares are gathered and thrown into fire. Thus by the end of the Tribulation all the unsaved will be removed from earth into Hades, so only the righteous by faith will remain to enter the Kingdom.

(3) Jesus made the same point in Matthew 25:31-46: **"when the Son of Man comes in His glory, and all the angels with Him, then He will sit on His glorious Throne."** This is the Throne of David in Jerusalem from which He will rule over the earth in the Messianic Kingdom. **"All the nations will be gathered before Him; and He will separate them from one another, as the shepherd separates the sheep from the goats; and He will put the sheep on His right, and the goats on the left."** Although it says 'nations' this is primarily a judgment of individuals. This is the word used for Gentiles, so it would better be translated:

"All the Gentiles will be gathered before Him." This is a judgment of all the Gentiles who have survived the Tribulation to determine which of them will be allowed to enter the Messianic Kingdom.

This Judgment is at the 2nd Coming and its location is on the earth, so this is different from the Great White Throne Judgment in Revelation 20, which takes place after the 1000 years. He separates them into 2 groups according to their nature. They are either sheep (believers) or goats (unbelievers).

In v34 He describes the sheep as blessed, that is, they possess eternal life: **"Then the King will say to those on His right: 'Come, you who are BLESSED of My Father, inherit the KINGDOM prepared for you from the foundation of the world."** They inherit the Messianic Kingdom.

But in v41 He describes the goats as accursed, under everlasting damnation: **"Then He will say to those on His left: 'Depart from Me, accursed ones, into the eternal fire which has been prepared for the devil and his angels."** All these unbelievers are removed from the earth to a place of everlasting punishment, first to Hades, to await their Final Judgment in the Lake of Fire. v46 concludes: **"These will go away into eternal punishment, but the righteous into eternal life."** It is clear that no unbelievers who survive the Tribulation will be allowed to remain alive to enter the Messianic Kingdom. Instead they are dismissed to a place of punishment. So only the believers alive at the 2nd Coming will possess the Kingdom.

(4) The Parable of the 10 Virgins (Matthew 25:1-11) teaches the same truth. The 5 who were without oil, who were not born again, at His 2nd Coming, are excluded from the Kingdom. A parallel passage in Matthew 7:21-23 describes Jesus rejecting some who professed faith in Him from entering the Kingdom, on the basis that He never knew them (they were never saved).

(5) We saw that Israel failed to possess the Messianic Kingdom because of unbelief, confirming that the condition to enter the Kingdom is faith in Christ.

Now if the Rapture happens at the 2nd Coming, then as well as all unbelievers being removed by death, all believers will also be removed by Rapture, leaving no one left to populate the Kingdom in their natural bodies. So the Rapture must take place a number of years before the 2nd Coming, in order for there to be enough time to produce a new crop of believers who will populate the Millennium. Only the Pre-Tribulation Rapture fulfils this requirement.

Revelation 7 describes a great soul-harvest in the 1st half of the Tribulation. Soon after the Rapture, God raises up 144,000 Jewish Evangelists who spearhead evangelism in the Tribulation (v1-8), resulting in the salvation of multitudes, seen in v9-17. Many are martyred, especially in the Great Tribulation, but those who endure to the end of the Tribulation will enter the Kingdom, and repopulate the earth. A Mid-Tribulation Rapture does not fulfil the requirement, because at Mid-Tribulation, the Mark of the Beast comes in when everyone will be forced to make their final decision. If they have not been saved by now, they will almost certainly take the Mark to survive, and once they take it they seal their doom forever.

2Thessalonians 2:9-12 confirms the cut-off point for most to receive salvation is at Mid-Tribulation: **"The coming of the lawless one is according to the working of satan, with all power, signs, and lying wonders** (this describes his activity at Mid-Tribulation according to Revelation 13), **and with all unrighteous deception among those who perish, because they did not receive the love of the truth, that they might be saved** (they rejected the Gospel in the 1st half of the Tribulation). **And for this reason God will send them strong delusion** (the mark of the beast), **that they should believe the lie, that they all may be condemned, who did not believe** (love) **the truth but had pleasure in unrighteousness."** So if all believers were raptured at Mid-Tribulation, hardly anyone would be left to populate the Kingdom. But a Pre-Tribulation Rapture followed by a great soul-harvest in the 1st half of the Tribulation, will produce a group of believers who will refuse the Mark and survive to the end.

*7. The Blessed Hope Argument. Many scriptures tell us to HOPE, LOOK, WAIT and WATCH for the personal Coming of the LORD for us, rather than expecting and waiting for the antichrist to kill us. If we were meant to go through the Tribulation, the Church would have been told to prepare and look for the antichrist, for he must come before Christ. But instead we are told to constantly expect and be ready for the Coming of Christ. Therefore, He must come before the Tribulation. 1Thessalonians 1:10 says that we are: **"to WAIT for His Son to come from Heaven whom He raised from the dead even Jesus who delivers us from the Wrath to come** (that is the Tribulation)."

Titus 2:13 says we are to be: **"LOOKING for the BLESSED HOPE and Glorious Appearing of our great God and Saviour Jesus Christ."** We are to look for the Blessed Hope of Christ, not the blasted hope of the antichrist! Our focus is to be on the Coming of the Lord - not the antichrist. Our hope is the Appearing of Jesus and our gathering to meet Him at the Rapture. If this is Pre-Tribulation then it is truly a Blessed Hope, but if we must first endure a time of Divine Wrath, and suffering at the hands of antichrist, it would not be such a Blessed Hope! If the Church was going through the Tribulation, we would not have a blessed hope of Christ, but would be looking in fear for the antichrist.

Paul concludes his teaching on the Rapture in 1Thessalonians 4 with the words: **"Therefore COMFORT one another with these words"** (v18). Likewise he concludes his teaching on the Rapture in chapter 5 with the words: **"Therefore, COMFORT each other"** (v11). Thus the primary effect of the true teaching on the Rapture is COMFORT, which encourages us to holiness and evangelism. Now the teaching of the Pre-Tribulation Rapture is obviously comforting for believers, whereas a Post-Tribulation Rapture, which teaches that we must first endure the wrath of satan, antichrist and God, is the opposite. The particular issue faced by the Thessalonians that called forth Paul's comforting teaching on the Rapture, was the death of some of the believers: **"But I do not want you to be ignorant, brethren, concerning those who have fallen asleep, lest you sorrow as others who have no hope"** (4:13). Paul had taught them to live in the imminent expectation of the Rapture, so when some died they sorrowed that these would miss out on this great event, which is why Paul affirmed this was not the case, but that the dead in Christ would rise first (v14-16). This sorrow that Paul addressed is understandable if they were Pre-Tribbers, but if they were Post-Tribbers they would have been glad their loved ones wouldn't have to endure the Tribulation.

*8. The Restrainer Argument (2Thessalonians 2:1-8). Daniel 9:27 and Revelation 6:1 say the Tribulation starts with the revelation of antichrist, making covenant with Israel and going forth in a bid for world-conquest. 2Thessalonians 2:1-3 says that the Day of the Lord (Tribulation) cannot come unless the Departure of the Church in the Rapture happens first (see Appendix 3), and then the antichrist will be revealed (signalling the start of the Tribulation). After describing antichrist's activity at Mid-Tribulation (v4-5), Paul explains why the revelation of the antichrist is so closely linked to the Rapture of the Church, and why he can only be revealed after the Church is removed. There is presently a RESTRAINER holding back the manifestation of antichrist, until he is TAKEN out of the WAY, and then the antichrist will be revealed (v6-8). Remember the subject under discussion is the Rapture - the 'Taking Away' of the Church from the earth (v1). So context demands that the CHURCH, indwelt by the Holy Spirit, is the Restrainer, who will be removed in God's time. Thus the antichrist cannot be revealed (and the Tribulation start) until the one restraining him (the Church) is removed (by the Rapture). This is in perfect harmony with what Paul said in v3 that the Departure (of the Church) must happen before antichrist can be revealed and the Day of the Lord begins. v6-8 repeats the same thought and adds the explanation. Thus a correct interpretation harmonises the whole passage.

The identification of the Restrainer as the Church is evident from other considerations. In the Church-Age, satan has opposed Christ and the Gospel (the spirit of antichrist). He does this by teachings denying the true Christ (His Person and Work). However, satan has not yet achieved his ultimate purpose of manifesting his final antichrist through whom he hopes to rule the world. He wants to use antichrist to completely remove faith in the true Christ. So God's agent in the earth set in opposition to the spirit of antichrist and restraining him is clearly the Church. By the power of the Spirit we are the salt of the earth, restraining corruption. As we use our authority as believers and release God's Word in testimony, preaching, praise, prayer and intercession, the forces of darkness are held back. So, the Church must be removed before evil can come to its fullness and be judged by Christ. Likewise in Revelation, after the Church is taken to heaven, there is a great release of evil on the earth, led by the antichrist.

The Restrainer is described as a 'He' (v7) and an 'it' (v6) indicating a 2-fold activity. The Restraining Ministry is carried out by the Holy Spirit working through the Church. In the Rapture, the Church is removed, but NOT the Holy Spirit, for as God He is omnipresent, and He'll be enabling people to be saved in the Tribulation. Just as the Spirit coming from Heaven to fill the Church in Acts 2 didn't mean He wasn't previously present on the earth, so likewise when the Spirit-indwelt Church is removed from the earth, this doesn't mean the Spirit won't be present on earth anymore. Thus when the Church is removed, although the Spirit is still present, His restraining Ministry through the Church will end.

*9. The Argument from Imminence

Perhaps the most important reason for believing in the Pre-Tribulation Rapture is that it is the only view that upholds the doctrine of imminence, which has great practical application to our lives. This vital New Testament doctrine says that **the Return of Jesus is imminent** - that is: **He could come AT ANY TIME.** Of course God knows when Jesus will return, but imminence means He has kept this knowledge from us, so that we are to live as if He could come at any time. The Church is told to look for and live in the light of His imminent Coming to translate us into His Presence. Therefore we are to live in constant expectancy, readiness and hope, watching, waiting and looking for His arrival. This blessed hope is a central teaching of the New Testament and is designed to motivate us to holy living and evangelism. It is used many times for this purpose.

For example Hebrews 10:24-25: **"Let us consider one another in order to stir up love and good works, not forsaking the assembling of ourselves together as is the manner of some, but exhorting one another and so much the more as you see the Day approaching."** We need to be in Church, and one key motivation given here is the Lord's imminent Return. Our zeal for God should increase as we see the Day getting closer. This motivates us to be faithful in Church attendance and service. We should run our Christian race every day conscious that at any time soon, we will stand before the Judgment Seat of Christ. This motivation is multiplied when we consider what will happen immediately after the Rapture - namely the Judgment Seat of Christ, when we will all stand before the Lord to give an account for our life and to receive our eternal rewards. Therefore, we should run our Christian race every day conscious that any moment, we will suddenly be raptured and find ourselves standing before the Lord.

Believing in the 'any-moment' Rapture motivates us to get ready and to make the maximum use of the short time remaining. It is NOT a teaching of defeatism and escapism, but creates an urgency and zeal in us to be found holy and occupied in serving the Lord when He returns. There is no doubt that the first generation of Christians lived in the light of the imminent Return of the Lord and that it was a major motivation, enabling them to turn the world upside down. Sadly, as the Church lost hold of the truth of the Pre-Tribulation Rapture, it also lost its vibrant faith in imminence, because the two go hand in hand. Without a belief in the Pre-Tribulation Rapture it's hard to believe in imminence, making it a neglected doctrine in much of the Church. To understand why imminence is only possible with a Pre-Tribulation Rapture, remember that Jesus will return in power and glory at the end of the 7-year Tribulation, which has well-defined Signs marking its start, middle and end. If the Rapture happens at the End of the Tribulation, then imminence is impossible, because it could not happen for at least 7 years. Also anyone in the Tribulation will be able to predict exactly when Jesus returns, since the exact timing of the Tribulation is revealed in Daniel and Revelation. Likewise, if the Rapture was at Mid-Tribulation, then it could not happen for at least 3.5 years. In both cases, a number of Signs must come first, so again imminence is destroyed. Therefore, immanency is only possible with a Pre-Tribulation Rapture, so if we can establish the imminence of the Lord's Return for us, then this would prove the Pre-Tribulation Rapture.

There is in fact overwhelming evidence for Imminence, because the New Testament writers frequently appeal to it to motivate their readers.

*For example, they describe His Coming as being AT HAND.

Philippians 4:5: **"The Lord is AT HAND."**

1Peter 4:7: **"The end of all things is AT HAND; therefore be serious and watchful in your prayers."**

Revelation 22:7,10: **"Behold I am coming quickly!...for the time is AT HAND."**

James 5:7-9: **"Be patient, brethren, until the COMING of the LORD... Establish your hearts, for the COMING of the LORD is AT HAND. Do not grumble against one another, brethren, lest you be condemned. Behold, the JUDGE is standing AT the DOOR!"**

Romans 13:11: **"Do this knowing the time, that now it is high time to awake out of sleep; for now our salvation** (resurrection) **is nearer than when we first believed. The Night** (the time of being on earth absent from the personal Presence of 'the Sun of Righteousness') **is far spent, the Day** (when we will stand in His glory) **is AT HAND. Therefore let us cast off the works of darkness, and put on the armour of light."**

Revelation starts by saying that the things it reveals: **"must shortly take place"** (1:1), and: **"the time is near"** (1:3), and ends by saying it has revealed: **"the things which must shortly take place"** (22:6).

Twice 1John 2:18 says: **"It is the last hour."**

*He is coming QUICKLY, so we are not to expect any delay. The language of 1Corinthians 15:51-52 describing the Rapture also emphasises its suddenness. Hebrews 10:37: **"For yet a little while, and He who is COMING will COME** and will NOT DELAY." Revelation 3:11: "Behold I am COMING QUICKLY (suddenly)! **Hold fast what you have, that no one take your crown."** It is particularly impressive that Jesus' final message to us in the final chapter of the Bible is a 3-fold emphasis on His imminent Coming in Revelation 22:7,12,20: **"Behold, I am COMING QUICKLY!... Behold, I am COMING QUICKLY and My reward is with Me to give every one according to his work... Surely I am COMING QUICKLY."** This is sometimes translated as: 'Jesus is coming soon', but literally it means quickly or suddenly, without warning - a plain statement of imminence. Therefore we must remain in a constant state of readiness for His Return, so that we can respond as Revelation 22:7 teaches us, by saying to Him: **"Amen. Even so, COME (now), Lord Jesus!"**

Jesus Himself taught imminence, when He compared the first phase of His Coming to the coming of a thief (Matthew 24:43-44, Luke 12:39-40, Revelation 3:3, 16:15, 2Peter 3:10, 1Thessalonians 5:1) - a clear statement of imminence. A thief comes suddenly and unannounced, with no warning signs. So His Coming in the Rapture will be unexpected, catching the world off guard and unprepared. He'll come, do His work and go away unseen by the unbelievers. The timing is also unknown to believers, but they have been informed about the event, and so if they believe and obey the Scripture they will keep themselves rapture-ready and so not get caught by surprise.

In His description of this dramatic event in the foundational passage in Matthew 24:36-44, His main repeating emphasis is on its imminence.
We see this in v36: **"But of that day and hour (of His Coming) no one knows."** v37-39 say there will be no special warning signs beforehand (another indication and proof of imminence), and v40-41 emphasise the suddenness of the event.
v42 emphasises that even believers don't know the time: **"Watch therefore (for the Lord, not for Signs), for you do not know what hour your Lord is coming."** v43 says His Coming will be sudden and without warning, like a thief. Then v44 totally demolishes any reasonings we may have that Jesus cannot return yet: **"Be ready, for the Son of Man is coming at an hour you do not expect"** (also Luke 12:40). Also 25:13: **"Watch therefore, for you know neither the day nor the hour in which the Son of Man is coming."** Thus Jesus said there will be no specific warning Signs before His Coming in the Rapture, for He would come as a thief, unlike His 2nd Coming in power and manifested glory, which comes after a

whole sequence of well-defined dramatic signs (Matthew 24:7-30). We do not know when the Rapture will be, so we have to always stay ready.

This combination of immanency verses in Matthew 24 answers a perverse interpretation of v36 used by some who want to fix the Rapture to the Feast of Trumpets. They say that this is coded language for the Feast of Trumpets, since it is the only Feast Day on the 1st of a month, and so is determined by the sighting of the new moon. This creates an uncertainty as it could be one of 2 days. Usually the 'Jewish Roots' card is invoked, claiming that any Jew would understand this (beware when people do this, for although there is much value in correctly understanding the true Jewish Roots, they are also often used as a Trojan Horse for false doctrines). It should be obvious that this interpretation of v36 reads ideas into the text that are simply not there. It is perverse, because it reverses the plain meaning that we simply cannot know when Jesus will return for the Rapture. Instead it claims the Rapture can only be on 1 of 2 days every year, and so it cannot be on any of the other days. But this interpretation is contradicted by v44, for if Christ had indeed clearly communicated to them in v36 that they were to expect Him to come at Trumpets, then why did He then say immediately afterwards that He would come at a time when they don't expect Him! Surely Jesus would not make a statement and then contradict it a few verses later.

Imminence is also revealed in the many scriptures that tell us to **WATCH, WAIT and LOOK expectantly for Christ Himself, in His Coming for us.**

The Church is never told to look or watch for the antichrist! We must be always ready, for at any moment we might be caught up to meet the Lord in the air! Some scriptures on watching tell us to look at and discern the Signs of the Times, but their overwhelming emphasis is that we should watch for the Lord Himself, that is, we should live every day with our spiritual focus upon His Return, living in the awareness and eager anticipation that He may come any time, and letting that stimulate and motivate our Christian lives. As a bride waiting for her bridegroom, we wait for Christ knowing our true future and destiny lies with Him.

*1. We are to WATCH for His Coming - not for the Tribulation or the antichrist!: **"WATCH therefore** (get ready, be alert that Jesus is coming soon and live accordingly) **and PRAY always** (do not be spiritually asleep and prayerless)

that you may be counted worthy to escape (in the Rapture) **all these things that shall come to pass** (in the Tribulation)**, and to stand** (resurrected) **before the Son of man** (in Heaven - by means of the Rapture)" (Luke 21:36). **"Take heed** (be alert) **WATCH and pray for you know not what hour your Lord shall come"** (Mark 13:33). See also Luke 12:37-40, Mark 13:33-37, Revelation 3:3, 16:15, 1Thessalonians 5:6.

2. We are to WAIT expectantly for His Coming and the Rapture (not for the antichrist). So we must be always ready for at any moment we might be caught up to meet the Lord in the air! We are to eagerly WAIT and look for His Appearing at the Rapture: **"Christ was offered once to bear the sins of many. To those who eagerly WAIT for Him, He will appear a second time, apart from sin, for salvation** (of the body)" (Hebrews 9:28). When someone important to us is coming to visit us, during the time we expect his arrival, we wait for him, to be sure we are ready to welcome him. We only wait for him if he could come at that time. If you know he won't arrive until tomorrow, then you won't be waiting for him today. So the fact we are to constantly wait for the Lord to come means that He could come at any time. The fact that this is a central truth for Christian living is seen by the fact that Hebrews 9:28 defines believers as those who are in a state of eagerly waiting for Christ to return. It assumes that this attitude is an intrinsic part of being a Christian.

Our expectation is not the Wrath of the Tribulation, but the Salvation of Christ

1Thessalonians 1:10 tells us that we are: **"to WAIT for His Son** (to come) **from Heaven, whom He raised from the dead** (we await the Rapture)**, even Jesus who delivers** (not delivered) **us from the Wrath** (Tribulation) **to come** (by the Rapture)**."**

The fact that we are WAITING for Jesus to come and rapture us is confirmed by Philippians 3:20-21: **"Our citizenship is in Heaven, from which we also eagerly WAIT for the Saviour, the Lord Jesus Christ, who will transform our lowly body that it may be conformed to His glorious body."**

1Corinthians 1:7-8: **"Eagerly WAITING for the revelation of our Lord Jesus Christ, who will also confirm you to the end, that you may be blameless in the day of our Lord Jesus Christ."**

See also Luke 12:35-36, Romans 8:23, James 5:7.

*3. We are to LOOK for His Coming, our Blessed Hope.

Titus 2:13: **"We should live soberly, righteously, and godly in the present age, LOOKING for the Blessed Hope and glorious Appearing of our great GOD and SAVIOUR Jesus Christ"** (also Luke 12:46, 21:28, Matthew 24:50, 2Peter 3:12, Jude 21). We are to LOOK for our Blessed Hope - the Appearing of Jesus in the Rapture, not the blasted hope of meeting the antichrist.

To the world, the Rapture will be like a Thief in the Night, removing the Church, but to us it is the coming and appearing of our Bridegroom for His Bride, taking us into the glorious light of His Presence forever (our Blessed Hope). So we are to live eagerly awaiting and preparing for His Return for us. If the Church were going through the Tribulation, we would not be looking for the blessed Appearing of Christ, but instead be looking in fear for the antichrist. We are to look for the Rapture, not the Tribulation. We have the blessed hope of the Rapture, rather than the dread of facing the Tribulation and antichrist. We are to LOOK for the Lord returning as our Bridegroom to take us home (John 14:1-3). So the Church is told to primarily LOOK for the Lord Himself, not for any Signs that must come first (1Thessalonians 5:6-10). This means His Coming must be imminent.

This is why Paul included himself in the 'we' who would be changed, rather than as one of the dead in Christ, who would be raised at the time of the Rapture: **"the dead in Christ will rise first. Then WE who are alive and remain shall be caught up together with them in the clouds to meet the Lord in the air"** (1Thessalonians 4:16,17). **"Behold, I tell you a Mystery: WE shall not all sleep, but WE shall all be changed - in a moment, in the twinkling of an eye, at the last Trumpet. For the Trumpet will sound, and the dead will be raised incorruptible, and WE shall be changed"** (1Corinthians 15:51,52).

Paul wasn't wrong to do this, for in obedience to God he lived in the expectation of the imminent Rapture. So the main focus for our lives now is to be ready for the Coming of our Lord. We need to live in constant hope, looking for His Coming, for at any time, He will suddenly come, without warning, to rapture us.

So our focus (our WATCHING, WAITING and LOOKING) is to be the Coming of the Christ, not of the anti-Christ. This will motivate us to walk before Him in holiness and serve Him zealously with our words and works. For immediately after the Rapture, He will give us a one-on-one interview with a searching examination of our lives, revealing, reviewing and assessing our works and motives, and giving us eternal rewards of glory according to our faithfulness to Him. **Imminence is a powerful motivation spurring us on to live godly lives, to be zealous in evangelism and good works**, so that when He returns, we will receive His commendation and eternal rewards. Many Scriptures motivate us by calling us to live in the light of His imminent Return, urging us to walk in love (1Thessalonians 3:12-13), patience and longsuffering (James 5:8-9), holiness (1John 3:1-3, Titus 2:11-14, I John 2:28, 1Thessalonians 5:23), to faithfully preach the Word and win souls (1Timothy 4:1-2, Jude 21-24. 2Corinthians 5:10-11), to be concerned with heaven and eternity (Colossians 3:1-4), to be steadfast in our labour for the Lord (1Corinthians 15:51-58), faithfully using the gifts that God has given us (1Corinthians 1:7-8), and to refrain from judging others (1Corinthians 4:5, James 5:8-9). The focus for our lives should be the moment we are ruptured and stand before Christ for His approval. But if the emphasis on imminence is removed they lose much of their urgency and motivating power.

Believing in imminence causes us to live our life looking for the Lord (consciously living in the light of His Coming), but if we don't have this belief, we will mostly focus instead on the Signs that must happen first, rather than the Lord's Coming, and this is unbiblical. It isn't a negative teaching of defeatism and escapism. Believing in the 'any-moment' Coming of Christ is a positive and exciting teaching motivating us to get ready and to make the maximum use of the short time remaining. It creates an urgency and zeal to be found holy and busy for the Lord when He returns. The focus for our lives should be that any moment, we will be ruptured and stand before the Lord to give an account for our life.

Now, the Bible's teaching on imminence is undeniable, so often those who reject Pre-Tribulation Rapture try to preserve a watered-down form of imminence, redefining it to mean that for every generation, Jesus could come in their lifetime. So they say that although He could not possibly come in the next few years, because of various events (signs) that must happen first, He could come in our lifetime. However, this does not reflect the immediate urgency of the imminence scriptures, and greatly diminishes their power to motivate us.

For example, imagine you received a letter from the Queen saying that she will pay you a visit any time and will want to tour your house. That would surely motivate you to get yourself and your house ready for inspection, and to stay ready.

But if it said she is coming, but not for a number of years yet, then the impact will be far less. There would be no immediate urgency to change or get ready. Much of the motivating power is lost. Likewise, when imminence is not taught, the church loses its urgency. Thus, one of the main Biblical motivations for godly living has been lost by much of the modern church. This is illustrated in <u>Matthew 24:45-51</u> by the servant who mistreated the other servants because he assumed His Master would delay His Coming. Then he is caught by surprise when the Lord suddenly returns and judges him very strictly. God knows there is something in human nature that slacks off if we think the deadline is a long time away, so He arranged it, so that we must believe He could come at any time.

There are 3 major kinds of motivation for believers in the New Testament based on FAITH, HOPE and LOVE. FAITH is based on the PAST, it says look what God has done for you, and live in the light of that. LOVE speaks of the new nature of Christ in our reborn spirit, and says live in the light of that. HOPE speaks of the future Coming of Christ, which is imminent, and says live in the light of that. Without a vibrant HOPE at best we are only firing on 2 cylinders, but believing in the imminent Rapture will enable us to move up a gear in our Christian life. In Church history when imminence was preached and believed, as in the early church it had the effect of breaking the power of worldliness, and produced increased zeal in evangelism and holiness.

*10. The Pre-Tribulation Rapture is consistently taught throughout the New Testament, in (1) the Teaching of Jesus (Matthew 24:36-44, Luke 21:34-36, John 14:1-3). **(2) the Teaching of Paul** (1Thessalonians 1:10, 4:13-5:11, 2Thessalonians 2:1-12)**, (3) the Teaching of Peter** (2Peter 1:19, Revelation 2:28, 22:16)**, (4) the Teaching of John**, throughout the Book of Revelation.

Objections to the Imminent Pre-Tribulation Rapture

Since the doctrine of Imminence (which requires a Pre-Tribulation Rapture) is such a Biblical doctrine, as well as being exciting and life-changing, it is strange that it is often strongly resisted. One reason might be that it is unsettling, preventing us from being too bound into life in this world. Those focused on this world and this life don't want to hear that at any moment it could all suddenly end, and they will find themselves standing before Jesus having to give an account. This realisation challenges and changes our perspective and priorities and makes us more heavenly minded. It shakes us out of our carnal thinking and complacency into action, because we want the Lord to find us serving Him when He returns. This is why the straw man commonly used by those who this teaching is so misleading. They say that those who believe in the imminent Rapture are escapists, who just want to disengage from this life and bunker down in a holy huddle waiting to be rescued in the Rapture. This is untrue - while it helps us to live with an eternal perspective, with our heart and treasure in heaven, rather than looking to this life alone and its pleasures, it does not create passivity. rather it encourages holiness and good works, especially evangelism, as we want to be found ready. It is true that we want to escape the Divine Wrath of the Tribulation, but we believe it because it is scriptural truth, because Jesus has promised His Church deliverance from wrath, not because of any desire to escape (what we believe will not change what happens, but it dies affect how we live now). The Imminent Coming of the Lord in the Rapture motivates us to live a strong Christian life for the Lord, so it's actually a very positive and practical teaching.

It does create a tension that some do not like, because it stops us from getting too comfortable in this world. Believing Jesus could come any time keeps us looking up and stops us from getting too entangled in the things of this life, but its also possible He will not come for some time, so we also have to live and build our lives accordingly. But we can't get too comfortable here because imminence keeps us on our toes and reminds us this is all temporary. I believe some resist imminence because they do not want to live in this tension. But its healthy for us to remember that our citizenship is in Heaven, and we are just pilgrims here, strangers in a foreign land, ambassadors on assignment, in the world but not of it, so we should not get too attached to it. This was the attitude of the heroes of faith (Hebrews 11:8-10, 13-16). Imminence is good for us spiritually, because it makes us more spiritual-minded, as it focuses us on the Lord Himself (Who is unseen), rather than Signs (which are seen). Many study Bible Prophecy with a carnal mind, with an unhealthy focus on the antichrist and his appearing, being more interested in who he might be, rather than in the Lord's Appearing.

One objection has been, if we are wrong then there will be a lot of people (the 'Pre-Tribbers') who will not be ready to meet the antichrist. First of all, we don't determine truth by weighing the consequences of being wrong and then taking the safe option. We follow where the scriptures lead us, according to literal interpretation. 2nd, there is no special teaching given to the Church to prepare it for the antichrist, apart from the information given in the New Testament about him, so 'Pre-Tribbers', if anything, will be more prepared as generally they are more interested in Bible Prophecy and know these scriptures well. So apart from the initial disappointment at being in the Tribulation they will be no worse off than anyone else. 3rd, there is a far more important meeting that we need to prepare for than any hypothetical meeting with antichrist, and that is our meeting with Christ at the Rapture when our whole life will be reviewed and rewarded. While other teachings focus on getting you ready for the Tribulation and meeting antichrist, the teaching of imminence focuses on getting you ready for your meeting with Christ, and this is surely is more important, and is the right emphasis that's true to the New Testament. Jesus could come at any time and call us to account. So it is vital we prepare ourselves and stay ready for this imminent meeting with Christ, rather than focusing on getting ready for antichrist.

Another objection is based on a misunderstanding of terminology. The most common term used for the final 7 years is the Tribulation, so people compare this to Jesus' words in <u>John 16:33</u> that: **"in the world you will have tribulation."** Therefore, they deduce (falsely) that it is unscriptural for us to be delivered from the Tribulation. They assume that the Tribulation is just like the Church-Age but a bit worse, not understanding it is completely different in nature (in a few years oat least 4-5 billion will die). Although 'the Tribulation' is a valid and scriptural term, the most common Biblical term is 'the Day of the Lord' signifying it is a time of Divine Judgment. So although it is a time of unprecedented tribulation (trouble) of all sorts, its key aspect is that it is a time of Divine Wrath from which the Church has been promised deliverance. Needless to say the Church has always suffered tribulation and persecution, so the teaching is not about avoiding tribulation, but avoiding the time of Judgment. Some say the Church needs to go through the Tribulation to be purified, a kind of Protestant Purgatory, but what about the majority of the Church over 2000 years, who never got the chance to go through the Tribulation, how will they get purified? My Bible says we are sanctified by the Blood of Jesus, and by the Spirit and Word of God!

I find that many objections to the Pre-Tribulation Rapture are appeals to emotion rather than logic, such as the persecution in China due to communism. Apparently the Chinese converts were taught the Pre-Tribulation Rapture, and on that basis believed they would not suffer persecution, but instead faced horrendous times, which led to a rejection of this teaching. The fact that Corrie ten Boom reported this adds emotional weight. But it should be obvious that either the Pre-Tribulation Rapture was taught wrongly to the Chinese or it was misunderstood, because it does not deny the fact that the Church suffers great persecution at times.

Another kind of emotional objection is particularly objectionable, revealing a kind of desperation in trying to discredit the teaching, rather than just judging it scripturally. I am talking about the attempts to discredit its ORIGINS. The claim is that it is a new doctrine discovered by J.N. Darby 200 years ago. To make matters worse, he got it from some dubious characters (Edward Irving and Margaret Macdonald)! This last accusation involving these 2 characters is mischievous and has now been proven false - Darby came to his conclusions from his own study of the scriptures. In any case we should not give these kind of considerations any weight, because that's not how we decide doctrine. Although the development of doctrine is a worthy study, we don't judge truth by who discovered it, or how recently it was (re)discovered. We judge truth by whether it agrees with the Word or not. Many truths known by the first believers were quickly lost by later generations and only relatively recently rediscovered, as many in the Church turned away from tradition and allegorical interpretation, and turned back to the Bible and its literal interpretation. If we say newly rediscovered truth must be wrong, then we must admit that the Reformers were wrong to teach justification by faith alone. I find it strange that this kind of argument is used against the Pre-Tribulation Rapture, when no one uses it against other doctrines. For example, Covenant Theology is not much older than Dispensationalism, but its relative modernity as a theological system is not used to discredit it, and rightly so.

I will conclude these thoughts by giving a potted history of prophetic doctrine. Obviously we believe the apostles had a clear grasp of the truth, but the early church fathers after them lost a lot of revelation, for example some of them believed in baptismal regeneration. Even so, they believed in a Tribulation, the imminent Coming of Christ and a literal Millennium to follow. They were all clearly Pre-Millennial, but the Tribulation issue is not so clear, as they did not have a developed theology on this issue, as we do today. However, there are early references to a Pre-Tribulation Rapture by the Shepherd of Hermas (95-150 AD), Victorinus, the Bishop of Pettau (270 AD), and Ephrem, the Syrian (306-373 AD) in his 'Sermon on the End of the World' wrote: *"Why therefore do we not reject every care of earthly actions and prepare ourselves for the meeting of the Lord*

Christ, so that he may draw us from the confusion, which overwhelms all the world? Believe me, dearest brother, because the Coming of the Lord is nigh, believe me, because the end of the world is at hand, believe me, because it is the very last time. Or do you not believe unless you see with your eyes? See to it that this sentence be not fulfilled among you of the prophet who declares: "Woe to those who desire to see the Day of the Lord!" For **all the saints and elect of God are gathered, prior to the Tribulation that is to come, and are taken to the Lord** *lest they see the confusion that is to overwhelm the world because of our sins."*

Therefore the doctrine of the Pre-Tribulation Rapture was not unknown before Darby. As Church history went on things got darker, especially as far as prophetic truth is concerned. Allegorical interpretation came in and controlled prophetic interpretation, especially when Augustine endorsed it, resulting in Amillenialism. Even when the Reformers called the Church back to literal interpretation, they broke this rule as far as prophecy was concerned and held to Amillennialism, so the Tribulation issue did not arise. Finally, 200 years ago there was a movement to take the prophetic scriptures literally, which allowed for a systematic study and exciting rediscovery of much truth. Initially, this led to the recovery of Pre-Millennialism as well as the Regathering and Restoration of Israel. Then, literal interpretation also led to the Pre-Tribulation Rapture. At this point we must give Darby credit for being the first to develop a systematic theology based on the literal interpretation of the prophetic scriptures. The truth was there in the Word all the time of course, but the Church did not have eyes to see it, because they did not take the Bible literally in that area. The rediscovery of this prophetic truth, which gained a great acceptance across many churches (not just the Plymouth Brethren, of which Darby was a leader), especially in America, played a large part in helping to motivate the great missionary movements of that time. Moreover, this truth was accepted by the Pentecostal movement 100 years ago and so played a key part in motivating holiness and evangelistic zeal. Another interesting observation is that this doctrinal development of prophetic truth is part of the larger process that's taken place throughout Church history. Church historian James Orr has pointed out that each different period of Church history has seen a different area of doctrine become the focus of attention and controversy, resulting in a systematic study of the scriptures and the development of a systematic theology in that area. The order in which this happened follows the standard order of chapters in any Systematic

Theology book. Appropriately, the last chapter, and the last area to be systematised (in the last 200 years) is Eschatology - the study of last things. So as the Church approached the end-times the Lord has restored understanding of the last things, just when it was most needed, so that we might know the times in which we live. Thus the fact that the Church has finally turned to the serious literal study of prophetic truth is another Sign of being in the end-times, for God told Daniel certain prophetic truths would be sealed until the time of the end, when many would go to and fro through the Bible and as a result prophetic knowledge would increase: **"Daniel, shut up the words, and seal the book until the time of the end; many shall run to and fro, and knowledge shall increase"** (Daniel 12:4).

One reason for this limitation on prophetic revelation was to preserve imminence, for this doctrine says God deliberately limits the prophetic knowledge of each generation, so that from their point of view Jesus could come at any time. So not only do we not know when He will return, but also if we say He can't return now or before a certain time, then we're contradicting His Word. Thus imminence says its God's secret, only He knows when Jesus will return (Matthew 24:36). Thus all we can do is speculate or try to discern it from types and shadows, but we cannot KNOW it, because He has not revealed it by any plain statement of Scripture. Therefore imminence means that in His Sovereignty He reserves the right to break into history at any time, and He says He will do it at a time we do not expect (Matt 24:44) which is a statement designed to confound and humble any human claim of knowing. This statement of Jesus trumps any human reasoning that says Jesus cannot come now. This is the simple answer to the final kind of objection to imminence, which is when people come up with reasons why Jesus cannot come yet, such as He is coming for a glorious Bride and she is not perfect yet. If that is the criteria, the Rapture will never happen, because we live in sinful flesh. The Bride will become perfect and glorious after the Rapture!

Another such argument is that the Gospel has not yet been fully preached to all nations, so Jesus cannot come yet. Now it is a valid motivation for world missions to say, by reaching out we are preparing the way for His Return, but ultimately only God can know and decide when this criteria is met to His satisfaction. It is foolish pride for us to put our reasoning above His plain statements of imminence. Some argue from the viewpoint of our more precise prophetic knowledge (based on the last 200 years of study and on world-events that have now happened), to say Jesus could not have come before 1948 for example, because we understand now that

Israel has to be back in the Land before Daniel's 70th Week begins. The answer is that imminence says that the knowledge of any generation was limited, so that **from their viewpoint** Jesus could come at any time. Also Jesus could have come at any time, because the Rapture is independent of any world-events. Although I believe the Tribulation will start on the day of the Rapture (Matthew 24:38-39, 1Thessalonians 5:2) that fact has rarely been understood. Moreover, there is nothing that says Daniel's 70 Weeks starts straight after the Rapture. In fact, if we knew Israel's covenant with antichrist happened straight after the Rapture that would destroy imminence. We assume it happens soon after, but there is an undefined time between the Rapture and the start of the 70 Weeks (the final 7 years of the Tribulation). Therefore any world event that has taken place before the Rapture (like Israel's Rebirth) could have also happened after it. In this way God has limited our knowledge to humble us and preserve imminence.

Finally, some construct special reasons why imminence was impossible for 1st century believers, for they knew certain prophesied events had to happen first, such as Peter's martyrdom (John 21:18-19) and Jerusalem's destruction prophesied by Jesus (Daniel 9:26, Luke 19:41-44, 21:6,20-24). The answer to the 1st point is that John's Gospel was written AFTER Peter's death, so imminence was preserved. The 2nd point has already been answered by what we said before that the Rapture is not directly tied to the start of the 70th Week, so hypothetically there was an unlimited time for such things to happen after the Rapture. 2ndly, the prophecies of Jerusalem's destruction could have been fulfilled in the Tribulation. Now, we know that is not the case, but the point is that this was a possibility for those living before the destruction (remembering also Revelation had not been written yet). The final answer to all these human reasonings against the plain statements of Scripture is that the 1st century believers, especially Paul, believed in, taught and lived in the light of imminence, and it was one of the keys to their spiritual effectiveness.

What about Matthew 24:31?

A favorite verse of the Post-Tribulationists is Matthew 24:31 (also Mark 13:27), which describes what Jesus will do after His 2nd Coming (v29.30): **"And He will send His angels with a Great Trumpet, and they will gather together His ELECT** (Israel) **from the 4 winds, from one end of heaven to the other."**

Those who say the Rapture will happen at the end of the Tribulation like to use this verse to support their view. They claim this is a description of the Rapture of the Church, at the same time as the 2nd Coming, but if that were true this verse contradicts their view in which the Rapture happens just before the 2nd Coming (the Church meets the Lord in the air as He is descending to the earth). This view violates the context, which is all about Israel, and we have already established that the elect in this passage must be Israel. Anyone who knows the Old Testament prophets, such as the disciples to whom Jesus was talking, would know He was speaking about the final Regathering of Israel from all nations at Messiah's Coming. He uses the term 'elect' to emphasise her status as His covenant People, and that He is regathering them in fulfilment of His Covenant with them.

The Regathering of Israel is one of the great themes of Bible Prophecy. As well as the initial partial Regathering before the Tribulation, with Israel in unbelief, when the Messiah returns there will be a complete and final regathering of Israel, with her now in faith. This is the subject of a number of Old Testament Prophecies which use **exactly the same language** as Jesus did in Matthew 24:31.

First, the context tells us that the elect in v31 is Israel who are now in faith. We have seen that Jesus will return to save His elect nation Israel at Armageddon, and then will complete the Regathering of Israel in preparation for His Kingdom, in fulfilment of many Old Testament prophecies. The elect here is not the Church, which did not even exist when He spoke these words. The disciples being Jews, who knew their prophets well, would have understood Jesus was talking here about the Regathering of Israel from the nations by the Messiah at His Coming.

Second, **a Great Trumpet** is only mentioned in one other place, Isaiah 27:12-13: **"You will be gathered one by one, O you children of Israel. So it shall be in that day the Great Trumpet will be blown; they will come, who are about to perish in the land of Assyria...and Egypt, and shall worship the Lord in the holy mount at Jerusalem."**

Third, **'the 4 winds of heaven'** is a Hebrew idiom meaning the same as the **'the 4 corners of the earth.'** The prophets often spoke of Israel and other nations being scattered to the 4 winds of heaven (for the Hebrew use of this metaphorical language see Jeremiah 49:32, 36, Ezekiel 5:10,12, Daniel 7:2, 8:8, 11:4, Zechariah

2:6), so this is a prophecy that God will now regather Israel, who had been 'scattered to the 4 winds' (to every nation). Those hearing Jesus' words would have understood His meaning (that He was talking about God regathering Israel to her land), because they knew what this language meant from the Old Testament. Likewise, we need to read the New Testament in light of the Old Testament background and use of language, rather that taking it out of context, and assigning our own meaning to it – namely, that it is talking about the Rapture). The direct link between the scattering of Israel and her Regathering is given in Jeremiah 31:10 **"Hear the word of the LORD, O nations, and declare it in the isles afar off, and say: 'He who SCATTERED Israel will GATHER him, and keep him as a shepherd does his flock."** Many are quick to believe that God scattered them in judgment, but are slow to accept that the same God will regather them in mercy, to fulfil His covenant promises to them.

Other prophecies speak of this final Regathering of Israel in similar ways.

Isaiah 5:26: **"He will lift up a banner to the nations from afar, and will whistle to them** (to Israel) **from the end of the earth; surely they shall come with speed, swiftly."** This is God calling and gathering His people, Israel.

Isaiah 11:11-12: **"On that day** (when the Lord returns to establish His earthly kingdom) **the Lord will again recover the 2nd time with His hand the remnant of His people, who will remain…and He will lift up a standard for the nations and assemble the outcasts of Israel, and gather the dispersed of Judah from the 4 corners of the earth."** See also Zechariah 10:8-10.

So it was prophesied in the Old Testament, using exactly the same language, that when Messiah returns He will blow a Great Trumpet to call his Elect (Israel) to gather them back to their Land. Where is Jesus at this time? From where is He blowing His Trumpet? Israel! So the Trumpet must be gathering people to Israel!

Partial Rapture?

Finally, we complete our study of the Rapture by asking: "Who will be taken up in the Rapture?" Is it all born-again believers of the Church-Age, or only those who are fully living for the Lord? The Partial Rapture Theory says that not all born-again believers will be raptured, but only the overcomers, those who deserve it. So, only 5 star Christians will go up, and the rest will have to go through the

Tribulation, which will function as a kind of Protestant Purgatory, to complete their sanctification, as they are not yet ready for heaven. Often people who say the Church needs to go through the Tribulation, think this way, believing that the suffering of the Tribulation is necessary to purify the Church, but my Bible says that we are cleansed by the Blood of Christ, and the Word and Spirit of God. You can see how a Partial Rapture makes for a good altar call: *"If you don't get your life straight you'll have to go in the Tribulation and the antichrist will get you. So you better repent."* However, this is not Biblical. It is based on human reasoning. The Rapture is part of our salvation by grace alone, apart from our works. Thus our works do not determine if we qualify to go up in the Rapture. The Rapture is the completion of our salvation - the resurrection of our bodies. In fact if we are in Christ and Christ is in us through the New Birth, when He comes we will automatically be drawn up to meet Him in the air.

This is clearly taught in the main Rapture passage, 1 Thessalonians 4:14-17: **"If WE believe that Jesus died and rose again, even so God will bring with Him those who sleep IN JESUS. For this we say to you by the Word of the Lord, that WE who are alive and remain until the Coming of the Lord will by no means precede those who are asleep. For the Lord Himself will descend from heaven with a shout, with the voice of an archangel, and with the trumpet of God. And the dead IN CHRIST will rise first. Then WE who are alive and remain shall be caught up together with them in the clouds to meet the Lord in the air."** Notice that those who are raptured are described as the ones who are alive when He comes, who believe that Jesus died and rose again. Also those who are resurrected at the same time are described as those who sleep IN JESUS, and as the dead IN CHRIST.

In saying: **"the dead IN CHRIST will rise first"**, it is clear that as far as those who have died are concerned, the only qualification for them to rise at this time is that they are IN CHRIST. In this group, some were faithful Christians, but others not so much. But as long as they are in Christ they will be raised at this time. It would be unrighteous of God to use a different criteria for the living believers. This is confirmed by what he says next. Having described the rising up of all the dead in Christ, he says: **"Then WE who are alive and remain will be caught up together with them in the clouds to meet the Lord in the air."** The 'WE who are alive' must also be those who are IN CHRIST, who are alive when the Rapture happens. 1 Corinthians 15:51 confirms that all living believers will be raptured: **"Behold, I tell you a Mystery; WE** (believers) **will not all sleep, but WE will ALL be changed."** Will Christ be presented with a disfigured Bride, with an arm, leg and eye and half her teeth missing? I don't think so! The whole body of Christ will rise to meet the Lord in the air.

Overcomers

The Partial Rapture theory says not all those in Christ will be raptured, but only the overcomers. Now it's true that there are promises given to the overcomers in Revelation 2-3, including the promise of the Morning Star (2:28). So it follows that only the overcomers will make the Rapture.

But what is the Bible definition of an overcomer? Revelation was written by the apostle John, so we should allow John himself to define who is an overcomer. 1John 5:4,5: **"Whatever is born of God overcomes the world; and this is the victory that has overcome the world - our faith. Who is the one who overcomes the world, but he who believes that Jesus is the Son of God?"**

So who is the overcomer? It is the one who is born again, who believes Jesus is the Son of God. So anyone born again is an overcomer. If you have put your trust in Christ, you are an overcomer. You do not have to try and be an overcomer. You are one already! Christ has already overcome the world (John 16:33), and in Him you are more than a conqueror (Romans 8:37). If you are in Christ, then through your union with Christ, all the promises of God are yours in Christ, including the promise of the Rapture (2Corinthians 1:20). To confirm this, if you study all the promises to overcomers in Revelation 2-3 you will discover they are promises given to all believers, and not just to a certain elite group.

The final proof that the partial-rapture theory is wrong is that both Romans 14:10 and 2Corinthians 5:10 say: **"WE** (believers) **shall ALL stand before the Judgment Seat of Christ."** ALL believers from the Church-Age will stand before the Judgment Seat of Christ to give an account and receive their eternal rewards. This will happen soon after the Rapture. Therefore, all true believers in Christ must be raptured together in order to all stand together before Christ.

This answers the main emotional motivation and appeal behind the partial-rapture position, which comes from the feeling that if all believers were in the Rapture, it would be unfair, for surely there should be a difference made between faithful and unfaithful Christians! Indeed there will be a big and eternal difference between believers according to their faithfulness, but this is not manifested in who goes up in the Rapture, but in what happens after the Rapture, at the Judgment Seat, for there we will receive eternal rewards of glory, opportunity and authority, which will differ greatly according to our works in this life. So how we live now is vitally important and will make a big difference to our eternal glory. Those who are lazy, careless servants will deeply regret wasting their time and opportunities, but those who faithfully walk with God and obey Him will be amazed at His generosity on that Day. Thus every blessing of salvation, including our resurrection body at the Rapture, is equally ours on the basis of grace, independent of our works. However, our eternal rewards will be reckoned to us according to our works. We will all have different degrees of reward depending on how we live now, according to our faithfulness to God.

*Differences between the Rapture and Second Coming of Christ

To summarise our discussion of the Rapture, we list the many differences between the Rapture and 2nd Coming, which mark them out as 2 separate events.

1. **In the Rapture, Christ returns to the AIR.**
   In the 2nd Coming, He comes to the earth.

2. **The Rapture is a joyous reunion.**
   The 2nd Coming brings terrible judgment.

3. **In the Rapture, Jesus comes is seen by believers only.**
   In the 2nd Coming He is seen by all.

4. **In the Rapture, He comes secretly, as a thief in the night.**
   In the 2nd Coming, He comes openly, in manifested power and glory.

5. **In the Rapture, He comes as the BRIDEGROOM.**
   In the 2nd Coming, He comes as the KING of kings and JUDGE of all.

6. **In the Rapture Christ comes FOR His Bride.**
   In the 2nd Coming He comes WITH His Bride.

7. **In the Rapture He removes believers from the earth by translation.**
   In the 2nd Coming He removes unbelievers from the earth by death.

8. **The Rapture brings in the Tribulation - the time of Jacob's Trouble.**
   The 2nd Coming brings in the Millennium - the time of Israel's Restoration.

9. In the Rapture, He comes as the Morning Star, which is during the night, but it heralds the soon-coming new day, only seen by those watching.

In the 2nd Coming, He comes as the Sun of Righteousness with healing in His wings, bringing in a new day, the rays of His glory shining upon the whole earth.

10. The Rapture is IMMINENT and SIGNLESS.

The 2nd Coming is preceded by many SIGNS.

11. The Rapture is related to the Church.

The 2nd Coming is related to Israel and the nations.

12. The Rapture is a Mystery.

The 2nd Coming is revealed in Old Testament Prophecy.

13. At the Rapture, all the believers of the Church-Age will be judged.

At the 2nd Coming, all the surviving Gentiles will be judged.

14. After the Rapture, Israel's everlasting Covenants still remain unfulfilled, but after the 2nd Coming, they will all be fulfilled.

15. After the Rapture, the earth will be unchanged, but after the 2nd Coming, the earth will be restored.

16. After the Rapture, evil and the antichrist will be released, but at the 2nd Coming, evil and the antichrist will be judged.

17. The Rapture comes before the Day of the Lord Wrath.

The 2nd Coming is the climax and conclusion of that Day.

18. Life before the Rapture will be going on as normal. Men will be saying: "Peace and safety." But in the Great Tribulation just before the 2nd Coming things on earth will be at their worst ever.

19. The Rapture is for believers only. The Second Coming is for all on earth.

20. The Rapture is the expectation of the Church, our blessed hope of being taken to Heaven. The 2nd Coming is the expectation of Israel, her earthly hope of inheriting the Messianic Kingdom.

*Chapter 10 - The Judgment Seat of Christ

A missionary came home from the field after many years of faithful work for God. During the voyage he was wondering what kind of welcome he would receive at the dock. As he approached the port there was a cheering crowd and band playing. His spirits were raised. All these had come to greet him. But his face fell as he saw whom they had come to see, for the Prince of Wales had been travelling on the same ship. As he got off he realised there was no welcome for him. In dejection he said to the Lord: "It's not fair. I've laboured and sacrificed for years, but at my homecoming I have nothing." Then the Lord simply said: "This is not your Homecoming." Our true Homecoming is to our true Home (Heaven). The Lord was telling him that his labour was not unseen nor would it be it in vain, for He sees everything we do and He will reward us accordingly, and part of that will be a joyful Homecoming. God does give blessings and rewards in this life, for our faithfulness, but our main payday is yet future at the Judgment Seat of Christ, when we receive our eternal rewards.

All men are created by God and are accountable to God, who is holy and judges us all without partiality and according to truth (Romans 2:2,11), that is, by His absolute moral standards as revealed in His Word, as Jesus said: **"Your Word is truth"** (John 17:17). He does not just look at the outward appearance of what we do, but also at the heart motivation (1Samuel 16:7). Therefore, there will be a time of final judgment for every person.

We have seen that each person's Eternal Judgment happens in **2 Stages**. The **1st Stage, immediately after death, determining our eternal innocence or guilt**, is according to our FAITH - whether or not we have put our trust in Christ alone for our eternal life. We are not saved by our works, but by trusting in Christ and His work for us. Salvation is by grace through faith, independent of our works. Our eternal salvation or condemnation is settled by this judgment. We either stand guilty before God in Adam on the basis of our own works and righteousness, or justified before God in Christ on the basis of His perfect work and righteousness. **The 2nd Stage, which happens immediately after our resurrection, determines either a man's eternal rewards if he has been found righteous, or his eternal punishment if guilty.** In either case the degree of punishment or reward is according to his WORKS. Thus **the 1st Judgement is according to our FAITH and the 2nd Judgment is according to our WORKS.**

In the Bible these 2 issues of faith and works are closely connected. Those who have truly repented and trusted in Christ will start to produce the fruit of good works. Although we have been SAVED from the judgement of our sins through FAITH in Christ, we still have to face the Judgement of our WORKS for our eternal reward. Although we are all equally saved through faith, we will have different degrees of eternal reward depending on our works in this life now.

Those who are alive for the Rapture are a special case, because they do not die, so the 2 Stages happen together. Anyone alive in Christ at that time will be raptured, and immediately find themselves standing before the Judgment Seat of Christ in their new bodies, to give an account to Him of their works, and receive their eternal rewards. This appointment with God will be the most momentous event of your life, an everlasting, irreversible judgment determining your eternal position and degree of glory, and it is imminent. So I must warn you about it, so you can prepare yourself, and make sure you are ready! We need to live our life and run our race with the conscious realisation and expectancy that at any time, we will stand before the Lord to give an account for our Christian life and service to God. This will motivate us to be on fire for God and put His Kingdom first.

Salvation v Rewards

Some find it hard to reconcile the idea of eternal rewards for our good works with our salvation by grace alone, through faith alone in Christ alone. These are 2 separate issues, which relate to the 2 most important days of your life:

(1) the day you received Christ as your Saviour,

(2) and (2) the day you will stand before His Judgment Seat.

Consider these 5 points of contrast:

*(1) SALVATION is provided for all sinners. On the other hand, **REWARDS are only awarded to the saints** (believers), God's rightful servants (Rev 11:18).

*(2) SALVATION is the same for all, but REWARDS differ, because they are proportionate to our acceptable service to God and man: **"The Son of Man will come in the Glory of His Father with His angels, and then He will reward each according to his works"** (Matthew 16:27), **"each one will receive his own reward according to his own labour"** (1Corinthians 3:8). See also Luke 12:47-48 and 2Corinthians 5:10. The Bible encourages us to labour for a 'great reward' (Luke 6:23) or 'full reward' (2John 1:8), so they cannot all be alike: **"Love your enemies, do good, and lend, hoping for nothing in return; and your reward will be great"** (Luke 6:35). To those faithful and courageous under persecution, Jesus said: **"Great is your REWARD in Heaven"** (Matthew 5:12).

*(3) SALVATION is God's gracious gift to the lost, but REWARDS are God's gracious wages to the saved, for their faithful service rendered after salvation, for being a willing and useful servant. **"Behold, I am coming quickly, and My reward is with Me, to give to every one according to his work"** (Rev 22:12). **"He who reaps receives wages, and gathers fruit for eternal life, that both he who sows and he who reaps may rejoice together"** (John 4:36). Whereas we just receive our salvation, we are active participants in earning our reward. Nevertheless these rewards are manifestations of grace, for God does not owe us anything, for when we obey Him, we are only doing what we ought to do. It is His gracious choice, not His obligation, to reward us according to our works. In the Parable in Matthew 20:1-16, a Landowner (a picture of Christ) gave wages to his labourers, above what they deserved. When challenged about this, He justified Himself by asserting His sovereign right to distribute His rewards as He pleases: **"Is it not lawful for me to do what I wish with my own things?"** (v15).

*(4) SALVATION is a present possession for believers, but REWARDS are a future possession. Payment comes after work is done, not before, based on what has been completed satisfactorily. Eternal rewards are awarded only as a result of your service being judged acceptable. This will happen at the Judgment Seat of Christ, which is yet future. Rewards are seen as future: **"If anyone's work which he has built on it endures, he WILL receive a reward"** (1Corinthians 3:14). **"The Crown of Righteousness, which the Lord, the righteous Judge, WILL give to me on that Day"** (2Timothy 4:8). See also Matthew 16:27 and Luke 14:14. Eternal rewards are not to be confused with the temporal blessings and rewards God gives us in this life. These blessings are nothing compared to our future eternal rewards that we will truly possess forever. Rewards are not given until we have run our race in this life and stand in the Presence of our Rewarder.

*(5). SALVATION is given on the basis of faith alone, but REWARDS are given on the basis of our works, the faithfulness of our service to Him. Ephesians

<u>2:8-10</u> gives the balance between these 2 aspects of faith and works. We are not saved by works (v8-9), but we are saved for works, for the purpose of doing good works (v10), that God might be glorified through our lives, and He chooses to affirm and celebrate these works by graciously crowning them with His eternal glory (our rewards). God has prepared a lifetime of good works for us to walk in and He will reward us according to how faithfully we have walked in His will for us. *"Blood washed believers will be spotless in God's sight, but not all will have the same service record. God is after (willing) obedience. Salvation gets us to Heaven, but works determine what we do after we get there"* (C.S.Lovett).

Ephesians <u>2:8-10</u> gives the balance between these 2 issues of (1) salvation by grace through FAITH apart from works, and (2) the importance of GOOD WORKS flowing from our faith: (1) **"By grace you have been saved through faith, and that not of yourselves; it is the gift of God, not of works, lest anyone should boast"** (v8-9). (2) **"For we are His workmanship, created in Christ Jesus for good works, which God prepared beforehand that we should walk in them"** (v10). Although the judgement for believers will be a searching exposure and strict judgment of our works, it will be far better than standing with unbelievers before the Great White Throne (Revelation 20) We will receive eternal rewards, but they will receive their sentencing unto everlasting punishment!

Rewards are often mentioned in Scripture, showing the importance of this subject (Genesis 15:1, Ruth 2:12, 1Samuel 24:19, Psalm 19:9-11, 58:11, Isaiah 62:11, Matthew 5:12, 6:3-4, 10:41, 16:27, Mark 9:41, Colossians 3:23-24, 2John 8). His rewards are a manifestation of His righteousness, love and grace in that it is His way of showing His approval of all that's good and right: **"God is not unjust to forget your work and labour of love which you have shown toward His Name, in that you have ministered to the saints, and do minister"** (Hebrews 6:10). Righteous authorities are like God in both punishing the evildoers and praising (rewarding) those who do good (1Peter 2:14, Romans 13:3-4). Rewards are God's idea, they arise from the heart of God. As fathers love to reward their children from love, and thereby motive them to greater things, so our heavenly Father loves to reward us, and uses His rewards to motive us to excel. He teaches us what He rewards (motives, faith etc.) to motivate these things in us.

The Timing of this Judgment

The Final Judgment does not happen to all people at the same time, for God judges different groups at different times. For example, the final judgment of believers happens 1000 years before the final judgment of unbelievers. Revelation 20 reveals that the 1st resurrection (of the righteous) takes place before the Millennium but the 2nd resurrection (of the wicked) is after the Millennium. Therefore the final judgment of the righteous, at the Judgment Seat of Christ, takes place at the Rapture and 2nd Coming, but the final judgment of the wicked, at the Great White Throne, takes place 1000 years later. So the judgment of believers for reward takes place before the judgment of unbelievers.

1Peter 4:16-17 confirms this: **"If anyone suffers as a Christian let him not be ashamed, but let him glorify God in this matter. For the time** (is at hand) **for JUDGMENT to begin at the House of God, and if it begins with us first what will be the end of those who do not obey the Gospel of God?"** Suffering believers can rejoice because they will be rewarded at this Judgment for being faithful and courageous under fire. Peter continues in v18: **"Now if the righteous one is scarcely saved, where will the ungodly and sinner appear?"**

The Judge

As with all judgments the Judge will be the Lord Jesus Christ, who said in John 5:22-23: **"The Father judges no one, but has committed all judgment to the Son, that all should honour the Son just as they honour the Father. He who does not honour the Son does not honour the Father who sent Him."** In v27 Jesus said that the Father: **"has given the Son authority to execute judgment also, because He is the Son of Man."** Because Jesus knows what it is like to live as a man this uniquely qualifies Him to be our judge. In the next verses (28-30), Jesus links this Judgment to the time of the resurrection.

When?

Next we establish the point that the Judgment for reward of the true Church happens straight after the Rapture. The principle of the Judgement for believers following their Resurrection is clear from Luke 14:14: **"When you give a reception, invite the poor, the crippled, the lame, the blind, and you will be blessed, since they do not have the means to repay you; for you will be REPAID at the RESURRECTION of the RIGHTEOUS."** When we act unselfishly to help those in need, who cannot pay us back, Jesus promises we'll be repaid at the resurrection. This confirms that the judgment for reward for the righteous takes place immediately after their resurrection - for us this means it will be straight after the Rapture of the Church. Likewise, Jesus said in Revelation 22:12: **"Behold, I am COMING quickly, and My REWARD is with Me, to give to every one according to his WORK."** So Jesus will distribute His rewards immediately after He comes in the Rapture.

In Luke 21:36 Jesus said that believers who escape the Tribulation in the Rapture will **"STAND before the Son of Man"**, who will be sitting on His Judgment Seat. This will take place in Heaven, for Jesus promised in John 14:1-3 that He will return for us in the Rapture and then take us to be with Him in Heaven. This again confirms a Pre-Tribulation Rapture, for in the Post-Tribulation scenario, Jesus raptures us at the 2nd Coming, and we then do a U-turn and return with Him to the earth.

1Corinthians 4:5 also confirms this Judgment will be when the Lord comes at the Rapture: **"Judge nothing before the time** (of judgment), **until the Lord comes, Who will bring to light the hidden things of darkness and reveal the counsels** (motives) **of the hearts. Then each one's praise** (reward) **will come from God."** 2Timothy 4:1: **"The Lord Jesus Christ will JUDGE the living and the dead:** (1) **at His Appearing** (the Rapture) **and** (2) **at His Kingdom** (His 2nd Coming)**."** In view of this Judgement, in v2 he urges ministers to be faithful in preaching the Word. In v8, Paul himself expected to receive a reward on the Day of His Appearing: **"Finally, there is laid up for me the Crown of Righteousness, which the Lord, the righteous Judge, will give to me on that Day, and not to me only but also to all who have loved His Appearing."**

Obviously, only those who are raptured will stand before Christ in this Judgment. So it is a judgment for believers only. It is for all believers of the Church Age, as Paul says: **"Why do you judge your brother? Or why show contempt for your brother? For WE** (brothers and sisters in Christ) **shall ALL stand before the Judgement Seat of Christ"** (Romans 14:10).

This is not a judgment to determine our salvation, for if we have received Christ, we have already been justified and passed from death to life. It is not a judgment of condemnation on our sins, for on the Cross Jesus already paid the penalty and took the judgment for our sins upon Himself, so there is no condemnation for us in Christ. It's not a judgment to determine PUNISHMENT for our sins, but to determine our REWARDS. It is not a judgment to determine if we are SONS of God, but to reward our faithfulness as His SERVANTS. In fact, only the Sons of God will be raptured to stand before the Judgment Seat. It is a judgment of all our WORKS, of our life and service as a Christian, to determine our eternal REWARDS - the glory, honour and authority that we will have throughout eternity. Our capacity for the eternal riches of His glory is determined by our faithfulness to God in this life. So it is not a judgment for punishment, but for reward. Our works will be rewarded, and our reward will determine our eternal capacity for God's glory.

Although God is merciful to forgive us our sins, we should take sin seriously, for it hurts our fellowship with God, and therefore our fruitfulness and eternal reward. But when we confess our sin, He blots it out with His Blood - praise God!   Isaiah 43:25 says: **"I, even I am He Who blots out your transgressions for My own sake and I will remember your sins no more."**

Our life is recorded on God's videotape, so any time out of fellowship is wiped blank and therefore nothing from that time can be presented for a reward. Only what is done in fellowship with God will stand and be rewarded.

Moreover, sin often undermines God's work and testimony, causing others to be discouraged and offended. This undoes the positive effect of your good works for the Lord, and so lessens or even destroys the reward you would have had. If a minister faithfully preaches the Word, but then falls into sin, the fallout will destroy much of the good that he had previously accomplished. As a result he will lose much of his reward, and his lack of faithfulness will disqualify him from opportunities to serve God in a greater way. What God would have entrusted him with, will now be given to another, who will take his crown. When we sin we don't lose our salvation, but we suffer loss of our eternal rewards and that is a serious issue. The subject of rewards is greatly neglected, but it is a major part of the teaching of the New Testament. We need to live our life in the light of the JUDGMENT SEAT of CHRIST.

The 4 major Passages on this Judgment for Reward

*The first is Romans 14:10-13: **"Why do you judge your brother? Or why do you show contempt for your brother? For we** (believers) **shall all stand before the Judgment Seat of Christ"** (v10). The word for 'Judgment Seat' is the Greek word 'Bema.' It is a high elevated Seat that the Roman Emperor would sit on to render judgment or give out rewards. For example, he sat on a Bema at the Olympic Games, before which the victors stood to receive their rewards (crowns). Likewise after the rapture, Christ will sit on His Judgment Seat and hand out His rewards to us. When we have run our race, we will all stand before the King to receive His rewards, that depend on how well we ran our race in this life, just as Olympians receive gold, silver or bronze medals. In light of this coming judgment, Paul points out that it is foolishness for us to set ourselves up as our brother's judge, since this job belongs to the Lord and He alone is qualified for it. We can judge actions against the Word of God, but we cannot know men's hearts or motives, so we are not qualified to be their judge. If we intrude on His work of judgment, we can expect a strict judgment ourselves. That is why Jesus said: **"Blessed are the merciful, for they shall receive mercy"** (Matthew 5:7), and: **"Judge not lest you be judged. For in the same way you judge others you will be judged and with the measure that use in judging others, it will be measured to you"** (Matthew 7:1,2). Likewise Paul says: **"Who are you to judge another's servant? To his own master he stands or falls"** (Romans 14:4).

Romans 14:11: **"For it is written: "As I live says the Lord, every knee shall bow to Me, and every tongue shall confess to God."** This is a quote from Isaiah 45:23, saying that one day, every man will stand before God and be judged. Paul applies this to the Judgment Seat of Christ, saying that Jesus is the Lord Judge. This proves that Jesus is God, and confirms the Father has given all judgement to His Son. Philippians 2:9-11 confirms Christ will fulfil this prophecy. v12: **"So then each of us** (individually) **shall give an account of himself to God."** In v10 it spoke of the Judgment Seat of Christ, but here it says we give an account to God, again showing that Christ is God).

So you have an appointment with God which you cannot miss. Are you ready? It could happen any time! We will all individually and personally give an account to God for our lives. God, Who sees all, keeps a perfect record of our every thought, word and deed, and will bring our whole Christian life before us, and we will have to give an account for how we have responded to people, situations and God's will. There will be no excuses, or blaming of others in that day, because whatever others do to us, we are responsible for our own actions.

In v13 he concludes: **"Therefore, let us not judge one another anymore, rather resolve not to put a stumbling block in our brother's way."** Rather than focusing on the failings of others we need to watch ourselves and make sure we do not cause others to stumble by our sin and harsh attitudes, and so incur an unfavourable judgment from the Lord on that day. Knowing that soon He will judge us should cause us to focus our attention on ourselves, rather than on others' faults and failings. We need to put all our energy into following God's will for our life, rather than wasting it by judging others. Rather than focusing on others, we need to focus our judging our own attitudes and actions by God's Word, for: **"If we would judge ourselves, we will not be judged"** (1Corinthians 11:31).

Scripture warns us that if we are judgmental against others, God will judge us in a stricter way. James 5:8-9: **"the Coming of the Lord is near. Do not complain, brethren, against one another, so that you yourselves may not be judged; behold, the Judge is standing right at the door!"** Imagine you are one of a group of people about to be judged, and are waiting in the court for the judge, and in his absence you decide to get up and sit in his seat and start to judge and pass out punishments on the others. What will happen when the judge walks in? Who is going to get the strictest judgment? That is why James also said: **"So speak and so act as those who are to be judged by the Law of liberty. For judgment will be merciless to one who has shown no mercy; but mercy triumphs over judgment"** (2:12-13).

Every day has great significance for how you live each day will make a difference to your eternal glory. Your future eternal rewards are at stake. The Judgment Seat of Christ is a strong inducement against sin, especially the sin of judging, which is a proud usurping of the Lord's place, and will result in a great loss of reward. Final judgment belongs to the Lord, so it is wise for us to walk in humility towards others, rather than pride and superiority, for we have such limited knowledge about people's history, situations and motives.

*The 2nd major Passage on Christ's Judgment Seat is 2Corinthians 5:9-11:

"We make it our aim to be well pleasing to Him... for we (believers) **must ALL appear before the Judgment Seat of Christ, that each one may receive his reward for the THINGS DONE in the BODY, according to what he has done, whether good or bad."** Again we see this is a judgment for believers only. It is a judgment of our works, 'the things done in the body', in order to determine our reward. It motivates us to live a life pleasing to Him. This will be a thorough searching examination of the quality of all our works, whether good or bad. God sees past the outward action, to the inward thought and motive behind it. Many works that seem good from a human standpoint are in fact they are dead works, done for selfish reasons not from love and faithful obedience to God, works of the flesh, not of the Spirit, to glorify self rather than God. On that day the true quality of all our works will be revealed. Every work is either good or bad, and will either be justified and rewarded, or condemned. Paul concluded in v11: **"Knowing therefore the fear of the Lord, we persuade men."** His awareness that soon he must stand before the Lord, produced in him the Fear of the Lord, motivating him to preach the Gospel and fulfil God's plan for his life.

This Judgment is on all   our WORKS and includes our WORDS. Matthew 12:36,37: **"for EVERY idle WORD men may speak, they will give account of it in the DAY of JUDGMENT. For by your WORDS you will be justified, and by your WORDS you will be condemned."**

God will reward our WORKS, not our good intentions. As Jesus said, idle, empty words where we promise to do something, but fail to follow through will get no reward, rather they will speak against us. Jesus made this point in Matthew 21:28-30: **"What do you think? A man had 2 sons, and he came to the first and said: "Son, go work today in my vineyard. He answered and said: "I will not", but afterward he regretted it and went. Then he came to the 2nd and said likewise. And he answered and said: "I go, sir", but he didn't go. Which of the 2 did the will of his father?" They said to Him: "The first."**

In evaluating the 7 Churches in Revelation 2-3, Jesus often said: **"I know your works"** (2:2, 2:19, 3:1, 3:8, 3:15). We may say: "He sees my heart." Yes, He does - but we will be judged by what we actually do in loving and serving Him, for this is the ultimate proof of what is in our heart. Jesus said: **"If you love Me, obey** my commandments" (John 14:15). Telling Him we love Him is good, but if we don't prove it by our actions it has little value.

*The 3rd major Passage on Christ's Judgment Seat is 1Corinthians 4:2-5:

"It is required in stewards (managers of God's resources) **that one be found FAITHFUL. But with me it is a very small thing that I should be judged by you or by a human court. In fact, I do not even judge myself. For I know nothing against myself, yet I am not justified by this, but He who judges me is the Lord. Therefore judge nothing before the time** (of Judgment), **until the Lord comes, Who will bring to light the hidden things of darkness and reveal the counsels** (motives) **of the hearts. Then each one's praise** (reward) **will come from God."** This passage shows that the quality God is primarily looking for in us is FAITHFULNESS in how we have used the gifts, time, money, energy and opportunities that He has given us, saying: **"It is required that one be found faithful."** It also confirms that: **"He who judges me is the Lord Jesus."** In comparison the judgments of fallible man are of little importance.

Again we see that when God judges, He does not just look at the outward work, but the inner motive behind it, for: **"He will bring to light the hidden things of darkness and reveal the counsels** (secrets) **of the hearts."** The true nature and motive of every work will be revealed, as Jesus said in Luke 8:17: **"Nothing is secret that will not be revealed, nor anything hidden that will not be known and come to light."** Hebrews 4:13: **"There is no creature hidden from His sight, but all things are naked and open to the eyes of Him to Whom we must give account."** God sees and knows everything, even your heart, so you can't hide anything from Him. He will bring everything to the light at the time of this final Judgment: Then: **"each man's praise and reward will come to him from God"** (v5). Again we see that it is a judgment for REWARD, not condemnation, but nevertheless it will be a fearful thing to have our whole life exposed to the light in such a way. But the more we judge ourselves and deal with our bad attitudes now, the less painful and embarrassing it will be for us then.

*The 4th major Passage on the judgment of our works is 1Corinthians 3:10-15 where Paul compares our life to the construction of a building: **"According to the grace of God which was given to me, as a wise master builder I have laid the Foundation and another builds on it. But let each one take heed how he** builds on it. For no other Foundation can anyone lay than that which is already laid, which is Jesus Christ" (v10-11).

Every believer has already received the Foundation on which to build his life, which is the Lord Jesus and His righteousness. This speaks of our salvation by grace through faith in Christ alone. This Foundation was laid by those who preached the Gospel to us. Once we trust in Christ, our life is established on that Foundation. We cannot add anything to this Foundation by our works to secure it, for it is already perfect. This means our salvation is secure, independent of our works. We are not saved by our works, but by the perfect work of Jesus. We must not trust in or build on any other foundation. If we trust in our own works for our salvation then we are building on the wrong foundation and all our works will be worthless and be destroyed, as with the man who build his house on the sand in Matthew 7:24-27. The true Foundation has already been laid when we trusted Christ for our salvation. The issue now is how we build on this Foundation.

v12-14: "Now if anyone builds on this Foundation with gold, silver, precious stones, wood, hay, straw, each one's WORK will become clear; for the DAY (of Judgment) will declare it, because it will be revealed by FIRE; and the fire will test each one's WORK, of what sort (material) it is. If any-one's WORK which he has built on it endures, he will receive a REWARD."

We build upon this Foundation of faith in Christ with our works, and all our works fall into one of 2 categories, they are either: (1) "gold, silver and precious stones", or (2) "wood, hay and straw." The issue is, with what kind of material are we building? At the Judgment Seat, all our works will be tested by the FIRE of God, that burns up everything unworthy. This fire will sweep through the whole of our life, works and ministry, revealing the true nature of every work. It will be a quality test, revealing if it was done in the Lord or in the flesh.

What is the FIRE? Revelation 1:14 says about Jesus: "His head and hair were white like wool as white as snow and HIS EYES like a FLAME of FIRE." Jesus will look into our life with His eyes of flaming fire, with penetrating and consuming insight. His fire will go through our whole life, burning up anything that can be burnt, and what remains of our works, having endured this test of fire, will become the basis of our eternal reward. The nature of fire means this judgment will be thorough, sparing nothing inferior in quality. Only what is of God will remain. The 2 kinds of works will be distinguished by their ability to stand the test of fire. The gold, silver and precious stones will be able to pass through without being consumed. But the wood, hay and straw will be consumed by the fire. Everything of bad quality will be destroyed, for nothing of the flesh can endure in God's Kingdom.

The fire will also purify the works done in God, which please and honour Him. So while some works will be burnt up, other works will be refined and rewarded. One kind of work is indestructible and will endure forever, having eternal value. The other kind is combustible, and will not stand the test of the fire of God's holiness. Thus the QUALITY of our works is more important that the QUANTITY, as everything of inferior quality will be destroyed.

Paul concludes by saying: **"If anyone's WORK is burned, he will suffer loss** (of his reward); **but he himself will be saved, yet so as through fire"** (v15). This proves this is not a judgment of a man's soul but of his works. Even if all his works are burned up, his soul will still be saved, because his salvation does not stand on his works, but on the foundation of Christ and His work. Remember this judgment only concerns those who have already rested their faith on the foundation of Christ. So someone whose life's work is burnt up will suffer loss of reward, but not loss of salvation, which rests on Christ alone. This searching examination will be a very difficult but purifying experience, as the light of Jesus exposes our true motives and reveals our lost opportunities, where what we did for the Lord is measured against what we should have done. There will be weeping in regret before the Lord wipes away our tears.

So there is a future Day of Judgement when the quality of our WORKS will be tested by fire and rewarded. It is not to decide our salvation, but to reveal how well we have built on the foundation of our salvation in Christ. Thus it is a judgment of our works to determine our eternal reward.

The 3 symbols of good works.

*1. GOLD symbolises the DIVINE NATURE. When were born again we received the nature of Christ (the fruit of the Spirit) within our spirit. **"God's love has been poured out into our hearts by the Holy Spirit"** (Romans 5:5). So these are works produced from the nature of Christ in us, which we possess through the New Birth. As we walk in the Spirit and Love of God, we produce works of Gold.

On the other hand 1Corinthians 13:3 says: **"If I have not LOVE, what I do profits me nothing."** That is, it brings me no reward.

*2. SILVER in the Bible represents REDEMPTION, so works of silver are works done in grateful response to Christ's redemptive grace, causing us to want to serve Him. They spring from faith in what He has done for us.

*3. PRECIOUS STONES are works of obedience to the commands of God, motivated by a desire to please God and receive His praise and reward, rather than the praise of man. Are we doing what we are doing, because we want men or God to recognise and praise us? If we are just doing it for man's approval, we will stop when no one is looking. But if we do it unto the Lord, to please Him and position ourselves for greater eternal intimacy and glory then we will endure, for we know that He sees all, even if no one else knows. Speaking of the moment of our resurrection when we will be rewarded, 1Corinthians 15:58 says: **"Therefore, my beloved brethren, be steadfast, immovable, always abounding in the work of the Lord, knowing that your labour is not in vain in the Lord."** God sees everything you do and will reward it on that Day.

Both Jesus and Paul said that a defining mark of a believer is that he is motivated by the praise (reward) of God. John 5:44: **"How can you believe, when you receive glory from one another and you do not seek the glory that is from the one and only God?"** Romans 2:29: **"he is a Jew who is one inwardly; and circumcision is that which is of the heart, by the Spirit, not by the letter; and his praise** (reward) **is not from men, but from God."**

The 3 examples of dead works (opposites to the 3 kinds of good work).

*1. WOOD represents HUMAN FLESH

These are works done in our own strength and self-will, independently from God. They might look good to man, but are wood.

*2. HAY represents human merit, works done in self-righteousness.

*3. STRAW represents human opinion and wisdom, works that proceed purely from human reasoning, rather than obedience.

Thus we must examine: (1) The POWER energising our works: Are we depending on the power of the Spirit through prayer or on our natural strength (the flesh)? (2) The MOTIVE for our works: Is it love for God and man, from a desire to glorify God? (3) The OBEDIENCE of our works: Do they spring from God's will or are we just following traditions and rituals we happen to like? What a motivation to live for Him now, doing good works of gold, silver and precious stones, and not wasting your life turning out wood, hay and straw!

God sees everything we do and will reward us accordingly: **"God is not unjust to forget your work and labour of love which you have shown toward His Name, in that you have ministered to the saints, and do minister"** (Hebrews 6:10). God does not just see our outward obedience, for He also weighs the heart (Proverbs 21:2, 24:12). **"The Lord does not see as man sees; for man looks at the outward appearance, but the Lord looks at the heart"** (1Samuel 16:7, c.f. 2Corinthians 5:12). **"Whatever you do, do it heartily, as to the Lord and not to men, knowing that from the Lord you will receive the reward of the inheritance; for you serve the Lord Christ. But he who does wrong will be repaid for what he has done, and there is no partiality"** (Colossians 3:23-25). He is looking for willing obedience (from the heart) for it is the willing and obedient who will be rewarded and eat the good of the land (Isaiah 1:18). So walk in fellowship with God, keep short accounts with Him, for any time out of fellowship can't be rewarded. If you sin quickly confess it, and He will forgive and blot out your sin (1John 1:9).

The 5 Crowns

The eternal REWARDS at the Judgment Seat include 5 CROWNS. The Greek word used for these crowns is 'stephanos', denoting a victor's crown won by athletes in the OLYMPICS. The Crown is given at the end of the race. The Christian life is like running a RACE. So when we have completed our race in this life, we will stand before the Lord and receive our crowns. Jesus said in <u>Revelation 3:10-11</u>: **"I will keep you from the hour of trial which shall come upon the whole world, to test those who dwell on the earth. Behold, I am coming quickly! Hold fast what you have, that no one may take your CROWN!"** This is a promise of Jesus' imminent Return to deliver us from the Tribulation by the Rapture. He confirms that this is the time He will judge and reward us by giving us a crown. He uses this truth to call us to stay faithful, so we do not lose our crown. So God has a crown waiting for you if you are faithful. But if you are unfaithful, you will lose your reward and someone else will get your crown, for doing what you should have done. So hold fast to your calling, walk in fellowship with God, and be faithful.

Let us now look at the 5 kinds of CROWNS we could receive on that Day.

*1. The INCORRUPTIBLE CROWN for walking in the Spirit and not following after the flesh, for exercising self-control and denying yourself in this life, in order to live a Spirit-controlled life, for living in victory over the sin nature. This crown goes to the man who puts God first, rather than the corruptible things of this life. In 1Corinthians 9:24-27 Paul compares him to a disciplined athlete: **"Those who run in a race run to receive the prize** (reward). **Run so to obtain the prize** (the crown)."** We need to have the same determination as Olympic athletes to run our best race and gain the eternal prize at the end of it. **"All who compete** (in the games) **for it** (the prize) **exercise self control in all things"** (v25a). Athletes go into strict training. They cannot just eat and drink anything, and waste their time and expect to win. Their eye is on the prize, so they dedicate themselves to run their best possible race, avoiding distractions and not indulging in things that would slow them down. They exercise dominion over the flesh, denying themselves when necessary. They sacrifice their comfort in the present for a greater and lasting future glory and honour. **"They do it for a perishable CROWN, but we for an IMPERISHABLE** (or incorruptible) **CROWN"** (v25b). The fact that it is incorruptible confirms that this is an eternal reward.

If they exercise self-control and denial for a temporal crown and glory, how much more should we be willing to control our flesh to gain an eternal crown! Whenever we deny ourselves to put the Lord and His work first, or suffer and sacrifice in order to do His will, we are gaining a greater eternal crown of glory, which will far outweigh anything that we have given up in this life.

v26-27: **"Therefore I do not run aimlessly...I discipline my body and bring it into subjection (in order to run with the purpose of fulfilling God's will), lest when I have preached to others I myself should be disqualified."** He is not talking about losing his salvation, but being disqualified from receiving his crown. 2Timothy 2:5 agrees: **"If anyone competes in athletics, he is not CROWNED unless he competes according to the rules."** In those days athletes had to follow strict rules of diet and exercise in their training, otherwise they were disqualified, just as today's athletes are disqualified for taking drugs. Likewise, if we do not do things God's way, but take shortcuts, we will lose our crown.

Paul said that rather than being body-ruled, he brought his body into subjection, so that he would qualify for an eternal crown. To be body-ruled is to dissipate one's life in the various works of the flesh, listed in Galatians 5, including drinking, gambling, sexual sins, strife and worry. The result is disqualification. Paul knew that even he could lose his rewards by letting his flesh rule him. The answer is to be filled with the Spirit and walk in the Spirit every day. We can live a Spirit-filled life, rather than a flesh-controlled life. Then we will gain a Christ-like character, which God will crown with His glory.

Romans 8:1-5 describes how we can walk in the Spirit:

*1. Realise the Mercy of God in Christ has forgiven all your sins and made you right with God (v1): **"There is therefore now no condemnation to those who are in Christ Jesus."**

*2. Realise that your reborn spirit (indwelt) by the Spirit has already overcome sin and death (v2): **"For the law of the Spirit of life in Christ Jesus has made me free from the law of sin and death."**

*3. Realise that on the Cross, Jesus judged and overcame the power of your sin-nature, just as He defeated satan. Therefore although it is still present in your flesh and tries to pull you away from God, it has no authority over you, rather your spirit now has dominion over it, and so you are well able to walk according to the Spirit and overcome it, and so fulfil God's law of love in your life (v3,4): **"For what the law could not do in that it was weak through the flesh, God did by sending His own Son in the likeness of sinful flesh, on account of sin** (our sin-nature in the flesh): **He condemned** (judged and defeated) **sin in the flesh, that the righteous requirement of the law might be fulfilled in us who do not walk according to the flesh but according to the Spirit."**

*4. The key now to walk in the Spirit is simply to set your mind on the things of the Spirit, trusting in His Word and depending on His Power (v5): **"For those who live according to the flesh set their minds on the things of the flesh, but those who live according to the Spirit set their minds on the things of the Spirit."** Galatians 5:16: **"Walk in the spirit and you will not fulfil the lust of the flesh."** In v21 he warns the works of the flesh will cause us to lose our inheritance (rewards) in the Kingdom. Then in v22-23 he describes the qualities of the fruit of the spirit that will be formed in us as we walk in the Spirit. The God will reward such things in us with eternal glory. These things are already in our spirit, but we need to walk in them: **"If we live in the spirit** (that is, if our spirit is alive to God by being born again) **let us also walk in the spirit"** (v25).

*CROWN 2 - The 'Crown of Rejoicing' or 'Soul-winners Crown.'

1Thessalonians 2:19: **"What is our hope or joy or Crown of Rejoicing? Is it not even YOU in the Presence of our Lord Jesus Christ at His Coming?"** Likewise in Philippians 4:1 Paul called his disciples: **'my JOY and CROWN.'** Again this shows that the Judgment for Reward will happen at His Coming in the Rapture. This Crown of JOY consists of all people we have shared the Gospel with, won to the Lord and discipled: **"He who reaps receives wages, and gathers fruit for eternal life, that both he who sows and he who reaps may rejoice together"** (John 4:36). It will be given to all who fulfil the Great Commission. Thus it is also called the Soul-winner's Crown. We are often too careless and indifferent. God tells us to speak to someone, or pray for them, but we are too busy. We put it off and so souls are lost. It is not enough to be ready for Heaven. We need to take as many as possible with us. We should share our hope with them and invite them to come to Heaven with us.

*CROWN 3: The Crown of Righteousness.

At the end of his life, Paul said in 2Timothy 4:7-8: **"I have finished the race, I have kept the faith. Finally there is laid up for me the CROWN of RIGHTEOUSNESS which the Lord will give to me on that Day and not to me only, but also to all who have loved His Appearing."** This Crown is for those who keep the faith, who stay in the truth of God's Word, persevering to the end. They run their race, staying in the right lane, staying in faith and in the will of God, walking in the righteousness until the end. They do this because they love His Appearing. They are focused on the end of the race when they will see the Lord face to face and receive His reward. Paul knew that he was at the point of death and had stayed true to the very end, despite every pressure to turn aside. So he knew he had receive a Crown of Righteousness from the Lord 'on that Day', that is, on the Day of His Appearing to the Church in the Rapture.

In Philippians 3 Paul describes his single-minded attitude as he ran his race keeping his eyes on the prize (eternal reward). In v1-9 he made it clear he was not trust in his own righteousness for salvation but rather in Christ's righteousness. Then in v10-14 he describes his motivation as a Christian: **"that I may know Him** and the power of His resurrection, and the fellowship of His sufferings, being conformed to His death, if, by any means, I may attain to the out-resurrection from the dead (a glorious resurrection in which he would receive great reward) not that I have already attained or am already perfected; but I press on, that I may lay hold of that for which Christ Jesus has also laid hold of me. Brethren, I do not count myself to have apprehended; but one thing I do, forgetting those things which are behind and reaching forward to those things which are ahead, I press toward the goal for the prize of the upward call of God in Christ Jesus (his eternal reward of glory)."

*CROWN 4. The Crown of LIFE given for enduring trials and patience faithfully. James 1:12: "Blessed is the man who endures temptation (tests and trials), for when he has been approved, he will receive the Crown of Life which the Lord has promised to those who love Him" Rev 2:10: "Be faithful unto death and I will give you the CROWN of LIFE." Therefore this Crown is especially for martyrs, those willing to lay their lives down for Him. This Crown is for those who are FAITHFUL to the Lord under testing, who continue to love and trust Him, enduring through trials, temptations and persecutions. If we continue to love Him through sufferings we will receive the Crown of Life. Peter reminds Christians who are suffering for Christ that they will soon stand before His Judgment Seat, so they can rejoice, because they will be rewarded for their faithful witness. Jesus promised those who remained faithful to Him under persecution: "Blessed are you when men hate you, and when they exclude you, and revile you, and cast out your name as evil, for the Son of Man's sake. Rejoice in that day and leap for joy! For indeed your reward is great in Heaven, for in like manner their fathers did to the prophets" (Luke 6:22-23).

*CROWN 5. The Crown of Glory for faithful leadership and ministry. 1Peter 5:1-4: "The elders who are among you I exhort...as a partaker of the GLORY that will be revealed: Shepherd the flock of God which is among you, serving as overseers, not by compulsion but willingly, not for dishonest gain but eagerly; nor as being lords over those entrusted to you, but being examples to the flock; and when the Chief Shepherd appears, you will receive the CROWN of GLORY that does not fade away."

Jesus will give this Crown of Glory at His Appearing in the Rapture. It is an eternal reward, that 'does not fade away.' It is for elders, and by extension for all who are faithful in positions of leadership, whether in their family, job or ministry. It is for exercising authority in the right way, with a willing and enthusiastic heart, loving, serving and inspiring those under you, setting a good example to them. The greater your faithfulness, the greater your eternal glory.

The more God entrusts to you, the more opportunity you have to prove yourself faithful and qualify for a more glorious crown. But the other side of this is: **"Everyone to whom much is given, from him much will be required, and to whom much has been committed, of him they will ask the more"** (Luke 12:48). As James 3:1 says: **"Not many should desire to be Teachers, for they will face a stricter judgment."** Usually God starts by asking us to be faithful over small things. Be content to be faithful in what God has called you to do, and then as you prove yourself faithful over little, He will entrust you with more.

Luke 16:10: **"He who is faithful in a very little thing is faithful also in much; and he who is unrighteous in a very little thing is unrighteous also in much."** One example of a small thing in which God requires you to be faithful is your money: **"Therefore, if you have not been faithful in the use of unrighteous wealth, who will entrust the true riches to you?"** (v11). The true riches include greater anointing and spiritual authority, as well as eternal rewards. v12: **"And if you have not been faithful in the use of that which is another's, who will give you that which is your own?"** What you possess right now, including your money, is not really your own, because you cannot take it with you to heaven. It belongs to the Lord and is on temporary loan to you to manage. But if you are faithful to use it right, on that basis, He will give you an eternal reward, which will be that which is truly your own, for you will possess it forever.

In Matthew 19:27-30 Jesus described the rewards for those who sacrifice to fulfil God's call on their lives: **"Peter said to Him: "See, we have left all and followed You. Therefore what shall we have** (as a reward)**?" So Jesus said to them, "Assuredly I say to you, that in the regeneration, when the Son of Man sits on the throne of His glory, you who have followed Me will also sit on 12 thrones, judging the 12 tribes of Israel. Everyone who has left houses or brothers or sisters or father or mother or wife or children or lands, for My**

Name's sake, shall receive a 100-fold, and inherit (more) **eternal life** (as a reward). **But many who are first will be last, and the last first."**

This last phrase tells us there will be many surprises in that Day. Many outwardly successful ministers will get little reward, because much of what they did was flesh and for their own glory, whereas others who seemed insignificant will receive great reward, because they were faithful in prayer, and in what God told them to do. So do not be jealous of those who seem to be more successful than you. It is unwise to compare your self with others for we all have a different calling (2Corinthians 10:12). Just be faithful with what God gives you to do, and in the end what will matter is your eternal reward.

Our Eternal Reward consists of the Eternal Glory we will receive

Our present body cannot handle the glory God wants to reveal in us. Only a resurrected body can do this. After standing before the BEMA in our new body and having our works purified by fire, our reward will be given to us by a release of GLORY through us. The Bible says the righteous will shine like the STARS in Heaven (Matthew 13:43), but each star has a different glory. Daniel 12:2-3:
"Multitudes who sleep in the dust of the earth will awake to everlasting life... Those who are wise will shine like the brightness of the heavens, and those who lead many to righteousness like the STARS for ever and ever." When we are resurrected, we will receive a degree of glory shining out of us, which will differ according to our eternal reward.

1Corinthians 15:40-42 says that in our heavenly resurrection bodies we will be like stars shining with God's glory. Not only will our heavenly body express a far greater glory than our earthly body, but like the stars, we will have different degrees of glory from one another. **"There are heavenly bodies and earthly bodies, but the glory of the heavenly is one, and the glory of the earthly is another. There is one glory of the sun... another glory of the stars; for star differs from star in glory. So also is the resurrection of the dead."** This glory will shine out of us, appearing as white glorious ROBES. It will also crown us. These CROWNS represent our capacity to give glory to God. We will also be given different THRONES of authority to reign with Christ (Revelation 3:21).

The degree of authority and glory we will possess in eternity will be determined by our faithfulness in this life. This should motivates us to follow the

Lord Jesus with all our heart, realising that any moment we will stand before Him to give an account and receive a reward that will be ours forever.

The eternal issue is not just whether we make it to Heaven. It is also how close to God's throne we will be, and how much opportunity, ability and capacity we will have to serve, know, love and glorify God throughout eternity. Our reward in Heaven will be our eternal glory, joy and authority. Much of our reward will be to have a greater capacity for God's life and glory, to have more of God. This depends on how faithful we are in doing God's will in this life, and how much we allow God to mould our character by His Word, and how much we let God's Spirit of love control us and flow through us. The depth of our character determines the amount of GOD'S GLORY we will be able to contain and express in eternity. We will be rewarded with position and glory in Heaven according to the character we have developed and our good works in this life. So what we do now greatly AFFECTS our FUTURE ETERNAL GLORY!

As we walk in the Spirit, there will be sufferings, but as we trust and love God in them, He is able to work a greater glory in us, which will only be manifested when our body is resurrected. Romans 8:17-19: **"If children, then heirs; heirs of God and joint heirs with Christ, if indeed we suffer with Him, that we may also be glorified together. For I consider that the sufferings of this present time are not worthy to be compared with the glory, which shall be revealed in us. For the earnest expectation of the creation eagerly waits for the revealing of the sons of God."** The size of our eternal inheritance depends on our faithfulness to Him in this life. Yes, we will all be perfectly happy and joyful in heaven. All our cups will be full and overflowing with God's life. We will all be filled with God to our full capacity. We will all be shining as stars at maximum strength. However, we will all have different capacities for God's life, joy and glory, depending on how we live now. As we love, trust and obey God, even through suffering, then a greater capacity for His glory is being worked within us. So the depth of our character that we develop now by following Christ determines how much glory we can possess in eternity,

As 2Corinthians 4:17-18 says: **"Our light affliction, which is but for a moment, is working for us a far more exceeding and eternal weight of glory, while we do not look at the things which are seen, but at the things which are**

not seen (including our eternal rewards). **For the things which are seen are temporary, but the things which are not seen are eternal."**

Galatians 6:7-10 also uses eternal rewards to motivate us: **"Do not be deceived, God is not mocked; for whatever a man sows, that he will also reap. For he who sows to his flesh will of the flesh reap corruption, but he who sows to the Spirit will of the Spirit reap everlasting life** (a greater abundance of life in eternity). **And let us not grow weary while doing good, for in due season we shall reap if we do not lose heart. Therefore, as we have opportunity, let us do good to all, especially to those who are of the household of faith."**

The choice we face is like choosing £100 now, which just lasts for a week, or having £10,000 next month lasting forever! We can either live unto ourselves now, but have no future reward, or live for the Lord, and later receive a great reward that lasts forever. Of course, our greatest reward will be to know that we have pleased our Lord and helped people. It will be to hear Him say to us: "Well done, good and faithful servant."

Objections to teaching of rewards

Although the teaching of eternal rewards and their use to motive us is everywhere in the Bible, some have trouble with the teaching of rewards. So we need to deal with some objections. Some think that being motivated by rewards is selfish, that doing things for reward is an invalid motivation, we shouldn't need a reward to do what is right. But this displays a misunderstanding of the nature of eternal rewards. We need to understand that rewards are not like sweeties that are unrelated to what we have done. Rewards are intrinsic to our decisions in this life, not extrinsic and artificial. For example, if your desire, as expressed in your life, is seek the Lord and follow Him and be close to Him and know Him, then your reward will include the fulfilment of that desire, resulting in a special closeness to Him, with a greater opportunity to know Him eternally. If your desire and joy is to serve the Lord and you did that faithfully, then your reward will include greater opportunities to serve Him. If you have been faithful with the authority that He has given you in this life, then your reward will be to be entrusted with greater responsibility and authority to rule for Him. So if your motivation in this life is to glorify God, your reward will be to have a greater ability and glory with which to glorify Him throughout all eternity. Therefore rewards are not selfish, but involve receiving more to use to give to God and others.

Another objection is that rewards are a form of works-righteousness, whereby we earn blessings by our good works, which is incompatible with grace. Indeed it is important to understand that our rewards are not some kind of payment that God is obliged to make for our good works. They are not wages for our good works. Jesus tells a parable about this in Luke 17:7-10: **"Which of you, having a slave ploughing or tending sheep, will say to him when he has come in from the field: "Come immediately and sit down to eat." But will he not say to him: "Prepare something for me to eat, and properly clothe yourself and serve me while I eat and drink; and afterward you may eat and drink. He does not thank the slave because he did the things which were commanded, does he? So you too, when you do all the things, which are commanded you, say: "We are unworthy slaves; we have done only that which we ought to have done."** That is: 'We have only done our duty'. This word 'unworthy' also translated 'unprofitable', but literally means 'unworthy of any special reward.' Imagine in your job, you faithfully get to work on time and do your hours for a few days, and then you go to the boss and say: *'I have faithfully done my job the last 3 days. You owe me a bonus.'* It would be inappropriate to expect a special reward doing a job you ought to do. Likewise when we serve God with all our heart, we are only doing what we ought to do. He does not owe us any special reward, for He created and saved us. He has done everything for us.

Therefore His rewards are all manifestations of His Grace. They are not what He is obliged to pay us. We do not earn them by our works. So although He chooses to give us rewards for obeying Him, He does not have to do it, so they are all gifts of grace that He chooses to reward us with. Is this why the 24 elders cast their crowns of glory down at Christ's feet (Revelation 4:10)?

Rewards in the teaching of Jesus

The final answer to those who object to the idea of eternal rewards, is that our Lord Jesus clearly taught much on the subject of REWARDS and considered it a valid and holy motivation. For example, when Jesus encouraged us to build up our treasures in heaven, He was speaking about our eternal rewards.

Matthew 6:19-21: **"Do not lay up for yourselves treasures on earth, where moth and rust destroy and where thieves break in and steal; but lay up for yourselves treasures (rewards) in Heaven, where neither moth nor rust**

destroys and where thieves do not break in and steal (they are eternal). **For where your treasure is, there your heart will be also."** If your treasure is your eternal reward in heaven, then your heart will be focused on heaven rather than entangled in the things of this life. It will be set on pleasing God. There are rewards and blessings in this life, but they are temporal and will pass away. Therefore, our most important and valuable treasures are our eternal rewards, which will never pass away and which will never be taken from us. These will only be given to us after this life. So if we have got any sense, we will build up our treasure in heaven by loving and serving God. If our main treasure is in heaven then that is where our heart will be also. In other words, our main motivation and focus will be on pleasing God, and we will put His Kingdom first.

Do not be like the old miser, who at last went to his reward and presented himself at the Pearly Gates, when St.Peter greeted him and escorted him to his new abode. Walking past numerous elegant mansions finally they arrived at a dilapidated shack at the end of the street. Much taken aback, he asked, "Why am I left with a rundown shack when all of these others have fine mansions?" "Well" replied Peter: "we did the best we could with the money you sent us."

In Matthew 6:1-4, Jesus told us not to do our charitable deeds to be seen by man, for then man's praise will be your only reward. Rather do your good work in secret before God, and then He who sees in secret will reward you openly.

Although it will be a thorough and exacting judgment, God will also be generous, rewarding even the smallest act of kindness. Jesus said in Mark 9:41: **"Whoever gives you a cup of water to drink in My Name, because you belong to Christ, assuredly, I say to you, he will by no means lose his reward."** God sees every good work of faith and love you do for Him, and will reward you generously for it with an extra measure of eternal glory. His reward is eternal, and so has infinite value, for it will continue to be ours forever, so whatever we sacrifice will be as nothing in comparison.

The Parables of Jesus

A number of Jesus' parables give teaching on rewards, for example: The Parable of the Workers in the Vineyard (Matthew 20:1-16), which emphasises they are gifts of God's grace, the Parable of the Rich Fool (Luke 12:13-21), which encourages us to be rich toward God, the Parable of the Unjust Steward (Luke

16:1-13), the Parable of the Minas (Luke 19:11-27) and the Parable of the Talents (Matthew 25:13-30). These all emphasise that God will reward how faithful and generous we have been with the money, gifts, time and strengths He has given us.

The Parables of the Minas and Talents are similar to each other and both depict the Judgment of Christ's servants at His Judgment Seat. In both He compares Himself to a Master who goes away to a far country (Heaven), and entrusts some resources to His servants (believers) to use while He is away. In Luke He gave them all one Mina (100 days wages), whereas in Matthew He gave each of the servants a different amount of Talents (15 years wages). In some ways we have all been given the same New Birth, Holy Spirit, and Word of God. But in other ways we all have different talents, abilities, positions, opportunities and gifts. But everything we have is ultimately His. The question is, are we using what we have to serve Him and forward His Kingdom, or are we just putting it in the ground and not using the opportunities that God has given us? He told them to occupy themselves and use His money (resources) productively. Some were faithful to use that money, but others were lazy and hid it in the ground.

When the Master returned (as He will at the Rapture) He called them to stand before Him to give an account of what they had done with His money. He then rewarded them according to their faithfulness. To the faithful ones He said: **"'Well done, good and faithful servant; you have been faithful over a few things, I will make you ruler over many things. Enter into the joy of your Lord"** (Matthew 25:21,23). So our rewards include an increased joy in His Presence, much of which is through knowing we have pleased Him. What a wonderful thing it would be to receive the Lord's commendation! There are degrees of reward for different degrees of faithfulness for in Luke He made one ruler over 5 cities, and another ruler over 10 cities, since he was twice as fruitful with the same money. This shows that our rewards also include ruling authority.

The principle of being rewarded for our faithfulness, rather than for our gifts, is seen in Matthew, where the 2 servants, one with 5 talents and the other with 2 talents are both equally faithful in doubling their money, and so receive the same reward. Therefore we are not to compare ourselves with others, for we all have different gifts. We are just required to be faithful with what God has given us. One of Jesus' favourite sayings is: **"Many who are first** (in earthly position and gifting) **will be last** (in heavenly reward), **and the last** (in position and gifting) **first** (in reward)" (Matthew 19:30, 20:16, Mark 10:31, Luke 13:30).

Although our good works do not save us, they are nevertheless vitally important in determining our eternal position and state of glory. In this way, God honours us by making us responsible and accountable for our life.

The lazy servants who did nothing with the Master's money were rebuked and suffered a total loss of reward and future opportunities to serve. The Master said: **"Take the talent from him, and give it to him who has 10 talents. For to everyone who has** (faithfulness), **more** (reward) **will be given, and he will have abundance, but from him who does not have** (faithfulness)**, even what he has will be taken away"** (Matthew 25:28-29). They had to go to a place of relative outer darkness further from the throne compared to the brightness of glory where the faithful servants lived. How sad it would be to be rebuked for being a lazy and disobedient servant. These are the ones that do not serve God but just do things that work for their own personal ends, advantage and glory. They will be shown what they should have done and the opportunities they missed because of their unfaithfulness and as a result: **"There will be weeping and gnashing of teeth"** (Matthew 25:30), in great regret as they realise they have suffered loss of eternal reward (1Cor 3:15) and feel deeply how they have failed their Lord. However, in His love the Lord will then wipe away all their tears.

It is significant that the reason for the laziness of this wicked servant was that he did not believe in the doctrine of eternal rewards (Matthew 25:24-26), that the master would not be gracious and generous in rewarding his efforts, and so he did not bother to make an effort or to take a risk or even just to invest the money. Understanding the teaching of rewards is a vital motivation for our life of faith.

Having dealt with His servants (at the Rapture) the Master then slays all His enemies (Luke 19:27). This speaks of His judgment of unbelievers (rebels who do not want Him to reign over them) in the Tribulation and at His 2nd Coming.

Make sure you are ready for this great Day. Remember that at any moment you will have to stand before the Lord and give an account as He reveals your whole life to you and assesses it, before then giving you your eternal reward. Make sure you walk in fellowship with God every day, being zealous for good-works, prayerfully bearing fruit for God. Focus on judging yourself rather than everyone else. Walk in love, and for your own sake repent of those bad attitudes.

*Chapter 11: Life after Death

We now turn to study the future and ultimate destiny of individuals. These are the foundational doctrines of **"the Resurrection from the dead and Eternal Judgment"** of Hebrews 6:2. This subject of Life after Death is clearly of great importance to us, and the Bible has much to say about how God will deal with each individual as they cross the threshold of this life into eternity.

Ultimately God, the Judge of all, will divide all mankind into 2 groups with 2 very different destinies. Whereas the judgments of God in time, on the scene of human history, may be upon a whole group of people, such as a family or nation (Exodus 20:4-6, Jeremiah 32:18), God's eternal judgment, determining each person's eternal destiny, will be solely a judgment of that individual.

God says in Ezekiel 18:1-4: **"The Word of the Lord came to me again, saying: "What do you mean when you use this proverb concerning the Land of Israel, saying: 'The fathers have eaten sour grapes, and the children's teeth are set on edge'? "As I live" says the Lord God: "you shall no longer use this proverb in Israel. Behold, all souls are Mine; the soul of the father as well as the soul of the son is Mine; the soul who sins shall die."**

The people were excusing their sin by blaming their fathers, so that God could not hold them responsible. But God rejects this excuse. Although the sin and historical judgment of the fathers does affect their children, God warns them that He holds each man individually responsible for his own condition, so that God's eternal judgment of each man will be solely based on his choices, character and conduct, independent of his ancestors or nation (see also Jeremiah 31:29-30).

The judgment of each individual soul by which its destiny is settled for eternity is described again in v20: **"The soul who sins shall die. The son shall not bear the guilt of the father, nor the father bear the guilt of the son. The righteousness of the righteous shall be upon himself, and the wickedness of the wicked shall be upon himself."**

The Bible teaches mankind generally goes through 3 Phases of Existence:

(1) The first Phase is THIS LIFE, where our spirit lives in a mortal (death-doomed) body. We are a spirit, we have a soul, and we live in a body. This phase ends at physical death when our spirit-soul leaves our body.

(2) The 2nd Phase is called the INTERMEDIATE STATE. When our spirit lays aside our body at death we continue to exist, but as a disembodied spirit. This is not how God designed us to be so this is just a temporary state in the interval between our death and resurrection.

(3) The 3rd and final Phase is the ETERNAL STATE, which starts at our physical resurrection, when our spirit puts on an immortal resurrection body.

An exception to this is those believers who are alive at the Rapture and at the end of the Millennium will go direct from Phase 1 to Phase 3, without experiencing the Intermediate State.

The Immortality of the Soul

The Bible teaches that after death the invisible part of man, his spirit and soul, will live on independently from his body. This is called the Immortality of the Soul. Although the body is mortal (that is, subject to death), because it is made from the earth, which came under the curse, man's spirit is immortal, because its origin is the breath of God.

Genesis 2:7 describes the creation of the first man: **"The Lord formed man of the dust of the ground** (his BODY) **and breathed into his nostrils the breath of life** (his SPIRIT) **and man became a living SOUL."** When the spirit was breathed into the body they fused and the result was a living soul or personality. Notice the material and immaterial parts of man are clearly distinguished. The body is dust that dies, but the spirit is made from God's breath, which can't die. Therefore the spirit-soul lives on after the death of the body.

In fact, physical death is simply the separation of the spirit from the body, when the body is no longer able to house the spirit. Physical death is the state of the body after the spirit has left, as James 2:26 says: **"the body without the spirit is dead."** Jesus said in Matthew 10:28: **"Fear not them who kill the body, but cannot kill the soul."** So our soul is not subject to death. It is not killed when our body is killed. It continues to exist.

The Bible speaks of the outward and the inward man. The man on the inside (the spirit-man) is the real us. The outer man or body is just the clothing of the spirit, allowing the inner-man to act and express itself in this world. The outward man is mortal, but the inward man is immortal. 2Corinthians 4:16-18: **"Even though our outward man is perishing, yet the inward man is being renewed day by day."** Even if the body decays and dies, the inward man continues to exist. **"For our light affliction, which is but for a moment, is working for us a far more exceeding and eternal weight of glory, while we do not look at the things which are seen, but at the things which are not seen. For the things which are seen** (including our body) **are temporary, but the things which are not seen** (including our spirit, our inward man) **are eternal."**

Both the Greeks and the Hebrews believed this, but some modern cults reject this and teach the false doctrine of Soul Sleep. They say that our soul cannot exist apart from our body, so at death it sleeps or becomes unconscious, and will only live again at the resurrection. But when the Bible talks about believers who have died as being asleep, it is describing the state of their bodies, not their souls. The word 'death' gives the impression of permanence, so the language of 'sleep' is used to remind us that physical death is just a temporary condition, for the Lord will cause these dead bodies to wake up again on the resurrection morning. In our study of the Intermediate State, we will see many scriptures that show that when both believers and unbelievers die, they continue to exist as spirits and are fully conscious. First, let us note some scriptures that declare that a believer's spirit continues to live on after death.

In the Old Testament, it often says that when someone died he was **'gathered to his people'** like Abraham in Genesis 25:8, or that **'he went to his fathers'**. In 1Samuel 12:23 David said when his baby son had died: **"I shall go to him, but he will not return to me."** The immortality of the soul is confirmed by Psalm 22:26: **"Your heart shall live forever"**, and Ecclesiastes 3:11: **"He has put eternity in their hearts."** Psalm 73:23-24 expresses the believers' hope: **"I am continually with You. You have taken hold of my right hand. With Your counsel You will guide me, and afterward receive me to glory."**

1Peter 3:4 says we should adorn ourselves with the qualities of: **"the hidden man of the heart, with the incorruptible beauty of a gentle and quiet spirit."**

The hidden invisible man of the heart is our reborn human spirit, which is incorruptible and indestructible. 1Peter 1:23 explains why, saying that our spirit has: **"been born again, not of corruptible seed, but incorruptible, through the word of God which lives and abides forever."**

Through the New Birth, believers are said to now possess everlasting life. Therefore we do not cease to exist at death, or go into an unconscious soul-sleep. John 3:16: **"whoever believes in the Son has eternal life."** John 5:24: **"whoever hears My Word and believes Him Who sent Me has** (possesses) **eternal life** (in his reborn spirit)." John 6:47: **"He who believes in Me has eternal life."**

John 11:25,26: **"(1) I AM the Resurrection** (for the body) **and (2) the Life** (for the spirit)**: he who believes in Me, though (1) he were** (physically) **dead yet shall he live** (by the resurrection of his body)**, and (2) whoever lives and believes in Me shall NEVER DIE** (his spirit will never die because it has eternal life)." Clearly this is not saying that our body will never die physically, but that our spirit will never die, for when we believe in Christ we receive God's eternal life into our spirit. This proves that our spirit continues to live on forever in God's Presence, even after our body has died, just as Romans 8:38-39 promises us that even death will not separate believers from the love of God in Christ.

Most Jews of Jesus' time believed in life after death, except the Sadducees, as Acts 23:8 says: **"the Sadducees say that there is no resurrection, nor an angel, nor a SPIRIT, but the Pharisees acknowledge them all."** So they did not believe man can live on as a spirit after death. Their belief contradicted the prophets, but they only accepted the Torah (the first 5 books of Moses) as God's Word. So, in Matthew 22:31-32, Jesus proved they were wrong from Exodus: **"Have you not read what was spoken to you by God, saying: 'I AM the God of Abraham, Isaac and Jacob'? God is not the God of the dead but of the living."** So many years after their death, Abraham, Isaac and Jacob were still alive in spirit before God. Luke 20:38 confirms this by adding: **"for ALL live unto Him** (even those who have died)."

So when we die physically we don't cease existing, because we are in essence a spirit, created in the image of God who is a Spirit. Our body is simply our earth-suit. The Bible compares it to clothing that we take off at the end of the day. Although in the Intermediate State we will be unclothed for a time, we will continue to be conscious, until we are clothed with an eternal body. The Bible also compares our present body with a tent, a temporary dwelling place, that we will lay aside one day, and then later in the resurrection we will receive a permanent house from God.

The Judgment at Death

The Bible also teaches that all mankind is divided into two groups, with two different eternal destinies, which is decided at death, when a permanent separation between the righteous and unrighteous takes place. **The condition of each soul at death will determine its destiny for eternity.** Of course we know it happens that someone can die and then be resuscitated, so we are talking about the moment when his body finally dies.

Ecclesiastes 11:3: **"Whether a tree falls toward the south or toward the north, wherever the tree falls, there it lies."** The tree falling represents a man dying. The position in which he falls in death, whether toward sin or toward God, decides the position he will be in forever. This is a very serious warning for every person is just a breath, a heartbeat away from stepping into eternity.

Are you ready for Eternity? Only now while you are alive do you have the chance to get right with God. After that your eternity is fixed, as God warns in Revelation 22:11, His judgment on you will be: **"He who is unrighteous, let him be unrighteous still, and he who is filthy, let him be filthy still, and he who is righteous -- let him be righteous still."** Every man either dies under condemnation or under grace, either **'in his sins'** or **'in the Lord.'** Man's problem is that he is born in a state of sin in Adam and so is automatically guilty. This is why Jesus said He did not come to condemn the world, for it was already condemned. Jesus came to save us through His perfect life, sacrificial death and victorious resurrection. He is man's only hope of salvation for there is salvation in no other Name. Each person has a choice to accept or reject Christ and His salvation. Those who trust in Christ are put into Christ and receive His salvation, and so they will die in the Lord. But those who reject Him continue to be in their sins and will eventually die in their sins and be lost forever. In John 8:24, Jesus said: **"you will die in your sins; for if you do not believe that I AM, you will die in your sins."** He is saying that it is essential to believe in the Deity of Christ to be saved. You must not just know Jesus as a good man, but as the God-man. The Christian confession of faith which is an evidence of our salvation is 'Jesus is Lord' (Romans 10:9), that is, He is God, for when Romans 10:13 says: **"All who call upon the Lord** (Jesus) **shall be saved",** this is a quote from Joel 2:32, where 'the Lord' translates the Divine Name 'Yahweh' or 'Yehovah'. Thus to be saved we must call upon and confess Jesus as God, the Son of God.

Those who receive Christ are baptised into Christ and His righteousness is imputed to us as a free-gift, and on that basis every blessing is ours, including eternal life in the Presence of God. That is why Revelation 14:13 says: **"Blessed are the dead who die IN THE LORD."** They will be eternally blessed.

Thus the first Stage of man's eternal judgment happens immediately after his death. If he dies in his sins in a state of unrighteousness then he goes down he goes down into Hades, to a place of torments (punishment), but if he dies in the Lord, in a state of righteousness, he goes up to be with the Lord in heaven.

The classic verse on this is Hebrews 9:27-28: **"As it is appointed for men to DIE once, but AFTER THIS the JUDGMENT, so Christ was offered once to bear the sins of many. To those who eagerly wait for Him He will appear a second time, apart from sin, for salvation."** God has appointed that man's Judgment takes place after death. His eternal judgment already starts from the moment of his death. This means when his spirit leaves his body, he faces a judicial sentencing from God. If he dies in his sins, he is found guilty and sent to a place of punishment in Hades. Then later, at his resurrection, he will stand before God a 2nd time to face his final sentencing and dismissal into the Lake of Fire, the degree of his punishment determined by his sins (Revelation 20:11-15).

However, Christ has made another eternal destiny possible for man. For in the Person of Christ, God became a man and identified with us, entering into the full human experience of life and death. Just as men die once, so Christ died once, but unlike all others He died as a righteous man, having lived a perfect life. This qualified Him to bear our sins in His death and bear the judgment that was due to fall upon us when we died, because of our sins. This means that those who trust in Christ and accept Him as their substitute sin-bearer, will not face a judgment of condemnation when they die, for Jesus has taken the sting of death (sin) for us. Thus when those who die in Christ face the judgment that comes immediately after death they are found to be forgiven and righteous through Christ and as a result go up to heaven. Now those who have died in Christ along with those who are still living in Him are eagerly waiting for His Return, when He will accomplish the 2nd Stage of our Eternal Judgment at our rapture and resurrection. The 2nd time He comes it will not be to save us from our sins, because He has already accomplished that, once for all, but rather to SAVE (manifest His salvation in) our bodies. He will resurrect the dead in Christ and rapture those in Christ who are still alive. We will then stand before His Judgment Seat, not for eternal condemnation but for eternal reward, the degree of which is determined by our works. The corresponding release of glory in and through our resurrection bodies at this time will releases us into our final eternal state.

This full salvation through Christ is described in 1Corinthians 15:54-58 (see Hosea 13:14, Isaiah 25:8): **"So when this corruptible has put on incorruption, and this mortal has put on immortality, then shall be brought to pass the saying that is written: "Death is swallowed up in victory. O Death, where is your sting? O Hades, where is your victory?" The sting of death is sin, and the strength of sin is the law.** (In His 1st Coming, Jesus took the sting of death for us, releasing us from condemnation under God's Law, so when we die we don't go to a place of punishment but to Heaven, so Hades has no victory over us. So although we still die, the sting of death has been removed - sin and its eternal judgment upon death. Moreover death itself will be completely defeated when we are resurrected). **But thanks be to God, who gives us the victory** (over Death and Hades) **through our Lord Jesus Christ. Therefore, my beloved brethren, be steadfast, immovable, always abounding in the work of the Lord, knowing that your labour is not in vain in the Lord** (this speaks of the eternal rewards we will receive at the Judgement Seat of Christ after our resurrection)**."**

Ecclesiastes 12:7 says that at death: **"the dust** (body) **will return to the earth as it was, and the spirit will return to God who gave it."** So when the spirit is released from the body it briefly comes before God, who then sends it to one of two locations - either a place of Punishment or a place of blessing called Paradise. At this point his eternal destiny is fixed. It is too late to repent.

This Intermediate State, as a disembodied spirit, is just temporary, until the time when God will reunite man's spirit with his body in the resurrection, in which he will stand before God for the 2nd and final Stage of His Eternal Judgment, when he will be released into his Eternal State.

(1) He who **'dies in his sins'** is in a state of unrighteousness, as He has not trusted in Christ and received His forgiveness and righteousness, and so will be judged as such, and sent to a place of initial punishment, to await his resurrection unto his Final Eternal Judgment. But (2) He who **'dies in the Lord'** is the one who has received Christ, and so is IN CHRIST, and has been clothed in His righteousness. Therefore He has been forgiven and declared righteous, and has already passed from death to life. **"Therefore there is no condemnation for those who are in Christ"** (Romans 8:1). So he is immediately released to go to Paradise to await his resurrection, when he will stand before the Judgment Seat of Christ where he'll receive his eternal rewards, releasing Him into his eternal state.

So, as with our court-system, Eternal Judgment is in 2 Stages.

Stage 1 happens immediately after death. This judgment determines a man's guilt or innocence, which depends on whether he has put their faith in Christ. At this point his eternal destiny is fixed, decided and determined forever, whether eternal life in heaven or eternal death in hell. Thus at death God separates people into 2 groups: the righteous and the unrighteous. The righteous spirits go up to Paradise, but the wicked go down to a place of punishment under the earth, called Hades, which is a holding cell, where they are kept until their final sentencing. For both groups it is a period of waiting (the Intermediate State between death and resurrection) until the time of the 2nd Stage of their Eternal Judgment.

Stage 2 happens immediately after a man's physical resurrection. The righteous will stand before the Judgment Seat of Christ to be judged for reward, and released into their eternal state of glory. Later, the wicked will stand before the Great White Throne for their final sentencing and dismissal to their eternal state and place of punishment, called 'Gehenna' or the Lake of Fire.

When the righteous are resurrected they will stand before the Judgment Seat of Christ, where they will be judged according to their works, to determine their degree of eternal rewards of glory, which depends on their faithfulness to God in this life. Then as that glory will be released in them, they will enter their eternal state. When the unrighteous are resurrected, they will stand before the Great White Throne for their final sentencing. This Judgment is not to decide their guilt or innocence, for that was already decided at Stage 1. In this Judgment, they will be judged according to their works, to determine the degree of their everlasting punishment, which depends on the degree of their rebellion against God and how much light they had rejected in this life. Then they will be sent into the Lake of Fire, where they will be forever. This is their final eternal state.

So generally the 1st Stage of Eternal Judgment (to determine guilt or innocence) is at the time of death, and the 2nd Stage (to determine the degree of reward or punishment) is at the time of resurrection. Whereas the first Stage is a private judgment, the 2nd Stage is public, when God will publicly reveal and review every man's works. So far in our study of man's ultimate destiny we've seen every man has 2 appointments with God that he can't miss, in which his eternal future is determined. First is his appointment with death (if the Lord doesn't come first). Immediately after his death is a judgment that determines if he goes up to Heaven or down to Hades. This seals him into a state of eternal salvation or condemnation. The 2nd appointment is immediately after his resurrection when he faces a judgment that decides the degree of his eternal reward or punishment. At this point he enters into his final eternal state.

The Intermediate State

After death a man enters the next phase of his existence, called the Intermediate State, which is the time between his death and resurrection. After leaving his body, he continues to exist as a disembodied spirit, and goes to one of 2 places depending whether he dies 'in the Lord' or 'in his sins.' God created man to exist in a body and to express himself through a body, so this is not God's ideal for man (as the Greeks believed), but just a temporary State. It is just a waiting time after death until the ordained time for the resurrection of the body.

First we will gather together all the Biblical data on the Intermediate State, focusing mainly on the situation before Jesus' resurrection. Both the Greeks and Hebrews believed that after death the spirits of men went to a special place under the earth. The Hebrews called this place of departed spirits: 'Sheol', and the Greeks called it 'Hades', so the Greek translations of the Old Testament always translate 'Sheol' as 'Hades.' While Psalm 16:10 used the term 'Sheol', when this verse is quoted in Acts 2:27,31 it is called 'Hades.' Psalm 16 predicted that at His death Messiah's soul would go to Sheol for a short time, before being raised from the dead. In Acts 2 Peter claimed this was fulfilled by Jesus in Hades. So both HADES and SHEOL are names for the same place - the invisible realm under the earth, a place of confinement, where departed spirits must wait until the time of their resurrection and final judgment, when they will be released into their final and eternal state. As men's bodies went into the grave at death, so men's souls descended to Hades in the heart of the earth, a holding cell for the dead, separated from the land of the living, and from heaven. Some say that Sheol or Hades are simply another words for the physical grave, and sadly translations often make this mistake. But a study of the 64 references in the Old Testament to Sheol and the 10 references to Hades in the New Testament proves that this is impossible.

We can make 9 deductions from these references to illustrate this:

(1) This was a place where both the righteous and the unsaved went at death (Psalm 89:48, Luke 16:19-31). The righteous expected to go down to Sheol in Genesis 37:35, 42:38, 44:29,31; Job 14:13, Psalm 16:10, Jonah 2:2. The unrighteous in Numbers 16:30,33, Job 24:19, Psalm 9:17, 49:14, Ezekiel 32:21. All peoples went to Sheol at their death (Habakkuk 2:5), so that it was continually enlarging itself to take in more people (Proverbs 27:20, Isaiah 5:14).

(2) It was a far worse experience for the unbelievers than for the believers (Job 24:19, Psalm 9:17, 49:14, Matthew 11:23, Luke 10:15, 16:19-31). Unbelievers are in a place of torment (punishment) and fire: **"A fire is kindled in My anger, and shall burn to the Lowest Hell** (Sheol)" (Deuteronomy 32:22). Likewise, in Luke 16:23 the rich man found himself: **"in Torments in Hades."** He said: **"I am tormented in this flame"** (v24).

(3) Sheol had different levels or compartments. For example, there are references to 'the lowest Sheol' (Deuteronomy 32:22, Psalm 86:13). Hades has at least 3 parts (Luke 16:19-31). Unbelievers went to a place called 'Torments' (Luke 16:23), also called in Hebrew 'Abaddon' (meaning Destruction). Believers went to a place called 'Abraham's Bosom' (Luke 16:22) or 'Paradise' (Luke 23:43). There was also a Great Gulf fixed between these 2 parts (Luke 16:26) called the 'Abyss' or 'Bottomless Pit', the prison for fallen angels and demons. Lucifer (satan) will be **"brought down to Sheol, to the lowest depths of the Pit"** (Isaiah 14:15). This will happen when He is cast into the Bottomless Pit and kept locked up there for 1000 years (Revelation 20:2-3).

(4) Its direction was always downward, for men always went DOWN to Sheol or Hades (Genesis 37:35, 42:38, 44:29,31, Numbers 16:30,33, 1Samuel 2:6, 1Kings 2:6,9, Job 7:9, 11:8, 17:16, 21:13, Psalm 30:3, Proverbs 5:5, 7:27, 15:24, Isaiah 5:14, 14:9, Ezekiel 32:21, Amos 9:2, Matthew 11:23, Luke 10:15).

(5) Sheol is a place of consciousness and those who go there are still fully conscious (Isaiah 14:9-10, Jonah 2:2, Luke 16:19-31). Though disembodied, they still experience stimuli and are aware of their location, surroundings, history and situation. They have feelings and can express themselves. References to their lack of knowledge (Ecclesiastes 9:5,10) refers to their ignorance of what is happening on the earth, as they now live in a place of separation, unable to communicate with those on earth, participate in or influence events there (v6). Even for believers it is a place of waiting for the next Stage of your existence, not a place where you can work usefully towards fulfilling your plans and vision (v10).

(6) Even men who were not buried in a grave were said to go to Sheol. One example is the antichrist (the final king of Babylon) in Isaiah 14, killed by Jesus at His 2nd Coming (2Thessalonians 2:8). The arrival of his soul in the underworld is in v4-11. v9-11 describes the response of the inhabitants of Sheol to his arrival confirming that the souls there are still conscious: **"Hell** (Sheol,) **from beneath is excited about you, to meet you at your coming. It stirs up the dead for you, all the chief ones of the earth; it has raised up from their thrones, all the kings of the nations. They all shall speak and say to you: 'Have you also become as weak as we? Have you become like us? Your pomp is brought down to Sheol, and the sound of your stringed instruments; the maggot is spread under you, and worms cover you** (your body)." (People speaking from the midst of Sheol is also recorded in Jonah 2:2 and Ezekiel 32:21). Then v12-14 is a flashback describing the rebellion of satan, his master, when God cast him down to the earth. Since antichrist submitted himself to satan, he must share the same punishment. This prophecy of satan's fall ends with the prediction that satan will be cast into Sheol in v15: **"you will be brought down to Sheol, to the lowest depths of the Pit"**, and indeed this happens at this time (soon after the 2nd Coming). Then in v16-21 the fate of his dead body is described. Many will gaze upon his body in disbelief that such a powerful man has died (v16-17). While the bodies of other kings rest in glorious tombs (v18), he is just part of a heap of bodies trampled underfoot (v19). He will not even get a burial (v20). The reason for this is that soon after his soul will taken from Sheol for his resurrection and casting into the Lake of Fire (Revelation 19:20-21). Thus although he does not go into a grave, he is described as going into Sheol, confirming that Sheol is not the Grave.

(7)   Sheol-Hades is a temporary place not an eternal one, for at the end of time it will be thrown into the Lake of Fire (Revelation 20:11-15).

(8) 'Sheol' (also called 'the Pit' in the Old Testament) is under God's jurisdiction (Job 26:6, Psalm 139:8, 1Samuel 2:6, Deuteronomy 32:22, Proverbs 15:11, Amos 9:2). Those who enter Sheol by death, can only return to the realm of the living by God's permission, as when Samuel's spirit rose up out of Sheol in 1Samuel 28, described as 'a spirit rising out of the earth' (v13). This strange event in 1Samuel 28:3-19 requires further comment. Saul goes to a witch to see if she can bring up the soul of Samuel from Sheol. Now spiritualist mediums do not have this kind of power. What normally happens is that they contact demons (familiar spirits) who impersonate the dead (for they have some knowledge of them). This is why the Bible forbids such occult practices in Deuteronomy 18:10-12, including: **"a medium, or a spiritist, or one who calls up the dead, for all who do these things are an abomination to the Lord."** But in this case God allows the real Samuel to come up, to the total surprise of the witch, showing she had nothing to do with it. God allowed Samuel to come up to pronounce His judgment on Saul, which was hastened by this act of occultism in disobedience to God's Command. There is no hint in the text that this was a demon, and both v15 and v16 name Samuel as the one speaking to Saul. The words of Samuel also confirm this. Samuel was not resurrected from the dead, but it was simply his immaterial part that came up from Sheol. The witch could see him but Saul couldn't: **"The king said to her, "Do not be afraid. What did you see?" And the woman said to Saul: "I saw a spirit ASCENDING out of the earth." So he said to her: "What is his form?" And she said: "An old man is coming up, and he is covered with a mantle." And Saul perceived that it was Samuel, and he stooped with his face to the ground and bowed down. Now Samuel said to Saul: "Why have you disturbed me by bringing me UP?"** (v13-15). So Samuel is seen as being fully conscious after his own death confirming the immortality of the soul. Moreover he came up from a place under the earth (from Sheol).

(9) Escape from the prison of Sheol requires the payment of a ransom, which God promises to do. Psalm 49:15: **"God will redeem my soul from the power of Sheol, for He shall receive me."** Hosea 13:14: **"I will ransom them from the power of Sheol."** Jesus paid this ransom with His blood on the Cross, enabling Him to release all the Old Testament saints from Hades, as we shall see. Because the ransom has now been paid the Church Age saints do not go down into

Hades when they die, but up to Heaven, fulfilling the promise of Jesus in Matthew 16:18 that the Gates of Hell (Hades) would not prevail against His Church.

So Sheol (the location of departed souls) is not the same as the Grave (the location of the dead body). In its first occurrence, Jacob says: **"I shall go down into SHEOL to my son** (Joseph) **in mourning"** (Genesis 37:35). Believing Joseph to be dead Jacob assumes Joseph is still conscious and still his son, and that when he dies he will go DOWN to Sheol and join him there. This statement does not make good sense if instead it is translated as 'Grave' as many translations have it. Hebrew has a different word for 'Grave' = 'Kever.' This is not synonymous with Sheol. This is evident in Isaiah 14, which gives 2 opposing descriptions of what happens to a particular man who has died in relation to Sheol and the Grave, showing they cannot be the same thing. He (his soul) goes down to Sheol (v9,11,15), but as a punishment his body is not given a burial in a Grave (v19,20). The translators of the Septuagint understood that Sheol is not the Grave, for they NEVER translated 'Sheol' into Greek as 'mneema' (grave); but always always as 'Hades' which is the Greek term for the invisible underworld where departed spirits go. Psalm 16:10 says the SOUL goes to Sheol, in contrast to the body in the Grave. Its location is the: **"lower parts of the earth"** (Psalm 63:9, Isaiah 44:23, Ezekiel 26:20, 31:14,16,18, 32:18,24, Ephesians 4:9), beneath or under the earth (Isaiah14:9, Philippians 2:10), **"in the heart of the earth"** (Matthew 12:40). By contrast sepulchres were often above the earth or in caves. Thus Sheol, below the earth, was used as the opposite of Heaven, above the earth (Psalm 139:8).

All 3 realms are seen in <u>Philippians 2:10</u> as being populated, and under the dominion of Jesus: **"at the Name of Jesus every knee should bow, of those in heaven, and of those on earth, and of those under the earth."** Further confirmation that 'kever' (burial place) is different from 'Sheol' is that 'kever' can be pluralised ('graves'), but Sheol is never pluralised. Also a grave is located at a specific site; but Sheol is never localised, but wherever a man dies he goes to Sheol, even if he has no grave. One can own, purchase or sell a grave (Genesis 23:4-20); but Sheol is never spoken of this way. Bodies are unconscious in the grave; but people in Sheol are conscious (Isaiah 14:4-7; 44:23; Ezekiel 31:16; 32:21; Luke 16:19-31). Moreover the verb 'kebar' (to bury the body) is always associated with 'kever' but never used of 'Sheol' (Genesis 23:4,6,9,19,20; 49:30,

31). So there is a consistent distinction between the two. All references to Sheol-Hades agree with the fact that this is a real place under the earth, where departed spirits go at death.

Some translations use the English word HELL to translate HADES, especially when referring to the compartment for unbelievers, which is the temporal place of punishment for the souls in the Intermediate State. What is confusing is that HELL is also used to translate another Greek word GEHENNA, which refers to the Lake of Fire, which is the eternal place of punishment for the bodies and souls of unbelievers. So HELL can either refer to the temporary place of punishment of souls in the Intermediate State, or to the final place of punishment of bodies and souls in the Eternal State.

So whereas the GRAVE is the temporary location of the body, SHEOL-HADES is the temporary place of confinement of the soul, where men await final judgment and release into their final destiny. So the body went to the grave and the soul went to Hades. The body without the spirit is under the power of Death, and the spirit without the body is under the power of Hades. Death demands the body, while Hades demands the soul. Because of the Fall, all men came under the power of DEATH and HADES, from which there was no escape.

That's why Death and Hades are often mentioned together in Scripture. Psalm 55:15: **"Let DEATH come deceitfully upon them; let them go down alive to SHEOL."** Revelation 6:8 describes the 4th Horseman of the Apocalypse as DEATH, going forth to kill men's bodies, with HADES following behind to capture their departed souls: **"Behold, a pale horse. And the name of him who sat on it was DEATH, and HADES followed with him. And power was given to them over 1/4 of the earth, to kill..."** Christ has triumphed over this deadly duo, which is why the risen Christ could announce: **"I have the keys of HADES and of DEATH"** (Revelation 1:18). 1Corinthians 15:55 (Hosea 13:14) describes Christ's final Victory over them both: **"O DEATH, where is your sting? O HADES, where is your victory?"** Therefore DEATH and HADES only have a temporary dominion over men's bodies and souls, for they are both cast into the Lake of Fire at the end of time, Revelation 20:13-14: **"DEATH and HADES delivered up the dead who were in them. And they were judged, each one according to his works. Then DEATH and HADES were cast into the Lake of Fire."** Therefore Hades is just a temporary place for departed souls, for they will eventually be released from it to stand resurrected before the Great White Throne, after which sent into their eternal home, the Lake of Fire.

Whenever people in the Intermediate State are described they appear as spirit-souls without bodies. In 1Samuel 28 the immaterial part of Samuel came up from Sheol and appeared as a spirit (v13), and he looked like he did when he was alive, because he was recognisable (v14). Thus a man's spirit-soul has the same appearance as his body. This is confirmed by the account in Luke 16:19-31 where the rich man, Lazarus and Abraham have left their bodies but are still recognisable as themselves in their Intermediate State. The appearance of Moses in the Transfiguration (Matt 17:3, Mark 9:4, Luke 9:30-31) is another example of someone who has died physically and is in the Intermediate State, yet is still alive and conscious in his spirit-soul, and appears as he did when he was in the flesh.

The New Testament reveals that a major change took place at the Resurrection of Christ. So first we'll study the situation BEFORE the Resurrection. Although at death everyone went to Sheol-Hades, the believers went to a different compartment than the unbelievers. The righteous were carried by angels to a place of conscious bliss called Paradise or Abraham's Bosom, but the wicked went to a place of punishment called Torments. For example in Luke 23:43, Jesus said to the believing thief on the Cross: **"Truly I say to you today: "You will be with Me in Paradise."** Paradise means the Palace Garden of a king, an enclosed walled orchard, like the Garden of Eden. Jesus assured him that as a believer he'd received God's forgiveness, and so was saved from going to a place of punishment after death, but instead he would go to Paradise, a place of blessing, where he would soon meet Jesus again. Thus Jesus spoke of Paradise as a real place.

Luke 16 - The Rich Man and Lazarus

The clearest description of Hades before the resurrection is given by Jesus in Luke 16, in the story of the Rich Man and Lazarus. Here Jesus clearly taught that men's souls live beyond death and continue to be conscious. He also described in detail what the Intermediate State in Hades was like for both believers and unbelievers. This passage of scripture totally contradicts soul-sleep, so those who teach soul-sleep try to explain it away as a Parable. But Jesus never said it was a Parable. In fact, it reads like a true story. And even if it was a Parable, it changes nothing for all the Parables of Jesus are true to real-life, teaching spiritual truths by comparing them to natural realities. They are not mythical stories. Therefore, if souls do not consciously exist after death, then in Luke 16:19-31, Jesus would be deceiving us about life after death.

Luke 16:19-23: **"There was a certain rich man who was clothed in purple and fine linen and fared sumptuously every day. But there was a certain beggar named Lazarus, full of sores, who was laid at his gate, desiring to be fed with the crumbs which fell from the rich man's table. Moreover the dogs came and licked his sores. So it was that the beggar died, and was carried by the angels to Abraham's Bosom. The rich man also died and was buried. And being in Torments, IN HADES, he lifted up his eyes and saw Abraham afar off, and Lazarus in his Bosom."**

Here we see that both men continued to exist after death, and were taken to a place called Hades, the invisible realm under the earth. But they ended up in 2 different compartments of Hades, reflecting the 2 divergent destinies of the righteous and unrighteous. Lazarus, as a believer, went to Abraham's Bosom (another name for Paradise), whereas the rich man, as an unbeliever, went to a place of punishment called Torments. However, they were both in the same realm, they were both in Hades, for they could see each other and even communicate with each other. So at this point, before Christ's resurrection, believers did not go to heaven when they died. Torments was below Paradise, for the rich man in Torments had to lift up his eyes to see Abraham in the distance.

v24-25: **"Then the rich man cried and said: 'Father Abraham, have mercy on me, and send Lazarus that he may dip the tip of his finger in water and cool my tongue; for I am tormented in this flame.' But Abraham said, 'Son, remember that in your lifetime you received your good things, and likewise Lazarus evil things; but now he is comforted and you are tormented."**
So believers went to a place of fellowship and comfort called 'Abraham's Bosom', where there was rest and refreshment. This name describes reclining at table with your head resting in Abraham's bosom, denoting close fellowship with him and other believers in a state of rest and happiness. This place is named after Abraham, as he is the spiritual father of all those who have been declared righteous on the basis of their faith, just as Abraham was. So having the same faith, in the afterlife they go to the same place as Abraham, who then welcomes his children on arrival. But unbelievers went to another compartment of Hades called Torments, a place of

punishment and flames, causing continual thirst. It is the Palace Dungeon, the holding-cell for those under the condemnation of the king, where they await their final sentencing and assignment to their final place of punishment.

v26: **"And besides all this, between us and you there is a great Gulf fixed, so that those who want to pass from here to you cannot, nor can those from there pass to us."** These 2 different compartments for believers and unbelievers were separated by a great Gulf fixed, also called the Abyss or the Bottomless Pit. Consistently in the Bible this is the place of imprisonment for fallen angels and demons. It is where satan will be locked up for 1000 years. So Hades has at least 3 compartments: Abraham's Bosom, Torments, and the Abyss. So at death a man's soul must go to one of 2 possible places: Paradise or Torments, depending on the choices he makes in this life. Abraham says that it is then **impossible to go from one side of the Abyss to the other, from Torments to Paradise.** In other words, **a man's eternal destiny is fixed forever at death**. After death it will be too late to change your mind. This true story about life in Hades gives a detailed description of conscious experience after death. The rich man saw, he willed, he heard, he desired, he felt heat, thirst and torment; he talked, and felt concern for his family. Also Lazarus and Abraham were conscious and felt comforted in Paradise, totally contradicting the idea of soul-sleep.

Therefore in the Old Testament times all went down to Hades when they died, even the believers, because before Jesus died and rose again, bringing in the New Covenant, it was impossible for anyone to be born again, and so it was impossible for their spirits to go into heaven. Jesus said in John 3:3-6 that the New Birth is essential in order to enter heaven: **"Unless one is born again, he cannot SEE the Kingdom of God...I say to you, unless one is born of water** (of his mother's womb) **and the Spirit, he cannot ENTER the Kingdom of God. That which is born of the flesh is flesh, and that which is born of the Spirit is spirit ...You must be born again."** So before the resurrection Heaven was not populated by man, as Jesus said in v13: **"No one has ascended into Heaven, but He who descended from heaven: the Son of Man."** This explains Jesus' statement in Matthew 11:11: **"Among those born of women there has not risen one greater than John the Baptist; but he who is least in the Kingdom of heaven is greater**

than he." Although John was the greatest of the prophets he wasn't born again, because he died before the Cross.

Now on the basis of their faith the sins of the Old Testament saints were forgiven, and they were legally counted as righteous. Therefore they went to Paradise, rather than a place of punishment. However, they only had an imputed righteousness, not an imparted righteousness. They were still spiritually dead in Adam, their spirits were not yet made perfect and alive to God, and so they did not qualify to enter heaven. Ezekiel 36:26-27 prophesied the New Birth: **"I will put a new spirit within you; and I will put My Spirit within you."** However this was not available until the New Covenant was established.

Our New Birth was accomplished by Christ. When we accepted Him, we were put in Him and were identified with His death and resurrection. Our old spirit-man was crucified and buried with Christ, and in its place we received a new spirit-man, which was made alive with Christ and risen with Him (Romans 6:3-11, Ephesians 2:4-9). By our union with Christ, His resurrection power was applied to our spirit, causing it to be reborn in His image. The New Man in Christ is holy, righteous and perfect (Ephesians 4:24). We are His workmanship created in Christ (Ephesians 2:10), His new creation, the old man has passed away and all things are new (2Corinthians 5:17). We are the righteousness of God in Christ (v21). 1Peter 1:3 says that we were born again through the resurrection of Christ, and v23 says we were born again through the incorruptible seed of God's Word, which lives and abides forever. Therefore, our spirit consists of the perfect incorruptible nature of the resurrected Christ. Jesus said that all who believe in Him will have (possess) God's eternal life in their spirit (John 3:16). Thus this amazing New Birth was made available through Christ's resurrection, and so the spirits of believers could only be reborn and go to Heaven after His Resurrection.

Although in the Old Testament men were counted as just (righteous), righteousness was not yet imparted to their spirits, so their spirits were not yet made perfect, and so couldn't go to heaven. But all that changed when Christ rose. Hebrews 11 lists the Old Testament heroes of faith, and concludes in v39 that although all these had: **"obtained a good testimony through faith, they did not receive the promise."** The context tells us what this promise is - it was the promise of heaven and the New Jerusalem (v10,16). Thus they did not go to heaven when they died. He explains why in v40: **"God having provided something better for**

us (New Covenant believers) **that they should not be made perfect apart from us.**" So they had to wait until the New Covenant to be made perfect in spirit and so be able to possess the promise.

But when Christ rose again the promise could be fulfilled and these Old Testament saints were born again and made perfect, and then transferred to Heaven, as Hebrews 12:22-24 confirms: **"You have come to Mount Zion and to the City of the Living God, the Heavenly Jerusalem, to an innumerable company of angels, to the General Assembly and Church of the Firstborn registered in Heaven, to God the Judge of all, and to the spirits of just** (righteous) **men made perfect."** Notice the Church saints are now in Heaven. We were registered in Heaven when we were born again, and became citizens of heaven. Believers are already seated with Christ in heavenly places, and when they die they go to heaven. There is also a separate group of people in heaven called: **"the spirits of just men made perfect."** This is a perfect description of the Old-Testament saints who were counted as just (righteous), but were only made perfect when they received the New Birth when Jesus rose from the dead.

Another way to see this is that Christ only opened up the new and living Way to heaven through His death and resurrection (Hebrews 10:20), so believers before the Cross couldn't go to heaven. But now that's changed. In John 14:1-3, Jesus promised to prepare a place in heaven for us, and then declared that He would be the Way to heaven, so we could come to God in heaven through Him. He also said there was no other Way, for no one can come to God except through Him (v4-6). He opened up this Way when He rose from the dead and ascended to His Father. Now we can understand John 14:12: **"Most assuredly, I say to you, he who believes in Me, the works that I do he will do also; and greater works than these he will do, because I go to My Father."** How can we do greater works than Jesus? He did many works, but He could not get anyone born again. But now He has died, risen again and gone to the Father, the New Birth is now possible and the way is opened to heaven. So now we can get people born again, where they receive eternal life in heaven. This is a greater work than the temporary work of healing or deliverance.

So by His death and resurrection establishing the New Covenant, Jesus brought in a major change. He prophesied this when He first announced the formation of His Church in <u>Matthew 16:18</u>: **"On this Rock** (which is Jesus Himself) **I will build My Church, and the Gates of HADES shall not prevail against it."** His promise to His Church, established after His resurrection, was that the Prison Gates of Hades would not prevail over us. Hades no longer has the right or power over a believers' spirit to hold us in its clutches. So when we dies we won't go through the Gates of Hades as the Old Testament Saints did. New Covenant believers will not go down to Hades, but rather up to Heaven. Man was under the power of Hades and Death. Hades controlled man's soul, Death had his body, but Jesus conquered both Hades and Death in His Death and Resurrection!

<u>In Revelation 1:18 He claimed</u>: **"I am He who lives, and was dead, and behold, I am alive forevermore. Amen. And I have the Keys of HADES and of DEATH."** By these keys He now has the power to release men's souls from the power of Hades, and man's bodies from Death. He demonstrated this at His resurrection. First, using His key to Hades, He set all the Old Testament believers free from Hades, and took them up to heaven with Him. Also when New Testament believers die, we will not go into Hades but to the Presence of God in Heaven. Second, at His resurrection He used His key of death to resurrect a number of believers who had died recently in Jerusalem (Matthew 27:52-53). They formed the first fruits offering to God, a token of the full harvest to come, the guarantee of our future resurrection from the dead. Jesus has defeated the power of Death and Hades for all believers, so we can declare <u>1Corinthians 15:55</u>: **"O DEATH, where is your sting? O HADES, where is your victory?"** Soon Jesus will use His key to Death again to raise us up at the Rapture.

<u>Philippians 2:9-10</u> confirms that Christ's victory included gaining authority over the realm under the earth: **"Therefore God highly exalted Him, and bestowed on Him the Name above every name, that at the Name of Jesus EVERY KNEE WILL BOW, (1) those who are in heaven, and (2) those on earth, and (3) those under the earth."** Those under the earth are all the inhabitants of Hades. Because Jesus identified fully with humanity, when He died His body was laid in a grave, but His human spirit went down to Hades upon His death, which is located in the centre of the earth, for <u>Matthew 12:40</u>, He said He would be: **"3 days and 3 nights in the HEART of the EARTH."** <u>Romans 10:7</u> says that **Christ descended into the Abyss.** <u>Ephesians 4:9</u> says that **Christ descended into the lowest parts of the earth** - the different compartments of

Hades. <u>Acts 2:24,31</u>: **"whom God raised up, having loosed the pains of death, because it was not possible that He should be held by it...so His SOUL was not left in HADES, nor did His FLESH see corruption** (in the grave)**."**

<u>1Peter 3:18</u>: **"Christ died for sins once for all, the just for the unjust, so that He might bring us to God** (in heaven)**, having been put to death in the flesh, but made alive in the spirit."** When He was made alive He went to Paradise, as He had promised the thief on the Cross, to preach the Gospel and take all the believers to heaven, just as <u>1Peter 4:6 tells us</u>: **"The Gospel has been preached even to those who are dead, that though they were judged in the flesh as men, they may live in the spirit according to God."** Though when they died they were judged as men in Adam and so had to go to Hades, yet now through believing the Gospel they were put in Christ and were born again, so their spirits received the life of God, and could go up to heaven. So Jesus went to the believers in Paradise and preached the Gospel to them, saying: *"I am the Messiah. I've died for your sins and have risen again, and established the New Covenant in My blood, so whoever receives Me will be born again and go to heaven with ME."* Paradise was already expectant for His arrival. First Joseph would have told them all about His conception, birth and childhood. Then John the Baptist would have arrived in Paradise and described His baptism and miracles. Then Lazarus made a 4-day visit there before they all heard Jesus calling him back to the earth, proving that He was the Christ. Finally the thief on the Cross arrived and told them about the Crucifixion and that He promised to meet him in Paradise.

When Jesus rose out of Hades He took the righteous dead with Him. Then early on the resurrection morning He ascended to heaven as the first fruits offering to God, and took them with Him into heaven. This is the ascension Jesus announced to Mary Magdalene in <u>John 20:17</u> when He said: **"Do not cling to Me, for I have not yet ascended to My Father; but go to My brethren and say to them, 'I am ascending to My Father and your Father, and to My God and your God."** This is when He took His blood into the heavenly holy of holies, and received all authority from the Father. This is when <u>Ephesians 4:8</u> (quoting Psalm 68:18) was fulfilled: **"When He ascended on high, He led captivity captive."** Those in captivity were the souls in Paradise. He led all the Old Testament saints up to Heaven as part of His Triumphal Procession.

This is why after the resurrection, Paradise, the dwelling place of the righteous after death, is now located in the 3rd Heaven, not in Hades as it was previously. We can see this from Paul's own experience in 2Corinthians 12:2-4: **"I know a man in Christ who, 14 years ago…was caught UP to the 3rd HEAVEN, he was caught UP into PARADISE and heard inexpressible words."** Paul was talking about himself when he was stoned to death in Acts 14:18-19, but was raised again through the prayers of the saints. If you work it out, he wrote 2Corinthians 14 years later. He died and left his body. Instead of going DOWN to Hades, He was caught UP to the 3rd Heaven into Paradise. **The 1st heaven** is the atmosphere, where the birds fly (Genesis 1:20,26, Jeremiah 4:25, Haggai 1:10, Matthew 8:20, 13:32, Acts 10:12, 14:17), **the 2nd heaven** is outer space, as it is where the sun, moon and stars are located (Genesis 1:14-18 22:17, 26:4, Matthew 24:29, Hebrews 11:12, Revelation 6:13), and **the 3rd heaven** is the special abode of God (2Cor 12:1-4), where the New Jerusalem and God's Throne is. Notice that Paradise has now been relocated to Heaven, so all believers now go up to Heaven when they die, rather than going down to Hades.

The Compartments of Sheol-Hades

Sheol (Hebrew) = **the Pit** (Hebrew) = **Hades** (Greek) describes the whole invisible realm at the centre of the earth (Matthew 12:40), in the lower parts of the earth (Ezekiel 26:20, Ephesians 4:9-10). It consists of 3 areas: (1) for righteous humans, (2) for unrighteous humans, and (3) for fallen angels and demons.

(1) Before the Resurrection the compartment of Hades for believers was called **Paradise** (Luke 23:43), the word for a Royal Garden. But at His resurrection Christ emptied Hades of all believers and took them to Heaven (Ephesians 4:8-10), and from that time any believer who dies goes up to Paradise in the 3rd Heaven (2Corinthians 12:4). The tree of life is now in the midst of the Paradise of God (Revelation 2:7), and it is also in the New Jerusalem (Revelation 22:2). Therefore Paradise is now in the New Jerusalem.

Another term for Paradise is **Abraham's Bosom** (Luke 16:22-23), a figure of speech describing a guest at a feast reclining on a friend's breast, describing a place of joyful fellowship between believers, Abraham being the spiritual father of this family. This term is related to Old Testament descriptions of the death of Old Testament saints as being 'gathered to his people', for example: **"Abraham** breathed his last and died in a good old age, an old man and full of years, and was gathered to his people" (Genesis 25:8). This cannot just mean being buried in the family grave, for Abraham's ancestors were buried in Ur and Haran (also 25:17, 35:29, 49:29, 33). A similar expression was to 'go to their fathers' (15:15), and in Genesis 47:30, Joseph distinguishes between spiritually joining his fathers and being physically buried with them. His joining them was years before his being buried with them.

(2)   **Abaddon** (Hebrew: 'destruction') is the name for the unbeliever's section of Sheol (Job 26:6, 28:22, 31:12, Psalm 88:11, Proverbs 15:11, 27:20, Rev 9:11), a place of punishment, cut off from God's goodness. Its Greek equivalent is **Torments** (Luke 16:23).

(3) **The Abyss or Bottomless Pit** is the transliteration of the Greek word 'Abyss' and so is only found in the New Testament. All 9 references confirm that this is the part of Sheol used to imprison fallen angels and demons. It is never associated with humans, except the antichrist, who has a special relationship with the devil (Revelation 11:7, 17:8). In Luke 8:31 the demons beg Jesus not to send them into the Abyss. Satan will be locked up in the Abyss for 1000 years (Rev 20:1,3). In the Tribulation, a demonic army is released on the earth which had been locked up in the Abyss (Rev 9:1,2,11). On the 3rd day, when Christ was made alive in spirit, He descended into the Abyss to proclaim His victory to the imprisoned fallen angels there (Romans 10:7, 1Peter 3:18-19). The Abyss is the **'Great Gulf fixed'** between Abraham's Bosom and Torments in Luke 16:26.

Another term which has a close relationship to the Abyss is the Greek word **Tartarus,** used in 2Peter 2:4: **"If God did not spare angels when they sinned, but cast them into Hell** (TARTARUS) **and committed them to chains of gloomy darkness to be kept until the judgment."** It is clearly a special prison for certain fallen angels who committed a particular sin, in connection with the days of Noah (v5). These same angels are mentioned in a parallel verse in Jude 6: **"the angels who did not keep their proper domain, but left their own abode, He has reserved in everlasting chains under darkness for the Judgment of the great Day."** Jude says that these have already entered into **"suffering the vengeance of eternal fire"** along with the sinners of Sodom and Gomorrah, as a demonstration (example) that God will judge sin and sinners (v7). Their sin is described in

Genesis 6:1-4, and it was one of the main reasons the Flood was necessary (for more on this, see my book: "Revelations at Caesarea Philippi"). It was designed by satan to prevent the Coming of the Messiah into the earth as a man in fulfilment of the Prophecy of 'the Seed of the Woman' in Genesis 3:15. For this reason, on the 3rd day the victorious Christ made a special visit to these angels in Tartarus to proclaim His victory, that despite their efforts He had been born and had accomplished His mission, sealing their doom. This is described in 1Peter 3:18-20: **"Christ also suffered once for sins, the righteous for the unrighteous, that he might bring us to God, being put to death in the flesh but made alive in the spirit, in which He went and proclaimed** (His victory) **to the spirits in prison, because they formerly did not obey, when God's patience waited in the days of Noah, while the Ark was being prepared."** Thus Tartarus is a special prison in the lowest part of the Abyss for these angels.

The Death of Believers Now

The Bible is clear that death not the end, but the doorway to the next phase of our existence. Death is the separation of the spirit-soul from the body: **"The body without the spirit is dead"** (James 2:26; also Job 4:10, 1Kings 7:20-22, 2Samuel 12:19-23, Luke 8:49-56, 16:22). The immaterial part of our being is able to separate from the material (physical) part. Thus when the body is no longer able to be a dwelling place for the spirit, the spirit will leave (depart from) the body, and this is the moment of death. 2Corinthians 5:8 describes death as being: **"absent from the body."** That is, at death we continue to exist as a spirit, but we no longer inhabit our body. Death is the departure of the spirit from the body. Paul said: **"My departure is at hand"** (2Timothy 4:6-8). In Luke 9:31 Jesus discussed His death with Moses and Elijah on the Mount of Transfiguration: **"who appeared in glory and spoke of His decease** (literally: His EXODUS) **which He was about to accomplish at Jerusalem."** His death is described as an Exodus or Departure. Thus death was not the end of His human existence, but rather in His death, He would go on a journey making an exit out of this world into another realm (Jesus being fully human as well as fully God had to enter into the full human experience, including human life after death). Thus 'death' does not mean extinction, but describes the state of the body when separated from the spirit. However, man's spirit continues to live and be conscious after death and goes to another place.

There is no intrinsic problem with spirits operating without bodies (for example God and angels function as spirits without physical bodies).

In 2Peter 1:13-14, Peter describes his approaching death: **"While I am in this tent** (body) **I stir you up by reminding you; knowing soon I must put off my tent** (body)." Notice how he distinguishes between his essential being, his inner man, his spirit-soul (called 'I') and his body or outer man, which he describes as his tent, his temporary dwelling place. Thus we are not our bodies, but we possess and indwell our bodies for a time. I have a house, I live in my house, but I am not my house. So if I leave my house, making it uninhabited, it becomes a dead thing, but I don't cease to exist. Likewise my body is not the real me. The real me is a spirit made in the image of God. I am a spirit who lives in a body and when I leave my body it becomes a dead thing, but I live on. I just change location. In v15 he describes his upcoming death as **"my departure."** In v14 he describes it as **his inner-man ('I') putting off his body**, just as you take off your clothes at the end of the day and lay them aside. You however live on, likewise your spirit lives on even after it has left the body.

Our body is like clothing that we wear around our spirit. As our clothes follow the movements we make, revealing the presence of a living being within, so the body expresses the actions of our spirit and reveals the presence of a living spirit within. Death, when our spirit puts off our body, is just like when we put off our clothes. They fall lifeless to the ground, but we continue alive as before, except we're unclothed. Now this is not an ideal state and it is just temporary, for soon we desire to put on new clothes. Likewise when we put off our body we will be unclothed (naked) and we will earnestly look forward to the resurrection when God will clothe us again with a new eternal resurrection body (a permanent house rather than a temporary tent, to use the other analogy). The Present State is temporary, because this body is like a weak tent, and clothing that will soon wear out. The Intermediate State where we are unclothed is also temporary, for this is not how God created man to be. The Eternal State is to be clothed with a new body, eternal in the heavens, that is strong and permanent like a house compared to the weak, temporary tent in which we presently live.

The classic passage that teaches all of this is <u>2Corinthians 5:1-11</u>. As we read this, notice the consistent clear distinction made between US (our spirit) and the house we live in (our body). This is the very distinction Paul made in the previous verse: **"the things which are seen are temporary, but the things which are not seen are eternal"** (2Corinthians 4:18). So, we are not destroyed when our house is destroyed, but we live on awaiting a new and better house.

<u>v1-3:</u> **"For we know that if our earthly house, this tent** (our present body) **is destroyed, WE** (our spirits) **have a building from God, a house not made with hands, eternal in the heavens** (our future resurrection body). **For in this** (present body) **WE groan, earnestly desiring to be clothed with our** (permanent) **habitation which is from heaven, because, having been clothed, WE shall not be found naked."** Our future desire and hope is not to be a disembodied (naked) spirit, although we may have to be that for a while in the Intermediate State, but to be clothed with our resurrection body - our permanent house from Heaven.

<u>v4</u>: **"For WE who are in this tent** (mortal body) **groan, being burdened, not because WE want to be unclothed, but further clothed, that mortality may be swallowed up by** (resurrection) **life."** We do not desire to be a disembodied spirit, but to be clothed in a glorious, eternal, immortal resurrection body. In v2-4 Paul is revealing the correct Biblical attitude for us as living believers to have a strong desire and expectation to be raptured (according to imminence), rather than suffering death and a time of being unclothed (as a disembodied spirit in the Intermediate State). We don't want to be unclothed by death, but rather to be given new immortal clothes by the release of God's life in our mortal bodies, that is while we are still alive in our mortal bodies. Notice it does not speak of the transformation of dead bodies but mortal bodies. Likewise, <u>Romans 8:11</u> doesn't directly speak of resurrection, but of the healing and rapture of our present mortal bodies: **"if the Spirit of Him who raised Jesus from the dead dwells in you, He who raised Christ from the dead will also give life to your mortal** (not 'dead') **bodies through His Spirit who dwells in you."**

<u>v5</u>: **"Now He who has prepared us for this very thing** (physical rapture and resurrection) **is God, who also has given us the Spirit as a guarantee** (that He will do it)." The Spirit within us is God's deposit guaranteeing that He will one day soon make good on His promise to complete our salvation by clothing us in a resurrection body. Even now He will give life to our mortal bodies if we call on Him (Romans 8:11). On that day, the Spirit will release the very same Power

within us that raised Jesus' body from death and transformed it into an immortal resurrection body, and we will receive an immortal, indestructible glorious body that is just like Christ's resurrection body (Philippians 3:21).

Although the Greeks also believed in Hades and in the continued existence of the spirit after death, they thought the disembodied state was the ideal, for then the pure spirit was free from evil flesh. That is why, when Paul spoke at Athens (the centre of Greek Philosophy) in Acts 17, they found it hard to accept his preaching on the resurrection of the body, when he proclaimed Jesus had risen! The Hebrew (Biblical) belief is that although the body is corrupted by sin (along with our whole humanity), it was created by God and so is essentially good and an integral part of our humanity. Thus a spirit without a body is unclothed and incomplete, and the Intermediate State is temporary until we receive a new body. Our ultimate eternal state is for our spirit to be clothed in a resurrection body.

v6-7: **"So we are always confident, knowing that: while WE are at home in the BODY, WE are** (physically) **absent from the Lord, for WE walk by faith, not by sight."** Notice again that WE are distinct from our body. The body is our dwelling place. Without it WE still exist. WE are spirits who live in a body. While we are in the body, it keeps us physically on earth, so that we are absent from the Lord in heaven, and cannot see Him. But when a Christian leaves his body he goes straight into the Presence of the Lord in Heaven, and sees Him face to face, as v8 says: **"We are confident, yes, well pleased rather to be <u>absent from the body and to be present with the Lord.</u>"** This proves that when we leave our body, we do not cease existing, our soul does not go to sleep, but we remain conscious and change location. We leave the earth and immediately go into the immediate Presence of the Lord, who is in Heaven. We are well pleased to do this because we will be in a state of greater blessing in His Presence, actually seeing Him, rather than just seeing Him though the eyes of faith as we do now. **"To be absent from the body is to be present with the Lord!"** - you can't have a clearer description of what happens to a believer at death. His spirit leaves his body and immediately goes to be with Christ in Heaven, entering into a state of heightened consciousness and blessedness.

v9-11: **"Therefore** (knowing that at any time this life might end by death or rapture), **we make it our aim, whether present** (with the Lord) **or absent** (from the Lord)**, to be well pleasing to Him. For we must all appear** (literally: 'be manifested') **before the Judgment Seat of Christ, that each one may receive the things done in the body, according to what he has done, whether good or bad. Knowing therefore, the fear of the Lord, we persuade men."**

Knowing that soon we must stand before Christ to give an account and be judged for how we have lived our Christian lives, and receive our eternal reward, helps to motivate us to live lives pleasing to Him. Paul considers this Judgment to be a fearful event for it will be a searching judgment in which all our thoughts, hidden motivations, words and deeds will be revealed, manifested and evaluated. 'Knowing the fear of the Lord', that he is under His authority and will be held accountable, motivates Paul to obey God with all his heart and especially to fulfil the Great Commission of persuading men of the truth of God's Word. 'Knowing the fear of the Lord' may also be a reference to God's even more fearful Judgment on unbelievers, so that knowing what will happen to those who die in a state of sin, makes Paul earnestly seek to bring as many as possible to salvation.

So Paul says believers who die become 'unclothed', that is they put off the clothing of their body (v4), and when they become absent from the body through death, they go straight up into the Presence of the Lord in Heaven (v8).

Philippians 1:21-24: **"To me to live is Christ, and to die is gain. If I live in the flesh, it is for the fruit of my labour: yet what I will choose I know not. I am torn between the two with a desire to depart** (this body) **and be WITH CHRIST, which is FAR BETTER. But abiding in the flesh** (in my body) **is more needful for you."** Paul describes his life as him (his spirit) living in the flesh (his body), and death, not as an end, but as a departure from this earth to be with Christ in Heaven! The moment we depart our body we will be with Christ, which is far better for us. This speaks of a state of intimate fellowship with Christ and conscious happiness in His Presence, which is FAR BETTER than anything this life can offer. Notice that to die is not non-existence, but 'to die is gain.' He says: 'to live is Christ' (to know and experience Him), but to die is gain. This must mean we will enter into an even greater knowledge and experience of Christ. So far as our personal blessedness is concerned, it's far better to be with the Lord in Heaven, even if unclothed, but as far as our usefulness to the Lord and our bearing fruit for eternity is concerned, it is better to abide in the body. Thus although the Intermediate State is a blessed state for believers, we won't have the opportunities to serve Him that we have in this life. It is a State of rest, waiting for the next Stage, which begins with the resurrection of our body.

Revelation 6:9-11 describes the SOULS of martyrs killed in the 1st half of the Tribulation in Heaven, as being CONSCIOUS and at REST in Heaven, in their Intermediate State between their death and resurrection: **"When He opened the 5th Seal, I saw under the altar** (in Heaven) **the SOULS of those who had been slain for the Word of God and for the testimony which they held. And they cried with a loud voice, saying: "How long, O Lord, holy and true, until You judge and avenge our blood on those who dwell on the earth?" Then a white robe was given to each of them; and it was said to them that they should REST a little while longer, until both the number of their fellow servants and their brethren, who would be killed as they were, was completed."** They are told to wait until the end of the Tribulation when they will be resurrected at the 2nd Coming of Christ. Revelation 14:13 confirms that the dead in Christ are in a state of REST as they await their eternal rewards when their works will be assessed at the Judgment Seat of Christ: **"Write: 'Blessed are the dead who die in the Lord from now on.' "Yes," says the Spirit, "that they may rest from their labours, and their works follow them."**

Revelation 7:9-17 reveals a greater number of martyrs killed in the Great Tribulation, who are clearly conscious, in Heaven, secure and at rest with all their needs met: **"behold, a great multitude which no one could number, of all nations, tribes, peoples, and tongues, standing before the Throne and before the Lamb, clothed with white robes, with palm branches in their hands, crying out with a loud voice, saying: "Salvation belongs to our God who sits on the Throne, and to the Lamb!"... "These are the ones who come out of the Great Tribulation, and washed their robes and made them white in the blood of the Lamb. Therefore they are before the Throne of God, and serve Him day and night in His temple. And He who sits on the Throne will dwell among them. They shall neither hunger anymore nor thirst anymore; the sun shall not strike them, nor any heat; for the Lamb who is in the midst of the throne will shepherd them and lead them to living fountains of waters. And God will wipe away every tear from their eyes."**

Stephen's death in Acts 7:55-59 describes the death of a New Covenant believer: **"Being full of the Holy Spirit, he gazed into heaven and saw the glory of God, and Jesus standing at the right hand of God** (ready to receive Him) **and said: "Look! I see the heavens opened and the Son of Man standing at the right hand of God!"** Heaven opened to receive him! **"They stoned Stephen as he was calling on God, saying: "Lord Jesus, receive my spirit."**

1Thessalonians 4:14 says that at the Rapture: **"God will bring with Him those who sleep in Jesus."** This proves the departed spirits of believers are now in Heaven, so when Jesus returns, He will bring them with Him to earth to be reunited with their bodies in resurrection power.

2Corinthians 12:2-4: **"I know a man in Christ who, 14 years ago...was caught UP to the 3rd HEAVEN, he was caught UP into PARADISE and heard inexpressible words."** When Paul was stoned to death, his spirit left his body and went up to heaven. Notice he was still conscious. Although he said he could not tell if he had left his body or not, the fact remains he considered it a real possibility that he had been in conscious existence in Heaven as a spirit who had left his body. Thus so he believed we continue to exist as a spirit after death.

Hebrews 12:22-24 describes the present inhabitants of the New Jerusalem in Heaven as including all the believers who have died in the Old Testament (**"the spirits of just men made perfect"**), and in the Church-Age (**"the Church of the Firstborn registered in Heaven"**). They are all alive and conscious.

At death, believers are escorted to Paradise by angels (Luke 16:22), or even by Christ Himself for His promise in John 14:2-3 can be applied to the moment of our death: **"I go and prepare a place for you, and I will come again, and receive you to Myself; that where I am, there you may be also."** When Thomas asked: **"how can we know the WAY** (to Heaven)" (v5), Jesus did not say: **"I will show you the Way"**, but instead He said: **"I AM the WAY** (to Heaven)" (v6), which means: *"I AM the WAY. I will take you there personally."*

The death of believers is described as 'sleep' (John 11:11-14, 1Thessalonians 4:13-15, 5:10; 2Samuel 7:12, Acts 7:60, 13:36, 1Corinthians 11:30, 15:6, 18,20,51; Matthew 27:52), but this refers to the body, not to the soul, since the soul does not sleep, but continues to be conscious, according to the abundance of Biblical evidence that we have seen. So sleep refers to the body, which looks as if it is asleep. The term is used to show there is a temporary suspension of physical activity. Thus 'sleep' indicates that death is only temporary and that the body will awake in the resurrection morning (1Thessalonians 4:16).

We have an exciting hope. When we leave the body we will be present with Lord in bliss, which is far better, and then we will a glorious resurrection! What a wonderful Saviour who made this all possible. So let us show our love for Him by living a life that pleases Him, remembering that soon (at any time, at a moment's notice), we will have to stand before His Judgment Seat and give an account to Him of how we have lived our life and used our time and our gifts.

The Death of Unbelievers now

Although Christ relocated the place where believers go at death, there is no change as far as unbelievers are concerned. Those who reject the grace of God, the work of Christ and the witness of the Holy Spirit still go down to Torments in Hades, a temporary place of punishment, a holding-cell for those who have already been found guilty and are waiting for their final sentencing at the Great White Throne, which will happen at the end of time (Revelation 20:11-15).

The present situation of unbelievers in the Intermediate State is described in 2Peter 2:9: **"The Lord knows how to keep the unrighteous under punishment for the Day of Judgment."** So when people die in a state of sin, they are judged as guilty and go to a place of punishment (Hades). They are now sealed in a state of unrighteousness forever, having rejected Christ in their lifetime. They have now lost their last chance to repent and no longer have any possibility of changing their situation. All they have left to look forward to is unending punishment. So we must preach the Gospel and tell them there is a Heaven to gain and a Hell to shun! Notice Peter says they are presently kept under punishment UNTIL the final Day of Judgment, when they are resurrected to stand before the Great White Throne, for their final sentencing and dismissal into their eternal abode, the Lake of Fire. Thus their present place of punishment (Hades) is just temporal, a holding-cell, until they enter their final place of punishment which will be eternal. At the moment only their soul is under punishment, but in the Lake of Fire both their body and soul will be under punishment, as Jesus said: **"Fear Him who is able to destroy both soul and body in Hell** (Gehenna)**"** (Matthew 10:28).

The Judgment of the Sheep and Goats (Matthew 25:31-46) also describes what happens to unbelievers at death. When Jesus returns He divides all those who are alive on earth into believers (sheep), and unbelievers (goats). The sheep enter (inherit) His Messianic Kingdom, but the goats are killed and sent to a place of fiery punishment. Since this judgment of unbelievers involves their physical death followed by what happens immediately afterwards, it is just like the judgment at the death of every unbeliever. v41,46: **"Then He will also say to those** (goats) **on the left hand: "DEPART from Me, you CURSED, into the EVERLASTING FIRE prepared for the devil and his angels** (the Lake of Fire)**... And these will go away into EVERLASTING PUNISHMENT."**

Now we know from Revelation 20 that they will not actually go into the Lake of Fire (their final place of punishment) for another 1000 years. However, the words of Jesus to them at the moment of their death make it clear that their future eternal destiny (of everlasting punishment) is decided and fixed forever at this time. Their status as guilty sinners under the curse (judgment) of God is determined forever at death and cannot be changed. Thus these terrifying words of Jesus also describe what is said to unbelievers at their death. He declares that they are guilty (cursed) and sentences them to face an everlasting punishment in the Lake of Fire, along with the devil who they have followed in rebellion to God (v41). Although they do not go immediately into the Lake of Fire (this can't happen until their day of resurrection), their everlasting punishment does start immediately (v46), for their departed souls go down to Torments in Hades, a place of fiery punishment, where they' will wait for their resurrection and appearance before the Great White Throne, when they will be sent into their eternal abode, the Lake of Fire. Therefore, as it will be for these sheep and goats, so it is for all people at their death. Based on their condition (nature) at that time, they'll immediately enter one of 2 possible eternal destinies - either a state of everlasting blessedness in God's Kingdom, or of everlasting punishment. In both cases the judgment (separation) is irreversible (it will be impossible to change one's state). Both face an initial time as disembodied spirit-souls until their physical resurrection, when they enter their final eternal state of blessedness or punishment involving both body and spirit-soul.

So every man's final destiny is fixed by God at the time of death, so it is essential that we share the Gospel with the lost before it's too late. The unsaved, being in a state of sin, are pronounced guilty by God and are under God's judgment of condemnation because of their sin and rejection of Christ. They go immediately into everlasting punishment (v46). Thus the time of punishment starts at death, but they don't go into the Lake of Fire until their resurrection at the End of Time.

Instead their soul goes to Torments in Hades, a place of punishment, a temporary holding cell for convicted prisoners, until they are called to stand before the Great White Throne and receive their final sentencing and dismissal into the Lake of Fire. Their degree of punishment is determined by the degree of their rebellion against God in their life. They are then sent to their final and permanent place of confinement and punishment - the Lake of Fire. Believers in Christ have already been forgiven and justified through their faith in Christ, and so will not be condemned like unbelievers, so when they die they go in spirit to Paradise, to await their resurrection and followed by the judgment of their works at the Judgment Seat of Christ, where He will assess their lives and service to Him, and reward them accordingly, so the more faithful they were to Him the greater degree of eternal glory, honour and authority will be released in and through them. Thus at this time we will enter into our Eternal State.

Though man's eternal destiny is determined at death (from the choices we make in this life), we still have to wait for the day of our resurrection and final judgment, which involves a searching public evaluation of all our works, before we enter our final eternal state. The final judgment of believers will determine the degree of our eternal rewards. Then He will release us into our eternal state of glory. The final judgment of unbelievers will determine the degree of their eternal punishment, before their release into their everlasting state of punishment.

The main false Theories about Life after death

*The first is the belief of atheism - there is a total **cessation of existence** at death.

*A 2nd false view is **reincarnation** or **the transmigration of the soul**, where each soul continues by entering a new body, which might even be that of an animal. But the Bible teaches we have but one life in this world, and one death, after which we are judged to determine our eternal future (Hebrews 9:27). Even when someone is resurrected the soul is reunited to the same body.

*A 3rd false view is **conditional immortality**, which is held by some cults and even by some believers. This says the soul is not inherently immortal, rather immortality is a gift for the saved only, so at death unbelievers cease to exist.

*A 4th false view is **Soul Sleep,** which denies the immortality of the soul, saying it can not exist without the body, so a man has no consciousness between his death and resurrection. Thus at death, the soul like the body 'sleeps' in a state of unconsciousness. We have already answered this theory by the abundance of scriptures showing that when people leave their bodies at death their souls continue to exist in a conscious state and in a particular location determined by God. In particular believers enter God's Presence (Phil 1:23, 2Cor 5:6-8, Rev 6:9-11). Also if soul sleep were true then the soul as well as the body would have to be resurrected, but the Bible only speaks of bodies being resurrected (Matthew 27:52).

*A 5th false view is **annihilationism**, which says the unsaved soul will eventually be annihilated by God after suffering a period of punishment. This is held by some evangelicals, who accept the demands of justice on a sinner must be satisfied, but reject the concept of eternal punishment.

*A 6th false view is that man is given an **intermediate body** between his death and resurrection. The main passage used for this is 2Corinthians 5:1-10, but it only says we look forward to being clothed in our eternal (resurrection) body. It also implies we'll be unclothed in the Intermediate State. There is no mention of any intermediate body. Although souls in this state are given robes in Revelation 6, robes are not bodies. The thrust behind this theory is the assumption that a disembodied spirit can't function without a body, but this is false, for God is a Spirit (John 4:24), yet can function without a body, likewise for angels (Hebrews 1:14). Although men without bodies may be limited in what they can do, they can certainly exist and operate on some level. Whenever men are seen in the Intermediate State they are seen as souls without bodies (Revelation 6:9-11).

*A 7th false view is **the 2nd Probation theory**, which says there will be a 2nd chance to be saved after death. **Universalism** teaches that all will eventually be saved. **Universal Reconciliation** teaches that there will be a temporary time of punishment in the Lake of Fire, but after that everyone will be reconciled, even satan. However we have already seen many scriptures that teach that the unsaved dead are in a fixed state, which cannot be altered. Also scriptures on the final judgment all teach that this judgment is based on what we have decided and done in the flesh, and not on what happens in the Intermediate State. Our final decision is made in this life (2Corinthians 6:2, Hebrews 9:27). Universalism plainly contradicts scripture (Matthew 25:46, John 5:29, Revelation 20:11-15).

*An 8th false view is the Roman Catholic view of **Limbus Infantum**, which (they say) is the place on the edge of hell where unbaptised infants go, if they die in infancy. He is not punished, but he is excluded from the blessings of Heaven. This false doctrine is based on another false doctrine, baptismal regeneration which says baptism saves a baby so it goes to heaven. This requires the invention of a special place where unbaptised babies go. But the Bible says nothing about such a place.

*An 9th view is the Roman Catholic view of **Purgatory**, a Latin term that means 'to purge.' It is a place of purification for those not bad enough to go to hell, but not yet good enough for Heaven. After spending some time in Purgatory he can go to Heaven. The time in Purgatory varies according to the person. It can be shortened by prayers, good works, Mass, penance and by buying indulgences. No scripture teaches that we face a time of purging after death to qualify us for Heaven. The main support is from 2Maccabees 12:41-45 in the Apocrypha. This is why they chose to make the books of Maccabees part of their Scripture, even though it was never accepted by the Jews as Scripture. However, even this passage of Maccabees does not support the Roman Catholic Purgatory, because the specific sin to which it refers is idolatry, a mortal sin, which cannot be solved by time in Purgatory, according to the Roman Catholic system of salvation, for a person who dies in a state of mortal sin must go to Hell, not Purgatory. The main problem with Purgatory is that it denies the Biblical doctrine of salvation by grace through faith in the finished work of Christ. The sins of believers have been fully forgiven and cleansed by the perfect Atoning Sacrifice of Christ, so they don't need to go through a period of purification from sins in Purgatory, before they can enter Heaven (Titus 2:14, Hebrews 1:3). Purgatory is a manifestation and logical consequence of the false doctrine of salvation through faith plus works.

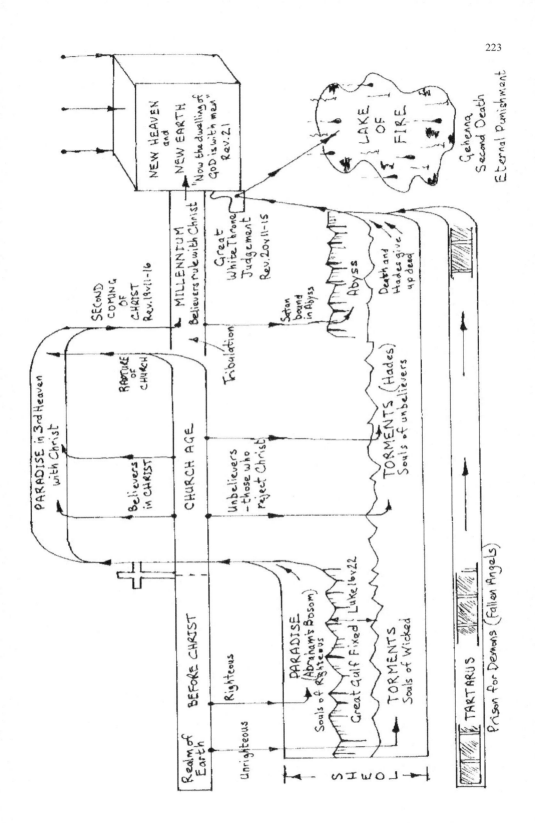

*Appendix 1: The 12 Keys (a Review of End Time Prophecy – Part 1)

In End Time Prophecy Part 1, we gave the 12 Keys to unlocking and correctly interpreting Bible Prophecy. Before studying Prophecy as it relates to the Church Age and the Rapture, we will first review these Keys, and add some supplementary material to enhance your understanding of these vital Principles.

*KEY 1 - Interpret Scripture Literally

*KEY 1 is the Foundational Principle for all Bible interpretation - **interpret Bible Prophecy literally,** according to its plain meaning, as it would have been understood by the original hearers. This is how we are to read all literature, which is why it is called LITERAL interpretation (according to the laws of reading literature generally). This should go without saying, but sadly Church History is full of people ignoring this principle when reading the Bible, especially its prophetic passages. It's important to say that literal interpretation allows for symbolic language, because symbols are a normal part of language. They are used all the time, and this is especially true in the Bible, which constantly uses natural this as symbols to teach us about spiritual things. There is a law that we instinctively apply in all our hearing and reading to determine if a symbolic interpretation is intended, which we should also apply to our Bible study. It says if the plain literalistic sense makes sense, seek no other sense. If it does not make sense then it must have a symbolic meaning. So when Jesus said: "I am the Door", we understand that He was not claiming to be a large rectangular piece of wood! So literal interpretation is not literalistic, for it takes obvious symbols into account. Why use symbols? (1) It adds interest because images create pictures in our mind, and (2) a picture is worth a 1000 words. When Jesus said: "I am the Bread of Life", He said in a few words what would otherwise take pages of text to explain.

Another thing it allows for is typology or spiritual applications. There is only one literal meaning, but there might be many applications. The important point is that these applications do not negate the literal fulfilment. Let us look at one example of the spiritual application of Scripture in typology, the story of Abraham offering up Isaac on Mount Moriah in Genesis 22. This is a picture, or type and shadow of the Father offering up his Son Jesus on Mount Moriah. But notice that the fact that this picture was fulfilled in Jesus does not negate the fact that Abraham actually and literally offered up Isaac on Mount Moriah. In fact the fulfilment rests on the fact that the type literally happened. So Genesis 22 records what literally took place, but by God's design it also includes a spiritual application to Christ. Thus if we insist on upholding the literal interpretation of a Scripture, this does not prevent us from making spiritual applications.

A big issue in Prophecy where we need to apply this rule is in regard to Israel. Many think the Church has replaced Israel, and so whenever they read prophecies about Israel they automatically assume that they must be fulfilled by the Church. Of course, our natural tendency is to make everything about us, so even if something is clearly promised to Israel the Church tends to just apply it to herself, while forgetting that the primary meaning must be for Israel. Replacement theologians say: *'If a prophecy predicts something good then it's about the Church, but if it predicts something bad then it must be for Israel!'* Now Israel is manifestly NOT the Church, so literal interpretation means that prophecies to Israel will be fulfilled to her. If it is speaking about Israel, then the literal meaning must be for Israel. Therefore, God has not finished with Israel and she is the focus of much end-time prophecy. When the Bible makes prophecies about Israel and promises to Israel, it means Israel. For example, consider the famous prophecy of <u>Jeremiah 31:31</u>: **"Behold, the days are coming, says the Lord, when I will make a New Covenant with <u>the house of Israel</u> and with <u>the house of Judah</u>."**

The fact the Church has entered into the blessing of the New Covenant in Christ (Hebrews 8:7-13) does not mean that Jeremiah 31:31-34 will not be literally fulfilled to the house of Israel, for this prophecy is primarily about the fact that God will remarry Israel through a New Covenant. God married Israel, as it were, at Mount Sinai through the Old Covenant of Moses, and He later divorced her because of her unfaithfulness, but He will remarry her at the 2nd Coming of Christ, when all Israel will be saved and enter into the New Covenant. As a Nation Israel rejected Jesus when He came the first time, so as a nation she could not enter into the New Covenant at that time. However, Jesus still established the New Covenant in His Blood, and made it possible for all who receive Him, Jew or Gentile, to enter into it. This is the Mystery: since Christ is the Seed of Abraham He could inherit all the covenant-blessings, and when we believed we were put in Christ, so through our union with Christ we share with Him in His covenant inheritance.

So we can receive for ourselves all the prophecies and promises in the Old Testament, which describe the blessings of the New Covenant that God will make with Israel through the Messiah, because in Christ we are in that same New Covenant. Therefore when Isaiah 60:1 says, **"Arise, shine; for your light has come and the Glory of the Lord is risen upon you"**, this is actually talking about what God will do for Israel, but we can also apply it to ourselves. However we should not deny its original literal meaning, which is a promise to Israel.

The fact that we can apply prophecies of New Covenant blessings to the Church does not negate the literal fulfilment of these prophecies for the nation of Israel, which will happen when she will accept Jesus at His Second Coming, when all God's covenants, promises and prophecies to her will be fulfilled.

So prophecies about Israel will be fulfilled by Israel, but it is also true that Israel is a type of the Church, and that the prophesied blessings for a future Israel under the New Covenant also apply to the Church under the New Covenant, for: **"God has blessed us with every spiritual blessing in Christ"** (Ephesians 1:3), and: **"all the promises of God in Him are 'Yes', and in Him 'Amen' to the glory of God through us"** (2Corinthians 1:20). We need to uphold God's purposes for both Israel and the Church. In replacement theology, the Church in its pride claims that God has finished with Israel and that the Church has permanently replaced her in God's purposes, although the Bible never said that. Indeed it says the opposite. This is a crucial issue in the interpretation of Prophecy

Even when the Bible uses symbols, that does not mean we are free to interpret them any way we would like. The Bible always supplies the correct interpretation of each symbol. It always gives you the key to crack the code! For example in Revelation 1:12-13 John describes a vision of Christ: **"Then I turned to see the voice that spoke with me. And having turned I saw 7 Golden Lampstands, and in the midst of the 7 Lampstands One like the Son of Man."** The 7 Golden Lampstands and the 7 Stars in His hand are symbols. But, we do not have to guess what they mean. We are not free to make up a meaning that suits us. The Bible always interprets itself, so you must look elsewhere in the Bible to discover the meaning of the symbol. In this case you do not have to go very far, for Revelation 1:20 says: **"As for the Mystery of the 7 Stars which you saw in My right hand, and the 7 Golden Lampstands: the 7 Stars are the angels of the 7**

Churches, and the 7 Lampstands are the 7 Churches." So the 7 Lampstands are symbolic of the 7 Churches and the 7 Stars are a symbol of 7 Angels.

By describing the Churches as Lampstands, the Bible speaks volumes in a simple image. This describes the main Purpose of the Church to be a witness of Christ, to shine the light of the Gospel of Christ. In the 7 letters Christ is judging these 7 Churches according to how well they have fulfilled this primary purpose of holding forth and living out the truth of God's Word. 'Angels' is the Greek word 'angelos' which also means 'Messengers.' So it is talking about the Churches and their Messengers or Pastors. The 7 letters are written to the 7 Pastors of the Churches. If the Lord wanted to communicate to angels, He would not need to send a letter through John! In these letters Christ holds these messengers accountable for what is happening in their Churches, which points to them being the leaders of these Churches. He rebukes their sin, calls them to repent, and encourages them to be faithful. This confirms that He is talking to men, not angels.

An interesting example of symbolism is Paul's thorn in the flesh. He says in 2Corinthians 12:7 : **"a thorn in the flesh was given to me, a messenger of satan to buffet me."** First of all we have to decide if this was a literal physical thorn in the flesh, or is he using symbolic language? Does the passage make sense if it was a literal thorn? If he really had a physical thorn in his flesh, would he really pray to God for it to be removed? No, he would pull it out himself or get someone to do it for him. It clearly was not a literal thorn, so it must be a symbol. Then we ask the next question: What does it symbolise? At this point many assume without justification that it represents a sickness. But we must let the Bible interpret itself rather than trust our human reasoning. We need to find where this same symbol is used elsewhere in the Bible to know what it really means, for God is consistent.

Numbers 33:55: **"If you do not drive out the inhabitants of the Land from before you, then it shall be that those whom you let remain shall be as irritants** (pricks) **in your eyes, and as THORNS in your SIDES** (flesh)**, and they will harass you in the Land where you dwell."** Joshua 23:13: **"the Lord will no longer drive out these nations from before you. But they shall be snares and traps to you, and scourges on your SIDES and THORNS in your eyes."** So a 'Thorn in the Flesh' is a figure of speech representing a person who troubles and opposes you. We have a similar expression: "He's a pain in the neck." So a 'thorn in the flesh' was a personality actively and physically opposing the progress of God's people. Paul identified it in the same verse as 'a messenger (angel) of satan.' There was an evil angel stirring up people against Paul wherever he went to try and stop his ministry. This is confirmed by context of this passage (2Corinthians 11:23-33). So Paul was praying for God to deliver him from this persecution.

Another example of symbolism is in Revelation 12:1-5: **"A great sign appeared in heaven: a woman clothed with the sun, with the moon under her feet, and on her head a crown of 12 stars. Then being with child, she cried out in labour and in pain to give birth. And another sign appeared in heaven: behold, a great, fiery red dragon having 7 heads and 10 horns, and 7 diadems on his heads. His tail drew a third of the stars of heaven and threw them to the earth. And the dragon stood before the woman who was ready to give birth, to devour her Child as soon as it was born. She bore a male Child who was to rule all nations with a rod of iron. And her Child was caught up to God and His throne."** We can easily identify the dragon, because v9 says: **"So the great dragon was cast out, that serpent of old, called the Devil and Satan, who deceives the whole world."** But who is the Woman? Is it the Church? Is it Mary? Is it Israel? We need to see where else in the Bible do we see a parallel symbol.

Genesis 37:9: **"Then he** (Joseph) **dreamed still another dream and told it to his brothers, and said, "Look, I have dreamed another dream. And this time, the sun, the moon, and the eleven stars bowed down to me."** The sun, moon and 12 stars were Jacob or Israel, his wife and his 12 sons (Joseph and his 11 brothers) who became the 12 tribes of Israel, as is clear from Jacob's response in v10. Thus this Woman is a picture of the nation of Israel, and Revelation 12 is describing how the Messiah came into the earth through Israel. She cannot be the Church for the Messiah brought forth the Church not the other way round!

So it is obvious when something is symbolic, because it makes no sense otherwise. When symbols are used, search the Bible for what that symbol actually means. You are not free to invent a meaning that suits your purposes.

*Let's now apply the principle of literal interpretation to 3 classic Scriptures.

*Prophecy 1: Isaiah 11:6-8: **"The wolf also shall dwell with the lamb, the leopard shall lie down with the young goat, the calf and the young lion and the fatling together; and a little child shall lead them. The cow and the bear shall graze; their young ones shall lie down together; and the lion shall eat straw like the ox** (even the lion will be vegetarian). **The nursing child shall play by the cobra's hole, and the weaned child shall put his hand in the viper's den."**

Literally interpreted, this predicts a future age when the curse on the animal kingdom will be lifted and all things restored to as they were originally in Eden. This plain literal sense makes perfect sense and so it will literally come to pass when Jesus returns and reigns on the earth. Those who reject the literal meaning have to spiritualise this to mean that in the Church there are various kinds of different people, some aggressive like wolves, and others like lambs. But in Christ, we will all get on together. I have no problem with this as a spiritual application to the Church, but it is surely not the original .

*Prophecy 2: Revelation 7:1-8 describes 144,000 of the 12 tribes of Israel, 12,000 from each tribe, whom God will seal in the Tribulation. They will be anointed to spearhead the evangelism in the Tribulation, for the rest of Revelation 7 describes the great harvest of souls from their ministry. Who are these 144,000? Do we take it literally as 144,000 from the 12 tribes of Israel, or is this symbolic of the Church? What about the claim of the Jehovah Witnesses that it's 144,000 JW's? Again we ask does the plain sense make sense? Yes. Would the Jewish writer (John) have understood it as 144,000 Jews? Yes. It makes perfect sense God would choose 144,000 from the tribes of Israel. Since the plain meaning makes sense, do not try and invent some other meaning. To submit to Scripture as the Word of God we must believe that God means what He says, and says what He means.

*Prophecy 3 is the major test case of how a person interprets Prophecy. In Revelation 19 we see Jesus return to earth in power and glory. Then Revelation 20:1-7 says He will reign on earth for 1000 years, with satan locked up in the Pit.

6 times it says 1000 years, so do we take these 1000 years literally or symbolically of a long period of time, namely part or all of the Church Age? We must ask: 'Does the plain sense makes sense.' Does it make sense that Jesus will

return to earth, establish His Kingdom here and reign for 1000 years? It not only makes perfect sense, but it agrees with many other prophecies about a future Golden Age when the Messiah will reign as king over all the earth. Therefore there is no reason not to take it as literal 1000 years. If it makes sense literally, take it literally. Moreover applying it to the Church Age leads to contradictions. For example, has satan really been bound so he does not deceive the nations any more?

In conclusion, **our first KEY: Interpret Prophecy Literally according to its plain meaning** is the foundational principle under girding our whole study of Bible Prophecy. This is based on God's integrity and faithfulness - He means what He says and says what He means. Obeying this principle shows we are submitting our thoughts to His thoughts, rather than replacing His thoughts with our thoughts.

*KEY 2 - Understanding the Dispensations

A direct consequence of the literal interpretation of Scripture is dispensationalism, which notes that there are distinctive periods of time and distinct groups of people, involved in the outworking of God's purposes, with different groups representing God at different times. The word 'Dispensation' comes from the Greek work 'oiko-nomia' (literally: house-law), describing a particular administration, management or stewardship of a household. Dispensationalism says that God rules the world according to different Dispensations at different times, just as American history is a sequence of different presidential administrations. It is like parents managing their household. The household-rules could be described as a dispensation. As the children grow up, some of these rules will change (for example, bedtimes). So there will necessarily be different phases or dispensations in the stewardship of their household. Likewise the Bible clearly reveals different Dispensations in God's dealings with the human race. At the moment we are in the Dispensation of Grace (the Church Age), but it will not always be so. We will see that these Dispensations are self-evident from a straightforward reading of Scripture. Many things remain the same, but whatever is changed is explained by God at the time. Some dispensations are in the past and are the subject of history, whereas others are yet future and are the subject of Prophecy. Thus all time is divided into different Dispensations or extended Ages of time characterised by a definite kind of Divine Administration.

God sets the rules for each Dispensation, and at key moments of history He intervenes to change the way He runs His household, bringing in a new Dispensation. Usually, an old Administration is brought to an end by a Divine Judgment and then a new Administration is established through a new Covenant that God makes with man. This means there is normally a relatively short transitional period in which the changes take place. This is encapsulated in the phrase: 'the times and seasons': **"concerning the TIMES and the SEASONS, brethren, you have no need that I should write to you"** (1 Thessalonians 5:1).

The words 'times and seasons' translate 'chronos' and 'kairos' in the Greek. Chronos is an extended period of time (a season), whereas kairos describes a turning-point or short transitional time when a major change is effected, bringing about a new 'chronos' or season. This applies to our own lives, which go through seasons. During a season things are stable for an extended period of time. But then suddenly a kairos moment happens, when there is a sudden change in our life, such as getting married, or having a child. Suddenly our whole life, priorities and rules change, and we enter into a new season. So the times and seasons in the Bible refer to God's dispensations and His dispensational changes. Each kairos is the result of a major Divine intervention, which moves God's dealings with man into a new phase, bringing in a new dispensation or season with different rules.

The fact that God rules over the Kairos (Transitional Times) and Chronos (Ages) is expressed in a Name of God: **'El Olam'** (Genesis 21:33). This is usually translated 'the Everlasting God', but could equally well be translated 'God of the Ages." Likewise: **"From everlasting to everlasting, You are God"** (Psalm 90:2) could be translated: **"from Age to Age, You are God."** Acts 1:7: **"the times and seasons** (dispensations) **which the Father has fixed by His own authority."** Hebrews 1:1,2: **"God, who at various TIMES (past dispensations) and in various ways spoke in time past to the fathers by the prophets, has in these Last Days** (the present dispensation) **spoken to us by His Son, whom He has appointed heir of all things, through whom also He made the worlds** (literally: 'the Ages')." Hebrews 11:3: **"By faith we understand that the worlds** (literally: 'Ages') **were framed by the Word of God."** So God framed the Ages by speaking His Word at each kairos time, and thus He defined the nature of the next Age. See also Acts 17:26-27, which says that God's ultimate purpose in all this is God's revelation to man, so that men might find God. Thus it is God who ordained and created the successive Ages of time, the different dispensations.

For example, there was a long period of time (an Age) from the Fall to the Flood, known as the Dispensation of Conscience. God ended that Dispensation by the worldwide Judgment of Noah's Flood (Genesis 7), and brought in a new Dispensation (of Human Government) through the Noahic Covenant (Genesis 8-9). The Transition Time, during which God's Judgment fell while He also saved the believers, was about a year. This is important for our study of End Time Prophecy, because we will see that the worldwide Judgment of the Flood bringing about a major dispensational change, was used by Jesus as a type of the worldwide Judgment of the Tribulation, that will be initiated by His Coming in the Rapture (Matthew 24:36-41). Thus the Tribulation is not a Dispensation in its own right, but a 7 year transition period of Judgment corresponding to the year of the Flood, between the Church Age and the Messianic Kingdom, which is why it is called 'the End ('suntelia') of the Age' (Matthew 13:39,40,49, 24:3, 28:20). This word 'suntelia' should be translated 'Consummation', because it does not mean the final end ('telos'), but the final short period of time in which things are brought to their conclusion. Thus people will be saved and born again under the New Covenant in the Tribulation, just as they are in the Church Age – there is no reversion to the Old Covenant Dispensation as some teach.

These dispensational changes are necessary as part of the way God progressively reveals Himself and His Plan to the human race. Understanding the Dispensations is a major key to understanding the overall progression of God's revelation in the Bible, helping us to trace God's progressive revelation through time, and to see the overall structure of history and prophecy from His perspective. To understand the big picture of Prophecy, it is vital to understand the past, present and future Dispensations of God, and the differences between the different periods of time. The Church has a self-centred tendency to think of herself and the Church Age as the only important group and time-period, and so ignore the rest. Dispensationalism gives due importance to God's progressive revelation through different groups of people and different time-periods, and so helps us to keep track of it. God does not reveal everything about a subject in one place, but progressively over thousands of years, each time building upon what He had revealed before. Often He introduces it in seed-form in Genesis and then He develops it all the way through to its climax in Revelation. So to comprehend the overall message of scripture on any subject, we need to trace it through the Bible from the beginning, seeing how God gradually develops His revelation in stages.

Dispensationalism also upholds literal interpretation in maintaining the distinction between different groups of people in God's Plan, especially between Israel and the Church: **"Give no offence either to the Jews, or to the Greeks, or to the Church of God"** (1Corinthians 10:32). The Bible consistently refers to Israel as the Jewish people, the physical descendants of Abraham, Isaac and Jacob. The Gentiles (represented in this verse by the Greeks) is everyone else, and the Church is a special group consisting of both Jews and Gentiles who have been called out through the Gospel to belong to Christ. The word: 'Church' comes from the Greek word 'ekklesia' meaning 'called out ones.'

The Dispensations are self-evident stages in God's Administration over man.

*1. **Innocence** (Genesis 1-2) from Creation (Genesis 1) and the establishment of **the Edenic Covenant** (Genesis 1:28-30, 2:15-17).

*2. **Conscience** (Genesis 3-7) The next kairos was the Fall when man sinned. God responded with **the Adamic Covenant** (Genesis 3:14-19), when He described the curse that would come upon them and the earth as a consequence of their sin. This was brought to an end by the worldwide Judgment of the Flood (Genesis 7 – 8:14).

*3. **Human Government** (Genesis 8:15 – 11:32) was brought in by the Covenant God made with man through Noah after the Flood, which is still in force today.

*4. **Promise** (Genesis 12 - Exodus 11). The next 'kairos' was God's Covenant with Abraham, Isaac and Jacob (Genesis 12-28), which is foundational to all the later covenants, in which God moves forward His Salvation and Kingdom Programs. This was an unconditional covenant of grace, promising Abraham a Nation, a Land and a Seed, through whom salvation (blessing) would come to the world.

*5. **Law** (from Exodus 12 to the death and resurrection of Christ). Having delivered Israel in the Exodus, God made a Covenant with Israel through Moses, which God used to prepare the way for the New Covenant in Christ, which alone can bring salvation. Most of the Old Testament comes from this dispensation. The Old Covenant was brought to an end by the death of Christ, who fulfilled it perfectly, and then He brought in the everlasting New Covenant in His resurrection.

*6. Grace - the Church Age (the Mystery). Jesus brought in a new Dispensation of Grace through the New Covenant. This does not mean that God did not give grace before this, but that this new period would be especially marked by God's Grace: **"The LAW was given through Moses, but GRACE and truth came through Jesus Christ"** (John 1:17). God had kept this Dispensation secret. It was hidden in God before the foundation of the world. The prophets saw the Coming of Messiah in 2 Stages: (1) to suffer and die for our sins, and then (2) to reign in glory as King over the earth. But it was not revealed to them that there was a significant time between His Suffering and His Glory. God kept this Dispensation as a secret or Mystery, because it was connected with Israel's rejection of Christ. Had Israel accepted her King, He could have established His Kingdom on earth fulfilling the vision of the Old Testament prophets. But since they rejected Him, this Kingdom had to be postponed and instead the Church Age was introduced. God only started to reveal the Mystery when Israel's rejection of the Messiah became clear, or else it would have infringed her freewill. The Mystery was that God would form a new body, distinct from Israel, consisting of Jews and Gentiles in Christ, which is the body of Christ, His Church, which is anointed to be God's representative and witness for this Age. The Church Age will be brought to an end by the Rapture, followed by the worldwide Judgment of the Tribulation (Revelation 4-19), which comes to its climax at the Second Coming of Christ, when He will establish His Messianic Kingdom on earth for 1000 years (the Millennium).

*7. The Kingdom Age or Millennium (Revelation 20:1-6), which is brought to an end by a Divine Judgement on a final rebellion (v7-9). Then satan and his angels are cast into the Lake of Fire (v10). Then the present universe is destroyed, and all unbelievers from all Ages are resurrected and stand before the Great White Throne for final sentencing and dismissal to the Lake of Fire, their final home (v11-15).

*8. Eternity (Revelation 21-22). Then God will usher in the Eternal State by creating a new perfect and everlasting heaven and earth.

On the next page is a detailed chart for further study showing how the Biblical dispensations and covenants are connected. The main alternative system of theology (Covenant Theology), is discussed in Appendix 2. Unlike Dispensationalism, Covenant Theology does not make a clear distinction between Israel and the Church, or interpret Scripture in a consistently literal way.

*KEY 3 - Premillennialism

*KEY 3 concerns one of these special periods of time called **the Messianic Kingdom or Millennium**, for Revelation 20 tells us it will last 1000 years. Israel has always looked forward to this Golden Age - when the Messiah, the Son of David will rule on the earth with Israel as the chief nation. All the prophets looked forward to it, which is why Peter in <u>Acts 3:21</u> called it: **"the Times of Restoration of all things spoken of by all the prophets."** As well as correcting Israel for her sins and prophesying upcoming events, all the prophets also looked beyond these to a glorious future Age of peace on earth under the personal rule of the Messiah. The Jews took these prophecies literally, and so should we, otherwise there is nothing to stop you making the prophecies mean whatever you want. The Bible says that all history is heading towards a climactic Golden Age of 1000 years under a one world-ruler, King Jesus (Revelation 20). He will establish His Messianic Kingdom on earth, when He returns. It will be a time of righteousness, prosperity and peace Mankind has always held a deep hope for such an Age. But foolish man thinks he can establish it himself. Starting with Nimrod at the Tower of Babel, men have tried to establish worldwide empires in their own name that would endure forever. The problem is that all these rulers were sinners, and so were unqualified to have that kind of power. So it always ends as a tyranny, controlled by the power of evil.

Throughout history the forces of darkness are in conflict with the Kingdom of God. Both want to establish their dominion on earth. Satan's programme is to set up a one-world government and religion and put his man (the antichrist) in charge thus gaining total control. But God is in control. He foiled this at Babel and will again at Armageddon. History is moving towards a great climax when satan's kingdom reaches its fullest outward form (in the Great Tribulation) and then Christ will return to judge and destroy it before all mankind is destroyed. Then God will establish His King and Kingdom on earth when Christ returns. So there is a coming world conqueror and ruler - Jesus! He will establish a literal Kingdom of peace on earth in fulfilment of all the prophets have spoken. He alone is able and worthy to

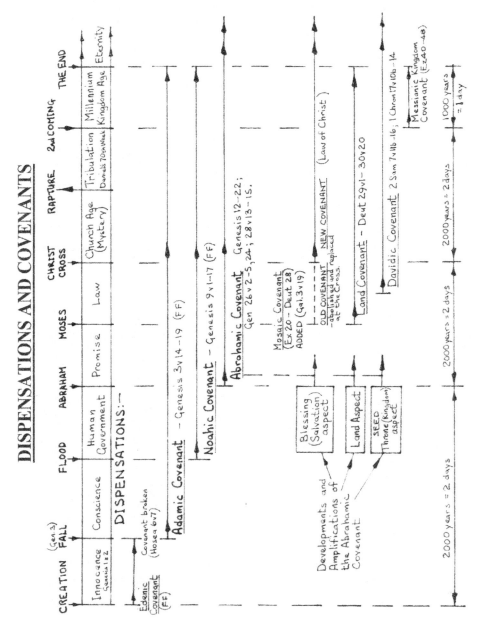

DISPENSATIONS AND COVENANTS

rule over the kingdoms of the earth! This future manifestation of God's KINGDOM on earth is a major KEY to understanding Prophecy. Its importance derives from the fact that it is the climax (the high point and focal point) of God's workings in time and history. All history is moving toward the time when God will literally and completely fulfil all His promises and covenants. All the rivers of history are flowing toward this destination - the Millennial Sea. So to understand Prophecy we must understand that all history is moving toward this Age. As understanding CREATION is foundational and essential, as it is the ORIGIN of all history, so understanding the MILLENNIAL KINGDOM is essential, because all history is flowing towards it.

Thus our view on the Millennium is a touchstone for how we read and understand all Prophecy. The Millennial Issue is a defining prophetic issue that separates the main streams of interpretation of Bible Prophecy (see Appendix 4 for an in-depth discussion of the various viewpoints on the Millennial Issue). What we believe about it governs our whole viewpoint of Bible Prophecy, and in turn, it controls our vision of the Church Age and how we should focus our efforts and energies, for example, whether primarily upon evangelism and discipleship, or upon kingdom building (the Church trying to establish dominion over the world-system). All agree that taking a literal approach to prophecy leads to a PRE-MILLENNIAL view. That is, Jesus Christ will return BEFORE the Millennium. Thus Jesus will personally establish His Messianic Kingdom on earth and literally reign on earth from Jerusalem for 1000 years in fulfilment of all the prophets.

The CONSISTENT VISION of all the Old Testament Prophets was that the Messiah, the son of David, would come in power to establish a literal Kingdom of God on earth, reigning from Jerusalem over the nations with a rod of iron. This Messianic Kingdom is the climax of Old-Testament prophecy. Even when the prophets rebuked Israel for sinning, they would always finish with this vision of a glorious future Kingdom, with Israel as the chief nation.

One example is Isaiah 2:2-4: **"It shall come to pass in the latter days that the Mountain of the Lord's House shall be established on the top of the mountains, and shall be exalted above the hills; and all nations shall flow to it. Many people shall come and say: "Come, and let us go up to the Mountain of the Lord, to the House of the God of Jacob; He will teach us His ways, and we shall walk in His paths." For out of Zion shall go forth the Law, and the Word of the Lord from Jerusalem. He shall judge between the nations, and rebuke many people. They shall beat their swords into plowshares, and their spears into pruning hooks. Nation shall not lift up sword against nation, neither shall they learn war anymore."** This is unfulfilled, no matter how much you spiritualise it. It's talking about world peace. The UN claims v4 for their vision, but it belongs to a future Dispensation. It is simply not true about the time we are living in. But it will literally come to pass when Jesus returns and establishes His Kingdom.

Isaiah 9:6,7: **"Unto us a child is born, unto us a son is given and the GOVERNMENT** (of the earth) **shall be upon His shoulder and His Name shall be called Wonderful, Counsellor, Mighty God, Everlasting Father** (the Source of Eternal Life), **Prince of Peace ...and of the increase of His government and peace there shall be no end, upon the Throne of David** (an earthly throne) **and over His Kingdom, to order it and establish it with judgment and justice from that time forward, even forever."** Right now Jesus is not sitting on the earthly throne of David in Jerusalem. He is sitting on His Father's throne in heaven. But one day when Jesus returns He will sit on the throne of the earth, the throne of David, and rule the earth from Jerusalem. That is what this prophecy literally tells us. The church world is so used to spiritualising these prophecies that we are in danger of missing the whole point of what they are really saying. The Old Testament prophets believed that their prophecies would literally come to pass. This Golden Age of the Messiah was the expectation of Israel in Jesus' time, and of the early church, and of the Orthodox Jews today. For the prophets it was the climax of history when all the promises of God's unconditional Everlasting **Covenant with Abraham** would be literally and completely fulfilled.

These Promises were 3-fold and were expanded in 3 later Covenants:

*1. The Promise of BLESSING (salvation) to all nations, that is, SALVATION, which is fulfilled through **the New Covenant**, which provides the New Birth and every spiritual blessing in abundance (Jeremiah 31:31-34).

*2. The Promise of NATIONHOOD and LAND to Israel through **the Land Covenant** (Deuteronomy 29-30), where God promised that Israel would ultimately enjoy full possession of her Land.

*3. Thirdly, the promise of a coming SEED of Abraham (Christ), who would bring all things to fulfilment. This promise was developed in more detail through **the Davidic Covenant**, which promised David an everlasting THRONE KINGDOM, and KING. God promised David that one of his sons would reign forever as King over Israel, and who also would rule over all the nations from David's throne in Jerusalem until the end of time.

All of these unconditional Covenants will be fulfilled through Christ in the Millennium. Thus Israel has always looked forward to a golden Messianic Age, when the Son of David rules upon the earth, with Israel as head nation. But many Christians do not believe this will happen. They say these promises to Israel are to be spiritualised and applied to the Church, so God no longer has a special role for national Israel - for the Church is the new Israel. This implies God has deceived Israel, giving her false hope. Thus this is a slur on His character, and if He deceived Israel how then can we be sure He will be true to His promises to us? They think the New Testament does not just clarify and expand on the revelation of the Old Testament but also that it changes its original meaning, as if it were not God's inerrant Word, to be understood in its plain meaning according to the laws of language. This is exactly what Jesus warned against in Matthew 5:17, saying that He had not come to abolish the Old Testament as the Word of God, but rather He would ensure it was all fulfilled. In fact, as we will now see, the New Testament perfectly confirms the revelation of the Messianic Kingdom in the Old Testament.

The New Testament confirms the Messianic Kingdom (Millennium). Although it does not contain as much material on the Messianic Kingdom as the Old, it has sufficient scriptures to clearly reaffirm that God has not changed His mind. He has not cancelled the hope of the Jewish prophets and covenants, but rather confirms their prophecies will still be literally fulfilled. The fact of the Church Age doesn't mean God's promises to Israel will never be fulfilled. The large amount of information in the Old Testament on this Kingdom meant it was unnecessary for the New to add much. The only missing information was how long it would last, and so Revelation 20 tells us (6 times) that it will exist for **1000 years**, which is why another name for the Messianic Kingdom is **the Millennium**.

*At Jesus' conception, the angel says to Mary in Luke 1:31-33: **"You will conceive in your womb and bring forth a Son, and shall call His name Jesus. He will be great, and will be called the Son of the Highest; and the Lord God will give Him the THRONE of His father David. And He will reign over the House of Jacob forever and His KINGDOM will have no end."** This refers to the fulfilment of the Davidic Covenant in the Messianic Kingdom. Jesus has not yet occupied the throne of David in Jerusalem, but He will when He comes again.

*Jesus said in Matthew 19:28: **"Assuredly I say to you, that in the regeneration, when the Son of Man sits on the throne of His glory, you who have followed Me will also sit on 12 thrones, judging the 12 tribes of Israel."** He was speaking of the Messianic Kingdom when the earth will be regenerated and nature made new. He assumed what the prophets had predicted was true. He confirms Israel will still exist with the 12 apostles sitting on thrones over the 12 tribes. He confirmed Israel's hope in a literal Messianic Kingdom.

*In Acts 1:6, when Jesus appeared to the apostles after His resurrection: **"they asked Him, saying: 'Lord, will You at this time restore the Kingdom to Israel?"** (). Clearly they still believed in the Messianic Kingdom. The fact they asked this question shows that Jesus, in His teaching to them, never gave them any clue that this concept of an earthly Kingdom should not be taken literally. They still expected it, and their question was simply about timing. They asked: *"Will you do it now or later?"* They knew Messiah will come to establish this Kingdom. Since He was the risen Messiah, it must have seemed like it was the right moment for Him to establish that Kingdom. Jesus answered them in Acts 1:7,8: **"It is not for you to know times or seasons, which the Father has put in His own authority, but you shall receive power when the Holy Spirit has come on you and you will be witnesses to Me in Jerusalem, and in all Judea and Samaria, and to the end of the earth."** In other words, the Father has fixed the time for the Kingdom to be established, but it was not that time yet. Instead of preparing them for this Kingdom He prepared them for the Church Age, but He never said to them: *"Don't you know that the Jewish prophets are not to be taken literally. I will now bring the Kingdom in through the Church."* His assumption is that the Messianic Kingdom will come to pass at a future time known to the Father.

*Acts 3:19-21 confirms that this Messianic Kingdom will be established at the Return of Christ. **"Repent and be converted, that your sins may be blotted out, so that times of refreshing may come from the Presence of the Lord, and that He may send Jesus Christ, who was preached to you before, whom Heaven must receive until the Times of Restoration** (or Restitution) **of all** things, which God has spoken by the mouth of all His holy prophets since the world began." Peter declares Jesus will return from Heaven in response to Israel's national repentance, and that His return will bring in the Time of Restoration of all things predicted by all the Old Testament prophets. This can only be speaking of the Messianic Kingdom. The word 'restoration' speaks of a return to previous condition of blessedness. The fall of man brought the curse on the earth. The Bible predicts that the Messiah will come and restore all things to their original state of blessing. Thus the Times of Restoration of all things must be talking about the Millennium. This is proven by Peter's observation that every prophet spoke of these times of restoration. It is a fact that all the prophets spoke of the coming Messianic Kingdom. So here Peter affirms that when Jesus returns from Heaven, He will bring in the time of restoration of all things, by establishing His Kingdom on the earth. This 'restoration of all things' must include the restoration of the Kingdom to Israel (Acts 1:6). Thus the Davidic House, Throne and Kingdom established by God, but now fallen, will be re-established on earth when Christ, the Son of David, returns to earth, and reigns on David's throne in Jerusalem.

*Amos 9:11-12 predicts this future literal restoration of the Davidic House and Kingdom, and James in the New Testament quotes these verses to show that what God was doing in the Church Age, namely saving Gentiles without requiring them to become Jews, was perfectly consistent with this prophecy of Israel's expectation. Acts 15:14-17: **"Simon has declared how God at the first visited the Gentiles to take out of them a people for His Name. And with this the words of the prophets agree, just as it is written: 'After this** (the Tribulation - see Amos 9:1-10) **I will return and will rebuild the Tabernacle** (the House and Kingdom) **of David, which has fallen down; I will rebuild its ruins, and I will set it up; so that the rest of mankind may seek the Lord, even all the Gentiles who are called by My Name, says the Lord who does all these things."**

Here Gentiles in the Messianic Kingdom are seen as being in covenant with God, while remaining as Gentiles and not having to become Jews. Thus James assumes and confirms the future literal fulfilment of Amos' prophecy in the Kingdom and says the salvation of Gentiles in the Church Age through the New Covenant agrees with it. Thus this new development does not nullify the promise of the restoration of the Davidic Kingdom. Rather it brings fresh light to it.

One aspect of literal interpretation is asking how the original hearers would have understood the words. Therefore there are other times when Jesus mentioned the Kingdom of God, which His Jewish hearers would have understood as referring to the Messianic Kingdom. For example, when Jesus preached: **"The Kingdom of God is at hand"** as well as the application to individual salvation, this would have been understood as the offer of the Messianic Kingdom to the nation of Israel. Had Israel received Him as King, He could have established His Kingdom soon after His resurrection. But because they rejected Him, the Kingdom was postponed and given to another generation. After telling a parable about His rejection by the leaders of Israel, Jesus said in <u>Matthew 21:43</u>: **"Therefore, the Kingdom of God will be taken from you and given to a nation** (people, a future generation of Israel) **bearing the fruits of it** (who have faith in Jesus as their Messiah)**."**

Likewise the disciples would have understood that Jesus was talking about the Messianic Kingdom in <u>Matthew 25:31-34</u>: **"When the Son of Man comes in His glory, and all the holy angels with Him, He will sit on the throne of His glory. All the nations** (gentiles) **will be gathered before Him, and He will separate them one from another, as a shepherd divides his sheep from the goats. And He will set the sheep on His right hand, but the goats on the left. Then the King will say to those on His right hand: 'Come, you blessed of My Father, inherit the KINGDOM prepared for you from the foundation of the world."** This is the Kingdom Christ will establish on earth when He comes again.

*The key passage around which most of the discussion is centred is <u>Revelation 20:1-7</u>. When interpreted literally, it is absolutely clear that when Christ returns He will establish the Messianic Kingdom on earth and it will last for 1000 years. <u>Revelation 19</u> describes Jesus' Return to earth in power and glory, and immediately after that He establishes His Messianic Kingdom upon the earth (Revelation 20:1-7), giving a clear confirmation of the Old Testament revelation.

<u>Revelation 20:1-7</u>: **"Then** (after His Return to earth in Revelation 19) **I saw an angel coming down from Heaven, having the key to the bottomless pit and a great chain in his hand. He laid hold of the dragon, that serpent of old, who is the devil and satan, and bound him for <u>1000 years</u>; and he cast him into the bottomless pit, and shut him up, and set a seal on him, so that he should deceive the nations no more till the <u>1000 years</u> were finished. But after these**

things he must be released for a little while. And I saw thrones, and they (resurrected believers) **sat on them, and judgment was committed to them. Then I saw the souls of those who had been beheaded for their witness to Jesus and for the word of God, who had not worshipped the beast or his image, and had not received his mark on their foreheads or on their hands. And they** (the Tribulation Martyrs) **lived and reigned with Christ for <u>1000 years</u>. But the rest of the dead did not live again until the <u>1000 years</u> were finished. This is** (completes) **the first resurrection. Blessed and holy is he who has part in the first resurrection. Over such the 2nd death has no power, but they shall be priests of God and of Christ, and shall reign with Him <u>1000 years</u>. Now when the <u>1000 years</u> have expired, satan will be released from his prison."**

<u>This passage states in the clearest possible language that when Jesus returns:</u> (1) Satan will be bound by an angel shut up in a prison for 1000 years, so that he can no longer operate on earth, deceiving the nations. (2) After the 1000 years he will be released back into the earth for a while. (3) All believers who have died will be resurrected at this time and given thrones (positions of authority) and they will reign with Christ for 1000 years. This agrees with the Old Testament revelation of the Messianic Kingdom: **"The saints of the Most High shall receive the Kingdom, and possess the Kingdom forever, even forever and ever... Then the Kingdom and dominion, and the greatness of the Kingdom under the whole heaven** (that is, on earth), **shall be given to the people, the saints of the Most High. His Kingdom is an everlasting Kingdom, and all dominions shall serve and obey Him"** (Daniel 7:18,27). The resurrection of all believers is called the first resurrection, even though different groups of believers (e.g. Christ, the Church, Old Testament Saints, Tribulation Martyrs) are resurrected at different times. This 1st resurrection is complete before the 1000 years start. (4) The rest of the dead (the unbelievers) are not resurrected until the end of the 1000 years, when they will face final judgment and the 2nd death in the Lake of Fire (v11-15). This is the 2nd resurrection that happens 1000 years after the first. Since this all makes perfect sense there is no good reason to reject the literal interpretation.

Although this New Testament passage clearly confirms and even expands the Old Testament vision of the Messianic Kingdom, sadly the Church has largely rejected a literal understanding of Revelation 20. As a result, alternative ways of understanding it have developed in Church history (see Appendix 4), and the way you interpret it reveals and governs your whole approach to Bible Prophecy.

*KEY 4 - Israel and the Church

This Key to unlocking Bible Prophecy is another consequence of Literal Interpretation – **ISRAEL and the CHURCH are two distinct peoples of God** whose destiny and prophecies are intertwined. If we confuse these two, we will be in confusion. 'Israel' means Israel, and 'the Church' means the Church! God has distinct programs for both peoples. The Bible is always consistent with its terminology. It is only human reasoning that confuses this obvious point. Thus whatever purposes, plans and promises God has for the Church, this does not nullify His plans and promises for the people and nation of Israel. Removing the distinction between Israel and the Church is the biggest cause of confusion and error in understanding Bible Prophecy. These distinctions are very clear in 1Corinthians 10:32: **"Give no offence either (1) to the Jews (Israel) or (2) to the Greeks (Gentiles) or (3) to the Church of God."** The New Testament upholds the distinction between Jews and Gentiles, but also introduces a new group called the Church, consisting of both Jews and Gentiles in Christ. When you become part of the Church you do not stop being a Jew or Gentile, and neither does the Church replace Israel in the purposes of God.

The Church is not Israel. Israel's membership is defined by natural descent, but membership in the Church is defined by a person's faith in Christ. In the New Testament the Church is something NEW, it is called a NEW MAN in Christ, which could only come into existence after His death, resurrection and ascension (Ephesians 2:13-16, 1:20-23, 4:7-13). The Church was born (had its beginning) on the Day of Pentecost (Acts 2, see Acts 11:15-16). In Matthew 16:18, Jesus said: **"On this Rock** (Jesus Himself) **I WILL build My CHURCH."** Also John 10:14-16. That is why the New Testament calls the Church a MYSTERY hidden in God from creation, but now revealed through Christ and His apostles (Ephesians 3:3-6). The New Testament never confuses Israel with the Church, or call the Church 'Israel', although Israel is a type of the Church, both being elect people's of God, so that we can learn from Israel's experiences (1Corinthians 10). Sometimes God distinguishes the remnant of Israel (the believers within Israel, 'the Israel of God' in Galatians 6:16) from Israel as a whole, but this is not talking about the Church, although of course the Israel of God are also part of the Church in this Age.

Although the Church has come into all the blessings of the New Covenant through her union with Christ, this does not contradict the fact that God will also bring the whole nation of Israel into the New Covenant, as Jeremiah 31:31-34 declares: **"Behold, the days are coming, says the Lord, when I will make a New Covenant with the house of Israel and with the house of Judah, not according to the covenant that I made with their fathers in the day that I took them by the hand to lead them out of the land of Egypt, My covenant which they broke, though I was a husband to them, says the Lord. But this is the Covenant that I will make with the house of Israel after those days, says the Lord: I will put My Law in their minds, and write it on their hearts; and I will be their God, and they shall be My people. No more shall every man teach his neighbour, and every man his brother, saying, 'Know the Lord,' for they all shall know Me, from the least of them to the greatest of them, says the Lord. For I will forgive their iniquity, and their sin I will remember no more."**

Having said that, the New Covenant promises of blessing, called 'the blessing of Abraham' also belong to the Church, for we are in Christ (the Seed of Abraham, who received all the blessing on our behalf), for Galatians 3:14 says Christ died for us: **"that the blessing of Abraham might come on the Gentiles in Christ, that we might receive the promise of the Spirit through faith."** Thus we are blessed, not because we are 'in Israel', but because we are 'in Christ.'

Replacement Theology is a false doctrine that says that Israel is now the Church, that is the Church is the true Israel of God, or 'spiritual Israel, so that 'natural Israel' is no longer relevant in God's purposes. In other words the Church has replaced Israel in God's eyes, so that the Church inherits all the covenant blessings promised to Israel, leaving Israel to take all the curses. This self-centred doctrine is a violation of the literal interpretation of the Bible, as it can only be upheld by a massive spiritualisation of scripture (rejecting its plain meaning). It is a misrepresentation of the heart of God, who says: **"I love you (Israel) with an everlasting love"** (Jeremiah 31:3). Surely anyone who has received God's poured into their hearts (Romans 5:5) will love Israel because God loves her and has chosen her. This false doctrine is responsible for much anti-Semitism in the Church throughout her history and deserves the strongest condemnation. Paul warns us against adopting this arrogant attitude against Israel in Romans 11:17-24, even warning that He will cut off those who stubbornly continue in this sin (v22), for they are manifesting their unbelief and rejection of God's Word.

The New Testament position on Israel is abundantly clear from Romans 11, so there is no excuse. It shows that despite Israel's unbelief, which resulted in the Church-Age of Gentile Salvation, God will still be faithful to His promises to Israel and establish the Messianic Kingdom through her. He maintains the balance between the present Church-Age with its emphasis on salvation going out to the Gentiles and the future restoration of Israel in the Tribulation resulting in the Kingdom Age, which will also release fullness of blessing on the Gentiles. It sets forth that although Israel has sinned in her national rejection of Christ, and is under Divine discipline, suffering judgment rather than receiving the Messianic Kingdom (v7-11,15,25), nevertheless she has not been rejected by God (v1,2,11), because she is God's elect nation, standing on God's unconditional covenants and promises to Abraham, Isaac and Jacob (v5,6,16). Moreover v28,29 says, even when Israel is unbelief she is still God's elect nation: **"Concerning the Gospel they are enemies for your sake, but concerning the election they are beloved for the sake of the fathers. For the gifts and the calling of God are irrevocable."**

Romans 11:1: **"Has God cast away his people? God forbid."** v11-12: **"I say then, have they stumbled that they should fall? Certainly not! But through their fall** (transgression), **to provoke them to jealousy, Salvation has come to the Gentiles. Now if their fall** (transgression), **is riches for the world, and their failure riches for the Gentiles, how much more their fullness!"** Israel has transgressed and stumbled by rejecting Messiah, but she has not fallen in such a way she will not rise up again. God even worked her transgression for good, for instead of the Kingdom being established, salvation now has been released to the Gentiles in the Church Age, where Jew and Gentile are equal in the body of Christ, so we can enjoy God's riches in Christ. He says if their failure brought riches for the Gentiles, how much more their fullness! Thus in the future God will restore Israel to her fullness, which will release even more riches to the world in the

Messianic Kingdom. v15: **"For if their being cast away is the reconciling of the world, what will their acceptance be but life from the dead?"**

God's response to her sin was to bring in the Church Age, whose primary purpose is the ingathering of a great harvest of Gentiles for salvation (v11,12,15,17, 25,30,32). But this does not mean God is finished with Israel, for once the Church Age is over and the fullness of the Church harvest is gathered in (v25), God will turn back to Israel (in the Tribulation), so that ultimately all Israel will be saved by receiving Christ and His New Covenant (v26-27, also 23-24,31,32), as a result of which great riches come to the whole world through the establishment of the Messianic Kingdom, which can only happen when Israel receives her King (v12,15). v25,26a: **"Blindness in part has happened to Israel UNTIL the fullness of the Gentiles has come in. And so ALL Israel will be saved."** During this Church Age, because of her rejection of Christ national Israel has been under a judicial blindness that is partial and temporary, UNTIL the fullness of the Church-Age Gentile harvest has been gathered in. Then all Israel will be saved and remain saved through the establishment of the Messianic Kingdom.

v30,31: **"For as you** (Gentiles) **were once disobedient to God, yet have now obtained mercy through their** (Israel's) **disobedience, even so these also have now been disobedient, that through the mercy shown you they also may obtain mercy."** Again Paul predicts that God will restore Israel and show her mercy, and the mainly Gentile-Church is called to be part of this. Literally it says: "through your mercy they may obtain mercy." We are called to show mercy to Israel both spiritually, through prayer and sharing the Gospel, and practically. God will use our loving witness to help them to reach the place of obtaining mercy from God. Unfortunately the Church has not fulfilled this calling very well, and has developed theologies, which have encouraged an apathetic or even antagonistic attitude towards God's people, Israel. Therefore sadly the official Church's teaching has historically been a major cause of anti-semitism and persecution against Jews. Even today Christian anti-semitism is widespread and manifested (1) politically as anti-Zionism, and (2) theologically as replacement theology.

*(1) Zionism simply supports the right of Israel to exist as a nation in her land. So an anti-Zionist is against the state of Israel and denies its right to exist. This is a form of anti-semitism. For example, if you were to say: "I'm not anti-British. I've got nothing against them, but I want the United Kingdom to be wiped

off the map", we would see through that. Clearly you are not just anti-Britain, you are anti-British. If you are against Israel as a nation, you are also against the Jewish people. Now Israel is like any other nation, it may do some things wrong, and is not above criticism, but that does not change the fact that God has chosen her and He is going to bring His purposes for her to pass.

*(2) We previously warned against Replacement Theology, which denies Israel's distinct identity and guaranteed future destiny as God's covenant people. Replacement theology says the Church has now permanently replaced Israel as God's people in His purposes, claiming the Church is now spiritual Israel or the Israel of God. It rejects the plain meaning of the Bible and it is an attack against God's integrity. We must always be on guard against anti-semitism, as it is a clear sign of the working of satan in man's heart, even when under a Christian cloak.

Gentiles and Gentile Nations will be judged primarily according to how they treat Israel. Speaking of Abraham and his seed God says in Genesis 12:3: **"I will bless those who bless you and curse him** (literally: treat him with contempt) **who curses you."** Those who teach replacement theology are in danger of this curse of, because they say Israel is as nothing now and has no right to exist. Replacement theology is not the teaching of the Bible, which says that although Israel as a whole is in unbelief concerning the Messiah she has not lost her place as the elect nation of God. Therefore the day is coming when she will repent and believe in Jesus as her Messiah and receive the Messianic Kingdom, when all God's Covenant promises to her will be fulfilled. Therefore God has not finished with Israel. In fact she is the only nation with a divinely guaranteed future. Whatever happens she is sure to survive, for she alone has a covenant with God. She is still the apple of His eye. In Jeremiah 31:35-37, God gives the strongest possible guarantee for Israel's future: **"Thus says the Lord, Who gives the sun for a light by day, the ordinances of the moon and the stars for a light by night, Who disturbs the sea, and its waves roar (The Lord of hosts is His Name): If those ordinances depart from before Me, says the Lord, then the seed of Israel shall also cease from being a nation before Me forever. Thus says the Lord: "If heaven above can be measured, and the foundations of the earth searched out beneath, I will also cast off all the seed of Israel for all that they have done, says the Lord."** So, whatever blessing God has for the Church does not nullify what He has already promised to Israel. He is the God of Israel. He will still fight for Israel and judge those who reject her right to exist and speak or come against her to harm her.

The Israel issue is very important because God's character and faithfulness is at stake. He has a wonderful Purpose for the Church, and a wonderful purpose for Israel. It is going to become increasingly important in these end-times as to where you stand on Israel, with the spirit of this world, which infiltrates the church-world, becoming increasingly anti-Semitic and anti-Israel. God is with Israel, so you will either be for or against God. It is very much a defining issue. Your position on this will determine to a great extent whether you are working for or against God's purposes. If the love of God has indeed been poured out into your heart by the Holy Spirit (Romans 5:5), then since God loves Israel (Jeremiah 31:3), you should have that same love in our hearts - if you are truly born again.

We should be grateful for Israel for giving us the Bible and our Saviour Jesus Christ. We have a great debt to repay her, and we can do this by supporting Israel and praying for her spiritual salvation and physical protection. Part of God's calling on the Church is to pray for the salvation of the Jews, that the veil of unbelief will be removed from their eyes, so they will see Yeshua is their Messiah. The Bible says there will be a great turning to the Lord in Israel. More and more Jews are becoming believers in Jesus, but there's a long way to go. Also we are to pray for the regathering and restoration of the nation of Israel, for this is God's End-Time Purpose, as revealed in the Bible. They face great challenges in what's happening right now, and they will go through a lot of difficult times in the future. We are also to pray for the peace (shalom) of Jerusalem for it is the city of the great King, the true capital of the earth, and the centre of great spiritual warfare (Psalm 122:6-9).

Like Ruth and Naomi, the destinies of the Church and Israel are intertwined. Thus we have seen a parallel restoration of God's 2 covenant Peoples: the Church and Israel over the last 120 years. For example, at the first Zionist Congress in 1897 the vision for the Jewish State was established, leading to increased Jewish immigration to the Land. This coincided with the Pentecostal Outpouring of the Spirit in the Church. Then when Israel was reborn as a Nation in 1948 there was a great restoration of the Gifts of Healing in the Healing Revival. Then the Recapture of Jerusalem in 1967 took place at the same time as the charismatic movement. Also according to Ezekiel 38-39 a future worldwide revival will take soon place in connection with a dramatic Intervention of God to save Israel.

In conclusion, when Christ came He offered Israel the Kingdom, but they rejected it, so it was postponed until a future believing generation of Israel will accept it. Instead God introduced the Church Age, whose purpose is to gather a harvest of souls for Jesus from the nations. Then after the Church Age, He will move His Kingdom Program forward by bringing down the kingdoms of the world in the Tribulation, and then establishing His Kingdom on earth through Israel.

*KEY 5 - the SUFFERINGS then the GLORY

There are 2 Streams of Messianic Prophecy: the SUFFERINGS then the GLORY. The Messiah would FIRST come in humility to suffer and die for our salvation, and THEN in power and glory to reign upon the earth. The time-period between His 2 Comings depended on Israel's response to Him. This 2-fold nature of Messianic Prophecy, reflects the 2-fold Programme of God throughout all history, namely (1) His SALVATION Program, and (2) His KINGDOM Program.

* KEY 6 - The Messianic Kingdom offered to Israel

When Jesus came the first time He offered the Kingdom to Israel. He not only came as the suffering Saviour to die for our sins, but also to offer the Messianic Kingdom to Israel, in order to fulfil all of God's promises to her. By establishing the New Covenant in His Blood, He laid the spiritual foundation for His Messianic Kingdom, and now all that was required was for the Nation of Israel to receive Him as Saviour and King. If the leaders of Israel had received Him, then He could and would have established His Kingdom right then.

*KEY 7 - The Kingdom Rejected and Postponed.

However, national Israel rejected the King and His Kingdom, and as a result He could not establish it at that time. Therefore the Kingdom was POSTPONED. It was not cancelled altogether for that would be impossible since it stood on the unconditional covenants and promises of God to Israel. Delay is not denial. Instead of establishing the Kingdom through Israel at that time, God brought in the Church Age, with its emphasis of Salvation going to the Gentiles. Now delay is not denial, and God must still fulfil His promises to Israel of establishing the Kingdom. But this will not happen until God has fulfilled His Purposes for the Church Age.

*KEY 8 - The Mystery of the Church.

In His Omniscience, God knew that Israel would not accept the Messiah and His Kingdom, so He always planned to bring in the Church Age. But He had to keep it secret, for had He revealed what would happen in advance, it would have violated Israel's freewill. She would not have had a genuine choice to accept or reject, if God had revealed her decision in advance. So God had to keep Israel's official rejection of the Messiah and the resulting Church-Age as a MYSTERY. So, although the Old Testament revealed the Sufferings of the Messiah in His 1st Coming and the Glories and Kingdom of the Messiah in His 2nd Coming, it did not reveal that there would be a Church Age between these 2 Comings. Thus the Church Age from Pentecost to the Rapture was a Mystery hidden in God. This means the Church is not the fulfilment of the Old Testament prophecies of the Kingdom, but is something new, which God had kept hidden as a Mystery or Secret in Himself from the foundation of the world, to only be revealed at the right time.

*KEY 9: Prophetic Gaps and Jumps

The Mystery of the Church explains an interesting characteristic of Old Testament Prophecy – namely prophetic Gaps and Jumps. When you read the Old Testament prophets, you will often find that they are describing events at the 1st Coming of Christ, and then suddenly they jump 2000 years to events around His 2nd Coming. Why do they jump over the Church Age as if it did not exist? The reason is that it was a Mystery, a Divine Secret. God had hidden it from them. Just like when we look at 2 mountains, one behind he other, we do not see the valley in between, so they did not see the Church Age. They did not know they were jumping across a Gap of 2000 years from Christ's 1st Coming to His 2nd Coming. So their prophecies flowed as if the events of the 2nd Coming happen soon after the events of the 1st Coming, whereas we know they jump 2000 years over the Mystery Age. These GAPS wonderfully illustrate the fact that in the Old Testament the Church was a Mystery hidden in God. So a common Prophetic Pattern is:

(1) Events at Christ's 1ST COMING in humility as a Suffering Servant.

(2) Then the Prophecy jumps 2000 years over a MYSTERY GAP. Nothing is said about this time, it remains hidden from view. The prophet cannot see into this time and so he has no idea how long it will last. The great difference between His Suffering and His Glory indicates there must be a time-interval between the fulfilments of the 2 parts of the prophecy but how long this time lasts, and what happens in that time was a Mystery to them.

(3) The Prophecy then describes events leading up to His 2nd COMING in power and glory as the Conquering King. The 2 parts of the Prophecy are

connected by a common theme that links them together and bridges the gap, thus connecting the events of 1st and 2nd Coming.

*KEY 10 – Understanding the Tribulation

Part 3 in this series of books will cover the Tribulation in great detail. Many Christians have no real concept of the Tribulation as a distinct period of time, but rather see it as just part of the Church Age, in which life on earth is a bit worse than usual. Neither do they appreciate its importance in the grand scheme of things.

At the End of the Age, just before the Lord's Coming in power and glory to establish His Kingdom, there will be a special period of time of unparalleled evil and distress on the whole world, called '**the Tribulation**' (or 'the Trouble' – Matthew 24:29). The prophets described it, as does Revelation in great detail in chapters 6-18. The New Testament confirms after the Church Age, evil will be allowed to come to its fullness (through antichrist and his kingdom), but only for a short time, for God will move in Judgement and destroy it, and then establish His Kingdom. God's wrath will be poured out on the evil world-system. Thus it is a time when the Lord will directly intervene in a worldwide Judgment, which is why its proper primary name is: '**the DAY of the LORD.**' The 'trouble' with the adoption of the term 'Tribulation' as the main way to describe this period, even though it is a Biblical term (Matthew 24:29), is that believers also experience a degree of tribulation (persecution) in the Church Age (John 16:33), and so many fail to see that 'the Tribulation' is a fundamentally different kind of time. Not only will it be a time of intensified worldwide evil and tribulation, well beyond anything experienced in the Church Age, the Tribulation, unlike the Church Age, will also be a time of Divine Judgment. It is this reality that most clearly distinguishes it from the Church Age, which is why the term most commonly used for it in the Bible is: 'the Day of the Lord.' It will be the climax in the war between good and evil. This time is brought to an end by Christ's Return to destroy all evildoers from the earth and establish His Kingdom (2Thesss 2:8, Revelation 19-20). Other names for the Tribulation are: **"The Hour of Trial which comes on the whole earth"** (Rev 3:10), '**the Wrath to come**' (1Thess 1:10), '**the Wrath**' (1Thess 5:9, Revelation 11:18), '**the Wrath of God**' (Rev 15:1,7; 14:10, 19; 16:1), '**the Hour of Judgment**' (Rev 14:7), '**the Indignation**' (Isaiah 26:20,21; 34:2; Daniel 11:36).

The Tribulation includes: **'the 70th Week of Daniel'** (Daniel 9:27). The Tribulation starts after the Rapture, and then has an unknown period of time (probably a few months) before the final 7 years (the 70th Week) begin, when the antichrist makes a covenant with Israel (see my: 'Chronological Commentary of the Book of Revelation' for full details). The Book of Revelation describes the Day of the Lord in great detail from chapters 6-19. It reveals that the Tribulation is initiated on earth by Christ breaking the 7 Seals in Heaven (Revelation 6). This proves the whole of the Tribulation is a time of Judgment, for it is Christ who initiates the Tribulation Judgements. The second half of Daniel's 70th Week is called **'the Great Tribulation'** (Matthew 24:21) described as a time far worse than any other time in human history (see also Daniel 12:1, Jeremiah 30:7). It lasts 3.5 years and is initiated by the Abomination of Desolation and the 7th Trumpet.

The final 24 hour day of His Return is called: **'the Great and Awesome** (lit: 'Manifest') **Day of the Lord'** (Joel 2:11, 31, Malachi 4:5, Acts 2:20). That is, 'the Great Day of the Lord's Manifestation' on earth, when He appears and completes His Judgment upon His enemies (Revelation 19) before establishing His Millennial Kingdom upon the earth (Revelation 20). So whereas 'the Day of the Lord' refers to the Tribulation as a whole or any part of it, the 24-hour day of the 2nd Coming is 'the Great and Awesome Day of the Lord'.

*There are 3 main PURPOSES of the TRIBULATION.

*(1) To end wickedness and wicked ones.

*(2) To bring a worldwide soul-harvest (Revelation 7, Matthew 24:14).

*(3) The Salvation of Israel (Romans 11:25-26), the basis of the 2nd Coming. The Tribulation is a time of trouble, especially for the Jews, for antichrist will wage a war of persecution against them, but in it Israel will turn back to God, as Jeremiah 30:7 says: **"it is the time of Jacob's Trouble, but he will be saved from it."** Although Israel starts the Tribulation as 'Jacob' by its end she will be 'Israel.'

The prophets also described this as a time of Birth Pains (Jeremiah 30:5-7), followed by the Coming of Messiah to bring His Kingdom to birth upon the earth, so it became known as the **Birth Pains of the Messiah**. Jesus described the coming Kingdom as bringing about a Regeneration or Rebirth in the earth (Matthew 19:28). Thus the earth is compared to a pregnant woman about to give birth to a baby - the Messianic Kingdom. Because of sin and the curse on the earth, just before this baby is born there are birth pains (Genesis 3:16-19), for the presence of sin in the body resists the birth. Likewise, as the Kingdom starts to forcibly push through into manifestation in the earth in the Tribulation, it will set off birth pains, as it comes into conflict with the kingdom of darkness ruling this world-system. Thus there will be a final time of birth pains, and then the Kingdom will be born upon the earth. When asked to give the Signs of His Return (the Birth), Jesus described the Birth Pains of the Tribulation in Matthew 24:7: **"Nation will rise against nation, and kingdom against kingdom. And there will be famines, pestilences, and earthquakes in various places. All these are the beginning of Sorrows** (literally: Birth Pains).**"** So just before the Birth of the Kingdom there will be at least 7 years of increasingly intensifying Birth Pains, and we are getting very close to that time.

The Tribulation commences after the Church-Age, and ends with Christ's Return. One reason why the Church must be raptured before the Tribulation is that the whole Tribulation (not just the 2nd Coming or the 7 Bowls of Wrath) is a time of Divine Wrath and the Church has been promised deliverance from the Wrath of God (Romans 5:9, 1Thessalonians 1:10, 5:9), and from this time of worldwide Trouble (Revelation 3:10-11). What Bridegroom would keep His Bride in a city He was about to bombard in His wrath, when He has the power to extract her first?

In Matthew 24:37-42, Jesus compared the worldwide Judgment of the Tribulation to the previous worldwide Judgment of Noah's Flood. Just as in the days of Noah, before the Flood fell, life in the godless world will be going on as normal (v38), until a key event that immediately triggers the worldwide Judgment, from which no one can escape. Thus this Judgment will suddenly fall and take the world by surprise. The key event in the days of Noah was the day when Noah entered the safety of the Ark. The corresponding end-time event is described as the Coming of Christ, which will trigger the 'Tribulation-Flood' Judgment: **"As the days of Noah were, so also will the Coming of the Son of Man be. For as in the days before the Flood, they were eating and drinking, marrying and giving in marriage, UNTIL the day that Noah entered the Ark, and did not know until the Flood came and took them all away, so also will the Coming of the Son of Man be"** (v37-39). Thus the Coming of the Son of Man is likened to Noah entering the Ark. In the days of Noah, once all the believers were removed to the safety of the Ark, God was free to release his Judgment, so the Judgment fell immediately after the believers disappeared into the Ark. It follows that a similar sequence of events will happen when the Lord comes. Thus this Coming of Christ is referring to His Coming in the Rapture to remove all believers from the earth, which then immediately triggers the Judgments of the Tribulation. It is not the 2nd Coming! So the Lord will come to call His own to Himself in the Rapture, just as He called Noah and his family into the Ark (a type of Christ). Then immediately worldwide Judgment will fall and no one will escape.

So <u>Jesus draws out 3 Points of Comparison</u>:

*(1) Life before Judgment falls will be going on as normal, so when it suddenly falls from above it will be a total surprise to the godless world (v37-38), **"so also will the Coming of the Son of Man be"** (v37).

*(2) The final event just before judgment falls was the disappearance of all believers into the Ark: **"until the day that Noah ENTERED the Ark"** (v38). Likewise, the final event just before the Tribulation-Flood falls upon the world will be Jesus COMING for us in the Rapture, so that we are gathered into Him (v39-42), **"so also will the COMING of the Son of Man be"** (v39). This is confirmed by the next verses: **"Then 2 men will be in the field: one will be taken and the other left. 2 women will be grinding at the mill: one taken and the other left. Watch therefore, for you know not what hour your Lord is coming"** (v40-42).

*(3) Immediately after the believers entered the Ark, the worldwide Judgment of the Flood suddenly fell, in which all unbelievers were killed. Likewise immediately after the Rapture, the worldwide Judgment of the Tribulation will suddenly fall upon the whole earth, so that there will be no escape. Moreover once all the Judgments are completed no unbelievers will be left alive on earth, so that only believers will left alive to be the initial population of the Messianic Kingdom (Matthew 25). However, because these Judgments are graciously spread over at least 7 years, many unbelievers will be saved during the Tribulation.

Finally it should be noted that 'the Day of the Lord' has a dual meaning in the Bible. There is the shorter Day of the Lord of 7+ years where He acts as Judge (the Tribulation and 2nd Coming), and the longer DAY of the Lord where He acts as King over the whole earth for 1000 years (remember one DAY to the Lord is as 1000 years to man - 2Peter 3:8). Then at the end of the Millennium He will destroy this present Universe. <u>2Peter 3:10</u> covers the whole 'Day of the Lord' including both its shorter and longer parts, describing both its start and its end: **"The Day of the Lord will come** (begin) **as a Thief in the night** (the Rapture –see Matthew 24:43, 1Thess 5:2); **in the which** (at its close) **the heavens shall pass away with a** great noise, and the elements shall melt with fervent heat, the earth also and the works that are in it shall be burned up (the destruction of the universe)." Then Christ hands the Kingdom to GOD, the Father (1Cor 15:28), bringing in a new eternal DAY, with a new heaven and earth (the Eternal State) called: 'The Day of GOD.' This is what Peter describes next: "looking for and hastening (towards) the Coming of the DAY of GOD, because of which the heavens will be dissolved, being on fire, and the elements will melt with fervent heat? Nevertheless we, according to His promise, look for new heavens and a new earth in which righteousness dwells" (2Peter 3:12-13). He uses the picture of a runner looking to the fixed finishing line and speeding toward it with all his might. Likewise the time of Christ's Return and the final End are fixed by the Father (Acts 1:7, Mark 13:32), and we are to run our race with all our might, keeping our eyes on the finishing-line, which is coming ever closer, motivated by the everlasting joy and reward set before us, when we cross that line and enter into eternity.

*KEY 11 - The Framework of Prophecy and the Framework Prophecies

The Framework of Prophecy refers to the overall outline and sequence of events that are prophesied in the Bible. We find that all of Bible Prophecy fits perfectly and consistently into this structure, this confirming it. Knowing this framework will enable you to accurately fit any particular prophecy into its correct position in God's overall Plan. We saw in particular that there are 3 major Prophecies that I call the Framework Prophecies, which reveal and establish this Framework, namely 'Daniel's 70 Weeks' (Daniel 9:24-27), the 'Olivet Discourse' (Matthew 24-25), and the Book of Revelation. In Part 1, we studied the first two of these Prophecies in detail, and in Part 3 we will also study Revelation in detail.

1. The First Coming of Christ, concluding with His death and resurrection.
2. Then the present Church Age, the Mystery.
3. The Church Age will end with the Rapture.
4. This initiates the Tribulation, the time of Birth Pains.
5. Christ then brings the Tribulation to its end by His Second Coming.
6. Then follows the Messianic Kingdom for 1000 years, the Millennium.
7. Then comes the destruction of the universe and the Great White Throne.
8. Finally there will be a new heaven and earth, and the Eternal State.

This Summary of what the prophetic Scriptures tell us is perfectly confirmed by the book of Revelation, which has the exact same structure:

1. The vision of the glorified Christ, who died and rose again (chapter 1).
2. The Church Age - the Mystery of the 7 Lampstands (chapters 2-3).
3. A Rapture - the transition to the things that must take place after this (4:1).
4. The Tribulation on earth initiated by Christ in Heaven (chapters 4-18).
5. Then the 2nd Coming of Christ, to save His people, judge His enemies and establish His Kingdom on earth (chapter 19).
6. The Messianic Kingdom, the 1000-year reign of Christ (chapter 20:1-6).
7. Then the present heaven and earth pass away (Revelation 20:11), followed by the Great White Throne Judgement (Revelation 20:11-15).
8. Finally a new heaven and earth is created (Revelation 21:1), and we enter the perfect Eternal State in Revelation 21-22.

Thus the book of Revelation perfectly confirms our Framework of Prophecy. In particular it confirms that the Church-Age ends before the Tribulation begins, for Revelation 1:19 gives the outline of the whole Book: **"Write the THINGS: (1) which you have SEEN** (1:1-19 - John's vision of the glorified Christ) **(2) the THINGS that ARE NOW** (1:20 - 3:22, which give an overview of the whole Church-Age, see Appendix 2). **(3) the THINGS that WILL take place AFTER THIS** (after the Church-Age, Revelation 4:1 – 22:21). This transition to the THINGS which must take place AFTER THIS takes place in Revelation 4:1: **"AFTER THESE THINGS I looked and, behold, a door open in Heaven, and I heard a voice like a trumpet speaking with me saying: 'Come up here** (picture of the Rapture) **and I will show you THINGS which MUST take place AFTER THIS** (after the Church Age)." In Revelation 4-5 we see the events in Heaven that prepare the way for the opening of the Scroll with 7 Seals (the Title-Deed of the earth) in Revelation 6, which in turn initiates the sudden release of the Judgments of the Tribulation. So this proves that the present Church Age (the things that are now) ends after chapter 3, and 'the things that will take place after this' (including the Tribulation) start in chapter 4. Thus the Tribulation or Day of the Lord is a distinct period of time that starts after the Church Age. In fact it starts immediately after the Rapture.

*Key 12 - FUTURISM

The reason for such a wide spectrum of beliefs in Eschatology (the study of 'the last things', *'eschatos'* = 'last') is that the Church has generally disregarded the sound principle of literal interpretation in this area. As a result, 4 main Schools of prophetic interpretation have arisen that govern how people interpret Prophecy, covering all 4 possibilities, for the Biblical predictions have either (1) been fulfilled in the past (Preterism), or (2) are being fulfilled in the present era (Historicism), or (3) are yet to be fulfilled in the future (Futurism), or (4) are timeless (Idealism). All books on Prophecy are written from the viewpoint of one of these Schools. If you consistently follow literal interpretation, you are a FUTURIST, as the end-time prophecies have not yet been fulfilled literally. For an in-depth explanation of these 4 Schools , and how they affect our vision of the Church Age, see Appendix 5.

*1. The PRETERIST School believes that what we see as end-time prophecies of the Tribulation and Second Coming (for example in Matthew 24 and Revelation) were fulfilled in AD 70, when Jerusalem was destroyed by the Roman armies, bringing the 'Jewish Age' to an end. But this clearly violates literal interpretation, and means that the Book of Revelation has very little relevance for us today.

*2. The HISTORICIST School seeks to make Revelation more relevant by saying the predictions typologically cover the whole Church Age, giving a symbolic coded prophecy of the Church Age, and so in Revelation we can see the events of the last 2000 years unfold, and trace the course of Church history. Again this requires a non-literal interpretation of prophecy, and is the product of human imagination.

*3. The IDEALIST School removes all time references and discourages us from trying to see specific fulfillments. For them Revelation portrays the eternal struggle between good and evil, and we can apply its truths at any time. Thus it treats prophecy as myth (using fictional events to communicate a moral or spiritual meaning). It's a product of liberal theology denying the literal truth of God's Word.

*4. The FUTURIST School (expounded in this book) is based on being faithful to the principle of literal interpretation for prophecy, as we do for all other areas of doctrine). We interpret prophecy in its plain meaning, according to the laws of language. Applying this principle, it is clear that most end-time prophecies have not yet been fulfilled literally, so they still await a FUTURE fulfillment.

*Appendix 2: The Church Age revealed through the 7 Churches

The Course of this present Church Age is revealed in Revelation 2 and 3 through Christ's 7 letters to the 7 Churches. Revelation gives an overview of events past, present and future, so <u>Revelation 1:19</u> gives its corresponding outline: **"Write the things (1) which YOU HAVE SEEN (chapter 1 - the vision of Christ) and (2) the things THAT ARE (chapters 2 and 3 - the Church-Age) and (3) the THINGS that will take place AFTER THIS"** (chapters 4-22). Thus His letters to the 7 Churches were designed to give a summary and overview of 'the things that are', and so should describe the history of the Church from its start to its finish.

Actually the section of Revelation summarised by 'the things that are' starts in 1:20, this is when chapter 2 should have started, for it introduces the Church as the Lord's LAMPSTAND: **"The Mystery of the 7 stars which you saw in My right hand, and the 7 golden Lampstands: The 7 stars are the angels** (messengers or pastors) **of the 7 Churches, and the 7 Lampstands which you saw are the 7 Churches."** This introduces Christ's letters to the 7 Churches in Revelation 2-3, and shows that the purpose of the Church in this Age is to be God's light-bearer to the world. The letters are Christ's evaluation of how the Church has fulfilled this ministry of being His anointed witness. Together they present a revelation of the whole course of the CHURCH-AGE, from the point of view of the Church fulfilling her ministry of witness through words and works.

The 7 letters are Christ's assessment of how true the Churches have been to the Word, in keeping and spreading it, and in resisting false doctrine. Of course, they were written to 7 literal local Churches at that time, but it is also clear that they also apply to all Churches throughout the Age. At the end of each letter Christ says: **"He who has an ear let him hear what the Spirit says to the Churches"** (3:13). The warnings and promises apply to all the Churches. Just as the promises in Paul's letters did not just apply to the Churches to whom He was writing, but to all believers in the universal Church, so it is with these 7 letters. A number of prophecies in these letters can only find their ultimate fulfilment on the scale of the universal Church, rather than just the local Church in question. The letters reveal the different kind of Churches that exist throughout the Age. But in any particular era of Church history, one kind of Church takes pre-eminence. This leads to the realisation that they also contain a prophetic revelation of the whole course of the Church Age, where each of these 7 Churches are chosen to be a TYPE of the Church that arises onto centre stage during a certain period of Church history. (In the case of the last 4 Churches, it is not so much that the new church displaces and removes the previous ones, but that it takes its place alongside the others, so that the new Era is characterised by a new kind of Church becoming a major force). **So together these 7 letters give a PROPHETIC PICTURE of the 7 main Eras of Church history.** The validity of this typological prophetic application is confirmed by the fact that a number of the promises and warnings use language that is designed to apply to something beyond that local church. That is, Christ addresses a real local situation, but that is only a type of something that will manifest on a greater scale during later Church history. Also there are promises and warnings that have a partial local fulfilment, but which can only find their full literal fulfilment through a future segment of the Church in the end-times, so again the local Church addressed in the letter functions as a type of part of the Church that develops in Church history, and continues until the end of the Church Age. It is remarkable how well these 7 Churches mirror the development of Church history, as I will endeavour to show. Even the meaning of their names agree with the main characteristics of each Era. It also provides further proof that we are living in the Last Days. I will develop the detail of these Church Ages and show how well the 7 Letters fit the 7 main Eras of Church History.

Each letter has a similar structure. Christ Himself addresses the angel (literally 'messenger') of the Church. It makes no sense to say this is a literal angel, as an angel would not have authority, responsibility and accountability for the state of the Church - that would fall upon the leadership, especially the Pastor whose primary role is as the Messenger of the Church, that is, to bring the Message of God's Word to the Church, so that the whole Church can be a light to the world. Moreover sometimes 'the angels' are corrected for sins and failures, which would be impossible if it were one of the elect angels. Also it makes no sense that Christ would communicate to such an angel through a letter by John, because he commands his angels directly by speaking to their spirits!

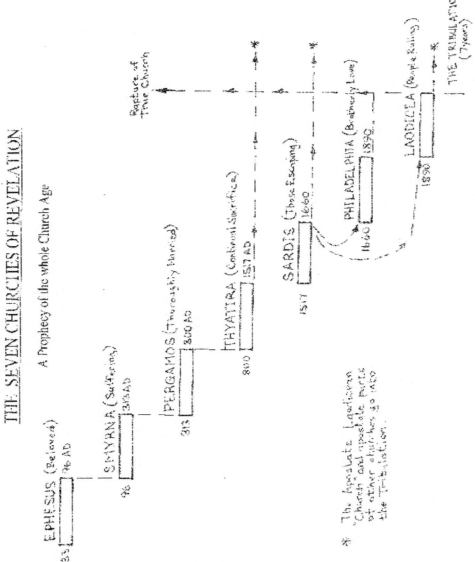

THE SEVEN CHURCHES OF REVELATION

A Prophecy of the whole Church Age

EPHESUS (Beloved) 96 AD

SMYRNA (Suffering) 313AD

PERGAMOS (Thoroughly Married) 800 AD

THYATIRA (Continual Sacrifices) 1517 AD

SARDIS (Those Escaping) 1660

PHILADELPHIA (Brotherly Love) 1890

LAODICEA (People Ruling) 1890

THE TRIBULATION (7 years)

Rapture of True Church

* The Apostate Laodicean "Church" and apostate parts of other churches go into the Tribulation.

Christ then identifies Himself according to a part of His description as given in chapter 1. The aspect of His character most relevant to the need of the Church is chosen, showing that our true faith and practice should ultimately flow from our knowledge of the nature of Christ. He then praises them for what they are doing right, and corrects them for what is wrong, giving guidance on what they should focus on doing, with promises for obedience and warnings for disobedience if they fail to obey, although some Churches only receive praise and others only censure. He concludes each letter by saying: **"He who has an ear, let him hear (and obey) what the Spirit says to the Churches"** showing that what He says applies to all the churches throughout the Church Age. He also gives a promise to the overcomers which is a title that applies to all born again believers (1John 5:4-5). These are all promises of what all believers will inherit as part of their eternal inheritance in glory. However, the size of our inheritance in each area will be determined by our eternal rewards received at the Judgment Seat of Christ.

*1. The Church at EPHESUS (2:1-7): **"To the angel** (messenger, pastor) **of the Church of Ephesus write: 'These things says He who holds the 7 stars in His right hand, who walks in the midst of the 7 golden lampstands**: **"I know your works, your labour, your patience, and that you cannot bear those who are evil. And you have tested those who say they are apostles and are not, and have found them liars; and you have persevered and have patience, and have laboured for My Name's sake and have not become weary. Nevertheless I have this against you, that you have left your first love. Remember therefore from where you have fallen; repent and do the first works** (evangelism), **or else I will come to you quickly and remove your lampstand from its place, unless you repent. But this you have, that you hate the deeds of the Nicolaitans** ('people-rulers'), **which I also hate. He who has an ear, let him hear what the Spirit says to the Churches. To him who overcomes I will give to eat from the tree of life, in the midst of the Paradise of God."**

The Church at Ephesus represents **the Church of the 1st century, the Apostolic Church.** Ephesus means: 'desired, beloved' and this spoke of the close loving relationship that the first generation of Christians had with the Lord. This was the time of 'first love' seen in the Book of Acts, when they were overflowing in love and witnessed freely, telling everyone about the Lord. The first works they did (fulfilling the Great Commission) flowed out of their first love (for Jesus, the Lover of their souls). However, in the 2nd generation their love for the Lord had begun to fade, although they still worked hard and were faithful and sound (Word-centred), resisting all false doctrine (both Judaising and Gnostic), but it had become more duty than love, and therefore their witness was in danger of fizzling out. Thus the loving Church had become the labouring Church. They began to forget what it is all about, or rather WHO it is all about. They were so busy doing the work of the

Kingdom that they did not have time for the King! Their devotional life had faded. That is why the remedy was to stir up their first love for Jesus by way of remembrance, repent for not having Him at the centre of their thoughts, and get back to their first works (pursuing a personal intimate relationship with Him through praise, worship, prayer and Bible Study, overflowing in witnessing to the lost and loving the brethren). In all our works and busyness we must not forget the Centrality of Christ, which is why He introduces Himself as the One in the midst of the Churches, the Head of the Church, holding the Pastors in His hand (see 1:13,16), and why He leaves them with a promise of eternal fellowship with Him in the Paradise of God. He warns them that if they did not repent they will lose their pre-eminence among the Churches (He will remove their lampstand from its pre-eminent position as the largest and leading Church).

The mention of the dangerous rise of the Nicolaitans (which literally means: 'ruling over the common people), whose doctrine became more established in the Pergamum Era (2:15), is an example of what happens when the Church stops looking to Christ as her Head. The result is increasing human organisation and control, without the leadership of Spirit. One manifestation of this doctrine of the Nicolaitans is the clergy-laity division, replacing the priesthood of all believers.

Christ's emphasis on them regaining their first love for Him shows what is important to Him. This speaks of the intimate love relationship that the Bridegroom desires with His Bride. He loves us with a passion and has proved it by sacrificing Himself for us, and He wants to constantly pour His love and life into us, but the depth of our fellowship with Him is determined by our response. We need to spend face-to-face devotional time with Him receiving His love and loving Him, so that He is the Centre, and the rest of our life flows out of this intimate love fellowship. This is how it is in the excitement of first love between a man and a woman. Initially this happens spontaneously, but after a time they will need to stir themselves up in love for each other to maintain this state of first love of continually pursuing deeper union with each other.

*2. The Church at SMRYNA (2:8-11): **"To the angel** messenger, pastor) **of the Church in Smyrna write: 'These things says the First and the Last, who was dead, and came to life: "I know your works, tribulation, and poverty (but**

you are rich); and I know the blasphemy (slander) of those who say they are Jews and are not, but are a synagogue of satan. Do not fear any of those things, which you are about to suffer. Indeed, the devil is about to throw some of you into prison, that you may be tested, and you will have tribulation 10 days. Be faithful until death, and I will give you the crown of life.
He who has an ear, let him hear what the Spirit says to the Churches.
He who overcomes shall not be hurt by the 2nd death."

The **Church at Smyrna** represents **the suffering Church**, especially in the era of the Roman Persecutions (96 - 313 AD). 'Smyrna' means 'myrrh, bitterness'. Myrrh is associated with death and embalming. Therefore Jesus introduces Himself to this Church suffering persecution and threat of death as the One who has conquered death (see 1:17-18). He reminds them He has suffered death, but rose again, and so will have the last word, so even if they suffer unto death, He will raise them up again. This Church suffered great persecution, but remained faithful to Jesus and He was pleased with them, giving them only commendation without correction. Even if though they were poor in this world, they will have much treasure in heaven. During this Era, Christians were persecuted and killed for refusing to worship Caesar as lord and god. Only the Jews had a special dispensation allowing them to worship their God, and none other, and this may have been a motivation for some Gentile Christians to Judaize, by adopting Jewish ways, forming a synagogue and perhaps even converting to Judaism. It seems that they separated themselves from the Church, seeing themselves as the only true Church, obedient to the Law, and also opposed the Church in Smryna, even instigating the persecution, for Jesus called it 'the synagogue of satan', and satan means 'the opposer.' They were not real Jews, but were pretending to be. So here Jesus was warning about one form of deviant Christianity that would arise, the Judaising faction, which Paul opposed in Galatians, which insists on believers submitting to the Law of Moses, either for salvation, or for sanctification and as a rule of life. This faction did indeed develop at this period of Church history.

Ignatius said in the 2nd century: *"it is absurd to talk of Jesus Christ and practice Judaism, for Christianity did not develop into faith in Judaism, but*

Judaism into faith in Christianity, in which people of every language who believed in God were brought together" and *"if anyone interprets Judaism to you, do not listen to him. For it is better to hear Christianity from a man who has received circumcision than Judaism from one who has not."*

Sadly in responding to this faction, which opposed them, the Gentile Church overreacted and adopted an anti-Semitic attitude and theology.

Jesus warned Smyrna they would suffer persecution for 10 days - symbolic of 10 periods of persecution that the Church would suffer in this Era, for indeed there were 10 Roman Emperors who officially persecuted the Church: (1) Domitian (96), (2) Trajan (98 - 117), (3) Hadrian (117 - 138), (4) Antonius Pius (138 - 161), (5) Marcus Aurelis (161-180), (6) Septimus Severus (193 - 211), (7) Maximin (235 - 238), (8) Decius (249 - 251), (9) Valarian (251 - 260) and (10) Diocletian (284 - 305). This Era corresponds to the first attack against the growth of the seed (Word of God) in the Parable of the Sower when satan sends 'persecution and affliction arising because of the Word' (to stop it spreading).

Jesus commends them for their faithful endurance (holding fast to the Word) in suffering, and asks them to be faithful unto death, promising that He will give them the crown of life as an eternal reward. Polycarp, the famous 2nd-century Christian bishop of Smyrna was martyred in AD 155. Christ's final promise to the overcomers, who are willing to die for Him, is that they will not suffer the 2nd death in the Lake of Fire (Revelation 20:6,14). Their persecutors will not only die once, but face a 2nd (eternal) death (unless they repent), but the believers will only die once and then it is glory! The Church at Smyrna is a perfect picture of the Church of this Era which stayed faithful under fire, and continued to grow rapidly despite the persecution.

*3. The Church at PERGAMOS(v12-17): **"To the angel of the Church in Pergamos write: 'These things says He who has the sharp 2-edged sword: "I know your works, and where you dwell, where satan's throne is. And you hold fast to My Name, and did not deny My faith even in the days in which Antipas was My faithful martyr, who was killed among you, where satan dwells. But I have a few things against you, because you have there those who hold the doctrine of Balaam, who taught Balak to put a stumbling block before the**

children of Israel, to eat things sacrificed to idols, and to commit sexual immorality. Thus you also have those who hold the doctrine of the Nicolaitans, which thing I hate. Repent or else I will come to you quickly and will fight against them with the sword of My mouth. He who has an ear, let him hear what the Spirit says to the Churches. To him who overcomes I will give some of the hidden manna to eat. And I will give him a white stone and on the stone a new name written which no one knows except him who receives it."

The **Church at Pergamos** represents the next era of the Church Age (313 - 800 AD), brought in by the Roman Emperor Constantine. The growth of the Church under persecution now led to new temptations, which always come with gaining power. Seeing that the outward attack had failed, satan moved to a far more subtle and seductive form of attack. Now the Church had grown sufficiently, he could start to draw her devotion away from Christ by tempting her with all the things the world has to offer, the outward trappings of political power, replacing true spirituality with pomp and ceremony, changing the focus from possessing the life of Christ within to outward show. Sadly, this internal attack succeeded where the external attack of persecution had failed, and worldliness, compromise and corruption started to enter the Church. This began a process, which became fully developed in the next Era of Church history.

'Per-gamos' means 'thoroughly married' and typifies the worldly, compromised church. In 313 AD Constantine issued the Edict of Milan, which reversed the persecutions of Diocletian and other former Emperors, creating religious tolerance of Christians throughout the Empire. Christianity soon became the official state religion, so it was now in a position of power. This may seem good, but through this marriage of Church and State, many pagan influences of the Roman Empire came into the Church. A ship is made to be in the sea, but if the sea gets in the ship it will sink. Likewise, the Church is in the world, but if the world gets into the Church, she will sink. The Church is to be married to Christ alone, so if she joins herself to the world, she commits spiritual adultery, and is corrupted. This marriage of Church and State opened the door for many wrong influences to come into the Church and the resulting mixture of good and bad meant her witness became compromised, for she lost her purity of heart, life, doctrine and practice. So

Christ comes to her as the One with the 2-edged sword (referring to His description in 1:16), to divide truth from error, right from wrong, flesh from spirit . They needed discernment from His Word to accept the good and reject the bad.

There was much that was good, for Christ commends their works, and the fact that they held fast to the central doctrines of the faith, especially concerning the Trinity and the Person of Christ: **"you hold fast to My Name, and did not deny My faith."** They resisted the false doctrines and left us the legacy in the form of the great Creeds that summarise the great truths of God and Christ. In His evaluation, Christ takes into account that they live where: (1) satan's throne is and (2) where he dwells (feels at home), for Pergamum was both (1) the political centre of Asia, and (2) the main religious centre (with 3 major temples, one dedicated to the worship of the emperor, another for the goddess Athena, and the Great Altar of Zeus, the king of the Greek gods, shaped like a throne, a symbol of 'the throne of satan.' It also had a healing centre called the Asklepion, built in honour of Asklepios, the Greek serpent-god. He knows the intense pressure they were under to compromise. Moreover politics and religion were combined, so failure to worship the gods and especially the Emperor would bring persecution from the State.

As well as the political pressure to conform, there was the seductive pull of the pagan idol feasts, where the worship of false gods was combined with food, drink and revelries, involving sex with temple prostitutes. Despite this, much of the Church at Pergagum had not compromised as typified by Antipas (which means 'against all), the bishop of the Church, ordained by John, who was martyred in AD 92, because the priests of Asklepios were upset that he had cast out so many demons, so they stirred up the Roman governor against him, claiming he was hindering the worship of their gods. The governor ordered Antipas to offer a sacrifice to a statue of the Emperor and declare that he was "lord and god." Antipas refused, and this rejection of the divinity of the Emperor was seen as a rejection of the authority of Rome, so he was killed. Because he stood and did not bow he was a faithful martyr (witness) of Christ.

However, under these pressures compromise had started to enter the Church through the doctrines of Balaam and the Nicolaitans. This was anti-nomianism, that as believers in Christ we are free from any kind of law, so we can indulge the flesh and do whatever we want. Although we are free from the Law of Moses, we are still under the Law of Christ as a rule of life, as defined by the New Testament (1Corinthians 9:21), which forbids idolatry and fornication. Compared to the Law of Moses it has very little ceremonial law, but its moral standards are even higher. Also in the New Covenant we have the New Birth and indwelling Spirit to enable us to fulfil the righteous requirement of this Law (Romans 8:4), which is to love God and man. Through this doctrine of false grace, satan was seducing some to compromise and conform to the world, in joining in with their idol feasts and sexual immorality, in the same way that Balaam's teaching led the men of Israel to be seduced by the Moabite women into immorality and joining in their idol feasts to Baal (Numbers 25). Through intermarriage these women would bring their idols and pagan ways of thinking and worship into God's community. The doctrine of Balaam might have been supported by false gnostic teaching that separated spirit and flesh so much that they said that only the spirit was important, so it does not matter what you do with your body, it does not affect your spiritual life. But in Biblical thought both are important.

The Nicolaitans were working in parallel with the Balaamites. Both said that instead of resisting the spirit of the world, and being different from it, the Church should fit in with it and follow its ways, whereas Christ wants us to shine as lights in a dark world. Whereas the teaching of Balaam appealed to one area of the flesh, the teaching of the Nicolaitans appealed to another - lust for power. 'Nico-laitan' means 'conqueror of the people' and represents an elite group who desired to have power, dominion and control over people in this life, both within the Church and in the world. For this reason they also advocated bowing to the world-system in order to advance their position, even it meant compromising their faith, for to them the ends justify the means. Desire for political power leads to compromise and sin. Together these groups had a persuasive message to the Church of intermarrying with the world, so it can enjoy all that the world can offer, but the inevitable result of this mixture of faith and worldliness is the loss of integrity, purity and effective witness, as salt mixed with powder loses its savour (Matthew 5:13)

Thus satan was finding inroads into the Church at Pergamum through these 2 groups, and **this was a picture of what he would do on a larger scale in the next**

Era of Church history. Having failed to destroy the Church by outward persecution from the State, satan tried the opposite tactic of compromising and corrupting the Church from within by causing her to be wedded to the State, thus offering her power, prestige, and relief from attack. This all seems good, but this set up a situation where the Church has divided loyalties, being wedded both to the Lord and the State, and no one can love two masters. James 4:4-5 says God wants our whole devotion, and that loving the world is spiritual adultery. Thus in order to keep her levers on power, she inevitably compromises her calling from God. Moreover, satan knows that until Jesus returns to destroy the kingdoms of this world and establish His Kingdom, satan has operational authority over the world-system, as the god and ruler of this world (2Corinthians 4:4, John 14:30, 16:11, Ephesians 2:2), all the kingdoms of the world having been given to him (Luke 4:5-6), so that the whole world is under his power (1John 5:19), which is why he will be able to give antichrist authority over all nations (Revelation 13:2-8). Satan still has his throne over the political systems of man (Revelation 2:13), so if the Church is seduced into taking a position of political power by a lust for dominion, she will inevitably become enmeshed with satan's principalities and powers and thus be compromised and weakened spiritually in her ability to obey the Lord and fulfil the Great Commission. This is the danger of Kingdom Now (Dominion) Theology. Through the pull of power it diverts the Church from its main mission.

Despite all the persecutions (represented by the heat of the sun in the Parable of the Sower and the Church of Smyrna) the Church had continued to grow, as it held faithfully to her Head, Christ. Seeing that the outward attack of intimidation on the seed had failed, satan moved to a different, far more subtle and seductive form of attack. Now that the Church had grown sufficiently, satan was able to start to draw her devotion away from Christ by tempting her with all the things that the world has to offer, the outward trappings of political power and wealth, replacing true spirituality with pomp and ceremony, changing the focus from possessing the life of Christ within to outward show. This corresponds to the next attack against the seed in the Parable of Sower - the thorns and weeds representing the desire for other things, such as riches, power, and pleasure. While they may be good in themselves, their danger is in claiming our affections and drawing us away from our commitment to Christ. Sadly, this internal attack succeeded where the external attack of persecution had failed, and worldliness, compromise and corruption started to enter the Church. What we see in Pergamos is the start of a process, which became fully developed in the next stage of Church history.

The **intermarriage of Church with State** meant an influx of unbelievers bringing in pagan ways and idolatry, rather than a pure Church reaching into the world. In absorbing them and enjoying the resulting outward growth, the Church also accommodated itself to their ways. Balaam's plan was for the pagan women to join the Jewish community by intermarriage, and so corrupt Israel by introducing their pagan beliefs, immoral practices and idol worship, thus bringing a curse upon Israel. Likewise satan's plan was for the pagan Roman State to be married to the Church, so the official Church would be flooded with the unsaved and their pagan ways, causing the Church to adapt its ways and worship to suit them. The world was joined to, and came into the Church, resulting in worldly morality, and heathen ways of worship being adopted, such as icons, images, idolatry, ritualistic worship, relics and other superstitious practices.

The rise of the **Nicolaitans** at Pergamum is a prophetic type of what Church started to become in this new era. Nicolaitan means 'one who conquerors', dominates and rules the people. With the Church becoming the established (state) religion, it began to take on the trappings (robes, ceremonies, titles) and authority structure of the pagan Empire. This was accelerated when Rome fell in 410 AD to the barbarians (soon after it became a Christian Empire). Many were puzzled why a Christian Empire would suffer such a defeat. The theologian Augustine wrote a famous book: 'The City of God' which explained that Rome's fall was due to her roots in idolatry, and argued that this was a good thing, because it will help them to take their eyes off the city of man and focus instead on building the City of God. Thus he said that Rome's fall will make way for the City of God to prevail. Whatever his intentions this was used as a basis for those desiring ecclesiastical and political power in the Church and State (the Nicolaitans in the Church) to say that the Church was the new Empire of God. An authoritarian structure arose. Regional Bishops were appointed, and the Roman Bishop (the Pope) took on the position and even the title of the Roman Emperor ('Pontifex Maximus). The 'Pope' means 'father' or chief bishop. The 6th century saw the beginning of the rise of the Bishops of Rome to a position of political power over kings (the ultimate ruler of the kingdoms within the Christian community), as well as being the highest religious authority. Thus the Church took on the authority structure of the Roman Empire with Bishops over regions instead of governors, and the Pope on his throne instead of Caesar. Needless to say this is all foreign to the New Testament, and is the result of a carnal desire for outward power and prestige.

When King Jesus returns He will establish His Kingdom and we will reign with Him on the earth, but that is for a future time. It is not the mission of the Church for this time to rule the earth, but rather to be His lampstand (His witnesses), humbly preaching the Gospel to the nations. Thus the nature of the Church changed, becoming more of an institution than a living body of believers. Thus the marriage of Church and State led to worldliness, the world's ways coming into the Church, with its emphasis on outward show and political power. She became larger, richer and politically powerful, but also compromised and spiritually weakened by the infiltration of pagan practices.

Another manifestation of the Nicolaitan spirit ('conquering the laity'), was the rise at this time of ecclesiasticalism, where the Church began to take more power for itself over the people. This included the rise of a ruling class of priests, creating a clergy/laity division, which increasing led to the Church being redefined as being the priesthood rather than the people, and this priesthood claimed to be mediators between God and the people, administering salvation through the sacraments and granting forgiveness through confession. To this end a magical view of the sacraments developed, conferring upon the Church (the priesthood) the power to save, so that salvation (from Jesus) could only be received by submitting to the authority and ordinances of the Church, rather than directly from Christ on the basis of faith (alone) in His Word. This was manifested in the doctrines of baptismal regeneration (you are born again when the Church sprinkles you with water) and transubstantiation (a priest has the power to turn the bread and wine into the actual body and blood of Christ, making it efficacious for salvation). All this greatly increased the power of the Church, as it held the power of heaven and hell over the people. Increasingly value was put on submission to the authority of the

Church, and the Pope as Christ's unique representative on earth, rather than on a personal faith in Christ through knowing His Word. All this bred nominal Christianity, for many did not have a personal relationship with God through faith, but just a second-hand relationship through the Church.

Once the idea of baptismal regeneration came in (through the Church's desire to have the power to mediate salvation), the high death rate among babies caused Christian parents to fear that if their babies died un-baptised they would not go to heaven. This resulted in a further corruption of baptism - the introduction of baby baptism, which only increased this nominalism. So now they had to believe that babies are saved and become part of God's Kingdom at their baptism (by their parent's submission to the Church ordinance), removing the need for the Gospel and a personal response of faith in Christ. This is a replacement and subversion of believer's baptism, the ordinance designed to emphasise and celebrate the new birth of a believer, highlighting the importance of our personal response to the Gospel. So he grows up under the presumption that he is already a Christian, which inoculates him against the Gospel, which requires him to come to God as a sinner for salvation. His 'baptism' makes him think he already is a Christian, so does not need salvation. Thus he never feels the need to personally come to Christ for salvation, so he has no personal saving knowledge of Christ, believing he is okay with God, because he calls himself a Christian, and because of his baptism and association with the Church. Instead of trusting Christ for salvation, he trusts in these other things, and as a result he is unsaved and does not even know it. He may attend Church regularly, but has no personal relationship with God and so is a nominal Christian (in name only). Even if he accepts his Christianity by being confirmed, if he's not really born-again in the first place there's nothing to confirm.

Adult baptism is the true confirmation of a heart, that's believed the Gospel and trusted in Christ. Thus the replacement of Biblical Baptism by baby baptism and confirmation has bred nominal (unsaved) Christians on a massive scale, and its effect is magnified when carried out by the State Church, for a baby born in a country where the Church and State are united is counted as a Christian, firstly by being born in a Christian country, secondly by being 'baptised', and because it is the State Church it is obligated to the State to carry out this 'baptism' for everyone in the State, even if they are not believers. Moreover this nominalisation increases over time in countries with a State Church, for with each generation a greater proportion of people come into association with the Church as 'Christians' through this process, rather than through hearing the Gospel, repenting and trusting in Christ. Thus over time only a small proportion of those who call themselves Christians are actually saved, and this is even true among those who faithfully attend a Church. Sadly this is exactly what's happened in what was called Christian Europe, whether we're talking about Roman Catholic or Protestant countries.

So in order to rule the people, the Church took the authority over men's souls and the power of salvation, which belongs to Christ alone, and claimed it for herself. She put herself between men and God, encouraging them to look to her, rather than Christ for salvation, and putting the main emphasis on obeying her. This ecclesiastical power was reinforced by the fact that people did not have access to the Scripture in their own language, so they had to depend on the priests to tell them what they said. Moreover the Church also increasingly took to itself the right to introduce new teachings (traditions) as equally authoritative as the Bible. As pagan priests used the power of superstition to control the people, so this kind of worldliness came into the Church. No wonder Jesus said He hated the deeds of the Nicolaitans (2:6,15), and was pleased that Ephesus Church had rejected them (2:6), and upset that they had got a foothold in Pergamum (2:15), and why He said if they did not repent He would come quickly and fight against them with the sword of His mouth (v12,16). This means He will judge them by His Word at His Coming (John 12:47-48, Psalm 119:60). He was telling this compromised Church (with the values of the world mixed in with the values of the Word), that they better get back to His Word and judge themselves by it, and repent of anything not in line with it, otherwise when He returns He will use His Word against them to judge them. The Word is shaper than any 2-edged sword and is able to separate spirit from soul, what is of God from what is of man (Hebrews 4:12). If they don't apply it to themselves to judge and cut out their worldly attitudes, then He will use it on them.

However if we judge ourselves and repent we will not be judged in that day, as well as avoiding unfortunate consequences in this life (1Corinthians 11:31).

Jesus is the only Mediator between God and man, the Way, and the only Saviour, and each person must come to Him in faith and call upon Him to be saved (Romans 10:13). The Church is help people by pointing them to Jesus and His Word, not to herself. The Church is authorised to preach His Word and the Gospel of Salvation, so men come to Jesus and put their trust in Him alone for salvation. This is why the Reformation was so vital in restoring the truths of the priesthood of all believers (that the Church is the people), that God's Word alone is our final authority for faith and practice (so our wills and consciences are only bound by the Word, not Church dictates and traditions), that salvation is from Christ alone, by grace alone, through faith alone, that each person can have a direct personal relationship with God through personal faith in Christ, so everyone needs to know God's Word for Himself (which led to Bible translations, fiercely opposed by the Nicolaitans, who did not want to relinquish their authority over men's souls, for if each person has access to God's Word, they come under God's authority, undercutting the false authority claimed by the Church hierarchy), and that the role and anointing of the Church is to help people in their relationship with God (not to take His place). Thus the Church is a body in which all the leaders and members play a part in ministering God's grace to each other (flowing from the Head) as the Church prays, fellowships and worships together. God uses all different gifts, ministries and sacraments of the Church as means of grace to build us up to become like Christ. Central to all this is the ministry of God's Word.

The attacks on the Church through the doctrine of Balaam (appealing to man's desire for worldly pleasures) and the Nicolaitans (appealing to his desire for worldly power) is the embracing of worldliness. The marriage of Church and State results in the Church being filled with the unsaved, causing the Church to be compromised in her doctrine, faith and life, losing her vitality, purity (holiness) and spiritual power, so she becomes less effective in her witness. These developments typified by the Pergamum Church laid the basis for worse to come.

Jesus wants us to focus and feast on what He has to offer, which has eternal value, instead of focusing and feasting on what the world has to offer (which will pass away), so in His conclusion He promises to give the overcomers: **"some of the hidden Manna to eat"** (v17). The Manna that came down from Heaven is a picture of Christ, of which we can eat and thereby receive His abundant and eternal life (John 6:32-35, 47-51). It is hidden because it is spiritual food, and because it speaks of the manna hidden in the Ark of the Covenant. This is a picture of the God's throne in the reborn spirit (holy of holies) of a believer (who is a Temple of God). In the chest under the Mercy Seat (throne) was the 10 Commandments (He has put His Word or Law in our spirits), Aaron's rod that budded (symbolic of the authority we have in Christ on the basis of His resurrection life in our spirit), and the hidden manna (the life of Christ Himself in us). Our true life is Christ Himself and we will feed and be sustained by His life, love and joy for all eternity. Knowing this helps us not to be charmed by the world's empty promises. Also Jesus promises: **"I will give him a white stone, and on the stone a new name written which no one knows except him who receives it"** (v18). Stones were used in court cases, so if a man was found guilty he would get a black stone, but if justified he would be given a white stone, which was the proof of his right to be free and enjoy the benefits of citizenship. Also stones with a person's name were used to give admission to a feast. So this is the promise that we will be given the right of access to the Kingdom of God and all its blessings. Jesus has prepared an eternal feast for us! The giving of a **new name** speaks of the manifestation of new aspects of our nature, and of us coming into a new position and new stage in the fulfilment of God's Purpose. It is a promise that Christ will release new potentialities and giftings in us, which are presently hidden within our spirit, so that we will be able to operate in new realms of our calling.

*4. The Church at THYATIRA (2:18-29): **"And to the angel** (pastor) **of the Church in Thyatira write: 'These things says the Son of God, who has eyes like a flame of fire, and His feet like fine** (burnished) **brass: "I know your works, love, service, faith, and your patience; and as for your works, the last are more than the first. Nevertheless I have a few things against you, because you allow that woman** (wife) **'Jezebel', who calls herself a prophetess, to teach and seduce My servants to commit sexual immorality and eat things sacrificed**

to idols. And I gave her time to repent of her sexual immorality, and she did not repent. Indeed I will cast her into a sickbed, and those who commit adultery with her into Great Tribulation, unless they repent of their deeds. I will kill her children with death, and all the Churches shall know that I am He who searches the minds and hearts. And I will give to each one of you according to your works. Now to you I say, and to the rest in Thyatira, as many as do not have this doctrine, who have not known the depths, of satan, as they say, I will put on you no other burden. But hold fast what you have till I come. And he who overcomes, and keeps My works until the end, to him I will give power over the nations: 'He shall rule them with a rod of iron; they shall be dashed to pieces like the potter's vessels' as I also have received from My Father; and I will give him the Morning Star. He who has an ear, let him hear what the Spirit says to the Churches."

The Church at Thyatira represents the Medieval Roman Catholic Church of the Dark Ages (800 - 1517 AD), where the negative developments from the last era came to their fullness. **Thyatira** means **'continual sacrifice'**, a reference to the Roman Catholic MASS, where the priest transforms the elements into the actual body and blood of Christ, and then sacrifices Christ again. This became central to the Roman Catholic System of salvation, enabling her to exercise great authority over people. Christ's attitude to what was happening in this Church is shown by His presentation of Himself as the One with the right and power to judge: **"the Son of God, with eyes as a flame of fire, and feet like fine brass"** (v18). As 'the Son of God', He has the authority to judge. The description of His eyes and feet comes from Rev 1:14-15. His possession of 'eyes as a flame of fire' (also 1:14, 19:12) speak of His omniscience, His ability to see all things, even to search out every human heart and shine the light on what is hidden and burn it up if it is combustible. In v23 He elaborates on this: **"all the Churches shall know that I am He who searches the minds and hearts** (with His eyes of fire). **And I will give to each one of you according to your works."** His feet like fine brass also speak of His right and power to judge, brass being symbolic of judgment, and feet represent the instruments by which He will judge, subdue and crush all that is opposed to God. 'Fine brass' is 'burnished brass', that is brass that has gone through a process of polishing and hardening of its surface by the application of great pressure, making it smooth, strong and shining. The original description in 1:15 adds a detail: **"His feet were like fine** (burnished) **brass, as if refined in a furnace."** This speaks of His human nature, which was perfected through suffering (Hebrews 2:10). As a Man, Jesus endured all the fires of affliction and judgment, being tested and tempted in every way, and passed every test, proving Himself perfect in every way. This now qualifies Him to be the judge of all men, for as a man He knows by experience what we face. Moreover, He has overcome sin and evil in all its forms and so has the right to judge it, and to crush it all under His feet.

Before explaining why He is warning this Church about His coming to them as the Judge, He first commends them for their many good works of loving service, so there were many individuals in the Church who truly loved and served Christ (v19). But then the bulk of His letter is devoted to strong correction and warnings of coming judgment. He focuses on 'Jezebel' as the main culprit, who by her teaching was leading believers to commit sexual immorality, and participate in the false worship of the pagan idol feasts (these two things often went together), just as we saw with the doctrine of Balaam. The teaching of sexual immorality represents the teaching of worldliness, that it is okay for us to conform to the moral standards of the world, so if a Church teaches that sex before marriage is okay, it is encouraging immorality, just like Balaam and Jezebel. The difference of the teaching of Jezebel from that of Balaam is that with Jezebel things have moved to a higher level of apostasy. This time the teaching is not just a seductive influence from a group within the church, but the direct official teaching coming from the place of authority, from the pulpit of the Church, for 'Jezebel' was the Pastor's wife. Remember the letter is written to the Pastor, and the word for 'woman' can also be translated 'wife.' Also her name was not actually 'Jezebel' (no one would actually be called that because of its associations), but He called her that to liken her to the Biblical Jezebel, wife of king Ahab. Now Ahab was in authority, but was weak and let his forceful wife take control, so likewise though the Pastor was in authority, he was weak and allowed his wife, who had a stronger personality and claimed to be a prophetess, to be a dominant voice in the church and like Jezebel of old she spoke evil things contrary to God's Word. So when Jesus said to the Pastor: 'that woman, Jezebel', He was saying 'that wife of yours, who's just like Jezebel.'

So there is a parallel being made here between the history of the Church and the history of Israel. God warned Israel against worldliness, adopting the ways and worship of the surrounding nations, but she sinned and corrupted her worship of God by introducing pagan practices (like the use of images and idols, such as the golden bulls). Then through Jezebel things got much worse, going to a new level of rejection of God's ways, because she introduced an entirely false system of worship, in which Israel no longer even worshipped God, but Baal instead. Worship based on a corrupted understanding of Scripture turned into worship based on a whole new set of principles that are not even in God's Word. Thus the doctrines of man (and satan) were substituted for God's Word as the basis for salvation and worship. Thus Jezebel led Israel to commit spiritual adultery against her true husband, God, by causing her to trust and worship another. She was the head of (and so represented) a new false religious system that forced itself on the people, taking away their religious freedom, and persecuting the true believers (so much so that Elijah thought he was the only one left). She was married to the king (the political power) and was able to control him, making him do as she pleased, and using his authority to enforce her will and religious system over the people.

This is a type of exactly what happened in the next Era of Church history. In the Pergamum Era the Church began to compromise to worldliness, but in the Dark Ages of Thyratira the institutional Church became a 'Jezebel' - a false religious system that had departed so far from the truth that it no longer represented God or His Way of Salvation. This Jezebel 'Church' was married to the State and came to rule over it. From 1000 - 1500 AD Papal power ruled over kings (the 2 crossed keys, worn by the Pope represent his supreme power over both Church and State). Thus this 'Church' was able to use the power of the State to launch the Crusades and the Inquisitions. It persecuted and killed those who did not submit to it, especially the true believers who held to God's Word. The Nicolaitans had now taken over all the levers of power and established a religious system where the doctrines (traditions) of man had been substituted for God's Word as the effective basis for salvation and worship. These doctrines combined to create a religious system that was totally unlike anything specified in the New Testament, and had the effect of transferring much of the power over men's souls from Christ to the Church, since it now mediated forgiveness and salvation (so you had to conform to this system to be saved), resulting in turning men's hearts from trusting in Christ alone for salvation, to looking to and trusting in the Church as well. Also their pure devotion and worship of their Bridegroom, Christ, was diverted to the veneration (worship) of Mary, saints (as exalted mediators), relics, and the worship of images and icons, which is clearly forbidden in scripture (Exodus 20:3-5, 1Corinthians 12:2, 2Corinthians 6:16, 1Thessalonians 1:9, 1John 5:21, Revelation 9:20). Even though it may be an image of Christ, the Bible says no image can be a true representation of God and so images are forbidden to be used as an aid to worship, for then you are not worshipping in truth, and you are in fact worshipping something other than God, a substitute for the true God - a mental fantasy.

Thus it led men to commit spiritual unfaithfulness (adultery). Like Jezebel, who brought the whole nation of Israel under the control of her religious system, so likewise the Church as a whole came under the control of this false Christianity (although I am focusing on the Western Church many of these things also apply to the Eastern Church), although of course there were always believers who stayed true to the Word and served Christ from their heart.

The dominion of this false system over people was achieved by: (1) seduction and (2) false teaching (v20). (1) Seduction is designed to draw the emotions by an appeal to the senses, hence the impressive ornate surroundings, priestly costumes (designed to project their special authority), images, icons, statues and ceremonial style of worship - all designed to impress the worshipper visually. On top of this is the projection of authority, importance and power through pomp and ceremony. The danger of all this is the seduction (drawing away) of people's focus, attention and affection from Christ to the Jezebel Church. (2) False teaching is designed to convince the mind of the rightness of this system. Since this system is totally other to what is in the New Testament, it was necessary for the Church to claim the right to introduce new doctrines that were equally authoritative and binding as the Word of God, as well as preventing the people from having direct access to the Bible, by forbidding its translation from Latin into their own language. As well as awakening the emotion (desire), it is also necessary for deception to convince the mind with a false logic. Once both emotion and mind are satisfied, then the way is open to take the will captive and demand its submission to a false religious system.

The warning of Paul in 2Corinthians 11:2-4 is very appropriate: **"I am jealous for you with godly jealousy. For I have betrothed you to one husband, that I may present you as a chaste virgin to Christ. But I fear, lest somehow, as the serpent deceived Eve by his craftiness, so your minds may be corrupted from the simplicity that is in Christ. For if he who comes preaches another Jesus whom we have not preached, or if you receive a different spirit which you have not received, or a different Gospel which you have not accepted, you may well put up with it!"**

*12 false doctrines became established as the official teaching of the Roman Church:

(1) Justification by works of faith (rather than through faith alone).

(2) Baby baptism and baptismal regeneration.

(3) Purgatory.

(4) Penance.

(5) Indulgences (all denials of salvation by grace alone).

(6) Worship of images (violating God's 2nd Commandment).

(7) Celibacy of priests (1Timothy 4:3 calls this a doctrine of demons).

(8) Transubstantiation (the Mass, a denial of the finality of Christ's sacrifice).

(9) Confession (to priests, as being necessary for forgiveness).

(10) Mariology (the worshipful veneration of Mary). Prayer to Mary (as a co-mediator with Jesus) is encouraged, as well as praying to the dead saints (forbidden by Scripture - Deuteronomy 18:11).

(11) Papal supremacy, claiming the Pope is the Vicar of Christ (standing in His place) and Pastor of the entire Christian Church, with full, supreme and universal power over the whole Church, a power which he can always exercise unhindered, so he has, by divine institution, supreme, full, immediate and universal power in the care of souls. This is based on his apostolic succession from Peter (also unbiblical).

Related to this is the doctrine that the Roman Catholic Church is the only true Church authorised by God, so all other Christians are separated brethren.

(12) The Church claims exclusive authority to interpret God's Word (so believers are not allowed to disagree, but are bound to accept all of the Church's official teachings). Also it claims the right to ADD doctrines to God's Word. Thus the official teachings, traditions and pronouncements of the Church are held to be just as much the infallible Word of God as the Scriptures. This is a common feature of false cults who use the Bible for their authority, but also add the writings of their prophets alongside the Scripture (such as Mormons and 7th Day Adventists). Although they claim to uphold Scripture, in practice they always end up interpreting Scripture through the lens of their other writings, and end up with an altogether different religion and way of salvation than what is in the Bible, which leads people to trust in something other than Christ (usually conformity to the rules of the cult in question), thus leading them to destruction, which is why God closed Scripture with the strong warnings of Revelation 22:18-19. The Bible claims to be uniquely God's Word, our only infallible authority and guide for faith and practice, sufficient for all man to know and teach the truth of God (2Timothy 3:16-17), and it does not point to the need for us to accept and hold another infallible authority alongside itself. In fact it strongly warns us against doing this, for we are not to go beyond what is written (1Corinthians 4:6), or add to the words of God (Deuteronomy 4:2, Proverbs 30:5-6), but only receive the Words of God (Matthew 4:4). Our Lord Jesus and the New Testament writers consistently appealed to Scripture as their only authority, so we should certainly imitate them in this matter.

What has happened in the Roman Church and in various cults in elevating the tradition of man to a place of infallibility alongside the Scripture, also happened in Judaism at the time of Jesus. In fact the parallelism is very close, so the attitude of Jesus towards this gives us an example for us to follow. The Pharisees had exalted their traditions to a place of equality with Scripture, by claiming it had been handed down by word of mouth from Moses (the Oral Law), just as the Roman Church claims their traditions have been handed down from the original apostles by word of mouth (needless to say there is no evidence for this), and later declared infallible by the church. In practice they interpreted Scripture in the light of these teachings, and so focused on and followed these traditions of men more than Scripture itself. These traditions resulted in them being blinded to the truths of Scripture, causing them to ignore Scripture in order to keep their tradition, thus nullifying the working of the Word of God in their lives. Jesus pointed this out to them in: **"In vain they worship Me, teaching as doctrines the commandments of men** (quoting Isaiah 29:13).' **For laying aside the Commandment of God** (in the Bible), **you hold the tradition of men... "All too well you reject the Commandment of God, that you may keep your tradition. ...making the Word of God of no effect through your tradition which you have handed down"** (Mark 7:7-13, see also Matthew 15:1-7). This always happens when other commandments (of men) are added to Scripture - people end up obeying them above and instead of Scripture, they usurp the place of God's Word. It is clear that Jesus only accepted the authority of the Word of God and rejected the authority of these traditions, and refused to bow to them. He judged them by the light of God's Word and often rejected them on that basis. Indeed a major cause of the conflict of the Pharisees with Christ, was the fact He did not accept their man-made traditions as divinely authoritative (especially their teachings on how to keep the sabbath), but instead held to the Scripture alone. In so doing, He challenged the whole basis of their special authority and ministry. Later on these traditions got written down as the Talmud, and Judaism became even more entrenched in the religious system they defined. This embrace of man's tradition alongside God's Word resulted in people being kept from the truth of God and from receiving Jesus: **"Woe to you, scribes and Pharisees hypocrites! For you shut up the kingdom of heaven against men; for you neither go in yourselves, nor do you allow those who are entering to go in"** (Matthew 23:13).

This principle of 'sola-scripture' is the fundamental issue, because if a church or cult claims the authority to add authoritative infallible teachings alongside the Bible, they not only deny the sufficiency and clarity of the Bible, but they can introduce any teaching they like (often designed to strengthen their hold on the people) as being fully authoritative from God, so that their members are obliged to obey it. Even if it does not line up the Word, the authority of the Church is invoked that says the teaching is inerrant, making it immune to questioning, so now the Scriptures has to be reinterpreted to fit with this new tradition of man. The result is that Scripture is subverted by the tradition of man. This unbiblical and anti-biblical doctrine, whereby the Church claims the authority to add new binding doctrines, which are not in Scripture, provides the basis for all 12 of these unbiblical doctrines introduced by the Church by its own authority (listed above), which together form the basis of a whole new religious system demanding the obedience of the people (and taking it away from Christ). Thus although they can't be found in the Bible and even contradict it, they are introduced by the Church by its own authority. Jesus alluded to these extra doctrines of 'Jezebel' in v24: **"this doctrine, who have not known the depths, of satan, as they say."** They (the false teachers) describe these teachings as 'the depths', that is the deeper teachings of God that go beyond the Bible, but Jesus says they are actually the teachings of satan, which uphold the false Jezebel system which leads men away from the true Way of Salvation, which is simply trusting in Christ alone. This is why 'Jezebel' fiercely resisted the translation of the Bible, for if people could read it for themselves, it would point them to Christ for salvation, as well as revealing her true nature, resulting in them rejecting her and embracing God's Word as the truth and their final authority. In v24 Christ defines the true believers in Thyatira as those who 'do not have this (Jezebel) doctrine' and His only requirement of them is to continue their rejection of it. Instead they're to faithfully hold fast to what they've already received (God's Word) rather than following after other 'new' doctrines.

These 12 'new' doctrines undergird a whole religious system (Jezebel) that forcefully claims to be God's mediator of salvation on earth. Those who really follow and submit to her teaching ('her children', v23) end up trusting in her for salvation rather than Christ, for they are led to believe that only by doing works of faith and by submitting to a complex system of sacraments, penance, confession and indulgences administered by the Church can they be justified. To the extent that they are still unworthy of going to heaven at death, they must do time in purgatory. All of this is a heretical denial of the perfect salvation purchased by Christ on the Cross and offered to us as a free-gift of grace. This leads to eternal death (v23), not eternal life, which comes only by believing the Gospel and trusting in Christ alone. So although there were many true believers within the Church (v19,24), as an Institution it became a false religious system, offering a different

Gospel and way of salvation (Galatians 1:6-8). This institution became so corrupted that Christ reckons it as a Jezebel, a false religious system ripe for judgment.

In v21 the 'Jezebel' in Thyatira is described as fixed in her unrepentance concerning her teaching and immorality (she'd been given time to repent but refused, so now judgment was inevitable). Likewise, the Roman Catholic Church is unrepentant concerning her unbiblical doctrines and must remain so, for she has bound herself to them by her doctrine of infallibility, for in order to maximise her authority and exalt the authority of her new doctrines to an equal status with God's Word, she declared her key doctrinal declarations infallible. Thus although she can change her presentation of her doctrine, the essential doctrines themselves must remain unchanged (including the pronouncements of the Council of Trent of anathama against those who believe the true Gospel of justification by faith alone). Although Rome, now that she has lost her political power and her monopoly, is much softer in her style of presentation of her claims and doctrines, we are not to assume that she has repented of her false teachings. Jezebel's teaching of sexual immorality is a type of this religious system leading people to be unfaithful to their true Husband, Jesus Christ, by trusting and submitting to another way of Salvation, and obeying the man-made commands of the 'Church' instead of His commands. Thus she leads them into spiritual unfaithfulness (immorality). Christ alone is the infallible King (Ruler of nations), High Priest (Mediator of Salvation) and Prophet (One who declares God's Word with absolute authority). He alone possesses inherent, absolute authority, although He delegates some of His authority to the Church to fulfil a task. When a Church (motivated by a desire for power) begins to take His place, claiming the authority to rule over people and nations, and to mediate salvation and to add new doctrines to God's Word, then it becomes a Jezebel religious system that's a barrier to people receiving salvation through Christ.

In v22-23 Christ declares He will judge the 'Jezebel' in Thyatira along with her children, and those 'who commit adultery with her.' This has a double meaning. It does not just refer to those who follow her teaching and immoral lifestyle, but also indicates that she was seducing some by sleeping with them. He will bring great trouble upon them, even death, unless they repent. Although judgment is now inevitable for unrepentant Jezebel, it was still possible for her followers to repent and avoid judgment.

The language used in this warning supports our prophetic interpretation of the letter, for He warns that He will cast Jezebel and her unrepentant followers into **Great Tribulation,** a phrase that elsewhere in the Bible always speaks of the last 3.5 years before Christ returns (Matthew 24:15,21, Revelation 7:14). Thus the complete fulfilment of this prophecy requires Thyatira/Jezebel to be a type of a Church that will exist in the last days and will suffer judgment in the Great Tribulation. Thus this letter looks beyond the local situation and uses it to predict developments in Church history leading up to Christ's Return. This means the letter to Thyatira speaks of a certain type of Church that will spring up at some point of Church history and continue until the Great Tribulation when it will be destroyed. During a certain Era (that we call the Dark Ages) it is completely dominant, before the next type of Church arises (represented by Sardis), however at that point it does not cease to exist but continues to the end. We will see that the same holds true for the remaining 3 Churches, and we will also find more evidence for this prophetic interpretation of these letters in other references where Jesus speaks of these Churches as continuing to exist until the end of the Church Age, even though these local churches no longer exist, for example: **"hold fast what you have till I come"** (v25). Thus they must be typical of a certain part of the universal Church.

Thus v22-23 is a prophecy that the Roman System (Jezebel) and those who 'commit adultery with her' (who've been seduced by her into trusting and obeying her for salvation, rather than trusting in Christ alone) will continue to the End of the Age and will miss the Rapture (because they are not born again) and continue into the Tribulation, when she will be judged. However she will continue to exist for the first half of the Tribulation, for v22 indicates that her destruction awaits the Great Tribulation, which starts at Mid-Tribulation, when all her 'children' will be killed. Jezebel's children are more closely associated with her than her followers, so they represent the priesthood. Amazingly Scripture elsewhere prophesies this very event at Mid-Tribulation, for that is when destruction falls on the Jezebel-like harlot called 'Mystery Babylon' of Revelation 17, who sits on the political beast and has dominion over the peoples of the world during the first half of the Tribulation, before the 10 kings destroy her at Mid-Tribulation. 'Mystery' indicates it is something from the Church Age. Whereas all born-again believers within the Catholic Church will be raptured (v28), the Roman Catholic system and those who trust in her will go into the Tribulation and form the core of the harlot church which will be destroyed at Mid-Tribulation to make way for the world-wide worship of the antichrist. The corrupted harlot church on earth in the Tribulation stands in contrast to the true pure Bride of Christ who has been raptured to Heaven.

Having told the true believers (the overcomers) to hold fast to the Word until He comes (v25), He then gave them His promise of eternal blessing, that they will receive at His Return. In fact, all the promises to the overcomers at the end of the letters will be fulfilled at His Return. To each Church He chooses promises that reinforce the message of the letter. In this case He says: **"To him** (the overcomer) **I will give power over the nations: 'He shall rule them with a rod of iron; they shall be dashed to pieces like the potter's vessels', as I also have received from My Father; and I will give him the Morning Star"** (v26-28). Here He confirms His Kingdom will rule over all the nations and the true Church will reign with Him, but this is not for the Church Age, it's for after He returns to establish His Kingdom. Right now we are in training for reigning, but our job is to fulfil the Great Commission, not to take power (as Dominion Theology says). So writing to the true believers living in this fully developed Nicolaitan Church, that desires and claims spiritual power over men's souls and earthly power over nations, He gives them these promises to help them to not be seduced into the system by the vision and desire for earthly power and prestige, or by the power and grandeur Jezebel seems to possess, but rather to stay true to Him and His commands. He reminds them that although this earthly power seems impressive, it is just temporal, and the real kingdom, power and glory of God on earth is yet future when He returns. He is keeping their vision on preparing for the future eternal Kingdom, which is the real deal, rather than trying to attain earthly power now. We are now to prepare ourselves for that time when we'll rule with Christ forever, by preaching the Gospel and inviting as many people as possible to be part of this future glorious Kingdom.

One reason why it is not yet time for the Church to rule over the nations is that while we have sinful flesh, power tends to corrupt, and when any religion controls the political power it becomes corrupted by that power and oppressive in using it, especially on those who believe differently. Therefore, that kind of power is only safe in the hands of perfect people, like Christ, and us once we have received our resurrection bodies, which is why Jesus finishes with the promise of the MORNING STAR (v28), which is speaking of the Rapture. The promise of the Morning Star is mentioned 3 times in the Bible. Here in Revelation 2:28, Jesus promises the overcomer: **"I will give him the Morning Star."** The context for this promise is His Coming for the Church (v25), so Jesus will fulfil this to believers at His Coming. In Revelation 22:16, Jesus says: **"I am the Bright and Morning Star."** Again the context is His Coming for the Church (v12). From these scriptures and from the nature of stars it is clear that the Morning Star is a manifestation of the Glory of Christ given to believers when He returns. This is confirmed by 2Peter 1:19: **"we have the prophetic word confirmed, which you do well to heed as a light that shines in a dark place, until the Day dawns, and the Morning Star rises in your hearts."** This speaks of 3 manifestations of Christ's light (glory). Now, with the world in darkness, we have the Light of God's Word to guide us, but there will also be 2 more manifestations of His Glory. The dawning of a new day speaks of the 2nd Coming of Christ, appearing as the Sun of Righteousness, when He will cover the whole earth with His glory. But just BEFORE the sun rises, while it is still dark in the world, the Morning Star rises, heralding the dawn. Peter says that this manifestation of Christ's Glory will not be seen by the world asleep in the darkness, but will take place in the hearts of the believers, for the Morning Star (the Glory of Christ) will rise (be manifested) in their hearts. Thus when Christ returns for His Church He will release the Spirit and Glory of God that already resides in our spirits, and it will explode through our hearts and transform our bodies to be like Christ's resurrection body. Thus the promise of the Morning Star to believers is the promise of the Rapture, which necessarily happens before Sunrise, when all shall see His Glory. This confirms the Pre-Tribulation Rapture.

It is also a happy coincidence that the 'Morning Star' promise in v28 also anticipates a major development that took place near the end of the night of the Dark Ages, about 100 years before the dawning of a new day (Era) of Church history brought in by the Reformation. 2 men, **John Wycliffe** in England (1302-1384) and the Czech **John Huss** (1369-1415) are called the **Morning Stars of the**

Reformation, for they were lights shining in the dark heralding the soon-coming end of the Dark Ages, and the dawn of a new day (represented by Sardis). They were the forerunners of the Reformation, for they preached its major themes, calling men back to the Bible and challenging the corrupted power of the Roman Church. Their aim was to reform the Church, for it to return to following the Bible. The Reformers, like Luther, were inspired by their teachings and courageous lives.

John Wycliffe, a top Oxford Professor, led the way. He formulated the foundational (formal) principle of the Reformation, the unique supreme authority of the Bible for the belief and life of the Christian. He was the first to translate the Bible into English, and his team of Lollards preached the Word and distributed the scriptures. He died of a stroke before he could be martyred. The Pope was so infuriated by his teachings and translation of the Bible, that 44 years after his death, he ordered his bones to be dug-up, crushed and scattered in the river! But even this could not stop the fire that Wycliffe started. His chronicler said: *"They burnt his bones to ashes and cast them into the Swift, a neighbouring brook running hard by. Thus the brook has conveyed his ashes into Avon, Avon into Severn; Severn into the narrow seas; and they into the main ocean. And thus the ashes of John Wycliffe are the emblem of his doctrine which now is dispersed the world over."*

John Huss was strongly influenced by Wycliffe and taught the same things in Europe. He nailed a statement called: 'The 6 errors' on his church door, which is where Luther (who was inspired by Huss) got the idea to nail his '95 Theses' to his church door, which act started the Reformation on 31st October 1517. One of these errors was that church members were required to believe in and obey the pope as God's representative. In contrast, Huss taught we should believe in and obey only God. He was the first of the Reformers to be burned at the stake in 1415 for his belief that the Church must conform to the Bible. At his death he gave an inspired prophecy. As the executioner was about to light the fire, he said: "Now we will cook the goose" (Huss in Bohemian means 'goose'). "Yes", replied Huss, "but there will come an eagle in 100 years that you will not reach." This was fulfilled 100 years later when Luther wrote his 95 theses. This leads us to Sardis.

*5. The Church at SARDIS (3:1-6): "To the angel (pastor) of the Church in Sardis write: 'These things says He who has the 7 Spirits of God and the 7 stars: "I know your works, that you have a name that you are alive, but you are dead. Be watchful, and strengthen the things, which remain, that are ready to die, for I have not found your works perfect before God. Remember therefore how you have received and heard; hold fast and repent. Therefore if you will not watch, I will come upon you as a thief, and you will not know what hour I will come upon you. You have a few names even in Sardis who have not defiled their garments; and they shall walk with Me in white, for they are worthy. He who overcomes shall be clothed in white garments, and I will not blot out his name from the Book of Life; but I will confess his name before My Father and before His angels. He who has an ear, let him hear what the Spirit says to the Churches."**

The Church at Sardis represents the next Era of Church History, the Reformation (1517 - 1660 AD). Sardis means: 'those escaping' or 'those who come out.' In our prophetic interpretation it must refer to those coming out (escaping) from Roman Catholicism. Although this was a step in the right direction, and their report card was certainly better than Thyatira's, nevertheless it is clear that there was still much to be desired. In fact, Christ describes it as a dying Church, which is why He introduces Himself as the One with the 7 Spirits of God, for He is the Source of the life-giving Holy Spirit for His people and the supplier of the anointing for His stars (pastors), and so they need to come to Him to receive His life, for the Church is becoming dead without the Spirit of God, and without born-again anointed Pastors.

By saying He knows their works, He acknowledges the much good work they did in reforming the Church, especially at the start. The fundamental principle of the Reformation was the restoration of the Bible as the sole final authority for faith and practice, thus rejecting many of the Roman ways, teachings and traditions that had no basis in the Bible (such as idols and images). Related to this is that each person is responsible to read and understand and obey the Bible for themselves, rather than teaching that only the priests can interpret its mystical meaning. This required the return to the principle of literal interpretation, that is, accepting its plain meaning according to the laws of language. This led to Bible translations in the language of the people, so all could read it for themselves.

The particular issue that triggered the parting of ways was over the issue of the Gospel and salvation. Roman Catholic teaching involves a complicated process administered by the Church, whereby a man's right-standing with God (justification) is achieved by a gradual process of faith and works done in conformity with the authority and sacraments of the Church (giving the Church great power over a man's salvation). Thus as man does works of faith in obedience to the Church, God imparts more righteousness to him. But Luther through his studies in Romans rediscovered the central doctrine at the heart of the Gospel - justification by faith alone (apart from works). This is based on the imputed righteousness of Christ, so that at the moment we trust in Christ His perfect human righteousness is accounted (given) to us as a free gift, so we can stand before God clothed in the white clean robe of Christ's righteousness. On this basis, God declares us perfectly forgiven and righteous in His sight. Thus in this way we are saved by grace alone, through faith alone, apart from any works (Ephesians 2:8-9). This is the Gospel, and the realisation that the Catholic Church preached a different (false) Gospel helped the Reformers realise that it had become a false Church, from which they needed to break away and come out from under its authority, in order to preserve and restore the truth of the Gospel (Galatians 1:6-8, 2Corinthians 11:4), thus forming the Protestant Churches. Those who had dutifully followed the false Gospel of 'faith + works' for salvation, trusting in their obedience to the Church, were not saved by that, for they were not trusting in Christ alone (so if anyone got saved it was in spite of the Church's teaching rather than because of it). By restoring the truth and centrality of the Gospel, new life surged into the Churches as more and more people were born again through trusting in Christ alone. Thus there was great growth of Bible-believing Protestant churches, which is why Christ said: '**you have a name** (reputation) **that you are alive**', for they started in life.

But because the Reformation did not go far enough in following through on their fundamental principle of going back to the Bible, a process of death started to happen in many Protestant Churches, so that today most Protestant Denominations are full of nominal (spiritually dead) Christians and dead Churches. Although this Sardis Church had a name of being alive because of her past, Christ said: '**you are dead.**' It is like a dead body that was alive once, but has become dead. However, it is not completely dead, for Jesus said to it: **"Be watchful, strengthen the things which remain, that are ready to die."** In other words: "WAKE UP, before it is too late." Even in its decline, it has a residue of truth, and 'a few' born again believers in it (v4). Our sources of spiritual life are God's Word and Spirit, which must take a central place, so He is calling them to go back to the foundational principle of putting the Word of God first, which is how they received life in the first place, thus reversing the process of death.

Jesus then explained the cause of this death process: **"for I have not found your works perfect before God."** Their work of reform was not carried through fully. Many of the old traditions, beliefs and ways were not changed. Yes, the doctrines of salvation and of the church were made biblical, but other areas such as Eschatology were untouched, because the literal interpretation of the Bible was not applied to them. The basic error of the union of Church and State persisted, along with the continued practice of baby-baptism, resulting in the growth of nominal Christianity in the Protestant Denominations, that came out of the Reformation, according to the process described under Pergamum. Thus the process of Reformation (applying Scripture to every area using literal interpretation) was cut short, opening the door to this death process, which would come to its head in the totally dead Laodician Church. Thus His description of Sardis is a very apt summary of what's generally happened in the traditional Protestant denominations. The Sardis Church started with new life, but fell into spiritual decline.

But it is not all bad news, and there are many vibrant Protestant Churches both within and without the historic Denominations. This is because another Church also came out of Sardis (our next Church - Philadelphia) which did strengthen 'the things which remain' (the core principles of the Reformation) which were 'about to die' and which has set about bringing the work of the Reformation to perfection, in restoring the whole truth of God's Word to the Church. Christ described this positive process in v3: **"Remember therefore how you have**

received and heard (the Word of God); **hold fast and repent."** By saying 'remember' He calls them back to their foundational principles, telling them to hold fast to them (guard and keep them), and build on them, being ready to repent of things that are not in line with them. In particular He says: **"remember HOW you have RECEIVED and HEARD** (the Word)**."** How did they receive the Word at the beginning? They received it as the inerrant Word of God, the only final authority for faith and practice, to be literally understood. This is the foundational principle to which He is calling them back, saying they should hold fast to this approach and apply it to all areas of the Bible, repenting accordingly (changing their thinking to line up with the Bible). This had logically led to its initial application in the area of salvation, for the central and entry-level message of the Bible is the true Gospel. He said they were to remember HOW they RECEIVED salvation, by HEARING God's Word and believing it (by faith alone). This was the 2nd key defining principle of the Reformation. They were to build on this foundation of the true Gospel of the Grace of God and learn to receive all the promises of God in the same way, that cover all areas of life and godliness (not just forgiveness). We will see that the Philadelphian Church started this process of restoration of truth and continues to do it.

Jesus warns those who did not do this, but rather stayed in the deadness of unbelief, that He will come to them suddenly as a THIEF in the night: **"if you will not watch, I will come upon you as a thief"** (v3). This is a picture of a sudden unexpected judgment and is used by Jesus, Paul, Peter and John as a reference to how unbelievers will experience His Coming in the Rapture when they will suddenly find themselves in the judgement of the Tribulation (Matthew 24:43, 1Thessalonians 5:2,4, 2Peter 3:10, Revelation 16:15). For believers the Rapture will be like the Bridegroom coming for His Bride (we will be clothed in white, God's glory shining from our resurrection bodies, v4-5), but for the unsaved (even if they are churchgoers) who will miss the Rapture and be left behind, it will be as if a thief had come and taken all the precious things (all the true believers) from the house (earth). Jesus used the history of the city of Sardis as a background to reinforce this warning of judgement. The city seemed impregnable being an acropolis surrounded by a cliff 1500 feet high, so it was easily defended. This made them overconfident, assuming they were safe. As result even though they were warned they did not keep watch and they were caught by surprise and defeated by an enemy scaling these cliffs and coming upon them suddenly like a thief in the night. This happened twice in their history.

This warning of judgment on this 'Sardis' Church at His Coming shows again that Jesus was not just talking to the local Church, but that Sardis must be a type of a section of the Universal Church that will exist at the time of the Rapture. Thus just as 'Thyatira' continues on until the End of the Age, even after its Era of total dominance had passed, so 'Sardis' will continue to the End even after its Era (when it came into being and arose to prominence) has passed. It will continue into the Tribulation, forming part of the One-World Church (the Mystery Babylon Harlot). Thus in the next Era marked by the rise of the Philadelphian Church, both the Thyatiran (Roman Catholic) and Sardis (historic Protestant State Churches) continue to exist alongside Philadelphia.

*6. The Church at PHILADELPHIA: "To the angel** (pastor) **of the Church in Philadelphia write, 'These things says He who is holy, He who is true: "He who has the key of David, He who opens and no one shuts, and shuts and no one opens." I know your works. See, I have set before you an open door, and no one can shut it; for you have a little strength, have kept My word, and have not denied My Name. Indeed I will make those of the synagogue of Satan, who say they are Jews and are not, but lie, indeed I will make them come and worship before your feet, and to know that I have loved you. Because you have kept My command to persevere, I also will keep you from the hour of trial which shall come upon the whole world, to test those who dwell on the earth. Behold, I am coming quickly! Hold fast what you have, that no one may take your crown. He who overcomes, I will make him a pillar in the Temple of My God, and he shall go out no more. I will write on him the Name of My God and the Name of the city of My God, the New Jerusalem, which comes down out of Heaven from My God. And I will write on him My new name. He who has an ear, let him hear what the Spirit says to the Churches"** (Revelation 3:7-13). Philadelphia means 'brotherly love' implying a healthy Church obeying Christ's commandment. In fact, along with Sardis, Jesus has nothing to say against her. The Church at Philadelphia represents the revived Protestant Churches. Although the Philadelphian Era is 1660 - 1890 AD, the Philadelphian Church continues today and is growing rapidly, and will continue to the Rapture. The appearance of the Laodician Church did not mean the end of Philadelphia. In fact Philadelphia & Laodicia represent 2 contrasting developments from the Sardis Church of the Reformation. The Churches that applied Christ's injunction to Sardis became Philadelphian, but those who rejected it and went the other way into theological liberalism became Laodician. Thyatira (Catholicism) on the other hand due to its centralised authority and claims of infallibility is not subject to change in its core beliefs. Although it can present itself and its ideas differently, and introduce new ideas, these new ideas cannot contradict previously established dogmas previously decreed by the Church's infallible decree. This has positive and negative aspects. Where the Church is holding forth the Word, for example the doctrines affirmed by the historic Creeds and in areas of Biblical morality, this refusal to change is positive. But when the Church holds to unbiblical traditions, especially a false gospel of justification by faith +works, this is negative.

On the other hand in the Protestant Churches the diminishing of the authority of the Church and its decentralisation (in order that each man may be directly under the authority of God's Word), has led to much greater change and diversification. This again can be both positive and negative. The positive effect is seen in Philadelphia, which endeavours to continue what the Reformation began, restoring the Church to the whole truth of the Word of God, by systematically applying the principle of literal interpretation, and throwing out old traditions that are found to contradict the plain meaning of Scripture. This resulted in great progress in restoring the truths of the independence of Church and State, believers baptism, sanctification (the Holiness Movement), the modern missions movement, the power and gifts of the Spirit (the Pentecostal and Charismatic Movements), Israelology and End-time Prophecy. But this freedom from the supreme centralised authority of the Roman Church and Pope also allowed the negative development represented by Laodicia where many Protestant Churches changed in the wrong way, falling into total apostasy through liberal theology, denying the very essentials of the faith.

This letter describes the first kind of response to Christ's challenge to Sardis, in contrast to the next letter, which describes the opposite kind of response of rejecting God's truth wholesale in favour of humanism. This wholly positive letter indicates that there will be positive developments from the Reformation through those continue to seek the truth of God's Word over man's traditions. Philadelphia means 'brotherly love' denoting a key characteristic of a Church that is determined to be true to the Bible, for the New Commandment of Jesus is that we should love one another as He has loved us (John 13:34-35). The restoration of true Doctrine results in a restoration of God's life and love in the Church. There were many great revivals, and evangelists like Whitfield, Wesley and Finney, and pioneers of the faith who restored more of the truth of God's Word to the Church, like Wesley bringing in the Holiness Movement. This Era also saw the start of great missions outreaches to the ends of the earth, with great missionaries like Hudson Taylor, Adoriam Judson and William Carey, restoring the Church to the fulfilment of the Great Commission, and the saving of the lost is the greatest demonstration of love for our fellow human beings who are eternally lost if they remain without Christ (John 3:16), and so this restoration and continuation of world evangelism is a major manifestation of the name and nature of Philadelphia. Then the start of the 20th century saw the restoration of the Baptism in the Spirit with speaking in tongues, and the Welsh and Azuza Street Revivals, and the Pentecostal and Charismatic Movements and the recovery of the supernatural gifts such as Divine Healing. It is hard to put an exact date on the start of the Philadelphian Era because even from early on in the Reformation there were 'Philadelphian' Churches like the Anabaptists, that is, Churches who believed the Reformation did not go far enough.

A key issue was believing in the separation of Church and State in contrast to the Protestant State Churches. This led to a strong emphasis on freedom of conscience in religion. They opposed the persecution so characteristic of their age. They denied the State had a right to punish anyone for their religious beliefs or teachings. This was revolutionary in the Reformation Era. This emphasis on freedom was also reflected in the restoration of Believers Baptism. They also had a greater emphasis on personal holiness. However these Churches were a persecuted minority on the margins. A larger movement of this nature were the Puritans who originally wanted to reform the established Church from within, but eventually felt they had separate from it, hence my date of 1660 (among these were the Pilgrims who settled in America to find freedom from the Established Church and its persecution). It should be noted that although a major Philadelphian characteristic is the separation of Church and State it is possible for a Church that is part of a State Church to be Philadelphian if its commitment to God's Word is greater than its commitment to its inherited traditions thus making it open to continued renewal and restoration. On the other hand a Free Church can become bound by tradition and resist further restoration and change and so lose its Philadelphian character.

Thus a Philadelphian Church holds to the supremacy of God's Word over man's tradition and seeks to apply this to every area of life and doctrine, resulting in ongoing restoration in increasing conformity to God's Word.

Christ introduces Himself as: **"He who is holy, He who is true"** (v7a), confirming them in their commitment to the centrality, truth and holiness of Christ. He also emphasises His supreme authority, as the One who possesses the keys (1:18): **"He who has the key of David, He who opens and no one shuts, and shuts and no one opens"** (v7b). The man with the key of David operated with the king's full authority (Isaiah 22:22), so that everything went through this 'right-hand' man, so no one could countermand his orders made in the name of the king. Likewise, Christ, who is at the Father's right hand operates with His full authority (Matthew 28:18), so that no one can countermand His orders. In particular, He has authorised and commanded the Church to fulfil the Great Commission (Matthew 28:19-20), and is able to open doors of opportunity to the Church. He commends them for their faithfulness thus far in keeping His Word and proclaiming His Name: **"I know your works... You have kept My Word, and have not denied My Name"** (v8), reflecting the restoration of the Biblical truth to the Church and the emphasis on evangelism and missions that characterises the Philadelphian Era.

He also tells them: **"See, I have set before you an open door, and no one can shut it, for you have a little strength."** He had used His keys to open a door of opportunity for them and they had been faithful in making use of it. As a reward

He promises to open new doors of opportunity to preach the Gospel and reach the lost for Christ. Thus the Philadelphian Church will continue to expand its outreach and growth until the Lord returns. The statement that they have a little strength or power is not a reference to their weak spiritual condition, for that would contradict the fact that this letter is full of commendation. Rather He is pointing out the fact that they only have a little natural power or influence in their society. Therefore He is calling them to look to Him, the One with all authority, Who promises to stand behind them as they reach out in His Name, trusting Him to open the doors. The Philadelphian Church has renounced the natural power, respectability and status that goes with being part of the establishment in order to operate in a greater spiritual power and to focus on being faithful to Christ alone, rather than balancing the demands of Christ and State. Thus the move from a Roman Church under the centralised authority of the Pope wielding great earthly power over all Christendom (Thyatira) to Protestant State Churches exerting power over individual States is taken one step further to Free Churches which have little power by comparison. However this is not all bad, for power tends towards compromise and a lack of spiritual purity and power, as Church History has demonstrated again and again. Although when Christ returns the Church will have power over the nations, our present mission is to witness to the world, not govern it, and it is not necessary to exercise great power to be successful in this, as Christ Himself and the Early Church proved. Dominion Theology which calls the Church toward the pursuit of power diverts it from its true call of evangelism which is primarily accomplished by means of spiritual power, exercised through prayer and proclamation, praying also for authorities that they would govern in such a way that doors would be open for the Gospel (1Timothy 2:1-4), just as Christ promised the Philadelphia Church.

This lack of natural power is also a consequence of the diversification into different denominations, networks and churches that resulted from the Reformation's emphasis on freedom from Papal authority and Church tradition and call for the Church to be restored to the truths of the Bible. As different truths were restored, different wineskins were needed to hold the new wine, but often the old-denominational wineskin was not flexible to adapt to change and rejected the restored truth. As a result new wineskins (new denominations or kinds of churches) were created that embodied and held forth these truths. (Of course divisions also happen for the wrong reasons). Now if the aim is political power this is a negative development for if the Universal Church existed as a single institution it would be very powerful. However, if the aim is to be a witness to the nations a diversity of styles, strengths and emphases is a positive thing. The creation of a centralised uniform institution is not necessary or desirable, as it would become encrusted in tradition, incapable of change, and would confer too much power on those at the top, inviting corruption, for there is the ever-present danger of the wrong people eventually gaining power, bringing the whole Church into darkness, and destroying her credibility and spiritual power, so she cannot fulfil her mission as a witness. Thus as God divided the nations at Babel as a protection from giving too much power to any particular sinful man, so in this Age He did not intend the visible Church to be conformed to a single institution under a single head (Pope). This is confirmed by how the apostles established the Church in the Book of Acts. God uses all kinds of Churches, Networks and Denominations as they seek to be true to His Word. He rejoices in unity, but not uniformity - unity in diversity and diversity in unity. The unity Jesus prayed for in John 17, is not an institutional unity, but the unity of believers with God, resulting in the spiritual unity of believers in truth and love. Together we are the body of Christ, so we are already one in Christ and we need to guard this unity. The essential basis for unity is that we believe in the true Christ and the true Gospel. We may disagree on other things that are of great importance, but we still have a unity of spirit as long as we agree on the essentials.

Thus the fact that Philadelphia had little natural power was not a problem for Christ, but rather our weakness is an opportunity for Christ to show Himself strong through us as we trust in Him (2Cor 12:9-10), and depend on Him to open doors for us to proclaim His Name. The missionaries from 1700-1900 had little natural power, and only a minority supported them, but they accomplished great things throughout the world. The nature of the church reflected the nature of the city. It was the least distinguished and powerful of the 7 cities, but it was influential, for Philadelphia was a missionary city from its beginning. It was not built as a military fortress to project power as Thyatira was, but as a centre of Greek civilisation to spread Greek culture and language (influence and light) to the regions of Lydia and Phrygia, in which mission it was very successful. It was located at the junction of several important trade routes and was called the Gateway to the East. Thus it had an open door to reach a whole region. So the missionary nature of this church fits with the calling and nature of the city. Another element of its background illustrates the message of the letter. In AD 17 there was a great earthquake with continuing aftershocks for the next few years, mentally shaking the inhabitants from being able to trust in their buildings. So many of them lived outside the city in huts. This disaster lived long in the memory of this city. Likewise the Philadelphian Church does not find its security in this world-system, but lives as pilgrims in this world, trusting in God's promise of being firmly established forever as part of God's eternal Temple and City which cannot be shaken (v12), for the Temple was the most secure structure built to withstand earthquakes (a promise to believers of their eternal security, and being inscribed with the names of God, Christ and His City confirm we will belong to Him forever and that we will have a permanent position in His Kingdom to His glory). So it does not make itself at home in this world, but goes out beyond its borders to reach those on the outside.

v9 predicts Philadelphia will have a successful mission also to the synagogue of satan: "who say they are Jews and are not, but lie." This group was initially seen in Smyrna (2:9). Satan means 'opposer', so this group was opposing the work of God in Philadelphia. This language of Gentiles claiming or pretending to be Jews or to be the true Israel fits two opposite errors or extremes, and significantly both of these arose in the Smryna Era: (1) the Judaisers who try to bring us under the Law of Moses on the basis that we have now been made part of Israel (misinterpreting Romans 11 and Ephesians 2). In Galatians, Paul denounced this as a false Gospel in opposition to the Gospel of Grace. (2) Sadly, in rejecting the Judaisers the Gentile Church went to the opposite extreme of Replacement Theology claiming that it was now the true 'spiritual Israel', having replaced natural Israel, ignoring the clear warning of Romans 11, resulting in theological anti-semitism infecting Christendom, causing it to be the primary cause of persecution of the Jews. Thus this false doctrine causes men to yield to the anti-Semitic spirit of satan that opposes the work of God, especially in relation to the elect nation of Israel.

v10-11 strongly confirms the prophetic typological application of these Letters to the Eras of Church History: **"Because you have kept My command to persevere, I also will keep you from the Hour of Trial** (Tribulation) **which shall**

come upon the whole world, to test those who dwell on the earth. Behold, I am coming quickly! Hold fast what you have, that no one may take your crown."

v10 describes the Tribulation, a unique time of worldwide judgment and Christ promises the Philadelphians that He will keep them from it. He does not just promise to protect them from the Trial, but from the very Hour of the Trial, from the time-period itself. He does not promise to protect them as they go through the Hour of Tribulation, but to keep them from ('ek' = 'out of') it. Since this Trial comes upon all who dwell on the earth, the only way Christ can fulfil this promise is by removing the Philadelphians from the earth in the Rapture. Hence in v11 He promises to come for the Philadelphians in the Rapture and reward them with crowns at His Judgment Seat. The language used by Christ requires a greater fulfilment than anything that might have happened to the local church at Philadelphia at that time. It can only find a complete fulfilment in the climactic end-time events of the Rapture and the Tribulation. Thus Philadelphia must represent a part of the Church that is alive at the Rapture (remember these letters are written to the whole Church, not just these local churches - v13). Thus v10-11 constitute a clear promise of the Pre-Tribulation Rapture for the believing Church.

Since these promises have not yet been fulfilled and the local church at Philadelphia only continued until the 14th century it follows that Jesus was not just talking to the local church. Whatever partial fulfilment might have taken place for that local church in the 1st century in terms of a deliverance from persecution and trouble in their region, it is clear that the full literal fulfilment of these verses has yet to take place. A complete fulfilment of these promises requires Philadelphia to be a type of a section of the universal Church that will exist at the time of the Rapture. This means the Philadelphia Church will continue until the Rapture, and since it is filled with true believers it will participate in the Rapture, and so be kept from the Hour (Time-Period) of the Tribulation. This means the letter to Philadelphia speaks of a certain kind of church that will spring up at some point of Church history and continue until the Rapture, for it is promised escape from the Tribulation by means of the Rapture. Even after the next kind of church arises (represented by Laodicia), it will not cease to exist but will continue until the Lord comes. Just as Thyatira and Sardis continue on until the End of the Age, even after other Church Eras have begun, so Philadelphia will continue even after its Era has passed. Thus each of these is typical of a certain part of the universal Church that continues to exist until the End of the Age.

  *7. The Church of LAODICEA: "To the angel (pastor) **of the Church of the Laodiceans write, 'These things says the Amen, the Faithful and True Witness, the Beginning of the Creation of God: "I know your works, that you are neither cold nor hot. I could wish you were cold or hot. So then, because you are lukewarm, and neither cold nor hot, I will vomit you out of My mouth. Because you say: 'I am rich, have become wealthy, and have need of nothing', and do not know that you are wretched, miserable, poor, blind, and naked, I counsel you to buy from Me gold refined in the fire, that you may be rich; and white garments, that you may be clothed, that the shame of your nakedness may not be revealed; and anoint your eyes with eye salve, that you may see. As many as I love, I rebuke and chasten. Therefore be zealous and repent. Behold, I stand at the door and knock. If anyone hears My voice and opens the door, I will come in to him and dine with him, and he with Me. To him who overcomes I will grant to sit with Me on My Throne, as I also overcame and sat down with My Father on His Throne. He who has an ear, let him hear what the Spirit says to the Churches"** (3:14-22)

  The Church at Laodicia represents the rise of **the apostate church** that came about through **liberal theology** (1890 onwards). Whereas the letter to Philadelphia is all positive, the letter to Laodicia is all negative. This leads some to criticise the overview of Church History based on the 7 Letters as being pessimistic, since it seems to predict that the Church Age will end in total failure. However this fails to take into account that once each kind of Church appears it continues to the End of the Age. So for example Philadelphia will continue to the end and be successful in gathering a final end-time harvest. So God will fulfil His purpose for the Church Age. So although this final Era of Laodicia is marked by the rise of a wholly unsaved apostate church, this is not the whole story, for the other kinds of churches will also continue to the end. Thus this overview of the Church Age is not pessimistic but realistic, describing both the bad along with the good, and indeed an

unprecedented rise of apostasy in the last days of the Church Age is confirmed by
1Timothy 4:1. The total contrast between the last two churches (one with a wholly
positive report of commendation, and the other with a wholly negative report of
condemnation) indicates that as the world heads towards the night of the
Tribulation, there will be an increasing polarisation between darkness and light in
the Church world, where one part of the church (Laodicia) becomes more and more
fully conformed to the moral and spiritual darkness of the world, whereas another
part (Philadelphia) becomes brighter and brighter. Thus the letter to Laodicia
predicts that near the end of the Church Age a major part of the Church will
become apostate, denying even the essentials of the faith. Although apostasy has
always been around, this final apostasy will happen in a unique way on a far greater
scale than has been seen before. This prophecy has indeed been fulfilled over the
last 120 years, confirming that we are now in the last period of Church history, and
so is another indication that we are near the end.

The Laodician apostasy (theological liberalism, which denies the very
fundamentals of the faith) has spread through both the Roman Catholic and
Protestant Churches, but its effect on the Protestant world is greater, for the Roman
Church (Thyatira) is more firmly locked into its official doctrine because of its
claims of infallibility. On top of this, its authoritative central control of doctrine
prevented liberalism from changing the official teaching of the church, even though
many parts of the church took on liberal theology. The Protestant Church (Sardis)
was more vulnerable to this apostasy taking over completely, which it did in many
denominations. The only protection for Sardis from apostasy was to stay true to its
founding principle - a strong commitment to God's Word literally understood, but
if that were to wane through the deadening growth of nominalism, then she would
be wide open to it. Therefore in church history Laodicia, like Philadelphia, should
be primarily seen as springing up from and coming out of Sardis. Christ saw Sardis
moving towards death ('about to die') and urged it to wake up and strengthen its
commitment to God's Word before it is too late (v2). Those who heeded this call
restored the truth of God's Word to the Church bringing renewal of life, and from
this came Philadelphia. But another part of Sardis ignored this call of the Spirit and

went in the opposite direction, totally rejecting the authority and truth of God's Word, as understood in its plain meaning, and as a result became a totally dead apostate church through liberal theology (represented by Laodicia).

The contrast between Philadelphia and Laodicia is seen by their attitude to the Name of Jesus. He commends the Philadelphians that they: **"have not denied My Name"** (v8). Thus they believe in His Deity and confess Jesus is Lord. In return Christ promises to declare and write His Name upon them (v12). But the liberal Laodicians deny His Name (His Deity and Lordship).

Thus there were 2 responses to the creeping deadness of Sardis, resulting in vibrant Philadelphia and apostate Laodicia. Between these were those who stayed in Sardis holding firm to the position of the Reformers, upholding the authority of Scripture in firm opposition to Thyatira and Laodicia, but resisting further recoveries of Biblical truth, especially the restoration of the supernatural gifts of the Spirit in the Pentecostal and Charismatic Movements, such as speaking in tongues, prophecy, healings and miracles). Instead they developed the doctrine of Cessationalism, which says that such things passed away after the apostles died.

'Laodicia' means **'people ruling'**. This is in contrast to God ruling in the Church, pointing to a rejection of the authority of God's Word, replacing it with man's opinions, reasoning and philosophy (humanism) - a perfect description of the belief of liberal theology. It is a church ruled entirely by men, for Christ is on the outside (v20) and the Holy Spirit is not present in His role as Guide, for the whole church is unsaved (v17,18). This is an accurate description of the section of the church that became dominated by liberal theology.

The roots of Protestant Liberalism were: (1) the rise of humanism through the 'Enlightenment' which elevated man's reason (rationalism) and individualism above any external authority, such as God and the Bible, (2) the rise of the anti-Biblical philosophy of Darwinian Evolution (1859) attacking the foundation of biblical truth in Genesis by presenting an alternative to Biblical Creation, and (3) Higher Criticism from German scholarship of the late 1800's which attacked the Divine origin, authority, inerrancy and veracity of the Bible.

Liberal Theology was inspired by these philosophies and essentially puts man at the centre rather than God, so that all religious knowledge finds its source within man. Human reason, experience and observation are all important. Human reason passes judgment on each belief. Man is free from all external authority (especially the Bible), and has the freedom to decide for himself what is right or wrong, according to his reason. So liberal theology rejects the Bible as the inerrant Word of God. Although it may say it has some spiritual value in communicating spiritual truths, it does not take it literally, and denies that God's interventions in history actually happened, especially the miracles, such as Creation (according to Genesis), the Virgin Birth and Resurrection of Christ, instead relegating them all to the status of myth - stories that teach spiritual truths. In fact it denies anything miraculous, even the power of prayer.

Most seriously, Liberal Theology denies the witness of the Bible concerning the Person and Work of Christ (the essentials of the Gospel). It rejects the Deity of Christ, seeing Him as just a holy man, denying the fact that He is the unique God-man (John 1:1,14), and so it preaches another Christ. Thus it denies the NAME of Christ, that is His DIVINE NATURE. This rejection of the true Person of Christ is why He is standing on the outside of the Church, seeking to gain entrance (v20). This is why He introduces Himself to them as: **"the Amen, the Faithful and True Witness, the Beginning** (Source) **of the Creation of God"** (v14, from 1:4,6,7). His witness to Himself in the Bible is faithful and true - He is the Creator God, fully God as well as being fully man. Moreover it denies the redemptive substitutionary DEATH of Christ for our sins, purchasing our salvation. Instead they say it was merely a martyr's death giving us an example of love and sacrifice. This is part of a rejection of the Biblical world-view of man's special creation, and fall into sin, so that he is under the Judgment of God (heading for Hell), and so needs the Salvation which God has provided through the Person and Work of Jesus Christ (thus man is spiritually poor and in desperate need of salvation as Jesus points out in v17).

Liberal Theology no concept of sin cutting man off from God or of man's accountability to God or judgment by God. It denies sin, judgment, hell and salvation. The only evils to be overcome are the social evils in this world such as poverty, for man is fundamentally good (no original sin). The world-view of liberal theology is humanistic and evolutionary, whereby through reason man is growing more enlightened in his religious and moral understandings, as he throws off the dogmas of the past. Thus Biblical faith with its emphasis on Divine revelation, authority and accountability is seen as a negative thing hindering man's progress in discovering his own potential and goodness. Even the existence of an objective transcendent God is thrown into doubt, with the focus moving to discovering the divine immanent within oneself. Therefore it also rejects absolute morality as defined by the nature of God, seeing the basis for morality as coming from man and what he feels and reasons to be right. Thus in practice, it conforms to the secular humanism of the world, and so possesses no spiritual life, only human pride.

Liberal Theology swept through most of the Protestant denominations and increasingly took over their top positions, especially the seminaries and training institutions for the ministers (stars), producing ministers who preached liberal theology in their pulpits, so that the churches became liberal, filling them with spiritual death. Thus a large part of the church world became apostate through liberal theology. The leaven grew quickly through the denominations through the seminaries. Many denominations were taken over by liberal theology, and some split as the believers departed from the liberal denomination to start a new denomination or network more true to the Biblical faith, or to form independent churches. Other denominations became divided between the liberals and evangelicals, which is also unsatisfactory as such a church is compromised (salt that has lost its savour), as it cannot speak with one voice concerning the essential spiritual and moral issues. Its mixed message has no power to influence the world, which is unimpressed, for the world is in this church, for in practice liberal theology conforms to the current worldly secular viewpoint, rather than the Divine viewpoint. Because it does not want to have open division with half the church in opposition to its message, it has no power speak against the declining moral standards in the world. Even worse, the liberal pressures mean the church offers little resistance to the inverted morality of the world, but rather tends to embrace it. Liberal theology also led to the Ecumenical movement and World Council of

Churches created to unify all churches on the basis of liberal principles. This theology also says that all religions are to be respected as equally valid expressions of man's spiritual quest to find God ('all roads lead to God'), and so this led to the interfaith movement, and the persecution of Bible-believers for being intolerant in claiming Jesus to be the only Way of Salvation (John 14:6, Acts 4:12).

Apostate churches are spiritually dead and so this led to the growth of cults and New Age (Eastern) religions, that offer to meet people's spiritual needs which these churches were not meeting. The rejection of Biblical authority and objective faith in a transcendent God, in favour of man's autonomy and subjective experience of the 'divine light' within man, opened the door for many to leave the Church and follow New Age spirituality. The response of others to the unclear, uncertain message of a church, that had rejected the absolutes of the Bible, is to turn to cults or other religions (like Islam), who offer authoritative clear-cut answers and certainty, in contrast to the feeble wishy-washiness of liberal theology.

Apostasy is the departure from the truth that one professed to have. This does mean that apostates necessarily once possessed the truth, simply that by being a member of a church an apostate minister professes to believe the doctrines of the church as stated in the creeds and statements of faith, but actually he denies the truths. Instead of doing the honourable thing and leave that church, he uses the respect given to his position to promote his apostasy. Such widespread apostasy has become a major characteristic of most Protestant denominational churches over the last century. It should be apparent that this end-time apostasy of liberal theology is far worse than anything that has happened previously in Church history.

This apostasy fits the Biblical descriptions of apostasy in the Church, which is predicted to come to its fullness in the last days. 1Timothy 4:1 speaks of a special last days apostasy are says it is demonic in origin: **"Now the Spirit expressly says that in latter times some will depart from the faith, giving heed to deceiving spirits and doctrines of demons."** 2Timothy 3:1-4 describes the breakdown of morality in society in the last days, then v5 describes apostasy in the religious world of the apostate church and cults: **"having a form of godliness but denying** its power. And from such people turn away!" They may use Christian language, be dressed in clerical robes and have religious titles but they deny the power of godliness - the Lord Jesus Christ, the Holy Spirit and the authority of the God's Word. This is a clear command to leave any church led by such a person.

2Peter 2:1-22 describes apostate ministers in great detail. He shows no tolerance towards them but castigates them. He first addresses their teachings: **"there will be false teachers among you, who will secretly bring in destructive heresies, even denying the Lord who bought them, and bring on themselves swift destruction"** (v1). Their teachings are described as destructive denials - denials that lead to eternal damnation: **"even denying the Lord who bought them."** This declares the Deity of Christ, and the first mark of an apostate is the denial of His Deity. The 2nd mark is the denial of His substitutionary death. Thus at the core of their apostate teaching is the denial of the Person ('Lord') and work ('who bought them') of Christ. Other passages give more detail about their denial of the central truths of the faith. They deny the Trinity (1John 2:22-23), the incarnation and virgin birth of Christ (1John 4:2-3, 2 John 7), and His 2nd Coming (2Peter 3:3-4). Behind these denials is the denial of the inspiration of the Scriptures. This denial of the authority of God and the Bible over human will, thinking and desire leads to immorality (in fact a major motivation of apostates in throwing off Biblical authority is to gain the freedom to sin). Thus the teachers are immoral and endorse and so encourage immorality: **"While they promise them liberty, they themselves are slaves of corruption; for by whom a person is overcome, by him also he is brought into bondage"** (2Peter 2:19, see Jude 18-19). They are also marked by mockery (Jude 17-18, 2Peter 3:3-4), mocking the fundamentals of the faith, from an attitude of pride and superiority. They also cause divisions (Jude 19), as when they deny and mock the essentials some agree with them and others do not, resulting in a split because the truths they deny are too fundamental to ignore. Throughout this Laodician Era there's been split after split caused by the entrance of liberal theology, dividing churches and denominations.

Jesus' description in v15-18 of the Laodician church perfectly describes the modern humanistic church of liberal theology. He has no good thing to say about them because it is an entirely unsaved church. Therefore it is heading for certain rejection and judgment: **"I know your works, that you are neither cold nor hot. I could wish you were cold or hot. So then, because you are lukewarm, and neither cold nor hot, I will vomit you out of My mouth"** (v15-16). In v17 He describes their unsaved nature, but in v15-16 He describes their works, that is their outward profession and actions. 'You' is in the singular, speaking of the Church. He characterises it as lukewarm, rather like the local water. Laodicea had an aqueduct that carried water from hot mineral springs 5 miles south, which became tepid by the time it descended to Laodicia, making it hard to drink. This was in contrast to the hot springs at nearby Hierapolis and the pure cold water of Colossae, both of which were preferable. This is a perfect description of an apostate church. 'Hot' describes a church full of truly saved believers. 'Cold' describes a group of unbelievers who do not claim to be believers. 'Lukewarm' describes a church full of people who call themselves Christians, but are unsaved. They are not cold for they profess a form of Christianity, but neither are they hot, for they are not true believers. Like the water at Laodicia this Church was once hot, but has now descended (fallen) into a lukewarm condition. This is what happened to churches and denominations as they came under liberal theology. He warns that this apostate church full of unsaved people is under His judgment being ready to reject them completely, spewing them out of His mouth as being unacceptable to Him (v16).

v17 confirms their unsaved nature: **"Because you say: 'I am rich, have become wealthy, and have need of nothing', and do not know that you are wretched, miserable, poor, blind, and naked..."** In the pride and self-sufficiency of their humanism they are completely unaware that they are spiritually destitute and desperately in need of salvation. They see man as the centre and answer to all things, but don't see their sinfulness before God. In the natural, Laodicia was rich and self-sufficient, a place of finance and banking. In 60 AD it was hit by a major earthquake, but refused help from the Roman Empire, and rebuilt the city itself. Their natural self-sufficiency was a picture of their spiritual self-sufficiency and overconfidence (trusting in themselves), imagining themselves spiritually wealthy, but they were totally bankrupt. They were also proud of their local clothing for the cloth trade of Laodicea was known for its special black wool. Man tries to cover his sinfulness (nakedness) with his works so as to appear respectable, but they are as filthy rags, black in nature. God sees right through them to the sinful heart, so they are naked in His sight. Even worse, they are blind to their true condition and so don't realise their need for salvation, for before you can receive salvation you must know you are sinner who can't save yourself. The fact they have an outward form of Christianity blinds them to the fact they don't have Christ, their lukewarmness blinds them to the fact they are not hot, for it is easier for a cold person to realise they need heat, which is one reason why He said it would be better for them to be cold than lukewarm, the other is that lukewarm churches present a dead compromised Christianity to the world, misrepresenting the nature of Christ.

Because they are unsaved, He extends an evangelistic appeal to them. Having convicted them of their sinful state, their desperate need of salvation, and their destiny of inevitable judgment ('wretched, miserable, poor, blind, and naked'), He urges them to come to Himself for salvation: **"I counsel you to buy from ME gold refined in the fire, that you may be rich; and white garments, that you may be clothed, that the shame of your nakedness may not be revealed; and anoint your eyes with eye salve, that you may see"** (v18). He offers them true eternal riches (purified gold, the perfect nature of Christ within, His imparted righteousness, and white garments (His imputed righteousness) to replace their garments of black wool, so that they might be able to stand before God clothed in His righteousness, and the eye salve of the Spirit, who will open their eyes and reveal the things of God to them, leading them into all truth. They also prided themselves in the area of physical sight for they had a medical school, with a famous eye-specialist, and a special eye-lotion came from their area. Likewise, they were proud of their spiritual insight (advanced understanding), but without Christ they were deceived and blind (in the dark), and they needed to come to Him and receive His Spirit in order to truly see.

"As many as I love, I rebuke and chasten. Therefore be zealous and repent" (v19). Jesus was strong with them in order to burst their bubble of self-righteousness, because He loved them, for while they are trusting in themselves they could not trust in Christ alone and be saved. In His love He confronts them and brings them under conviction of sin so they might repent and be saved. He reminds them of the urgency of their situation ('be zealous') and calls them to repent of trusting in themselves. Then in v20 He gives one of the greatest salvation verses of the Bible calling them to receive Him by faith (as in John 1:12): **"Behold, I stand at the door** (of your heart) **and knock. If anyone hears My voice** (through the Gospel) **and opens the door, I will come in to him and dine with him, and he with Me** (eternal covenant fellowship)" (v20). He speaks this to the Church as a whole and to each individual in it ('if anyone'), for as they are all unsaved, He stands on the outside of the Church and of each person, until they hear His voice, believe and open the door of their heart and invite Him in as their Lord and Saviour. Some have denied that this is a salvation verse since Jesus spoke it to a Church, but they miss the plain fact that the people He is addressing are unsaved, having only an outward form of Christianity.

His promise to those who respond to Christ's invitation to repent and believe and receive Him, and so overcome the spirit of worldly pride is: **"To him who overcomes I will grant to sit with Me on My Throne** (the Throne of David on earth), **as I also overcame and sat down with My Father on His Throne** (in heaven)" (v21). They will rule on earth as kings with Christ in His everlasting Kingdom, starting with His Millennial reign. But for those who do not respond awaits only rejection and judgment, for He will spew them out of His mouth. The fact that they call themselves Christians and were part of His visible Church on earth will not save them. He will reject and disown them and cast them out of His Presence forever. Moreover He will do the same thing to the apostate Laodician Church after the Rapture. At this point the institutional Church on earth will be totally unsaved, made up of those remaining from Thyatira, Sardis and Laodicia, and these will unite to form a false church (the Harlot, Mystery Babylon, a counterfeit Bride of Christ - see Revelation 17). Jesus will spew this church out of His mouth, giving it over to certain judgment. She will sits on the beast in a position of great power and influence for the first half of the Tribulation, and will persecute the true saints, but at Mid-Tribulation God puts it in the heart of the beast to destroy her. Even today we see the beginnings of spiritual forces at work to unite Christendom into a one-world apostate Church.

*Appendix 3: Dispensational Theology verses Covenant Theology

As far as Eschatology is concerned there are 2 main systems of Theology: (1) Covenant and (2) Dispensational Theology, into which mould the scriptures are made to fit, so they can be understood together as a unity. These 2 systems take you to 2 very different eschatological destinations, as they are based on different foundational assumptions. Therefore it is important to understand them and their differences. This book develops a Dispensational Theology, because it is the result of the fundamental assumption that the discovery of the truth comes from interpreting the prophetic scriptures literally. Covenant Theology may take some prophecies literally, but will spiritualise others when necessary, in order to make them fit into its theological system. Whereas Covenant Theology is a system of covenants that is imposed upon Scripture, whereas Dispensationalism is built inductively from the covenants revealed within Scripture.

Covenant Theology

The unconditional Biblical Covenants (Abrahamic, Davidic, Land, New) give us the foundation for understanding God's prophetic Program. However Covenant Theology is not based on these Covenants, neither is it named after them. The covenants of Covenant Theology are 3 theological covenants, postulated by theologians, into which straightjackets the whole of Scripture is squeezed. They are known as the covenants of works, redemption and grace (some combine the last 2 covenants into one covenant).

In Covenant Theology all Scripture is interpreted on the basis of these covenants. This system was formulated in Europe in the 16th and 17th centuries. It teaches that before the Fall God made a **Covenant of Works** with Adam, promising eternal life for obedience and death for disobedience. Adam was put on temporary probation to see what he would do, and he failed, so came under death, and as he was the head of the human race, spiritual and physical death came upon all mankind also. After Adam's sin, God graciously established **the Covenant of Grace** with mankind, through which men could receive salvation from this problem of sin and death, through Jesus Christ. It is the gracious agreement between the offended God and the offending, but elect, sinner, in which God promises salvation through faith in Christ, and the sinner accepts this by faith, promising a life of faith and obedience. In this system each Biblical Covenant and Dispensation is just another stage of the progressive manifestation of this same Covenant of Grace throughout history. Thus this Covenant of Grace becomes the unifying principle of all Scripture. Those who by faith become a part of this covenant form the people of God. Thus from this perspective, there is and always has been one and only one people of God, the Church, the true Israel. This gives the basis for the unscriptural blurring of the distinction between Israel and the Church, and the adoption of replacement theology. The **Covenant of Grace** is based on **the Covenant of Redemption**, made in eternity past between the Father and the Son. The Son agreed to die on the Cross to provide Salvation, and the Father agreed the Son would be the Redeemer and Head of the Church. Thus in this system the whole purpose of God is the salvation of the elect.

There are a number of problems with Covenant Theology in the way that it affects and controls ones interpretation of Bible Prophecy.

*1. Covenant Theology sees all Scripture, whether history or prophecy through the lens of the Covenant of Grace. This controls and directs their interpretation of Scripture, and when necessary it's used to trump the principle of literal interpretation. Thus it frequently spiritualises scriptures to make them fit within the system of Covenant Theology, even when their plain sense makes perfect sense. To make the Biblical Covenants (made to Abraham and Israel) conform to the system, it is necessary to depart from the literal sense when interpreting them. Thus promises to Israel are interpreted as promises to the New Testament Church. It allows no place for the fulfilment of God's covenant promises to national Israel, so either cancels them on the basis of Israel's sin, or transfers them to the Church, as well as spiritualising their content. This is an abuse of Scripture, which denies God's veracity and faithfulness. These are everlasting, unconditional covenants made by God under oath and He is obligated to fulfil them to the same people with whom He originally made the Covenant. We have no right to tamper with the promises of these covenants by spiritualising them. This approach is inconsistent because Covenant Theologians will generally take

Scripture literally, but when facing many prophetic scriptures they use a different method of interpretation. This need for this dual-hermeneutic reveals the weakness and inadequacy of their system in summarising the whole of Scripture.

*2. In attempting to impose a unity on Scripture it does not do justice to the distinctions found in Scripture. While observing the abiding similarities in God's dealings and relationship with man it ignores and fails to account for the emphatic differences. Thus whatever the merits of these 3 covenants as theological ideas, the basic error is in trying to reduce all Scripture to make it fit within this unifying framework. The result is a massive oversimplification, based on this unfounded reductionist assumption. This causes confusion - the mixing together of 2 things that should be kept distinct. For example, in the name of this artificial imposed unity, it fails to see any significant difference between Israel and the Church, between the Abrahamic and Old (Mosaic) Covenants, and between the Old and New Covenants. Such major distinctions must be accounted for, for if a system denies fundamental differences it must lead to invalid interpretations, for any attempt to harmonise 2 different things, by emphasising similarities and playing down any differences, will require much spiritualising (torturing) of scriptures to make them agree, resulting in one's prophetic scheme leading you into error.

The Biblical Covenants are manifestly not simply progressive manifestations of the Covenant of Grace, for they contain much material that does not pertain to personal salvation. Thus any attempt to squeeze them into this mould is bound to fail. Moreover Galatians 3:15 says that once a covenant is ratified no one can add conditions to it. But this condition is violated by Covenant Theology when it says the Mosaic Covenant was a newer phase of the Covenant of Grace, which had been previously established, yet it instituted many conditions that had not been introduced before. Also it has to claim that the Covenant of Grace in the New Testament (the New Covenant) is essentially the same as the Covenant of Grace in the Old Testament (the Old Covenant). For them 'New' cannot denote an essential contrast between these 2 Covenants, which flies in the face of what the New Testament itself has to say, especially in Galatians. The attempt to unify these 2 very different Covenants inevitably results in much wrong interpretation. Thus the Biblical Covenants simply do not fit into the mould of the Covenant of Grace and it is wrong to try and force them to fit. Instead we should allow them to speak for themselves concerning the things yet to come, and accept what they tell us. This is the approach of Dispensational Theology.

*3. Another problem with Covenant Theology is that its goal and purpose of history is too narrow. Although it is right to stress the importance of the grace of God in our Salvation and the centrality of Christ, it has gone too far in saying that the salvation of the elect is the only and all-inclusive purpose of history. By limiting the scope of history to this one program and one people of God, the result is the neglect of other areas of revelation, and unwarranted conclusions such as saying that Israel has no future as a nation. God has various distinct purposes and programs operating through history, for the Church, Israel and the Gentiles, the saved and unsaved, as well as the holy and fallen angels, and the physical universe. There is the Kingdom Program as well as the Salvation Program. These cannot all be reduced to the Covenant of Grace, and they must all be contributing something to an ultimate Purpose of God, which is greater than any of them.

This ultimate Purpose of God must be large enough to incorporate all of these programs, peoples and purposes, not just one of them. **This ultimate Purpose can be no other than the Glory of God – which is the unifying principle of Dispensational Theology.** Thus by reducing the purpose of history to the salvation of the elect, Covenant Theology oversimplifies things and so fails to discern between the different purposes, peoples and programs of God in history (especially in connection with Israel, Gentiles and the Church), all of which contribute to the ultimate Purpose of God's Glory, which will be fully and finally manifested in the Eternal State, when all these things will be brought together to perfection in unity (reconciled) in Christ under God's Kingdom.

Dispensational Theology

Dispensational Theology, on the other hand, builds its view of history and prophecy from an inductive study of the Scriptures, based on a consistently literal interpretation. Dispensation, from the Greek word 'oikonomia' means 'stewardship' or 'administration', the management of a household, where the one in authority delegates duties to those under him. A steward is told what to do and is held accountable for what he does, with reward for faithfulness or judgment otherwise. The administration and stewardship may be changed at the discretion of the Lord of the house, and this will especially happen in the case of a major failure. The roles of different stewards may be changed when the administration changes. The word is used in this way in Luke 16:1-4, 1Corinthians 9:17, Ephesians 1:10,3:2,9, Colossians 1:25, 1Timothy 1:4). In theology, a Dispensation is a distinguishable administration of God over the household of mankind, which forms part of the outworking of God's total purpose in history. So although each Dispensation is associated with a certain period of time, it technically refers to the Government of God operative at that time. Dispensationalism observes that the successive Divine Interventions in history, when He makes Covenants with man, necessarily create new and distinguishably different Administrations (Dispensations) of God. In this way, He brings in a new Age of history with new conditions (although many things stay unchanged). Thus He is Lord of the Ages, and God's progressive revelation throughout history can be understood as a succession of Dispensations.

Moreover, as well as recognising the different Administrations of God, Dispensationalism also recognises that the Lord may have different roles and purposes for different peoples in His household. Thus it does not try to blur the scriptural distinctions between Israel and the Church. Unlike Covenant Theology, which is guided by a system and assumption imposed on Scripture, Dispensationalism is guided by Scripture itself in its understanding of both Dispensations and Peoples. Thus it springs from an inductive study of Scripture literally understood. Paul uses the word 'oikonomia' in its theological sense in Ephesians 1:10, 3:9). He distinguishes the present 'Mystery' Dispensation of the Church Age from the previous one that was governed by the Law of Moses, and from the future Divine Dispensations - the Age to come (the Millennium, Hebrews 6:5) and the Dispensation of the Fullness of Time (the Eternal State).

The Dispensations are not different ways of Salvation, but different ways God administers His rule in the world. Each has unique features that mark it out. These new responsibilities and blessings are given by revelation of God. In a new dispensation many things stay the same (continuity), although there are also changes (discontinuity). A study of the relevant Covenants reveals clearly what stays the same and what changes. The Mosaic Covenant resulted in much discontinuity both at its start at Sinai and at its end at the Cross, as it was a temporal Covenant. Other Covenants (Noah, Abrahamic, New) remain in force throughout all time once they have been introduced. The Adamic Covenant (Genesis 3:14-19) will remain in force until the start of the Millennium, when the 2nd Adam takes dominion over the earth, and fulfils God's Kingdom Purpose revealed in the original Edenic Covenant (Genesis 1:26-28).

The 3 essential characteristics of Dispensational Theology are: (1) a consistent literal hermeneutic, (2) a clear distinction between Israel and the Church, as 2 distinct elect peoples of God, so that God has distinct programs for them both (the Church has not replaced Israel nor taken over her place in the covenants), and (3) the Glory of God is God's ultimate Purpose for history.

Prophetically it follows from these facts that since there are many covenant promises to Israel that God has not yet literally fulfilled, national Israel has an important future in God's Plan, putting her at the heart of the prophetic scenario, and the fulfilment of these promises against all odds will be to God's Glory, whereby He'll show Himself to be the God of Abraham, Isaac and Jacob (Israel). Indeed it will be essential to His Glory. Thus Israel's miraculous Rebirth and continuing survival is a vindication of Dispensational Theology, for many in Covenant Theology equate Israel and the Church, and so dismiss the Rebirth of Israel as an accident of history, despite the fact it this a literal fulfilment of prophecy and that Covenant Theologians have a strong doctrine of God's Sovereignty. To square the circle, they have to spiritualise prophecies to Israel and transfer them to the Church.

The New Testament never equates the Church with Israel nor suggests that the Church is fulfilling the promises originally given to Israel: (1) The Church began at Pentecost 1500 years after the birth of national Israel (Matthew 16:18). (2) The Church was a Mystery hidden in God, which means it was not even revealed in the Old Testament. It was new and in many ways dissimilar to national Israel, especially in the unity and equality of Jews and Gentiles in the Body of Christ. (3) The New Testament distinguishes Israel, Gentiles, and the Church or 'One New Man' (1Corinthians 10:32, Ephesians 2:11-16, Romans 11). Also in Acts, Israel and the Church are consistently distinguished. (4) The terms Israel and the Church are not used interchangeably in Scripture, which would be the case if they were the same. The name 'Israel' is always used either for the entire nation of Israel, or for the believing remnant of Israel, but never for the Church. It is never called 'Israel', 'spiritual Israel' or the 'new Israel.'

Believing Gentiles are called 'the seed of Abraham' through being in Christ, the Seed of Abraham, and so inherit the blessing of Abraham (Galatians 3:14,16,29), in fulfilment of God's promise that all the nations would be blessed through Abraham and His Seed (Genesis 12:3, 22:18). However, this Gentile inclusion into the blessing of the Covenant through our union with Christ, in no way does away with Israel's historic identity or nullifies the covenant promises to Israel or remove her right-standing in the unconditional covenants God made with her. The Bible uses the term 'the seed of Abraham' in a number of ways. First, it literally denotes all physical descendants of Abraham, but the Bible emphasises the sons (inheritors) of his covenant, which is limited to the physical line through Isaac and Jacob. On the same basis the term is sometimes limited to the believing remnant of Israel, since the blessing (salvation) is received by faith (Romans 9:6-8). Now Christ is the unique Seed of Abraham who inherits all the promises, and when Gentiles believe in Him they are put 'in Christ' and so become the spiritual seed of Abraham, and so inherit all the blessings of salvation. However, the spiritual seed of Abraham is never called 'Israel', and it is never said to fulfil the covenant-promises given to national Israel (the physical seed of Abraham).

*Appendix 4: The meaning of 'Apostasia' in 2Thessalonians 2

One of the key Rapture passages is 2Thessalonians 2, whose correct interpretation depends on the correct identification of the meaning of *apostasia* in v3: **"Let no one deceive you by any means; for that Day** (the Day of the Lord) **will not come unless THE APOSTASIA comes first, and the man of sin is revealed."** It is often translated FALLING AWAY based on the view that it refers to a religious defection (apostasy) or falling away (departure) from the faith in the last days (c.f. 1Timothy 4:1), after which the antichrist is revealed. This view became dominant through the 1611 King James Version. One problem with this view is that Paul is using *'the apostasia'* as a well-defined sign of a specific event that must happen before the Day of the Lord, as confirmed by the use of the definite article, yet apostasy has always taken place throughout the Age, and Paul does not seem to give any further guidance as to what is special about this unique 'falling away.' Neither are we told elsewhere in the New Testament of a unique end-time event in the form of a special defection from the faith. Some appeal to 1Timothy 4:1ff, but this does not describe a unique event but a growing trend that was already present. Also 2Timothy 3:1ff does not describe an apostasy from the faith, but the increasing lawlessness of evil men in the latter days (see v13). Also 1 and 2 Timothy were written many years after 2 Thessalonians. Therefore there are a number of guesses as to what it is, varying between apostasy in the world, the Church or Israel. Some would prefer to translate it as the Revolt or Rebellion denoting a more forceful rejection of God. Either way it is an unsatisfactory situation as it means that God has provided a Sign, but in such a way that we have no way of knowing for sure what it is, and so can't recognise it when it happens!

Unfortunately the common translation of Apostasia as 'the falling away' or 'the apostasy' feeds in an interpretation that closes the mind to other possibilities. It would be better to translate it as 'the Departure' as the older translations did, as this is the basic meaning of the word. Since Paul did not specify what kind of departure he was talking about (as he did in 1Timothy 4:1 when he said many will **"depart from the faith"**), it would be better to follow suit and leave the possibilities open for now. Translating it as 'the Departure' allows for the meaning of 'Departure from the faith', but it also allows for other possibilities.

For the first 15 centuries translations consistently rendered *apostasia* as 'departure' leaving it open as to what kind of departure was meant (whether a departure from the faith or a spatial departure). The 4th century Latin translation by Jerome (the Vulgate) reflects this standard understanding by using the Latin word *discessio* meaning 'departure.' Thus the earliest English versions used the neutral term 'departure', namely the Wycliffe Bible (1384), Tyndale Bible (1526), Coverdale Bible (1535), Cranmer Bible (1539), Breeches Bible (1576), Beza Bible (1583) and Geneva Bible (1608). Later Beza, a member of the Geneva Bible Translation Committee and disciple of Calvin, was the first to break this trend by transliterating the Greek term *apostasia* which pointed to a religious defection or falling away (apostasy). The fact that *apostasia* is similar to our word 'apostasy' (defection from the truth) is beside the point as we don't interpret Scripture on the basis of a transliterated word to which a certain meaning has been given, but on the basis of what the Greek word meant to the first century reader. Perhaps Beza thought it would help his cause in the theological battle with Romanism, by relating it to the popish apostasy, who he believed was the man of sin. Soon after the King James Version (1611) continued in this direction by translating it 'falling away', and in so doing inserted their interpretation of it rather than giving the basic translation. Since then translations have generally followed the practice of the KJV in not using 'departure', but instead 'rebellion', 'falling away', 'rejection of God', 'great revolt' or 'apostasy.' Had they simply translated the word instead of interpreting it, they would have better rendered it by the word 'departure.'

If we allow that 'apostasia' essentially means 'departure', an alternative view presents itself, which solves all the problems of this passage, and for which I argue in this book, that *the apostasia* in v3 refers to **the Rapture, the Departure of the Church from the earth,** before the Day of the Lord (Tribulation) begins with the revelation of the man of sin. If this is true then this passage clearly teaches the Pre-Tribulation Rapture, and so it is understandable why many would resist this interpretation. However, sadly, even among Pre-Tribulationists this is a minority view. This is unfortunate for, as I will endeavour to show, the case for identifying *the apostasia* as the Rapture is stronger than is generally realised. The most well known proponents for this view are E.Schuyler English, Kenneth Wuest, Thomas Ice and Wayne House. Those who have argued against it include Robert Gundry, Paul Feinberg and William Combs. In this chapter, I summarise the evidence in these previous works, and point to a piece of evidence that has not been mentioned yet in the debate, and introduce a new line of argument, which tips things firmly in favour of the *apostasia* in 2Thessalonians being the Rapture.

Word meanings

First we need to determine the semantic range of possible meanings for this word to see if 'apostasia' can mean a physical, spatial departure as well as a spiritual departure. In so doing, we will point to vital evidence that has been over-looked in previous discussions. Then we will apply the law of context to determine the specific meaning of *apostasia* in this passage. If the noun *apostasía* can refer to a physical departure, then the context of 2Thessalonians 2 strongly points to Paul using this word to describe the Rapture. To decide if a physical departure is a possibility it is necessary to study the possible range of meanings of the word *apostasia*, gathering evidence from its etymology (roots), history and usage.

*The associated (root) verbal form from which the noun *apostasia* is derived is *aphistamai* (the present middle of *aphistemi*). The simple verb *histemi* means "to stand," the prefix *apo* means "off, away from," and the compound verb, "to stand off from" denoting a departing to a distance, a separating apart. The word does not mean "to fall" (as in 'falling away') which would be the word *pipto*. Thayer defines it as: *"to make stand off, cause to withdraw, to stand off, stand aloof, to desert, to withdraw from one"; in contexts where a defection from the faith is in view, it means "to fall away, become faithless."* The verb *aphistemi* is clearly used of physical departure in both Testaments. In the Septuagint (LXX) it is used in Genesis 12:8 of Abram's departure from Shechem toward the hills east of Bethel, of David's departure from Saul (1Samuel 18:13), and the physical separation of the wicked from God's presence (Psalm 6:8). The use of the verbal form in the LXX is primarily used for a spatial departure. In the New Testament there are clear examples of the use of the verb to express physical departure or separation. Luke 2:37 says Anna never left the temple, and in Acts 19:9 Paul taught

in the synagogue in Ephesus for 3 months before departing when they rejected him. In this case, as in many others the physical departure has a spiritual basis, so the word may carry both aspects (that is, we should beware of overdoing the Greek thinking that separates the physical and spiritual as either/or, when often both may be involved). The KJV translates it 'to depart' (Luke 2:37; 4:13; 13:27; Acts 12:10; 15:38; 19:9; 22:29; 2Cor 12:8; 1Tim 4:1; 2Tim 2:19; Heb 3:12), 'withdraw' (1Tim 6:5), 'fall away' (Luke 8:13), 'drew away' (Acts 5:37) and 'refrain' (Acts 5:38). So it is used 15 times in the New Testament, of which only 3 have anything to do with a spiritual departure from the faith (Luke 8:13, 1Tim 4:1, Heb 3:12). So the predominant translation of the verbal form is 'to depart', and when it is translated differently, the context adds the idea of 'falling away' to the verb, which action is still a departure. In most cases, a physical departure is primarily in view. So the verb often means to physically depart in both the Greek Old and New Testaments, and this departing may be good or bad from the perspective of the writer. So we would expect this basic meaning of the verb to carry over to the associated noun.

The standard response to this evidence is that it does not necessarily follow that the related noun form (cognate) should carry the meaning of the verb (that is, the idea of spatial separation), although both counterexamples that Feinberg produces fail upon closer inspection ('ana' also means 'again', and 'eperotema' does actually mean 'request' and is best translated as such in 1Peter 3:21). A 3rd example used is another cognate noun from this verb meaning 'divorce', which they say is a 'relational separation.' But does not divorce also include the idea of physical separation? To 'send her away' is as much a physical as relational act. In reality, in many 'departures' both spiritual and physical elements are present together. So it won't do to just plead the 'root fallacy' and use it to dismiss all evidence of this nature. It may not be conclusive in itself, but it is certainly good evidence in favour of this position, which should be taken into account even if cognates do not provide absolute proof. If the verb form primarily means spatial separation then that at least creates a presumption that the noun includes that idea within its range of meanings, even if it is not a winning argument in itself. So the verb is a valid help in helping to establish the meaning of derivative nouns.

From this verb are derived 4 nouns. Compared to the large number of uses of the verb in the literature, there are relatively few uses of the 4 related nouns: (1) *Apostasion* (masc) is found with a fixed meaning in both Testaments, related to the breaking of the marriage covenant (Mal 2:14), and means 'a certificate of divorce' (Deut 24:1,3; Isaiah 50:1; Jer 3:8; Matt 5:31; 19:7, Mark 10:4), which results in physical separation. (2) *apostates* - a rebel or deserter, someone who separates himself physically from a group he was in due to differences of belief, (3) the other cognate *apostasia* (fem) is the word we are studying. So far we have seen that the primary use of the verbal form (root) is to describe a physical departure in a general sense, and is by no means limited to a specialised meaning of rebelling against God or forsaking the faith. Therefore we would expect this to transfer to the related noun, at least as a possible meaning. Since a noun takes its meaning from the verb, the noun is likely to have a similar semantic range as their cognate verbs. In most cases the meaning of the underlying verb carries over to its derivative noun. Generally nouns and verbs stay within the same field of usage, so nouns participate in the meaning of their root verb (this is true as a rule, even if there are exceptions). So the Complete Biblical Library says: "its (*aphistemi's*) meanings of 'go away' and 'depart' can also be applied to *apostasia* to give a secondary meaning of removal or departure." (4) *apostasis* is an earlier form of *apostasia* that was used in classical times, and it includes 'physical departure' among its meanings, which implies *apostasia* can probably have this meaning also, based on its origins.

Obviously we must also study a noun's own usage to fully establish its meaning. We will see that this actually supports the evidence from the verb, for although the majority of the uses of the noun *apostasia* in the literature emphasise the spiritual aspect, it did sometimes carry the idea of spatial departure, and this is true for the classical, koine and patristic eras. Considering the mere handful of uses of *apostasia* we have in the literature, it's significant that we can still find evidence of its spatial use in each era, establishing the fact that although it is a secondary meaning, it is within the semantic range of the word, and therefore if it is the meaning that makes best sense from the context, it is the correct meaning.

So now we go on to the usage of the noun *apostasía* in each of the 3 eras.

*For the Classical Period, the LSJ (Liddell-Scott-Jones Lexicon), the primary Greek-English Classical Lexicon, says *apostasia* is a late form for *apostasis* and gives the following meanings for *apostasia/apostasis*: 1. defection, revolt, esp. in a religious sense, rebellion against God, apostasy, **2. departure, disappearance**, 3. distinguishing, **4. distance.** Thus it gives spatial departure and distance (separation) as secondary meanings, indicating that the meaning of 'spatial departure' can be found in classical Greek. Although *apostasia* as such does not occur in the classical period, it is a later construction of *apostasis* (and so is essentially the same word), which was used of spatial departure in classical Greek.

*The evidence used from the Koine period (from Alexander the Great through New Testament times) is used by opponents of the *apostasia* Rapture, as the proof positive for their view, claiming that in the koine period no example of spatial departure or separation is to be found. However, this is incorrect, as is the assertion that *apostasia* first occurs in Greek literature outside the Bible in the 1st century BC. At this point I need to point out a piece of evidence, which seems to have been overlooked in this debate, which I believe changes the whole balance of the argument (I thank Andrew Chapman for bringing this to my attention). In 'The Sand Reckoner' by Archimedes (287-212 BC) he clearly uses *apostasia* in a spatial sense, of physical distance or separation. This text reads: **"the circle in which the earth is supposed to revolve has the same ratio to the distance (*apostasian*) of the fixed stars as the centre of a sphere to its surface."** This has special importance as it is the very first use of the word *apostasia* in our possession, and it proves that the idea of physical separation was within the possible range of meanings of the word in the koine period (this is related to the idea of physical departure, which causes a separation). This first use of *apostasia* suggests that the basic physical sense was originally its primary meaning (like the verb), even if it later became a secondary use of the word. Thus its original simple meaning (like its root verb) is physical departure or separation, even if later it was often used to describe a religious separation, defection or rebellion.

apostasia is found 5 times in the LXX (the Greek Old Testament, 3rd/2nd century BC): Joshua 22:22 (rebellion); 2Chron 28:19, 29:19; 33:19 (unfaithfulness); Jer 2:19 (wickedness); 1Maccabees 2:15. It also occurs 7 times in Aquila (Deut 15:9; Judges 19:22; 1Kgdms 2:12; 10:27; 25:17; Proverbs 16:27;

Nahum 1:11), once in Theodotion (3Kgdms 21:13), and twice in Symmachus (1Kgdms 1:16; 2:12). In each of these instances, the meaning is religious or political defection. In addition there are a couple of papyrus fragments, quoted by Moulton and Milligan, where the word means 'a rebel.' This is evidence that the primary meaning of the word became a departure in a religious or political sense rather than a simple physical sense. However the relatively small number of these cases do not exclude the possibility that this word had a secondary sense of physical departure, and **the Archimedes quote, at about the same time as the LXX, establishes beyond doubt that a simple physical departure or separation is a possible meaning of this word.**

In the New Testament there is only one other time than in 2Thessalonians 2 that this noun is used and that is in <u>Acts 21:21</u> where Paul is accused of teaching Jews to depart from Moses: **"they have been informed about you that you teach all the Jews who are among the Gentiles to forsake** (*apostasia*) **Moses, saying that they ought not to circumcise their children nor to walk according to the customs."** Here the emphasis is on a spiritual departure, but it is Greek thinking to totally separate the spiritual from the physical (as if it were one or the other). In Hebrew thinking these two are closely connected, for a spiritual departure always results in a physical departure. In this case, spiritually departing from Moses would result in physically departing from the synagogue and not participating in the many physical customs, just as this verse points out. Thus the 'apostasia' in this verse includes a physical departure from the Jewish community as well as (resulting from) a spiritual departure from Moses. In any case, this one verse cannot possibly be used to limit the meaning of *apostasia* to a spiritual departure, and exclude the possibility of a physical departure.

*Later in the Patristic era, there is no question that *apostasia* included the idea of physical departure within its range of meanings. **Jerome** (347 - 420 AD) chose to translate it into Latin as 'discessio', a word that means departure (usually in a physical sense), pointing to the fact that in his time, this meaning was understood to be part of the range of meanings of *apostasia*. Another example from the **6th century AD** is **Olympiodorus Meteorology. 320.2.**

Lampe's Patristic Greek Lexicon also gives an example of a spatial departure from a **5th century** New Testament apocryphal work: 'The Assumption of the Virgin.' The amazing thing about this example is that in it *apostasia* is used to describe a physical translation or rapture! Sections 31–32 read: **"The Holy Ghost said to the apostles and the mother of the Lord: "Behold, the governor has sent a captain of a thousand against you, because the Jews have made a tumult. Go out therefore from Bethlehem, and fear not; for behold, I will bring you by a cloud to Jerusalem." The apostles therefore rose up straightaway and went out of the house, bearing the bed of their lady the mother of God, and went forward towards Jerusalem: and immediately, just as the Holy Ghost said, they were lifted up by a cloud and were found at Jerusalem in the house of their lady."** This clearly describes a 'rapture' of the apostles and Mary. Section 33 continues: **"But when the captain came to Bethlehem and did not find there the mother of the Lord, nor the apostles, he laid hold upon the Bethlehemites... For the captain did not know of the departure of the apostles and the mother of the Lord to Jerusalem."** This 'rapture' is now described as a 'departure', the Greek word being *apostasia*. Here is clear evidence that *apostasia* can refer to a 'rapture.'

Thus we have seen that in the Classical, the Koine and the Patristic eras, the times before, during and after the New Testament times, *apostasia* certainly included within its range of meanings the idea of spatial separation or physical departure, as well as a spiritual departure from the truth, and this is only to be expected considering that this is the basic and primary use of the verb from which it is derived. This is illustrated by fact that when Paul used the related verb in 1Timothy 4:1: "some shall **depart** from the faith", he had to qualify 'depart' by a phrase indicating that he was speaking of a spiritual departure, showing that the word itself did not inherently carry this meaning. Although Jewish literature in particular mostly came to use *apostasia* metaphorically to describe a spiritual departure from the truth, this does not justify eliminating its basic literal meaning. It is understandable, since the ideas of departure from the faith of Israel and rebellion against a foreign power were major themes of their literature at that time, that *apostasia* was used repeatedly in a religious sense in such contexts. But the word does not intrinsically carry the meaning of defection or revolt. In each biblical case it is only given that particular meaning by a qualifying phrase and/or by the context. We only know it has this meaning, because the context makes it clear. Thus as the Archimedes quote confirms these are acquired meanings of the word supplied by the context in which it is used, not its original, basic, literal meaning, and so should not be imposed on the word when the context does not point to such meanings, as in the case of its use in 2Thessalonians, where it has no qualifying phrase and the context does not refer to a religious defection, but to the Rapture.

This brings us back to my 2nd main contribution to this debate, the argument that unlike Greek thinking, which makes a strong separation between the spiritual and physical, the Hebrews saw the two as working closely together, as indeed they often do, and so would naturally have maintained both meanings in their use of the word, and even would have often seen both aspects together when used in a particular situation. It would have been unnatural to their way of thinking to sever off the physical meaning from the spiritual. This tendency is the result of Greek-type thinking that is better at dividing things into separate compartments (analysis), than holding them in synthesis, creating a bias towards 'either/or' thinking rather than 'both/and' thinking. I am saying this to correct the bias that presumes the word lost its original basic physical meaning, when the starting presumption should be the opposite, and indeed we have shown that the evidence from its usage in all eras bears this out, for although the primary use is religious, there are clear cases when it is used in a physical sense. Considering the relatively few uses of this noun in the surviving literature this is surely significant. The apparent lack of use of *apostasia* in referring to a physical departure in the koine period (except arguably 2Thess 2:3 itself) has convinced many against its application to the Rapture, especially as this is the time-period leading up to the New Testament. But **the Archimedes quote changes all that** as it shows the word was indeed used in a physical way at that time. Although Feinberg's database search revealed no instances when the word was used in a physical sense during this time, this is because he chose to search only from the 2nd century BC to the 1st century AD, thus missing the Archimedes quote, which was from just before his starting point.

Sadly this bias is manifested in overstating the case. House has to correct Gundry's claim that *apostasia* and its cognates occur over 40 times in the LXX and all carry the idea of political or religious defection. In fact there are over 220 occurrences, of which at least 66 express spatial separation, compared to religious defection (x 53) and political defection (x 8). If he meant to speak of the noun alone, he should not try and hide the relatively small number of usages by including the cognates in the total number quoted. Another example of this kind of smoke and mirrors is Feinberg's claim: *"If one searches for the uses of the noun 'apostasia' in the 355 occurrences of the 300 year period between the 2nd century BC and the 1st century AD, one will not find a single instance where this word refers to a physical departure."* In fact 355 is the number of occurrences of the noun and its cognates, and so if he is focusing on the use of the noun he should have used that number, which is a small fraction of 355, and so obviously far less impressive for his case. Moreover by limiting the range of years as he did he excluded the Archimedes quote, which invalidates his claim in any case.

This word, with its basic root meaning of a physical departure, but also often denoting a spiritual rejection, used by a Hebrew mind which naturally holds both physical and spiritual aspects together, makes *apostasia* the perfect word to describe the Rapture, and is no doubt the reason Paul chose it. For the Rapture is not just a simple physical event, it is also filled with great spiritual significance. Paul would not have been bound into the oversharp Greek-style separation of physical and spiritual and would have wanted a word that did not merely describe the Church's physical departure, but which also carried a sense of its spiritual significance, which would add depth to his explanation of its connection to the Day of the Lord. When we study the context of 2Thessalonians 2:3 we will see how perfectly *apostasia* does this. Thus Paul chose *apostasia*, because it lent itself to the fusion of both the spiritual and physical aspects of the Departure of the Church, for it can refer to a physical departure from a place, which has a spiritual significance (basis), or a spiritual rejection and rebellion against a system, which results in a physical withdrawal from it. This fusion perfectly describes the nature of the Rapture, which is a decisive departure and withdrawal of the Church from the earth, based on a rejection of the evil world-system, which is about to come under the judgment of the Day of the Lord. The Rapture is the Church departing from an evil world that is about to be judged, being separated from it, so that it does not share in its judgment, just as righteous Lot departed unrighteous Sodom, just before judgment fell. Paul was saying that they were not yet in the Day of the Lord (v2), for the Day of the Lord cannot come unless the *apostasia* comes first (v3). By using *apostasia* for the Rapture he was not just stating the fact of the Pre-Tribulation Rapture, but also explaining its necessity, for the true Church is identified with Christ and not with this world-system, in fact it has forsaken it and stands in opposition to it, and this spiritual reality will be manifested by her removal from it in the Rapture, when it comes time for Christ to judge this world, for it is not right for her to partake in its judgment.

Paul had made this very point in 1Thessalonians 5, when he discussed the timing of the Rapture (v1), saying that: **"the Day of the Lord** (Tribulation) **comes** (begins) **as a thief in the night** (the Rapture, Matthew 24:43)" (v2). He then defined 'the Day of the Lord' as the time of labour-pains and destruction (the Tribulation, Matthew 24:7,8) that will come upon the whole world (v3). He then explained why the Rapture of the Church must take place before this time of worldwide judgment: **"THEY** (the world) **shall not escape** (the destruction of the Day of the Lord). **BUT YOU, brethren, are not in darkness, so that this Day should overtake YOU as a thief. You are all sons of light and sons of the day. We are not of the night nor of darkness"** (v3-5). The Church is contrasted to the world in darkness, believers (the sons of light) do not belong to the darkness of this world-system, and so will not come under its judgment. We belong to the kingdom of light, whereas the world in darkness is under God's wrath, that will be released in the Day of the Lord. Since no one on earth will escape it, the Church must be removed from the earth before it starts. Therefore, because of the contrasting natures of the Church and the world, of light and darkness, they will have 2 very different destinies: **"For God has not appointed us to wrath** (the Day of the Lord), **but to obtain salvation** (in the Rapture) **by our Lord Jesus Christ"**(v8).

Therefore the physical event of the Pre-Tribulation Rapture is seen as a moral and spiritual imperative, that she will not share in the Day of the Lord

Judgment upon the world, because although she is in the world, she is not of it. She shines as a light in the darkness of this world. Thus the Rapture is a physical event that expresses her spiritual rejection of what it stands for. Her physical departure from the world and gathering to Jesus, is a manifestation of her previous spiritual departure from the darkness of this world, by coming to Jesus. The departure of the Church from the earth unto Jesus above, opens the way for Him to start the time of judgment, called 'the Day of the Lord' upon the earth.

This revelation of the spiritual basis for the Rapture explains why *apostasia* is the perfect word for God to have chosen in 2Thessalonians 2, as it fits the context perfectly, expressing and enriching the main thought. The opposition of the Church to the spirit of evil in the world is also confirmed in v6-8, where the Church (with the Holy Spirit) is described as the one restraining evil, so that only when it is removed (in the Rapture) can the antichrist be manifested and then judged (in the Day of the Lord). Finally, it is striking how similar this is to Jesus' instructions to His disciples on leaving a place that has rejected their witness to Him: **"Whoever will not receive you nor hear your words, when you depart from that house or city, shake off the dust from your feet"** (Matthew 10:14). Mark 6:11 and Luke 9:5 explain that this functions: **"as a testimony against them."** This was a sign that they were guilty and deserving of judgment for having rejected the message. So if having completed their witness it was rejected, they were to physically depart the place and spiritually disassociate themselves from any of its defilement, symbolised by shaking off its dust. This will ultimately be fulfilled at the Rapture. When the Church has completed its witness to the world, it will leave it and its dramatic and rapid departure will demonstrate its rejection of the world and all it stands for. This *apostasia* will be a sign to the world that judgment is about to fall, but God in His mercy will still give people a chance to repent, for this dramatic warning sign will be a wake up call to many, causing them to turn to Christ for forgiveness and salvation.

CONTEXT

Having established that physical departure is within the semantic range of meanings of *apostasia*, we will now show that the context of 2Thessalonians 2 points clearly to the Rapture as the correct interpretation. The importance of context is magnified in this case, because 'the *apostasia*' in v3 has the definite article ('the') and no qualifier explaining its meaning. This combination only happens when what the word refers to is a definite event, which is so well-defined to the reader's mind that no qualifier is needed. Thus it must be obvious from the context. The only other case of *the apostasia* arising in this way is in 1Maccabees 2:15, and reading the preceding 46 verses makes it absolutely clear that it refers to a religious defection. This is why the term with the article needs no further qualification, even though it could potentially have a variety of possible meanings. Applying this same logic to *the apostasia* in 2Thessalonians, leads us to conclude that it must refer to a definite event whose nature is clear and well defined by the preceding context. On this basis we'll see the only valid candidate is the Rapture.

The meaning of this *apostasia* should be obvious from the prior context of 2Thessalonians 2:3, that is, 1Thessalonians and 2Thessalonians 1:1 - 2:2. That is, there should be a well defined end-time departure or defection discussed in this section of Scripture that corresponds to the *apostasia* of 2:3 in such a way that the readers would easily recognise it as such. There is nothing in these chapters corresponding to a religious defection or political rebellion. However, the single topic discussed more than any other in these chapters is the Departure of the Church in the Rapture. Almost every chapter in 1Thessalonians has a direct reference to it (1:9-10, 2:19, 4:13-18 which gives the most complete statement on the Rapture, and 5:1-11).

Finally and most importantly, the verses immediately before 2Thessalonians 2:3, which begin and introduce the passage under consideration, announce that the subject under discussion is the Rapture: **"Now, brethren, concerning the Coming of our Lord Jesus Christ and our gathering together to Him"** (v1). In this way, Paul emphasises his previous teaching on the Rapture in 1Thessalonians, causing us to remember it and focus upon it as we read what he has to say next on this subject. Thus it is the key to interpreting the following verses correctly. So in v3 when Paul refers to 'the Departure' without specifying what departure he was talking about, the law of interpretation says it must be obvious from the context, so we should ask: "Is there an obvious departure in the context which is marked so clearly that it was unnecessary for Paul to clarify any further what this Departure was?" The answer is a resounding 'Yes' - the Departure of the Church in v1, which is not only the declared subject of the passage, but the major topic of the Thessalonian epistles! Context determines meaning, so the fact *apostasia* is often used to mean religious defection in other kinds of contexts is irrelevant to this situation. In these other passages the context naturally points to a defection, but this is not the case in 2Thessalonians, where the context naturally points to the departure of the Church.

Alternative interpretations, which do not involve the Rapture, are not only inconsistent with the preceding context, but also with the rest of the passage in 2Thessalonians 2, for they have Paul announcing in v1 that the main subject under discussion is the Rapture, but then in their reading of the following verses the Rapture is never mentioned after that! Yet for those who have eyes to see the central theme is the Rapture and its relationship to antichrist and the Day of the Lord (which opens with the revelation of the antichrist). Thus following the law of context points strongly to the Rapture being the Departure in v3.

In v2 Paul explains the purpose of his teaching in this passage: **"we ask you not to be soon shaken in mind or troubled, either by spirit or by word or by letter, as if from us, as though the Day of the Lord had come."** The perfect tense of the verb 'to come' used here indicates that a false rumour had arisen that the Day of the Lord had already arrived and was present, and this was troubling the Thessalonians. Every use of the perfect tense of this verb agrees with this meaning, and there is no question that this is the correct translation. This fact confirms what we deduced about the Day of the Lord from 1Thess 5:2-3, namely that 'the Day of the Lord' here cannot be the 2nd Coming, for it would be plain to all that the Lord had not returned in glory. Neither could it be the Rapture for again it would be obvious to all that this had not happened, and so they would not have taken seriously any claims to that effect. Instead 'the Day of the Lord' must be the Tribulation, which is consistent with its Old Testament usage denoting a special time of judgment in the end-times. This also explains why they were disturbed, for they had been taught the Pre-Tribulation Rapture by Paul in 1Thessalonians and orally (v5), so when they were told that the Tribulation had overtaken them and they had not been raptured, so they will have to go through this terrible time of wrath, their reaction is understandable. The KJV translation: 'the Day of the Lord was at hand' is invalid and is driven by theological not grammatical reasons, for if you assume the Day of the Lord is the 2nd Coming, then the literal translation ('the Day of the Lord has already come') makes no sense. The literal statement only makes sense when you understand 'the Day of the Lord' is not the 2nd Coming.

In v3 Paul then explains why they could not possibly be in the Day of the Lord: **"Let no one deceive you by any means; for that Day will not come unless** *the apostasia* (departure) **comes first, and the man of sin is revealed."** We have established that the only candidate for this departure in the prior context is the Rapture of the Church. Moreover, when the passage is read from this viewpoint it makes perfect sense. Thus Paul is saying that the Tribulation will not start until the Departure of the Church comes first, and only then will the man of sin be revealed, that is, only then will the Tribulation begin (the revelation of antichrist happens at the start of the Tribulation - Daniel 9:27, Revelation 6:1-2). Thus Paul answers by reaffirming the Pre-Tribulation Rapture, that the Church must be removed before the Day of the Lord begins and antichrist is revealed. This is exactly the answer we would expect from Paul if he taught the Pre-Tribulation Rapture. To those claiming we are already in the Day of the Lord, the most obvious reply of a Pre-Tribber would be that we cannot possibly be in the Day of the Lord because the Rapture has not happened yet, and the antichrist has not been revealed, and that is exactly what Paul said. For a Pre-Tribber to interpret *apostasia* in any other way creates difficulties, for in that case Paul failed to make the obvious point that would have clearly settled the issue (that the Rapture must happen first), and instead he appealed to some specific but undefined apostasy that must happen first, which is not mentioned in Thessalonians, or in the rest of Scripture, but that the Thessalonian readers knew about from Paul's oral teaching. For this reason there are many theories about what this apostasy is, but we can't know it, so we can only speculate, and we cannot recognise it when it happens. This is unsatisfactory for it contradicts the sufficiency of Scripture, especially as this is an end-time sign needed most of all by the end-time generation.

Thus any Pre-Tribulation interpretation that does not see *apostasia* as the Rapture is unsatisfactory, and so it is disappointing that this interpretation has not yet been accepted widely in the Pre-Tribulation camp. The main reason has been the argument that 'physical departure' is not one of the viable meanings of *apostasia*. However, the evidence presented in this article shows that this is simply not so. Therefore, I appeal to my fellow Pre-Tribulationists to embrace the Rapture interpretation of *apostasia* in 2Thessalonians 2:3 as it makes perfect sense of the passage and agrees with the context, as well as being consistent with word usage. Furthermore, if *apostasia* speaks of a defection from the faith which must happen first, it is hard to understand why Paul would use it as a means of bringing comfort to the troubled believers, as he seeks to do in this chapter (v2,3,17), just as he does in 1Thessalonians 4:18 and 5:11 where the Rapture is the basis for comfort.

This view also has the advantage of harmonising v3 with v6-8, as they contain parallel thoughts, for in v3 the *apostasia* is followed by the revelation of the man of sin, and in v6-8 the taking away of the Restrainer is followed by the revelation of the lawless one: **"And now you know what is restraining, that he may be revealed in his own time. For the mystery of lawlessness is already at work; only He who now restrains will do so until He is taken out of the way. And then the lawless one will be revealed."**

If the *apostasia* is the Rapture every-thing fits perfectly. Having reminded them that the Departure of the Church from the world must happen before the antichrist is revealed to the world (v3), on the basis of this knowledge he expected them to know what was presently preventing and restraining his revelation (v6). Simple logic dictates that the 'WHAT is restraining' has to be the Church. But of course it is not the Church on its own, but the Holy Spirit indwelling the Church, so in v7 the description of the Restrainer shifts from 'WHAT' to 'HE who now restrains.' Thus the present Restrainer of the antichrist could be described as the Holy Spirit working with and through the Church, or as the Church empowered by the Spirit. Logically this restraining ministry will continue until the Restrainer is 'taken out of the way' in the Rapture (v7), and then this will allow the antichrist to be revealed (v8). Thus we can see how v6-8 repeat and develop the thought of v3. Having declared that the antichrist cannot be revealed until the Departure of the Church (v3), in v6-8 Paul explains the reason for this fact. It is because the Church, indwelt by God's Spirit, is presently holding back the antichrist from being revealed and will continue to do so until its Departure from the world, so that only when it is taken out of his way (by its removal in the Rapture) will satan be able to manifest the antichrist to the world.

Whereas in alternative interpretations both the *apostasia* and the identity of *the Restrainer* are left undefined by the context and so become a matter of speculation, this interpretation allows *the apostasia* to be defined by the context, which in turn allows us to determine the identity of *the Restrainer* from the context. Thus it brings harmony and coherence to the whole passage, whereas other interpretations are left with a collection of undefined and unconnected ideas. Thus this literal interpretation of *apostasia* harmonises the whole passage with its context and central theme and solves all its problems. It's the only interpretation that explains why Paul was able to just call it *the apostasia* without adding any explanation. He clearly expected them to know what he was talking about, so it must be clear from the prior context, and the only 'departure' in the prior context is the Rapture. Moreover this literal interpretation transforms 2Thessalonians 2 from a passage that can be harmonised with the Pre-Tribulation Rapture to a passage that plainly declares it, in fact it is the main point of the passage. Thus Pre-Tribulationists should embrace it, not resist it.

In response to the question as to whether there is a single passage of the Bible that reveals the 2 phases of Christ's Return (Rapture and 2nd Coming) separated by the Tribulation, we reply that 2Thessalonians 2 is one such passage. The Rapture (His initial coming to the air for His saints) is in v1 ('our gathering together to Him'), and His 2nd Coming to the earth to destroy antichrist and establish His Kingdom here is in v8. The coming of antichrist during the Tribulation is clearly located between the 2 phases of Christ's Return (his activity is described in v3-12). Thus a straightforward reading of this passage demonstrates the Pre-Tribulation view. If in addition *the apostasia* is recognised to be the Rapture, then v3 is a plain statement of this view, which is then reinforced further by the further explanation of the Restrainer in v6-8.

In closing, I want to answer a couple of possible objections. There is a Post-Tribulationist interpretation that claims *the apostasia* is the rebellion of antichrist described in the later verses, and so is in the context.

This must be rejected for 2 reasons: (1) Common sense dictates that the assumed knowledge of v3 must come from what has previously been said in the verses before it. Paul expects the reader of v3 to understand what he means, because he has already discussed it, not because he will explain it later. A basic principle of good communication is to define your terms first so people know what you are talking about. (2) This interpretation of v3 says the Day of the Lord cannot come unless the *apostasia* (rebellion of antichrist) happens first, and (thus) the man of sin is revealed. This then requires the Day of the Lord to be the 2nd Coming of Christ, which makes a nonsense of verse 2, which describes what occasioned Paul's discussion. The Thessalonians were disturbed because they thought the Day of the Lord had come, and Paul had to explain to them why it had not. If they understood the Day of the Lord was His glorious Return this would be nonsensical, as it was obvious He had not returned. Also if the Day of the Lord had suddenly come upon them in some way, then they would not have been 'troubled', but rather they would have been rejoicing, for their rapture and gathering together to Christ (to be with Him forever) was now imminent. The only way to make sense of v2 is that the Day of the Lord is an extended period of judgment, from which the Church is promised deliverance by Rapture, so those who thought they might already be in it were naturally troubled. In this case, the rebellion of antichrist is an event within the Day of the Lord, and so it cannot be the *apostasia* of v3, which must take place BEFORE the Day of the Lord.

Another technical issue is the implication of the word FIRST in v3: **"that Day** (of the Lord) **will not come unless *the apostasia* comes FIRST, and the man of sin is revealed."** Does it mean that the Day of the Lord will not come until BOTH *the apostasia* and the revelation of the man of sin has taken place? Or does it mean that the Day of the Lord will not come until the *apostasia* comes first, and then the man of sin will be revealed (as the key event at the start of the Day of the Lord)? Both interpretations are grammatically possible, but other prophetic scriptures tell us that the revelation of the antichrist takes place at the start of the Day of the Lord (Revelation 6:1-2, Daniel 9:27). In fact, it is the definitive event on earth that marks the start of the Tribulation. Therefore the latter view must be correct. Paul assumes that they understood that the Day of the Lord is the time when the antichrist comes to power, which was why they were troubled at the thought that they were in that time, so he was saying this time won't come unless the Rapture comes first, and then the antichrist will be revealed, which is equivalent to describing the start of the Day of the Lord.

One can discern 2 clear points in v3: (1) the *apostasia* comes before the Day of the Lord (from the first part of the verse), (2) the *apostasia* comes before the revelation of antichrist (from the 2nd part of the verse). It does not necessarily say that the revelation of antichrist comes before the Day of the Lord (Tribulation), and this would contradict other scriptures. Clearly it makes better sense as a parallelism, where the coming of the Day of the Lord is equivalent to the manifestation of antichrist. Since there are 2 main aspects of the Tribulation that would trouble anyone: (1) it is a time of Divine Wrath (the Day of the Lord), and (2) it is the time of the antichrist's manifestation as ruler, in v3 Paul gave a 2-fold assurance, comforting them that they were not in this time, for *the apostasia* had not yet happened. This is then confirmed in v6-12 which say that the Church (Restrainer) must be removed (in the Rapture) before the antichrist is revealed and deceives the world in the Tribulation until Christ returns to destroy him.

*Appendix 5: The 3 Viewpoints on the Millennium

What we believe about Revelation 20 and the MILLENNIUM governs our whole viewpoint of Prophecy. We will now look at the 3 main viewpoints, which define the 3 main prophetic Camps and you will be in one of them. You can know which basic prophetic view any person has by his position on this issue. Thus this is a touchstone revealing a person's general approach to Prophecy.

*1. Pre-Millennialism. The first view is PRE-MILLENNIALISM. 'Pre' means 'before'. So Pre-Millennialism says the 2nd Coming of Christ comes BEFORE the Millennium. In other words, at His 2nd Coming, Christ will personally establish the promised Kingdom on earth, fulfilling the vision of the Old-Testament prophets. He will reign as King of kings over this earthly Messianic Kingdom for 1,000 years (Revelation 20), before time moves into eternity. This was the view of the Early Church for the first 3 centuries. In older literature it was also called Chiliasm from the Greek word for 'a thousand.' A literal reading of Bible Prophecy says that this Church Age will lead into a time of Tribulation, after which Christ will return to establish His Millennial Kingdom, during which He will be present on earth in His resurrected body and reign as King over the whole earth. All the believers will all be raised to reign with Him over a Kingdom of righteousness and peace, on a renewed earth from which satan and all his demons will have been removed. At the end of the 1000 years satan is released and gathers together all the unbelievers who have submitted outwardly to Christ's reign but inwardly have rejected their rule over them. Their rebellion is thus revealed for the purpose of judgment. Christ will then resurrect all unbelievers who have died and they will stand before Him for Final Judgment, after which we will all enter the Eternal State in a new heavens and earth.

I am pre-millennial, simply because it follows from taking prophecy literally. In fact all the camps agree that if you take prophecy literally then you will be Pre-Millennial. The clearest way to see this is in the book of Revelation. Revelation 19 describes the Return of Christ. Then in Revelation 20:1-6 He reigns for 1000 years. So its plain meaning is that Jesus will return to earth and establish His Kingdom for 1000 years - the Millennium. So one immediate consequence of the literal interpretation of prophecy is Pre-Millennialism. If you are not pre-millennial then you do not take prophecy according to its plain (literal) meaning.

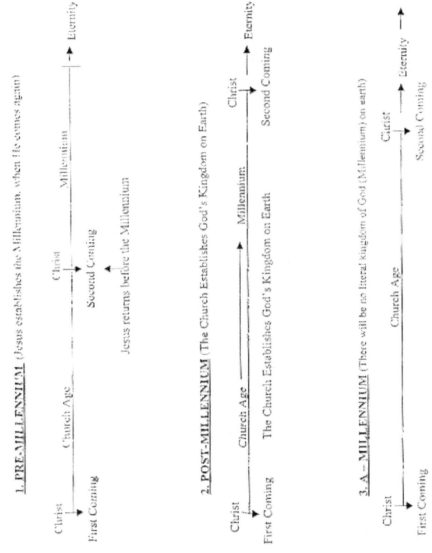

THE THREE VIEWS ON THE MILLENNIUM

1. PRE-MILLENNIUM (Jesus establishes the Millennium, when He comes again)

2. POST-MILLENNIUM (The Church Establishes God's Kingdom on Earth)

3. A–MILLENNIUM (There will be no literal kingdom of God (Millennium) on earth)

You might be shocked to know that because of developments in Church History, most Christians do not take prophecy literally, which accounts for the widespread ignorance and confusion concerning Bible Prophecy. So most Christians belong to one of the camps other than Pre-Millenialism.

There are 2 forms of Premillennialism: **(1) Covenant or Historic Premillennialism**, which bases its view solely on a literal interpretation of

Revelation 20:1-6, and does not use the Old Testament prophecies to support its view of the Millennial Kingdom. The result is that Israel has no special place in this version of the Kingdom, even though it is the fulfilment of the covenants and promises to Israel. This is because covenant theologians like George Ladd apply Old Testament promises to the Church, even though they were made originally to Israel. Thus like the Amillennialists they regularly spiritualise the Old Testament prophecies. Because they take this approach and don't clearly distinguish between Israel and the Church, they generally believe in a Post-Tribulation Rapture.

(2) Dispensational Premillennialism also sees the Millennium as the literal fulfilment of Revelation 20, but it also sees it as the literal fulfilment of the many prophecies in the Old Testament of a coming Golden Age when the Messiah will reign over the earth from Jerusalem, with restored Israel as the chief nation. It is also when the everlasting unconditional covenants of Abraham and David will be fulfilled to Israel by the Messiah. We previously saw how a number of other New Testament scriptures confirm this restoration of the Kingdom to Israel.

Covenant Premillennialism is the less consistent view because although it takes Revelation 20 literally, it spiritualises the Old Testament prophecies of the Kingdom, applying them to the Church, which is falsely termed 'spiritual Israel.' Thus it fails to give Israel its proper place in the program of God, and it does not glorify God in showing how God will fulfil His Covenants to Abraham and David in this Kingdom (see Appendix 2). It also misuses the concept of progressive revelation, using the idea that the New Testament helps us to understand the Old, to justify changing the clear plain meaning of Old Testament prophecies. On the other hand Dispensational Pre-Millennialism emphasises the application of a consistently literal hermeneutic. The many Old Testament Prophecies of a messianic Golden Age are not literally fulfilled by the Church, so must have a yet future fulfilment. These prophecies fit perfectly with the earthly Millennial Reign of Christ.

Both forms of Pre-Millennialism agree that Christ Himself will return to earth before this Kingdom is established, so the present heavenly rule of Christ is not the Millennium. It is a future Kingdom that will suddenly be established at the Lord's Return, rather than coming in gradually over a period of time. It will be brought in by the Lord Himself not by man's efforts or by the Church. Both forms believe it will be a literal kingdom of universal righteousness, joy, peace and glory on this earth, with the Edenic curse and satanic forces removed, ruled over by

Christ Himself, who is physically present, and will be the centre of attention and worship. Both believe in 2 physical resurrections separated by 1000 years according to Revelation 20:4-6. The 1st resurrection refers to the resurrection of all believers before the start of the 1000 years, the 2nd resurrection is the resurrection of the wicked at the end of the 1000 years.

Both forms of Pre-Millennialism believe that this Messianic Kingdom will only be established after all the human kingdoms of this earth are destroyed. This is clear from the prophecies of Daniel 2 and 7, which describe 4 human kingdoms that exist before God's Kingdom is established by the Messiah who comes down from heaven during the 2nd phase of the 4th kingdom (the 10 toes and 10 horns), the empire ruled over by the antichrist. At this time Christ will suddenly and completely destroy that kingdom, along with the vestiges of all other human kingdoms. Only then will He establish God's Kingdom on earth (Daniel 2:32-35, 44-45). **"The Stone** (Christ) **that struck** (and totally destroyed) **the image** (representing man's kingdoms) **became a great Mountain** (the Messianic Kingdom) **and filled the whole earth. ...in the days of these kings the God of heaven will set up a Kingdom which shall never be destroyed... it shall break in pieces and consume all these kingdoms** (of the world), **and it shall stand forever"** (v35,44). There is no coexistence between God's Kingdom and the kingdoms of this world. Neither is there a gradual peaceful take-over by God's Kingdom as Postmillennialists say. This proves that the Millennial Kingdom was not established at Christ's 1st Coming as suffering Servant, but rather it must happen at His 2nd Coming in power and glory as King of the whole world.

Some refer to John 18:36 to support their objection to an earthly Kingdom: **"Jesus answered** (Pilate)**: "My Kingdom is not of this world. If My Kingdom were of this world, My servants would fight, so that I should not be delivered to the Jews; but now My Kingdom is not from here."** It is important to note the difference between being 'of the world' and 'in the world.' Jesus made this very distinction just before in John 17:11-16. So His Kingdom is not 'of this world.' It will not originate from this world or be of the same nature as the kingdoms of this world. It will be of an entirely different order. He is telling Pilate that it will not be established in the normal ways, through insurrections or military victories of early armies. However, it will come to be established 'in the world' when He returns to the earth as King of kings. He confirmed this when He said in v37: **"You say rightly that I am a king."** Revelation 19 describes the Lord's Return bringing a sudden destructive end to the kingdoms of this world, and it is the Lord alone who personally accomplishes this judgment (not earthly armies, the church or even heavenly armies), and then in Revelation 20, He removes all evil demonic powers and establishes His Kingdom on earth. Thus this scripture fits with the Pre-millennial view, but it does contradict the Postmillennial view, and especially the viewpoint of Dominion Theology, for Jesus said His Kingdom does not come from within this world and so His servants here do not fight to establish it. Those that do so are not acting as servants under His orders, but are following their own impulses just as Peter did when he took his sword and cut off Malchus' ear. Such misdirected action is futile and useless to God and hurts the witness of the Gospel. Instead His Kingdom will come from above, from outside this world. It will invade this world and destroy all its kingdoms. Moreover His servants will not fight to establish it for the King Himself will do all the fighting.

The Kingdom of God

It is important to realise that there are different uses of the term 'Kingdom of God' in the Scriptures, referring to the reign of God and the realm over which He exercises His authority. There is God's **Universal Kingdom** for He reigns over all His creation. The **Spiritual Kingdom** of God refers to God's rule over believers in all ages. In the Old Testament men were subjects or servants of His Kingdom, but not sons or citizens. This was true even of John the Baptist, but Jesus brought in a new phase of the Spiritual Kingdom of God, consisting of those who are sons of God by the New Birth (Matt 11:11, John 3:3-6). During the Church Age this Kingdom is the same as the true Church. In the Old Testament God's rule over the nation of Israel is called the **Theocratic Kingdom** under the Mosaic Covenant and Law. But this was temporary, a preparation for the **Millennial Kingdom** to be established ruled over by Christ under His Covenant and Law, when the Abrahamic, Davidic and New Covenants will all be fulfilled. Israel expected the Messiah to establish this Kingdom when He came, but because of her national rejection of Christ, He established the **Mystery Kingdom** instead, which is the form of the Kingdom in the Church-Age, and includes all those who are related to the Church, whether or not they are born-again. After the **Messianic Kingdom** comes the **Eternal Kingdom** when God's Kingdom enters its Eternal State of perfection (Rev 21-22), although from another point of view Christ's everlasting reign (kingdom) begins with the Messianic Kingdom (Daniel 2:44, Isaiah 9:6,7, Rev 11:15). Thus the Everlasting Kingdom of God will be manifested in 2 phases: (1) the Messianic Kingdom for 1000 years, when Christ rules with a rod of iron (sin is still present), followed by (2) the perfect Eternal State (1Corinthians 15:23-28).

2. A-Millennialism The 2nd view is A-MILLENNIALISM, which became the dominant view in Church history. 'A' is Greek for 'no.' So this says that there will be no Millennium, no literal 1,000-year Messianic Kingdom on earth. It says that when Christ came He brought in the Church Age, so that is how God fulfilled the prophecies of the Kingdom, spiritually through the Church, rather than literally through Israel. Thus these prophecies are all to be interpreted as symbolic of Christ's spiritual rule through the Church. The 1,000 years of Revelation 20 is just picture language for the Church-Age. They believe that one day Jesus will return and take us to Heaven, but He will have no earthly Kingdom and there will be no literal fulfilment of the Old Testament prophecies. This is considered to be unspiritual and overly literalistic. This depends on a system of Bible interpretation that allegorises or spiritualises all references in the Bible to Christ's reign upon the earth and the fulfilment of the Old Testament promises to Israel, and so denies the literal meaning and fulfilment of these promises.

It was Augustine in the 4th century who promoted this idea. Until then the Church took Prophecy literally, but he thought the idea of a literal rule of Christ for 1000 years on earth was too materialistic and did not seem very spiritual. Since he was such a dominant theologian this became the accepted view in the Roman Church. Even though the Reformation generally stood for returning to the literal reading of the Bible, sadly in the area of Bible Prophecy the Reformers were inconsistent and stayed with Augustine. Therefore this is also the general view in the historic Protestant denominational churches. They believe the Millennial Kingdom began at Christ's 1st Coming and will end at His 2nd Coming. Thus they interpret the Millennium of Revelation 20 as a picture of the Church Age with Christ ruling with the Church, and satan bound by Christ on the Cross, although they have to admit he is on a very long leash. They claim satan's influence over the nations has been reduced, so that the Gospel can be preached to the whole world. Those who are said to be reigning with Christ for 1000 years are Christians who have died and are reigning with Christ in Heaven. Thus Christ's reign is heavenly (He is not physically present on earth). The 1000 years are not to be taken literally, they are a figure of speech for a long period of time. Since the Old Testament Prophecies are fulfilled by the Church, this view leaves no room for the fulfilment of God's Purposes for Israel. Thus the great importance and significance of Israel is discarded by this view. Having fulfilled her purpose of bringing forth the Messiah, Israel has been set aside by God. Also in this view, when Christ returns believers and unbelievers will be resurrected together at the same time, when the final judgment of all men takes place, and we all then enter the Eternal State of blessedness or punishment. Thus it is a simple scheme as it has most of the main end-time events happening together immediately after Christ's Return.

Amillennialists have to set aside the literal interpretation of Revelation 20.

*The binding of satan in v1-3 is the binding that Jesus accomplished in His 1st Coming, which He spoke about in Matthew 12:28-29. This restraint on satan enabled the Gospel to be preached to the nations. However in Revelation 20 it is an angel who does the binding and it is at the 2nd Coming. Moreover the restraint on satan is much more extensive than what we see presently in the Church Age. Satan is not just bound, but thrown into the Abyss, which is sealed. This is a prison for angels and demons (Luke 8:31, Revelation 9:1-2,11). Thus satan will be totally removed from any active influence on the earth. This does not fit the situation during the Church Age where he is still very active on earth (1Peter 5:8, Acts 5:3, 1Cor 10:20, 2Cor 4:4, Ephesians 2:2, 6:12, 1John 5:19). Yes, satan has been defeated at the Cross by Christ, who now has all authority in heaven and earth, but until Christ Himself uses His authority to dethrone these principalities and powers and remove them from their positions of authority in the 2nd heaven, they will continue to rule the darkness of this world. This will initially happen at Mid-Tribulation when Michael casts them down to the earth's surface, and then at the 2nd Coming Christ will lock them up in the Abyss for 1000 years. Revelation 20 speaks of a time when satan will no longer be able to deceive the peoples of the earth, yet that is exactly what he is doing now (Revelation 12:9, 18:23).

When v4 speaks of the souls of martyrs 'coming to life' and reigning for 1000 years, Amillennialists have to say that this does not mean they receive a physical resurrection, but simply that upon death they come into a heavenly existence and live a higher life with Christ, reigning with Him there. In this view 'the 1st resurrection' (v5) is not a physical resurrection, but a coming into God's

Presence in Heaven. Likewise, when v5 describes unbelievers coming to life after the 1000 years, this means their coming into God's Presence for Judgment. Thus they interpret 'coming to life' as 'coming into God's Presence in Heaven.' However, all these interpretations defy the normal meaning of the words used.

First, Revelation 20:1 indicates that this passage is focused on events taking place on earth, not in heaven, for it says: **"Then I saw an angel coming down from Heaven."** So when v4 says that souls, who had suffered physical death on earth, 'came to life' in the 'first resurrection', this clearly means they received a physical resurrection after death, enabling them to reign on earth. Also, the verb 'to live' used in the phrase 'came to life' NEVER takes the meaning of 'come into God's Presence.' In fact the same phrase 'came to life' is used to describe Jesus' resurrection in Revelation 2:8. Also the word 'resurrection' never means 'going to heaven', but rather it normally signifies a physical resurrection. Moreover believers in Heaven in the Intermediate State are never said to be reigning with Christ, rather they are in a state of waiting (Revelation 6:9-10). Whenever the New Testament promises believers will be given authority to reign with Christ over the earth, it speaks of a future time, not as something that is happening now (Luke 19:17,19, 1Corinthians 6:3, Revelation 2:26-27, 3:21, 5:12). This confirms the Premillennial interpretation of v4, that the reigning with Christ is something yet future rather than present, as Amillennialists have it. Furthermore those who come to life in v4 are described as those who did not bow to the beast of Revelation 13, who has not yet come on the world scene. So this whole event described in v4 must still be future. Thus Revelation 20:4-6 cannot describe the Church Age, but instead must describe the future Millennial Reign of Christ.

Amillennialists argue that only one passage (Revelation 20) teaches a future Millennial reign of Christ, and that it is obscure, so it is unwise to base a major doctrine on one passage of uncertain and disputed interpretation. First we should say that the Bible only needs to say something once in order for it to be true and something we are obliged to believe. Also it's simply untrue to say that Revelation 20 is obscure. It is very clear in teaching the Pre-Millennial position if read in a straightforward way. Obscurity only enters in when the reader tries to find in it something different. Moreover, although this is the only passage that speaks of its duration as being 1000 years, there are a multitude of Scriptures that speak of this Messianic Kingdom, especially in the Old Testament. These passages fit neither the present Age nor the Eternal State. Rather they speak of a future Age that is far greater than the present Church Age, but which still falls short of the Eternal State, because sin and death is still present on earth albeit greatly reduced, and there is still the need for strict government. These passages portray an Age identical to the Millennium of Revelation 20. Let us now look at some of these.

Isaiah 65:20: **"No more shall an infant from there live but a few days, nor an old man who has not fulfilled his days; for the child shall die 100 years old, but the sinner being 100 years old shall be accursed."** Unlike in this Age there will be no infants who die in infancy or old men who die prematurely, life spans will be lengthened, so someone aged 100 will be considered to be as a child. But sin and death (by capital punishment) will still exist. Isaiah 11:2-9 describes a renewal of nature and the animal kingdom to like its Edenic State, but v10,11 show that it is not yet the Eternal State, for the Lord is still calling the nations to seek Him, and is regathering the remnant of Israel to the Land. Psalm 72 describes the glories of Messiah's future righteous reign over all nations, as long as the sun endures (v5,8,11), but it still falls short of the Eternal State, because the King still has enemies (v9) and has to deliver the needy from oppression and violence (v12-14). This speaks of conditions very different from the present Age, but the continued presence of sin, suffering and the need for strong government restraining evildoers means it falls short of the Eternal State. Likewise Zechariah 14:5-21 describes a transformed earth where the Lord is King over all, but where there is also sin, rebellion, suffering, death, and the necessity for strong government.

There are also New Testament passages that portray an Age identical to the Millennium of Revelation 20. Revelation 2:26-27, 12:5, 19:15 (c.f. Psalm 2:9) speak of a future Age when the Messiah will rule over the nations with a rod of iron, with believers reigning with Him. This suggests a rule of force over rebellious people. This does not fit the present Age or the Eternal State, but it does fit perfectly with the Millennial Kingdom when the glorified saints will rule with Christ on earth. Finally, the sequence of events in Revelation 20 (2nd Coming, 1st Resurrection, Millennium, 2nd Resurrection) is confirmed by 1Corinthians 15:23-26: **"Each one** (will be resurrected) **in his own order: Christ the first fruits, THEN** (after that) **those who are Christ's at His Coming. THEN** (after that) **comes the END** (of time), **when He delivers the** (Messianic) **KINGDOM to God the Father, when He puts an end to all rule and all authority and power. For**

He must REIGN till He has put all enemies under His feet. The last enemy that will be destroyed is death." Both words translated 'THEN' indicate a period of time separating the successive events, described as 'the KINGDOM' and the 'REIGN' of Christ. Thus after Christ's Coming, when all the saints are resurrected, there will be an extended period of time (the Millennial Kingdom). Then at its end, He will complete the destruction of the final enemy (death) by resurrecting all the dead unbelievers. The Eternal State will begin once every enemy has been completely put underfoot. Before that there is a period of time when Christ reigns in His Kingdom actively subduing His enemies. This is not the Church Age, for although Christ reigns over the Church in this present Age, while He sits at the right hand of God, it is not yet the time for Him to subdue His enemies and start putting them under His feet (Psalm 110:1). Thus this must be speaking of the future Messianic Kingdom, when He will have physically left the Father's throne in order to sit on His earthly throne and personally reign over the earth, subduing His enemies. Thus 1Corinthians 15 agrees with Rev 20 that Christ will establish His Messianic Kingdom at His Coming. In fact the process of leaving His Father's throne and forcefully using His authority to subdue His enemies begins with the Tribulation, culminating in His 2nd Coming to usher in His Kingdom. That's why both the Tribulation and Messianic Kingdom are called 'the Day of the Lord'.

Another argument they use is that some scriptures seem to teach only one resurrection, of both believers and unbelievers, rather than 2 resurrections separated by 1000 years (John 5:28-29, Acts 24:15, Daniel 12:2). First Revelation 20 explicitly speaks of the 1st resurrection implying there's also a 2nd resurrection. v5-6 distinguishes between the blessed and holy ones who are part of the 1st resurrection from 'the rest of the dead' who do not share in it. These are raised 1000 years later (in the 2nd resurrection) and then experience the 2nd death (condemned to eternal punishment separated from the goodness of God). So the Bible here clearly teaches there are 2 distinct resurrections. The other passages above do not exclude the idea of 2 resurrections at different times, they simply do not make it clear if believers and unbelievers are raised at the same time or not. In fact, Jesus in John 5:28-29 points to 2 resurrections, 'the resurrection of life' and 'the resurrection of judgment.' Likewise Acts 24:15 speaks of the resurrection of the just and (the resurrection) of the unjust, whereas Luke 14:14 speaks of 'the resurrection of the just' in isolation. Daniel 12:2 describes the resurrection as consisting of 2 groups, some to everlasting life, and the rest to everlasting contempt, without specifying if there is a time-interval separating them. When Jesus said in John 5:28 that "the hour is coming" when all the dead will be raised, remember that in John's Gospel 'hour' can refer to a long period of time (John 4:21-23, 5:25, 16:2). In the same way, we might tell a group of university students that 'Graduation Day' is coming for all of them, but some will graduate this year and others may graduate in a few years. We say 'Graduation Day' rather than Days because we are simply speaking of the kind of day it is. Thus all these verses agree that on the certainty of the resurrection of all men, and that they will be raised in 2 groups (the just and the unjust) without giving the relative timing. This differential timing is revealed by Revelation 20:4-5,12, and is confirmed by 1Corinthians 15:23-24. Thus the Scriptures are all consistent on this issue.

Amillennialists also struggle with the idea of resurrected saints being on earth in the Millennium alongside people still in their natural sinful bodies. But although this may seem strange to us, because it is outside our present experience, there is no good reason why this could not happen. In fact, Jesus lived in this way on earth for 40 days after His resurrection, interacting with His disciples, and also a number of other saints who were raised at the same time appeared to people in their natural bodies (Matthew 27:53). This mixture of peoples is also anticipated in the Transfiguration, which is a prophetic preview of the Messianic Kingdom, with the glorified Christ and Moses and Elijah fellowshipping with the disciples.

Another objection they have to a literal Millennium is that it teaches the ongoing presence of sin on earth even after Jesus has returned and is present in His glory, this sin being manifested in a great rebellion at its end. However, there is nothing impossible about persistent unbelief in the Presence of Christ and His power. Consider Judas and the Pharisees who saw His many miracles. Remember satan and his angels fell from their place in the Presence of God in Heaven. This objection is based on not understanding the deep-seated and irrational nature of sin, and that genuine conversion is fundamentally moral (volitional) in nature, so that no proof can compel it. Therefore men can continue in their rejection of God even in the face of overwhelming evidence to the contrary. Now most people in the

Millennium will be saved and overall it will be an Age of Righteousness (Daniel 9:24), but it is not hard to see that sin will also continue in men's hearts.

Amillennialists also cannot see the point or purpose of the Millennium. Once Christ has returned why would He delay the Eternal State by 1000 years? God's overarching Purpose through all the Ages is His GLORY, and in the Millennium He will reveal His Glory in new ways. He will fulfil all His covenants and promises, thus showing Himself faithful. Christ will be revealed in His glory as the righteous King and Judge, and His power over nature, sickness, satan and the curse will be fully demonstrated. It will be a fitting and glorious climax to history before the Eternal State is inaugurated, providing the opportunity for the salvation of billions of more souls. Probably more souls will be saved in the Millennium than the rest of history combined. It will be glorious time with Christ exalted as King over the whole world, and we (the glorified Church) will reign with Him over the earth in the heavenly places (presently occupied by the principalities and powers).

With the restraint on sin and removal of the curse through Christ's Presence, this Age will provide the opportunity for God to reveal His wisdom and goodness in providing for man's individual blessing, as well as for his corporate blessing through the Divine Institutions of family and government, with the disruptive influence of sin broken. The rightness and blessing of living God's way under Divine Government will be revealed and manifested as never before. The Millennium will also reveal the true nature of sin and so vindicate God's righteous judgment against it, for even in a perfect and peaceful environment under a perfect government, with no poverty, and all demonic influence removed, some will still continue in sin and rebellion against God. Thus the issue must be the deep-rooted sinfulness of men's hearts, vindicating the justice of God in the final Judgment.

The Lord of Ages unfolds His purposes and reveals His glory progressively through the different Ages of time. Therefore it is fitting that before the Eternal State, He has ordained one more final stage in the progression of His Kingdom Program and the revelation of His glory. The Millennium as revealed in the Bible is perfectly consistent with this progressive revelation of God through the Ages of time, providing a fitting climax to His self-revelation in history, where Christ, the God-man, is revealed in His power and glory, victorious over sin, satan, sickness, and curse, exercising dominion over all nature, including mankind, and the blessedness of this reign will demonstrate His worthiness to rule as King over all.

This final Stage of the manifestation of the Kingdom of God on earth before the Eternal State begins (with sin still present) will reveal what it is like when God's righteous government is fully in charge. The overall effect will be to demonstrate the rightness of Divine Government, and the sinfulness and destructiveness of sin. For it will show that God is good and gives us life and peace (shalom, wholeness) when we submit to Him, and that the curse of suffering, sickness and death only comes because of sin (man's rebellion against the will of his Creator). Thus if there were no Messianic Kingdom there would be something vital missing from the unfolding drama of the revelation of God's glory in history. It would be as if the last act of a play, where all the threads of the plot are brought together to their conclusion, was not shown. It would be an unsatisfactory anticlimax and not so glorifying to God if history ended with the worldwide darkness of the Tribulation. How much better for God to demonstrate His glory with a victorious climax to history with a golden age of righteousness and peace under the rule of Messiah! Although there is a final rebellion that is not the characteristic of the Age and it probably involves just a small minority, considering the population explosion in the Millennium. Thus it provides a fitting closing act to the drama of history.

In conclusion, Amillennialism is to be rejected because it spiritualises the prophecies of the Messianic Kingdom, explaining them away and denying their literal fulfilment, making God unfaithful to His Word and a covenant-breaker. It also clearly fails to provide a satisfactory explanation of Revelation 20.

*3. Post-Millennialism The 3rd view is POST-MILLENNIALISM. 'Post' means 'after.' So these believe in a literal 1,000 year political Kingdom of God on earth, but that the 2nd Coming of Christ will only comes AFTER these 1000 years of peace. In other words, this Millennial Kingdom will be established by the Church, and not by Christ directly. In this view, the progress of the Gospel and the growth of the Church will gradually increase, so that an increasing proportion of the world will be Christians, and society will increasingly conform to God's standards under the rule of the Church, gradually resulting in a 'millennial age' of righteousness and peace (some say it will last for 1000 years, others say this is just symbolic of a long period of time). Finally, at the end of this period, Jesus will return in response to the Church saying: *"We've conquered the world for You, so now You can come back!"* When He returns He will resurrect believers and unbelievers and the final judgment will happen, and we will all enter the Eternal

State in a new heaven and earth. So in this scenario, the Church will restore all things and inaugurate the Kingdom without Christ's personal Return. We will possess political power in every nation, controlling all aspects of its life, so that the world will eventually be Christianised. Thus Christ in Heaven will reign through His Church on earth for 1000 years (or a long time), but not be present physically on earth. He will return only after this millennial reign of the Church. It is attractive in its optimism about the power of the Gospel to change lives and societies. During times of revival, times when there is an absence of war, and progress is made towards overcoming evil and suffering in the world, and times when the influence of Christianity is growing, this view naturally gains support.

It provides an exciting, positive and optimistic vision, but its problem is it is unscriptural, and has to reject the principle of literal interpretation. It ignores the great body of scriptures that speak of the whole Church Age being 'evil' (Galatians 1:4), with satan being 'the god of this age' (2Corinthians 4:4), and that evil will even increase and come to its fullness as this Age moves towards its End (in the Tribulation), and that it will only be vanquished by Christ Himself at His Return. The Biblical view is more balanced. It says the world is getting darker and will reach its darkest in the Tribulation just before Christ returns, as described in Revelation. The Bible says that Jesus alone is able to defeat the forces of darkness and establish His Kingdom. This is not a negative view, simply a realistic view that only the Lord Jesus can put this earth right, and our main focus needs to be on saving souls. On the positive side, as the world gets darker, the Church will get brighter, and will be successful in fulfilling the Great Commission and bringing in a great soul harvest from all nations, for Revelation 5, at the end of the Church Age shows multitudes in Heaven saved from all nations.

Postmillennialism argues that since Christ, who possesses all authority, has commissioned the Church to disciple all the nations, we should expect a triumphant outcome, especially as He promises to be with us as we fulfil this commission (Matthew 28:18-20). This is confirmed by some Parables, such as the Mustard Seed (Matthew 13:31-32), which indicate a great growth of God's Kingdom and its influence in this Age. In response, I would say that although the Scriptures, including some Parables, do indicate that the Gospel will be preached as a witness to the nations, nowhere do they say that the whole world will be Christianised as a result. In fact the prophecies of the End of the Age before Jesus returns indicate quite the opposite. Not only do the Parables not tell us the extent of the Kingdom's growth in this Age, they also reveal a parallel negative growth of evil through satan's counter sowing.

Those who say the Church will establish (restore) the Kingdom also point to <u>Psalm 110:1</u>: **"The Lord** (God the Father) **said to my Lord** (Christ): **"Sit at My right hand** (in Heaven), **until I make Your enemies** (on earth) **Your footstool."** This points to an unknown time-period from Messiah's ascension until His return to earth when God subdues all His enemies under His feet. There is no indication here that this is the job of the Church - the only 2 persons involved in this are the Father and Son. During this time He rules from Zion (Heaven) over a priestly army, the Church, who live in the midst of His enemies (v2-4). Thus His enemies are active and not crushed during this time. God makes His enemies His footstool at His 2nd Coming, in the Day of His wrath, when He judges the nations and establishes His Kingdom (v5-7). Thus v1 does not mean Christ is passively sitting waiting for God or the Church to crush all His enemies underfoot, but He is told to wait until it is the God-ordained time for Him to return and do this. The Father will authorise it, and the Son will implement it. This thought is developed in another favourite postmillennial verse, <u>1Corinthians 15:25</u>: **"He must reign till He has put all enemies under His feet."** Again there is nothing in the context that says that He will do all this in the Church Age through the Church. It's in His 2nd Coming and Millennial reign that God subdues all His enemies under His feet. The interpretation that says His feet are the Church, and that Christ must stay in Heaven until the Church has defeated every enemy for Him, is impossible for it is immediately contradicted by the next verse: **"The last enemy that will be destroyed is death"** (v26), which takes place when all the dead have been resurrected (v23,24). All agree that this last enemy must be destroyed by Christ Himself at His Return, not by the Church during the Church Age, so it is impossible for the Church to destroy all enemies BEFORE His Return. This is actually speaking of the 2nd resurrection at the End of time (v24) after the Millennium (Rev 20:12-13). Thus Christ is in Heaven until the time for Him to actively start judging, reigning and destroying all enemies on earth, which He will start to do at His 2nd Coming (actually even before that in the Tribulation) and will continue to do throughout the Millennium and will complete this by completing the destruction of the last enemy at the End of Time.

The attempt to uphold a Postmillennial view against this logic leads to the 'manifest sons of God' heresy which says the restored victorious Church will go from glory to glory until by faith she overcomes death itself and receives immortal bodies before the Return of Christ, and thus will be able to complete her mission of overcoming all enemies for Christ. In this way Christ will come for a glorious Church. Thus the Church must 1st become fully restored, glorified and victorious before Jesus can return. The Bible never says that Jesus is coming for a glorious Bride, but rather that: **"He might present her to Himself a glorious Church"** (Ephesians 5:27). The Church only becomes glorified after Christ's Return when He resurrects and raptures her, cleanses her from her dead works at the Judgment Seat and then glorifies her, and then presents her to Himself as His glorious Bride. Those who think this is all attained in the Church Age forget that this glorious Bride does not consist just of those still alive but also those who have already died in Christ. So most of the Bride has already died without attaining to this level of super-sanctification and glory. So this verse can only be fulfilled after the Rapture.

Another favourite Restorationist passage (Romans 8:18-23) only confirms what we are saying, when read carefully. The present age is characterised by suffering, but it is a preparation for a future age of glory (v18), which is eagerly awaited by all creation which is presently labouring under the curse (v19,20,22), until it is removed at the time of: **"the revealing (manifestation, glorification) of the sons of God"** (v19), when it will: **"also will be delivered from the bondage of corruption into the glorious liberty of the children of God"** (v21). So they say that as the Church is fully restored and revealed to the world in her anointed-glory the curse will be pushed back, and the millennial kingdom of peace will be established on earth. However v23 tells us that this manifestation (glorification) of the sons of God (the Church) takes place at: **"the redemption of our body."** In other words, this is not fulfilled during the Church Age, but at the 1st resurrection, which is at Christ's Return. Again we can see how the 'manifest sons of God' heresy arose as an attempt to make this passage support a restorationist position in a consistent way. Thus because there is no clear scriptural basis for Post-Millennial Restorationism, the relevant scriptures are either handled very loosely to make them sound as if they support this position, or their attempt to be more consistent with these scriptures while upholding their vision forces them into heresy.

Another passage used by those who say the Church will restore the Kingdom is Acts 3:19-21: **"Repent ...that He may send Jesus Christ, who was preached to you before, whom Heaven must receive until the Times of Restoration of all things, which God has spoken by the mouth of all His holy prophets."** They interpret this to mean Jesus must be held in Heaven until the Church has restored all things, so that He can return when the Church is fully restored and victorious over all enemies. This must be wrong because Peter defines the Times of Restoration of all things as the fulfilment of all the Old Testament prophets, whose consistent vision was the restoration of the earth and the ruling House of David, by the personal Return of the Messiah, the Son of David to the earth. Actually Peter is calling national Israel to repent, because only then can God fulfil His covenants to Israel by sending Christ back to the earth to establish His Kingdom (restore the Kingdom to Israel). Thus 'the Times of Restoration of all things' predicted by all the prophets is the Messianic Kingdom, which must be brought in by Christ Himself (not the Church, which does not even appear in Old Testament Prophecy). Thus He must remain in Heaven until it is the time for Him to return and restore all things according to the prophets. What must happen on earth to make this possible is the national repentance of Israel, not the conquest of the Church over the world.

In response to Postmillennialists pointing out that the Church has grown and spread throughout the earth, even in places of great persecution, we can point out that the world is also becoming more evil. Scientific modernisation, which brings much good, has not only failed to improve man's morality, but has also enabled evil to spread all the more. Secular humanism and Islam increasingly dominate the cultures in different parts of the world. What we observe of the parallel growth of good (through the Gospel) and evil in the world perfectly agrees with the Premillennial view, whereas the postmillennial view has trouble explaining the persistence and growth of evil, even after 2000 years of the Church.

Several New Testament Scriptures contradict the Post-millennial view. Jesus said that few go through the narrow gate and walk the narrow way of life (Matthew 7:13-14). See also Luke 18:8. Descriptions of the Church Age in the Last Days (2Timothy 3:1-5, 12-13, 4:3-4), and of the Tribulation (Matthew 24:7-30, Revelation 6-18), do not describe a Christianised world, but a world of great evil and suffering. Even those who admit there will be a final rebellion before Christ's

Return, can't answer the fact that these Scriptures reveal a dominant non-Christian culture in the world just before Christ's Return. This is far removed from the Postmillennial vision of a Christian world brought about by the Gospel. A period of rebellion against a dominant Kingdom of righteousness is very different from a Tribulation period where evil dominates and believers suffer great persecution. Not only does Matthew 24 contain no hint of a Millennium of righteousness and peace before the Lord's Return, it shows Him coming after a period of Great Tribulation. The clear contradiction of Matthew 24 with Postmillennialism has led to Preterism, which reinterprets it symbolically, as a prediction of the destruction of Jerusalem in AD 70, rather than a prediction of events leading up to the 2nd Coming. This interpretation does great violence to the natural reading of the text.

Also there are many scriptures which we will see later in this book that command us to look for and live in the light of the imminent Coming of the Lord, for He could return at anytime soon, so we must be ready for Him. This is used by the New Testament writers as a major motivation for holiness and evangelism. If these Scriptures are true, then Postmillennialism is impossible, for it requires a long period of time for the (1) the Church to bring in the Millennium and (2) the Millennium itself to run its course, before the Lord Jesus can return. Although Postmillennialism sounds positive, it creates a false hope in believers who will ultimately be discouraged when they see the world getting worse rather than better. Thus it does not properly prepare believers for the realities of this Age. It replaces the New Testament heavenly hope of the Lord's imminent Return by an earthly hope, putting the Coming of the Lord into the distant future. By taking the focus off the Lord's Return it inverts the emphasis of Scripture.

Though Postmillennialists take the Bible more literally than Amillennialists in acknowledging there will be a special period of time on earth called the Millennium, where God's Kingdom is manifested in a greater way than it is at present, nevertheless 'the Millennium' of a Postmillenialist is very different from 'the Millennium' of a Premillennialist, which has Christ physically present and reigning on a renewed earth, together with his glorified saints. Thus they do not take literally the many Old Testament Prophecies of the Messianic Kingdom, with the Messiah personally ruling on earth from Zion. Moreover they not take Revelation 20 literally, and they ignore the fact that the Millennium of Revelation 20 follows on immediately from the 2nd Coming of Christ in Revelation 19 (they generally interpret the rider on the white horse as Christ being victorious through the Church and the preaching of the Gospel). This is the latest view to have appeared on the scene being only initially developed in the 17th century by Daniel Whitby, a Unitarian minister. It quickly gained wide acceptance as the most popular millennial view in the 18th and 19th centuries as it resonated with the optimism of the times. But its idea of man's steady progress towards the golden age of the kingdom was dealt a terrible blow by the world wars, by the end of which very few Post-Millennialists were left.

Alongside the Postmillennialism of Bible believers, who saw the irresistible advance of the Kingdom through the Gospel, there also developed a Liberal Postmillennialism, which focused on societal transformation rather than personal conversion (the social gospel). It upholds the unbiblical view of the basic goodness of man and sees the real evil to be overcome as that which is 'out there' in society. If we can just improve conditions on earth all will be well. So they see the great purpose of the Church as saving society from social evil, liberating man from poverty, racism, disease, war and injustice, rather than preaching the Gospel to sinners. It denies the Gospel because it denies that men are sinners who need saving, which is why Jesus had to die on the Cross, thus it also denies the Cross. Although we would all support these causes, and should work to overcome these evils, they are just the symptoms of a deeper problem - sin in every human heart, man's rebellion against God for which the Gospel of Christ is the only cure, and the main purpose of the Church is to faithfully proclaim the Gospel, which will surely have positive effects on society as more and more people get saved. Whereas the more Biblical form of Postmillenialism puts its confidence in the Gospel to establish the Kingdom on earth and Christianise society, Liberal Postmillennialism puts its confidence in man's efforts in an evolutionary process.

More recently Postmillennialism has seen a resurgence in the form of Calvinistic Reconstructionism (Theonomy) and Charismatic Dominion Theology, also called 'Kingdom Now' or Restorationism (although this last term is also used by some for the belief in the Restoration of Israel). These newer forms combine the 2 emphases of the original Biblical and Liberal Postmillennialisms. That is, they say the Church has 2 equally important mandates. As well as the Great Commission, they say the Church is called to fulfil the dominion or cultural mandate of subduing the earth, given to Adam in Genesis 1:26-28. The dominion lost by Adam in the Fall is now restored in Christ, the 2nd Adam, and so we are to use that authority to transform society and take cities for God. The non-charismatic Reconstructionists believe that the Church is to take dominion by restoring the Law of Moses to society, whereas a charismatic Dominionists believe that the restoration of anointed governmental apostles and prophets, along with new techniques of spiritual warfare, will cause the Church to rise up and take dominion over the various structures (mountains) of society.

Neither view has any Biblical basis. The dominion given to Adam was over the earth and the animals, not over people, so cannot be used as a basis for our right to have dominion over people, society or the world-system. The Fall meant that Adam lost his relationship to God and became a slave of sin, making it much harder to subdue the cursed earth, so Adam did lose his freedom and right to exercise full dominion as tenant-possessor of God's earth. Adam also had dominion over satan which he lost, when he submitted his headship of the human race to satan, thus putting mankind (including the world-system) under the power of satan, for Jesus did not contradict satan's claim in Luke 4:6 that the kingdoms of the world had been delivered to him. Now Jesus, the 2nd Adam, our Kinsman Redeemer has redeemed us and the earth with His blood, and so He has all authority to take possession of the earth and its kingdoms (see my commentary on Revelation 5). He has all authority in heaven and earth (Matt 28:18). So anyone in Christ has been delivered from the authority and dominion of satan and our authority over satan has been restored and we reign in life as far as our personal lives are concerned (Romans 5:17, Col 1:13, James 4:7, Ephes 2:4-6, 4:27, Mark 16:17, 1Peter 5:8).

Moreover by giving us the right to use His Name to do His works of healing and deliverance, Jesus delegated some of His authority on earth to us, so that we can take authority over satan and his works in other people's lives as part of fulfilling the Great Commission (Matthew 10:1, 28:18-20, Luke 10:19, Mark 16:15-20, John 14:12-14, 20:21, Acts 1:8). However at no time did Jesus delegate authority to the church to take dominion over the world. He alone as the Kinsman-Redeemer has the right to do this and He will only do this in the Day of the Lord (Tribulation and 2nd Coming). At that time He will share this ruling authority with us, so that we will then rule and reign with Him over the world, but this is after the Church-Age, as the future tense is used in all these verses (2Timothy 2:12, Revelation 2:26-27, 3:21, 5:10, 20:6). Revelation 5 takes place at the start of the Tribulation and the reigning is still future tense. In fact, we can only be trusted with that kind of power when we are in our resurrection bodies for our sinful flesh disqualifies us from inheriting the Kingdom of God (1Corinthians 15:50, Romans 8:17-19). If we presume to unlawfully claim these powers now we shall be in pride and come under satan's power and become corrupted in the process. This is why it's always disastrous when the Church is in bed with the political powers.

Thus we have no authority to displace satan from his present position of prince of the power of the air (Eph 2:2), god of this world or age (2Cor 4:4), ruler of this world (John 12:31, 14:30, 16:11), ruler of the darkness of this age (Eph 6:12), so that the whole world lies under his power (1Jn 5:19). These scriptures apply to the whole Church-Age, called 'this evil age' (Gal 1:4). 1Cor 2:6 describes satan's principalities and powers as 'the rulers of this age, who are coming to nothing.' Although they have been defeated by Christ, and are doomed to destruction, they still rule during this Age. Moffatt's translation of 'dethroned powers' is okay in the sense they now have no authority over those in Christ, but is misleading if taken to mean they have lost their place of rulership over the world-system. They have a right to be there given them by Adam, which they will keep until Christ personally enforces His authority over them and removes them. While we can restrain these evil forces through prayer as part of fulfilling the Great Commission, we cannot remove them from their present position over the world-system granted to them by Adam. Only the 2nd Adam can do that when He returns. If we want to damage the kingdom of darkness we must go and preach (shine the light of) the Gospel (Romans 1:16).

Thus the results of Adam's sin such as a cursed earth, physical death, and satan's position of rulership over unsaved mankind and his world-system (Genesis 3) will continue until Christ's Return when He will assert His dominion and fully remove the curse and satan from the earth (otherwise Christians would be able to resist death and live as long as they want). Meanwhile we can walk in victory over sin and satan reigning in life through the blessing of the New Covenant in Christ and share the Gospel, so that as many as possible can be saved, and be made fit to be part of God's future Kingdom on earth, before judgment falls and it is too late.

Dominion Theology is based on a bad interpretation of <u>Matthew 28:18-20</u>:
"All authority has been given to Me in heaven and on earth. Go therefore and make disciples of all the nations, baptising them in the Name of the Father and of the Son and of the Holy Spirit, teaching them to observe all things that I

have commanded you." All authority belongs to Christ (v18) and the part He delegated to us is defined by the job He gave us (v19,20), namely the Great Commission to preach the Gospel to people and make disciples by baptising and teaching people. If a boss says I have all authority over this business, now go and take charge of sales, He is giving you authority to do the sales, not to take over the building program or manufacturing! Dominion theology rejects the normal meaning of 'making disciples' (well established in the Jewish culture as what a Rabbi does in training a group of men, as modelled by Jesus Himself with His disciples - clearly He was saying *'as I discipled you, disciple others, not just Jews, but people from all nations'*) and redefines it to mean 'disciple nations' as in taking over nations (changing the focus from individuals to institutions), thus bringing their political structures and institutions under the Dominion of Christ, to establish His Kingdom upon the earth. This was clearly not the way that the disciples understood Jesus, for when they went to the nations they baptised and taught people, and made no direct effort to change the culture and politics of the nations. It must mean to disciple people from all nations, for you can only baptise people. How do you baptise institutions? This is another example of when you don't take the Bible literally you can make it mean whatever you want it to mean.

Although neither Christ nor the apostles adopted this Dominionist approach, for many it is more exciting vision than simply fulfilling the Great Commission. However, it contains within itself the seeds of liberal apostasy, since to the extent that the Gospel is not given first and central place it subtly denies the inherent sinfulness of man, as in practice it thinks it can change the world for God apart from the Gospel. Social and political action for good causes is to be commended, but it is not a substitute for the Gospel, which is what usually happens when we do not consciously hold the Gospel as being of supreme importance. Good works are vital in supporting and giving credibility to the proclamation of the Gospel, but we must also let the light of the Gospel shine before men, otherwise they will glorify us rather than God (Matthew 5:16). God calls believers to different positions in society and government and they are to fulfil their role with excellence and be faithful to share the Gospel as opportunities arise, but it is not about not building an earthly kingdom, but preparing people for the heavenly Kingdom (there will be a future Kingdom of God established on earth, but it's not of or from this world, it will descend from heaven to earth at the 2nd Coming).

Dominion Theology has great dangers, especially in distracting us from our mission of fulfilling the Great Commission, and in setting us up for the compromise that comes from loving this world. We are called to shine as lights in a dark world by holding forth the Gospel (Philippians 2:15-16), for the Gospel is man's only hope of salvation and transformation. But if our vision is turned toward gaining position and dominion in this world-system we will compromise our faith and witness to gain it. As we try and climb our mountain satan will come to us, as he did to Jesus, and offer us that power, fame and influence if we will only bow to him (agreeing to keep the Gospel hidden). Those with a Dominionist ambition will reason that by bowing they can attain a position where they can be a greater force for good, but by the time they get there they are so compromised and silenced they are little use to God or the Gospel. Whenever the Church covets political power it ends up compromised, entangled with principalities and powers and unable to fulfil her real mission of reaching the lost. Jesus' mission was to seek and save the lost and He sent us to continue what He had started, saying: 'as the Father has sent Me, so I send you.' In His 1st Coming Jesus did not try to fulfil a dominion mandate, and take on the Roman Government as the false Jewish Messiah's did. Likewise the apostles preached the Gospel but did not try and implement any kind of dominion mandate. Yes, 'they turned the world upside down' but that was the result of reaching so many people with the Gospel. Thus whatever good works and institutions and areas of society the Church gets involved with, the fulfilment of the Great Commission must be our primary aim and vision. Everything else we do should be to support that. The moment we are ashamed of the Gospel and relegate it to a secondary issue we are disloyal to God's call and are compromised. Jesus warned us that we cannot be loyal to 2 masters (2 governing visions), for we will end up loving one and hating the other. When the Dominionists emphasise as our primary call the extension of the Kingdom by climbing the mountains of influence and success in this world, and by getting involved in social and political action, it leads to the Church compromising the Gospel, because the Gospel is offensive to the world (it says all human goodness is as filthy rags before God and that you can only be saved through Christ), and so declaring its truths will get in the way of your promotion in the world-system. Jesus promised us persecution and rejection by the world when we are true to Him, just as they rejected Him. So yes, Christians should obey God when He calls them into different positions and roles in society, but our primary role is not to 'take over' this world, but to fulfil the Great Commission, saving the precious souls by sharing the Gospel, supported by our godly and loving example. That is how the early church actually 'changed the world'.

So all our social and charitable action must have as its ultimate aim the fulfilment of the Great Commission. The idea that we can transform society apart from the Gospel is a denial of the Gospel, which says that mankind is so lost in sin, we can only be changed by receiving Christ. So attempts to improve things any other way are bound to ultimately fail. Moreover the Christianising of society apart from the centrality of the Gospel has the danger of creating a society of people of unsaved nominal Christians and moralists who think they are okay because they accept an outward form of godliness (Christianity) in its moral codes, but deny its power (not having a personal relationship with Christ), which only comes by being confronted with the Gospel. We see this all too clearly in Europe.

Instead of being motivated to evangelism by the hope of the Lord's soon Return, Dominion Theology motivates the Church to try and build an earthly Kingdom of God, and considers any focus on the Lord's soon Return as an escapist distraction. Thus main danger of this view is that it takes our focus off the main purpose of the Church, which is the fulfilment of the Great Commission, the salvation of souls through evangelism and discipleship. Instead it presents us a new vision of trying to attain political power and position, taking over the structures and institutions of this world, which are going to be destroyed anyway by Christ's Return. Thus it diverts the main energies of the Church away from her main assignment of evangelism into a project that must ultimately fail.

Yes, Christians are meant to be engaged in this world. We need Christians in politics, law, the media and arts, IT, and every sphere of life. But our ultimate purpose is to let the light of the Gospel shine all the more, for the higher the elevation of a light the greater its impact and reach (Matthew 5:15). Our God-given mandate for this age is to preach the Gospel and win people to Christ, not take over the world, as Jesus made clear when He gave us His marching orders at the start of the Age, telling us to be His witnesses to the ends of the earth (Acts 1:8).

The literal view is Pre-Millennial. To submit to the Bible, we must take it according to its plain meaning - that Jesus will come before the Millennium. The other views have to spiritualise prophecy and apply Israel's promises to the Church.

*Appendix 6 – The 4 Schools of Prophetic Interpretation

*1. The PRETERIST School believes that most (if not all) prophecies (especially the Olivet Discourse and Revelation, as well as the Old Testament prophecies about the judgments of 'the Day of the Lord') have already been fulfilled in the events surrounding the destruction of Jerusalem by the Romans in AD 70! Unbelievably they believe that this fulfilled the prophecies of Christ coming in power and glory. They believe the references to the last days or end times, characterised by apostasy, refer to the last days of Israel's Age of favour (AD 33-70), after which the earth entered a new phase of history, with the Church forever replacing Israel as God's people. Thus these prophecies were written for the first century Christians to prepare them for what was shortly going to happen (the candidates for antichrist being the Roman Caesar Nero and the false Jewish Messiah's of that time), so these prophecies have little relevance for us today as they have already been fulfilled.

However, anyone adopting literal interpretation has to reject this approach for it is clear that these prophecies have not come to pass yet in any literal sense. Sadly most seem to feel free to abandon literal interpretation whenever necessary into order to promote their vision of what they think the future should be, rather than accepting God's revelation at face value. The Preterists are especially guilty of this tendency. Also Preterism requires Revelation to have been written before AD 70, but all the best historical evidence points to the fact it was written during the reign of the Roman Emperor Domitian, in about AD 95, which proves that it is false (see 'Dominion Theology: Blessing or Curse?' by Wayne House/Thomas Ice).

Preterism finds its main basis in <u>Matthew 24:34</u>: **"Assuredly, I say to you, this generation will by no means pass away till all these things take place."** They assume that 'this generation' is the generation to which Jesus is speaking, but the context, which describes the Signs leading up to the 2nd Coming, indicates that Jesus is speaking about the end-time generation that sees the beginning of these Signs. Preterism comes in 2 forms. Full Preterism says that the destruction of Jerusalem fulfilled all end time prophecies, including the resurrection of the dead, Jesus' 2nd Coming, and the Final Judgment. Partial Preterists realise that the consequence of following this system of interpretation leads to heresy and so modify it and call themselves Orthodox Preterists. They believe there are prophecies yet to be fulfilled by the Return of Christ and a future resurrection and judgment. Once people become partial Preterists there is a tendency to go all the way into full Preterism because it is the more logically consistent version.

The Olivet Discourse consists of Jesus' answer to the 3 questions of Matthew 24:3 about the signs of the destruction of the Temple, the 2nd Coming, and the end of the world (or age). The Full Preterists say that these must have all been fulfilled by AD 70 because of v34 ('the end' being the end of the Jewish age). But even though it is the logical consequence of their position, the partial preterists step back from the brink of saying that the Bible does not reveal the 2nd Coming of Christ and the Final Judgment, by admitting that parts of Matthew 24 and Revelation do prophesy events that are yet to take place at the end of time, which will be initiated by the literal Return of Jesus. Although full Preterists often try to maintain their orthodoxy by affirming their faith in the Return of Christ and the Final Judgment based on the historic Creeds of the Church, this requires them to reject 'Sola Scripture' (the sufficiency of Scripture) which is foundational to our faith, the rejection of which leads to even greater heresies (Revelation 22:18-19).

A literal approach to the Olivet Discourse is that Jesus' prophetic answer to the 1st question about the destruction of the Temple (recorded in Luke 21:20-24) was fulfilled in AD 66-70), but His answer to the other questions concerning the End of the Age (Tribulation) and the 2nd Coming, have clearly not yet been fulfilled. What could possibly have motivated this unnatural reading of scripture? It originated from a Roman Catholic scholar who realised the Protestant Reformers were making effective use of Revelation in proving the Roman Church was apostate, fulfilling the prophecies of 'the woman riding the beast' in Revelation 17, with the Pope being an antichrist ('vicar of Christ' literally means 'in the place of Christ', which is a possible meaning of anti-christ). So he was motivated to create an alternative way of interpreting Revelation and the other prophetic scriptures. Another hint as to its dark origins is the way it could be used as a basis for anti-semitism as it denies any future for Israel in God's Plan.

Preterism also appeals to those who want to promote Dominion Theology, because a normal reading of the Bible's Eschatology contradicts their vision of the Church taking over the world. They want to have what they would call a 'victorious eschatology' (as if the glorious truth is not victorious enough - of Christ returning for us as the Bridegroom coming for His Bride, then judging and cleansing the world of all evil and establishing His Kingdom of righteousness, joy and peace on earth). Not content to stay with Christ's marching orders by fulfilling the Great Commission by evangelism and discipleship, they go beyond this by saying that we also have a dominion mandate, which requires us to Christianise the world, transform society, taking over the culture, taking our cities for God (not so much saving the people, but changing the institutions). Such a vision is certainly optimistic and appeals to man's desire for outward success and power. But Dominion Theology has dangers, as discussed in Appendix 5. Its main problem is that it has no clear scriptural support, which is strange for something so important. Moreover the idea of the Church increasingly taking dominion over the world-system, so that Christ is held in Heaven waiting to return when the Church has put all things under His feet, plainly contradicts the scriptural description of the future, which reveals apostasy in the Church and the whole world lying under the power of satan throughout this present Age (2Cor 4:4, Eph 2:2, 1John 5:19). Also this Age will end with the Tribulation, a time when evil comes to its fullness and becomes dominant, with the whole world being ruled by the antichrist. Therefore, the kingdoms of this world will only become the Kingdom of our God through the intervention of King Jesus, who will personally establish His Kingdom on earth at His Return. But Partial Preterism says that all these 'negative' prophecies have been fulfilled, allowing the dominionist to believe that things are going to get better and better as God's Kingdom is advanced through the Church until she has taken over all the systems of the world for God. This view is overly optimistic as the Lord has never authorised the Church to do this. Moreover, it is dangerous for it means the Church will not be on guard against the increasing apostasy in the end-times, and it will relax its hold on the Gospel in order (1) to unite with other religious groups in its attempts to maximise its power to change the world, and (2) be less offensive to the world in its attempt to gain a greater position in it.

Doctrine is not determined by us choosing the most optimistic view possible but by being true to what Scripture actually says. The Biblical view of the end-times is realistic, containing both optimistic and realistic elements. It is victorious because it reveals Christ's total and final victory over the powers of evil, but neither does it deny the power and growth of evil in this world. Also in it the glory rightly belongs to Christ, not to the Church. On the one hand, the world and the apostate church that denies the Gospel will get darker and darker until God judges them in the Tribulation and 2nd Coming. On the other hand, there are Biblical grounds for optimism that the true Church will get brighter and brighter as it holds forth the Gospel and brings in a great soul-harvest from all the nations, thus fulfilling her real mission (the Great Commission) before Christ establishes His Kingdom, when His saints will reign with Him (Mark 13:10, James 5:7, Revelation 5:9,10, Romans 11:25). Often this issue is presented as a choice between an overly pessimistic view of the Church failing and becoming totally apostate and an overly optimistic view of the Church taking over and driving satan off the planet. The present and future realities are more complex. Apostasy within the church and evil in the world will continue to grow, but that is not the whole story. At the same time God will fulfil the Purpose of the Church Age, by calling out many from every nation to belong to Him through the Gospel. There is every hope for revival, and the pattern of earthly harvests (after the former and latter rains) give good reason for hope that the last days of the Church Age will see the true Church having great success in fulfilling her mission to bring in a great soul harvest. Indeed this is happening now for the worldwide Church has been growing rapidly over the last 100 years as it's faithful to spread the Gospel. The imminence of the Rapture is preserved, because only God knows when the full measure of the harvest of the nations (the fullness of the Gentiles) will be gathered in. Sadly many following a Dominionist vision will compromise the Gospel to gain power in this world and establish a working unity with other groups, and will end up as part of the apostate church in the darkness, for without the Power of the Gospel we have nothing to offer this world (Romans 1:16-17). Thus what has taken place over the last century, the parallel growth of the light of the Gospel and the darkness of sin and religious deception, will continue until the End of the Age.

Thus we see that the correct Eschatology keeps us focused on our heavenly hope and our God-given earthly mission to reach people with the Gospel and so gather the precious fruit of the earth, whereas a false Eschatology diverts our energies to fulfil an futile earthly hope of establishing the Kingdom now, so that after we have spent all our time and energy in our 'kingdom building' we have little left to do what we are actually called to do. Those who like to call themselves apostles and prophets should make sure they are building on the foundation already established by the Biblical apostles and prophets (Ephesians 2:20), as recorded in Scripture, rather than presenting visions that are created in their own imaginations as to what a victorious Church-Age should look like.

Another danger of the Preterist or Dominionist view is that it effectively creates a new dispensation after AD 70, so that much of what the apostles wrote before that time no longer applies today. For example, the warnings about apostasy and the man of sin and the end-time events. Also they claim that satan has now been fully dethroned from his place of authority over the world-system (Rev 12), so that the way is clear to the Church to take dominion and displace him and his principalities and powers. Thus the scriptures given to the apostles for their Age, which focus on a humble ministry of preaching the Gospel, being ready to face persecution from a hostile world ruled by satan, no longer apply today.

Moreover it follows that these scriptures are inadequate for our present Age when the 'glorious church' is being called to rise up and take dominion in the earth, the manifestation of the sons of God. New revelations are therefore needed for the Church, especially in the areas of prayer, spiritual warfare and taking dominion, and these are being provided by the new apostles and prophets who increasingly claim a status comparable to the foundational apostles and prophets, because they see themselves as laying the foundation for the future Church which will operate on a higher level than the early church. These new theologies and methods do not come from Scripture, but from the authority of these false apostles and prophets. Beware those who teach from their own thought and make only passing references to Scripture when it fits their ideas! There are true apostles and prophets today but they do not have the authority to add to Scripture, which is now complete and sufficient for us. Therefore any teaching that is not based in Scripture has little value, and distracts us from what is really important. It is not enough for them to say that no new revelation from God is allowed to contradict Scripture, for this is exactly what the Roman Church and all other cults do when they add their new relations (traditions) to the Bible. The result is always that the group follows the exciting new and now revelation and increasingly depart from the Bible.

Church history sadly confirms these facts. Whenever the Church adds to Scripture it goes into error and ends up with a false Gospel. Moreover, whenever the Church has pursued and gained political power (as with the Medieval Roman Church) its lust for power causes it to become compromised and corrupted. It becomes an oppressor denying religious liberty and ends up persecuting the true believers. Through these deceptions satan has greatly hindered the preaching of the Gospel and the salvation of the lost. Also those who submit to the power of the Church are led to believe that in so doing they are citizens of heaven, but this is a deception for salvation is only through the means of the Gospel. Moreover, modern charismatic attempts to take cities for God have signally failed despite great efforts at unbiblical dominionist spiritual warfare, whereas the church has made great strides forward wherever it is faithful to the Great Commission.

*2. The HISTORICIST School seeks to make Revelation 6-19 more relevant by saying its predictions cover the whole Church Age. Thus it equates the current Church-Age with the Tribulation, and relates the Seal, Trumpet and Bowl Judgments to major historical events (usually centred on European history). It gives a symbolic coded prophecy of the Church Age, so it sees the Book of Revelation as tracing the course of the last 2,000 years. It has been the standard Protestant approach from the Reformation until 200 years ago, when many returned to a more literal view. It is the view of 7th Day Adventists, Mormons, and Jehovah Witnesses. It was used to equate the Roman Catholic institution and popes with the antichrist, and some use it to identify America as Babylon. Again this is an allegorical approach requiring a non-literal interpretation of prophecy.

*3. The FUTURIST School (which is expounded in this book) is based on taking prophecy literally (using the same rules of interpretation as other areas of doctrine). That is, we take it in its plain meaning, according to the laws of language. If the literal meaning makes sense, then read it that way. Applying this principle it is clear that Revelation 4-22 has not yet been fulfilled; it still awaits a future fulfilment. Most end-time Bible Prophecy describes the future climax of the battle between good and evil. In this way, we don't have to make forced interpretations of prophecies in trying to show that they have already been fulfilled.

One criticism of FUTURISM is that the prophecies do not apply to us today, so studying prophecy has little value for us. But this is shortsighted. The same argument could be used to say it is pointless to study Bible history, as Prophecy is just His-story that has not happened yet! By revealing what God will do, we discover more about His character, power and purposes, and how we fit into the scheme of things and how we are to focus our lives and what purposes we should give ourselves to. Understanding the times in which we live and what lies ahead stabilises us in difficult times, when evil is increasing. Also by showing us the End of this Age in great detail the Bible helps us to interpret what is happening around us, for this world is necessarily moving closer and closer to the conditions described in Revelation. By comparing our times with what the Bible says about the end-time, we can see how close we are to the climax. This also helps us understand the forces at work in the world, so that we can unmask the disguises of evil. Prophecy also builds our hope that God is working out His Purposes and will be victorious! Knowing what will happen strengthens and guides us in our life today. The key qualities we need are: "faith, hope and love", and HOPE is developed through the study of Bible Prophecy. Our hope in the imminent Coming of Christ keeps us watchful, alert and occupied in His work. Therefore, End-Time Prophecy very much applies to our lives today.

There are also prophecies that apply to this present Age. Moreover, by applying TYPOLOGY to some literal prophecies (without denying their primary literal fulfilment), we will gain prophetic insights into our present time. In Appendix 1, we do this with the 7 Churches in Revelation 2 and 3. In my book: "the 7 Times of the Gentiles" I do this for the 7 TIMES typology in Daniel 4. But this is different from taking the HISTORICIST and PRETERIST approach to prophecy, which denies the literal fulfilment and replaces it with an allegorical interpretation, when the plain meaning makes perfect sense. For example, just because we see a deeper spiritual meaning in the typology of Abraham offering up Isaac (Genesis 22), does not justify us denying that this event actually happened. Literal interpretation requires the literal fulfilment of prophecy, but also allows us to perceive spiritual truths in the prophecy and make typological applications.

*4. The IDEALIST view removes all time references to the fulfilment of prophecies, and discourages us from seeing specific fulfilments. Thus Revelation portrays the eternal struggle between good and evil, and we can apply its truths to any time. Thus it treats Bible Prophecy as myth, describing fictional events that carry a moral or spiritual meaning. This amounts to a denial of the truth of God's Word and a denial of such events as the Second Coming and the Final Judgement. Of all the views it is the greatest manifestation of man's refusal to take God's prophetic word seriously in its plain meaning, emptying it of its meaning. It is a typical example of the kind of thinking of unbelief produced by Liberal Theology.